D·N·ANGEL

BY YUKIRU SUGISAKI

VOLUME 5

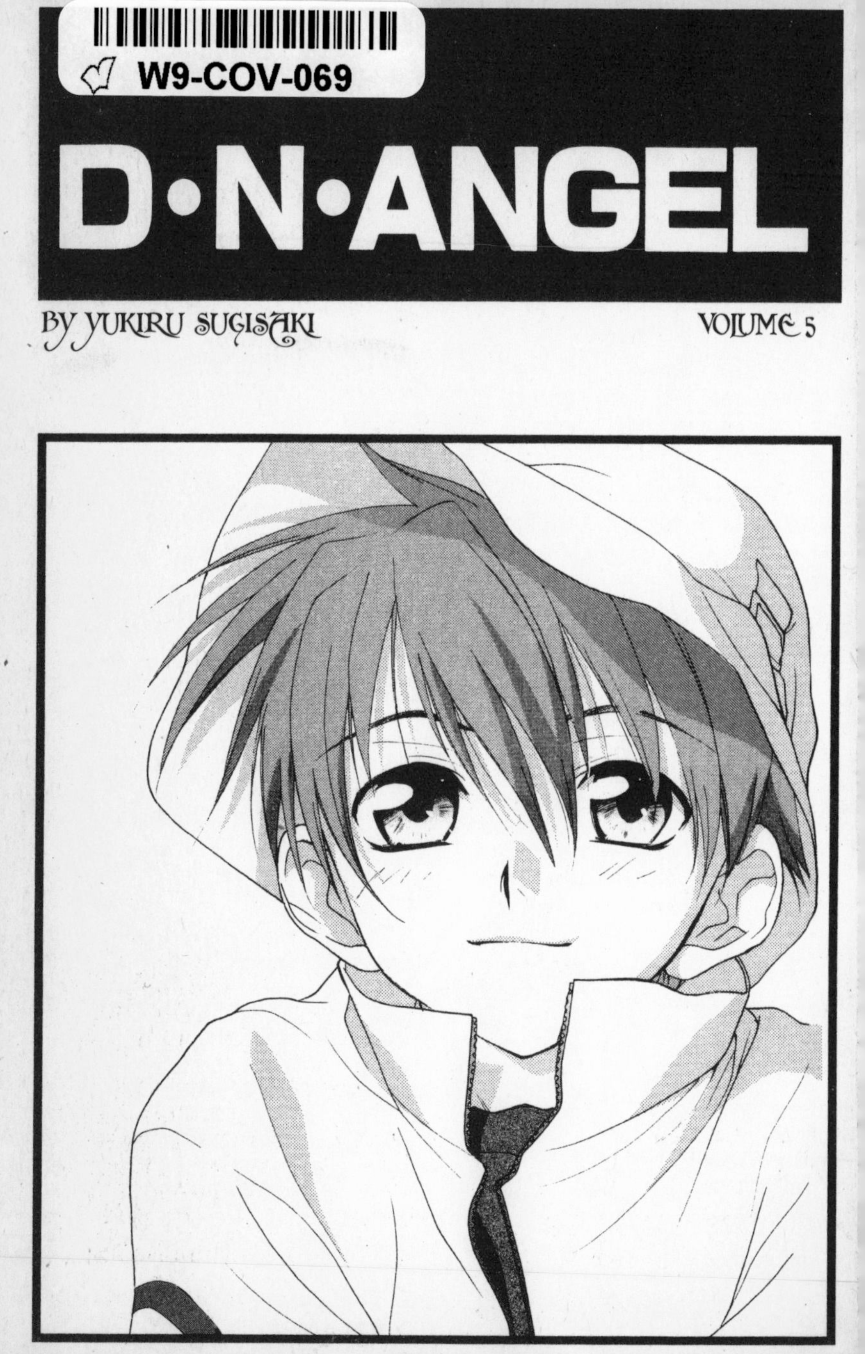

CHARACTERS & STORY

Before now:
After many misunderstandings, Daisuke and Riku were able to finally confess their feelings for one another. They expected to relax together on their class trip to a small island, but Riku kept bumping into Daisuke while he was in compromising situations with her sister, Risa! And if that wasn't bad enough, Satoshi finally trapped Dark inside a mirror called "the Sage of Sleep"—and then transformed into the white-winged villain, Krad!

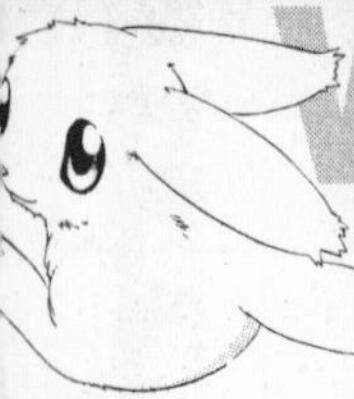

Wiz
A mysterious animal who acts as Dark's familiar and who can transform into many things, including Dark's black wings. He can also transform himself into Dark or Daisuke.

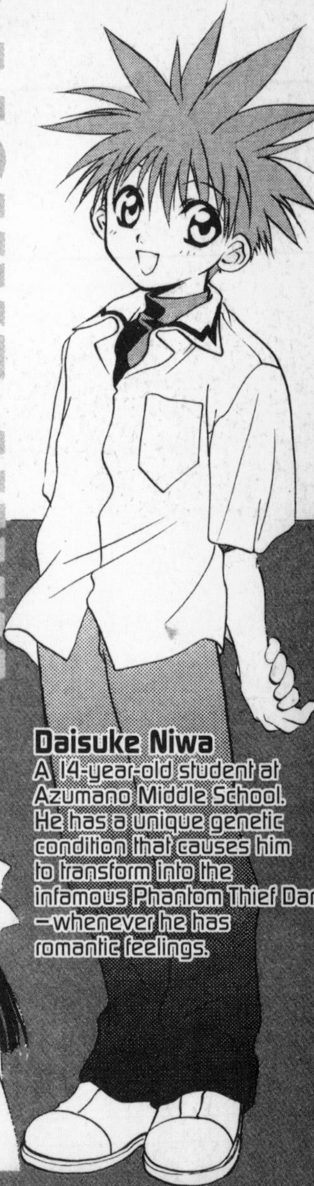

Daisuke Niwa
A 14-year-old student at Azumano Middle School. He has a unique genetic condition that causes him to transform into the infamous Phantom Thief Dark—whenever he has romantic feelings.

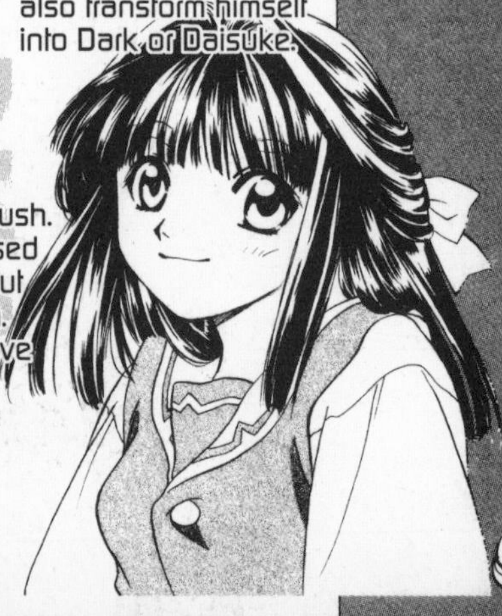

Risa Harada
Daisuke's first crush. Daisuke confessed his love to her, but she rejected him. She's been in love with Dark since the first time she saw him on TV.

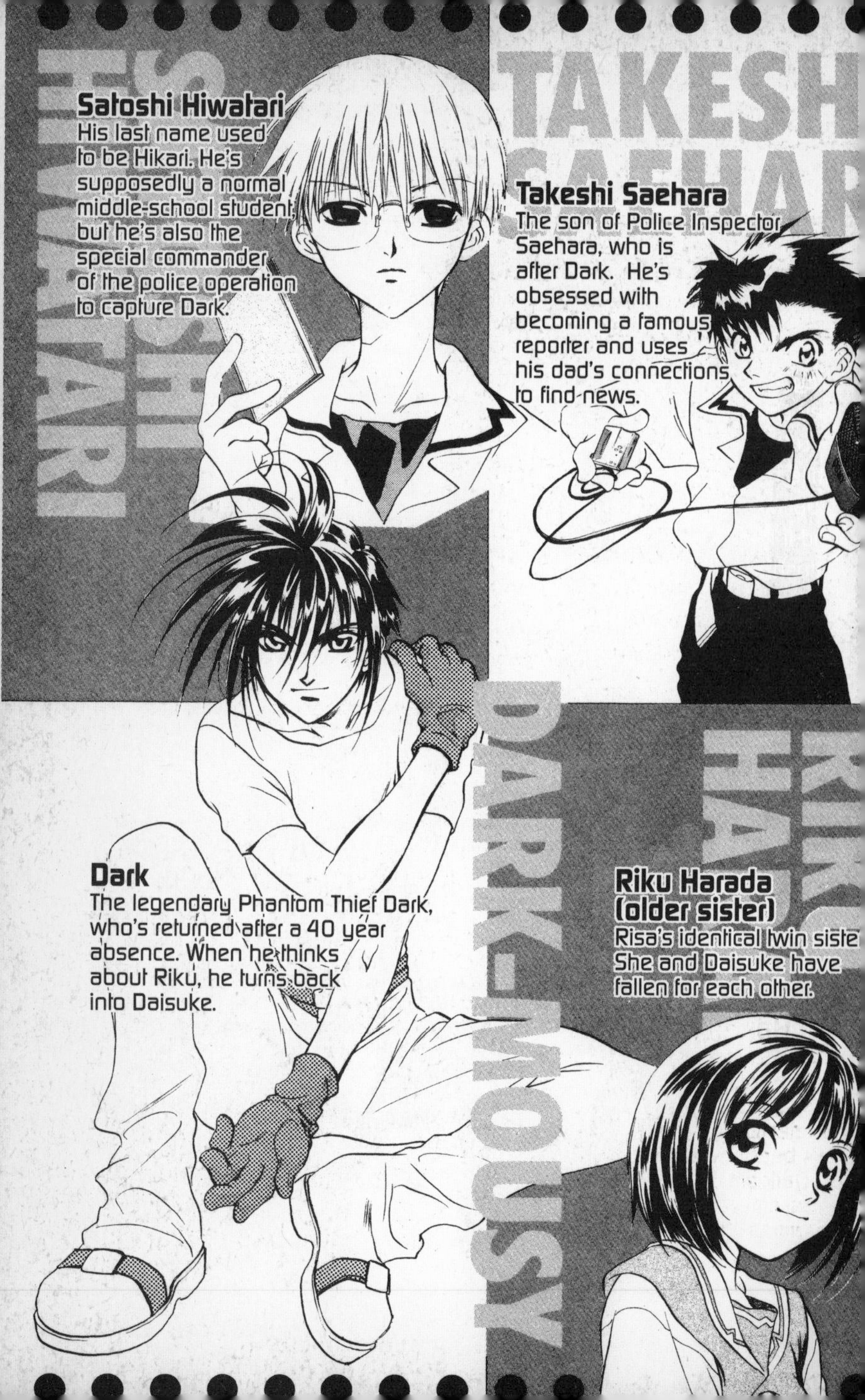
TAKESHI
Takeshi Saehara
The son of Police Inspector Saehara, who is after Dark. He's obsessed with becoming a famous reporter and uses his dad's connections to find news.
Satoshi Hiwatari
His last name used to be Hikari. He's supposedly a normal middle-school student, but he's also the special commander of the police operation to capture Dark.
Riku Harada (older sister)
Risa's identical twin siste She and Daisuke have fallen for each other.
DARK-MOUSY
Dark
The legendary Phantom Thief Dark, who's returned after a 40 year absence. When he thinks about Riku, he turns back into Daisuke.

D•N•ANGEL Vol. 5
Created by Yukiru Sugisaki

Translation - Alethea Nibley, Athena Nibley
English Adaptation - Sarah Dyer
Copy Editor - Peter Ahlstrom
Retouch and Lettering - Paul Tanck
Production Artist - John Lo
Cover Layout - Gary Shum

Editor - Bryce P. Coleman
Digital Imaging Manager - Chris Buford
Pre-Press Manager - Antonio DePietro
Production Managers - Jennifer Miller and Mutsumi Miyazaki
Art Director - Matt Alford
Managing Editor - Jill Freshney
VP of Production - Ron Klamert
President and C.O.O. - John Parker
Publisher and C.E.O. - Stuart Levy

A  Manga

TOKYOPOP Inc.
5900 Wilshire Blvd. Suite 2000
Los Angeles, CA 90036

E-mail: info@TOKYOPOP.com
Come visit us online at www.TOKYOPOP.com

ISBN: 1-59182-803-1

First TOKYOPOP printing: December 2004
10 9 8 7 6 5 4
Printed in the USA

D·N·ANGEL

Volume 5

By
Yukiru Sugisaki

HAMBURG // LONDON // LOS ANGELES // TOKYO

CONTENTS

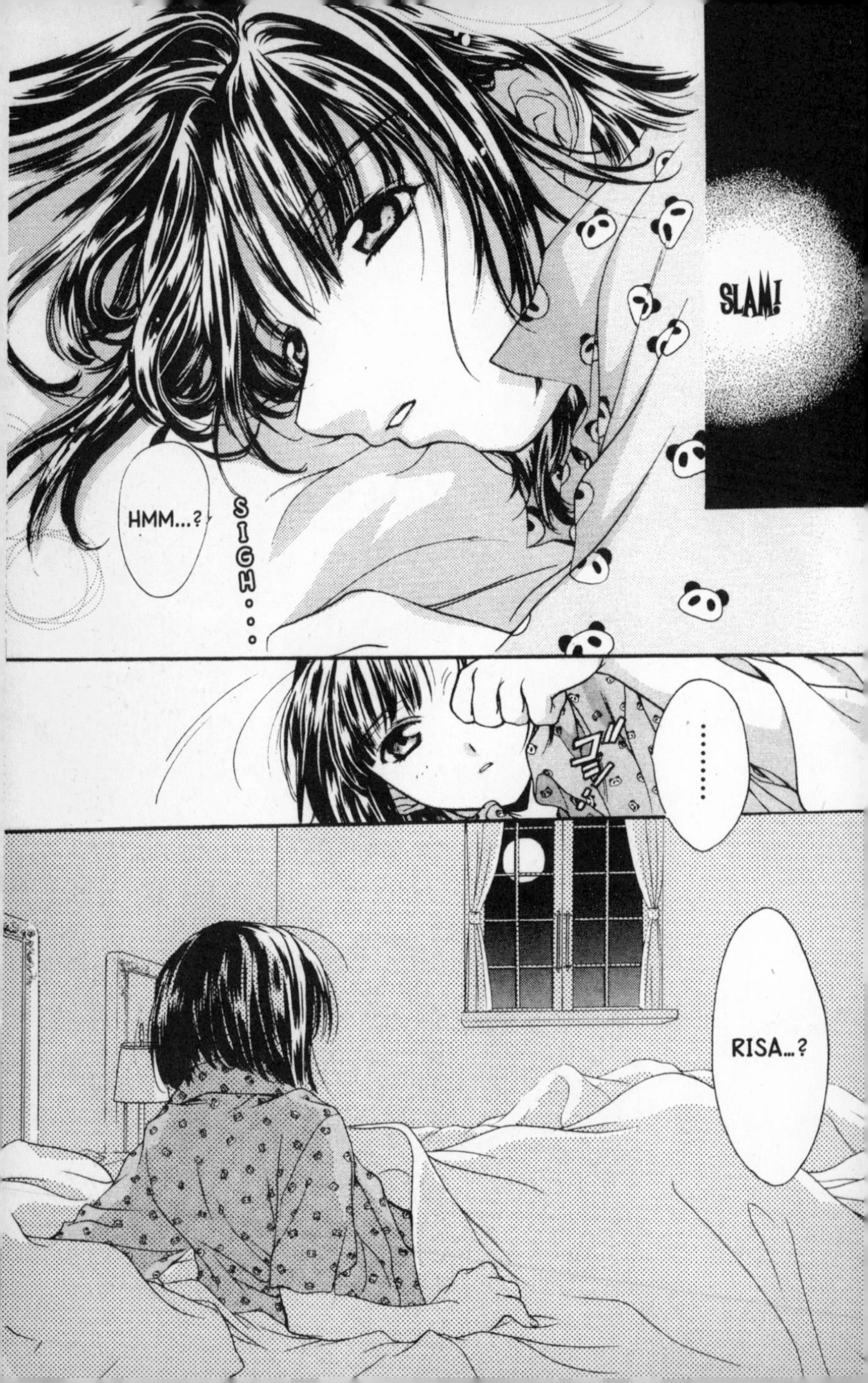
SLAM!
SIGH...
HMM...?
......
RISA...?

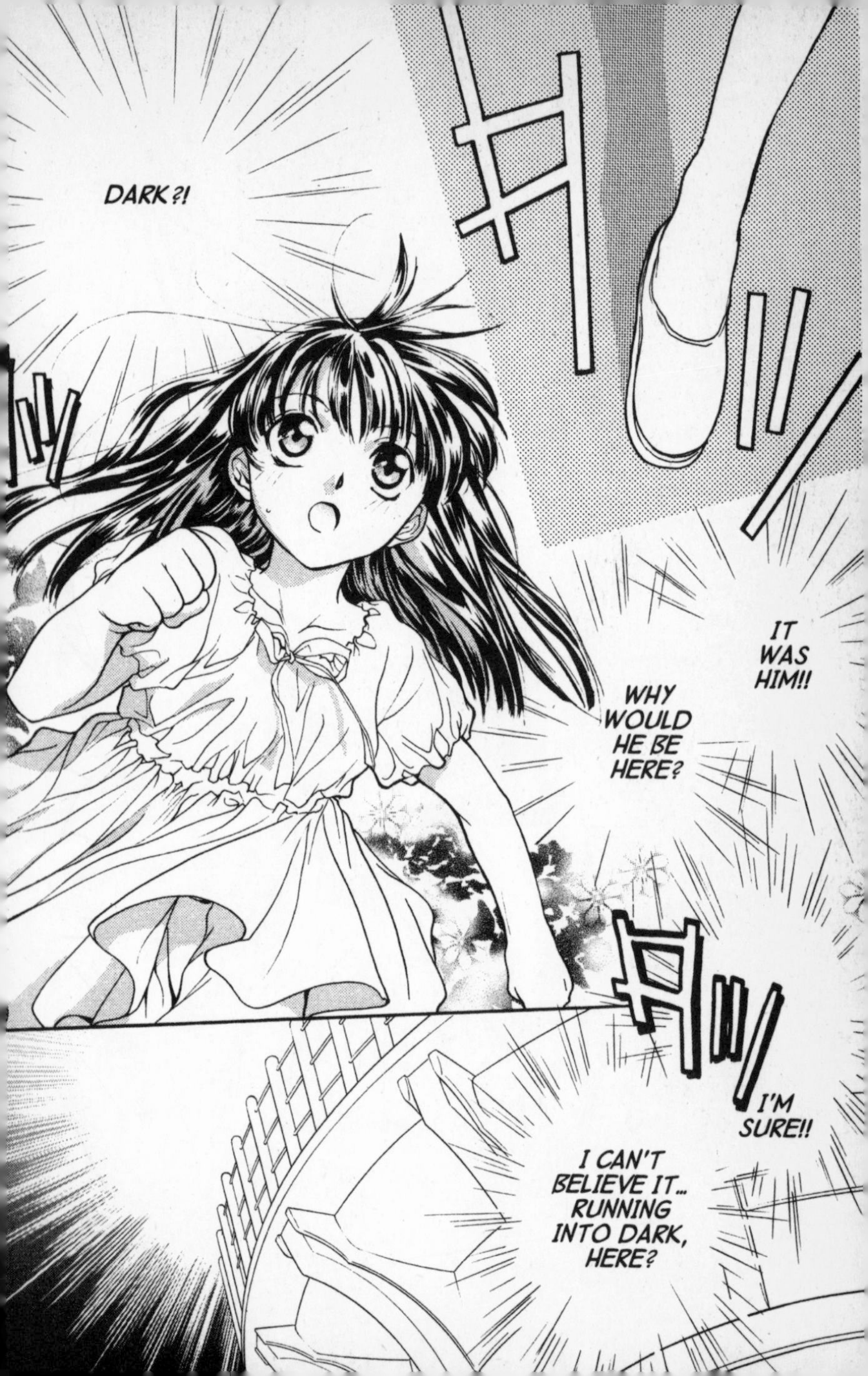
DARK?!
IT WAS HIM!!
WHY WOULD HE BE HERE?
I'M SURE!!
I CAN'T BELIEVE IT... RUNNING INTO DARK, HERE?

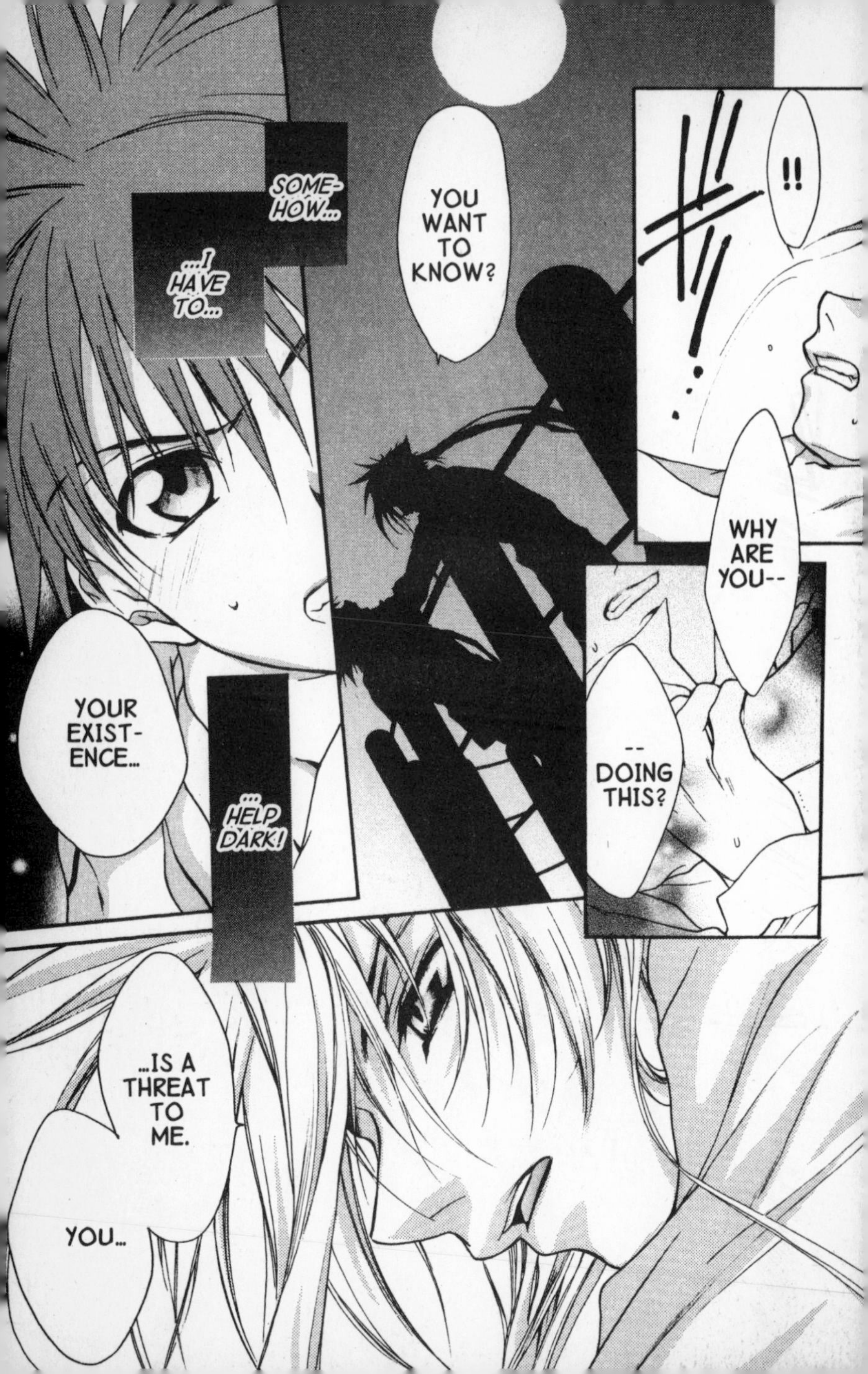
!!
WHY ARE YOU--
-- DOING THIS?
YOU WANT TO KNOW?
SOME-HOW...
...I HAVE TO...
...HELP DARK!
YOUR EXIST-ENCE...
...IS A THREAT TO ME.
YOU...

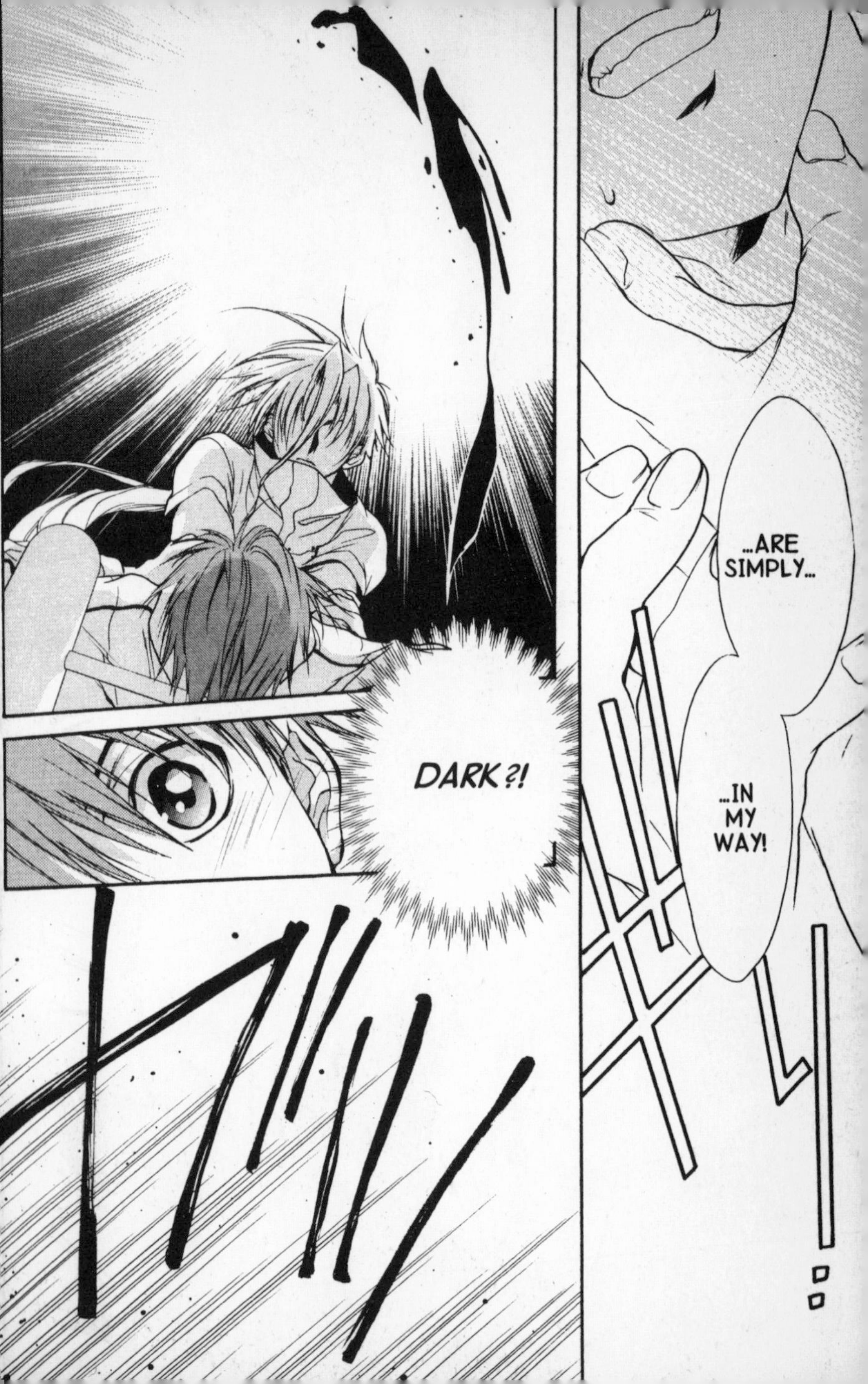
...ARE SIMPLY...
...IN MY WAY!
DARK?!

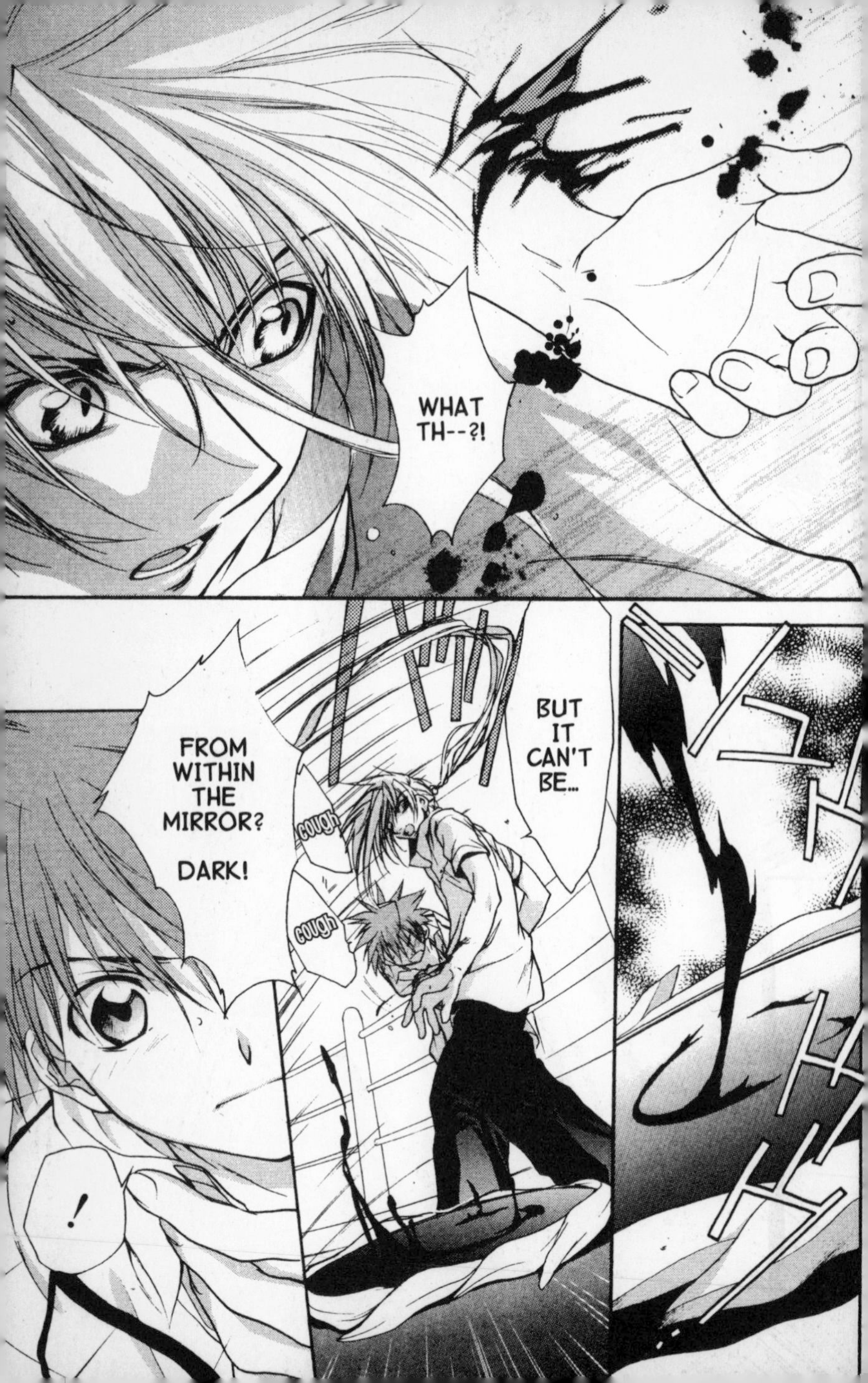
WHAT TH--?!
BUT IT CAN'T BE...
cough
cough
FROM WITHIN THE MIRROR?
DARK!
!

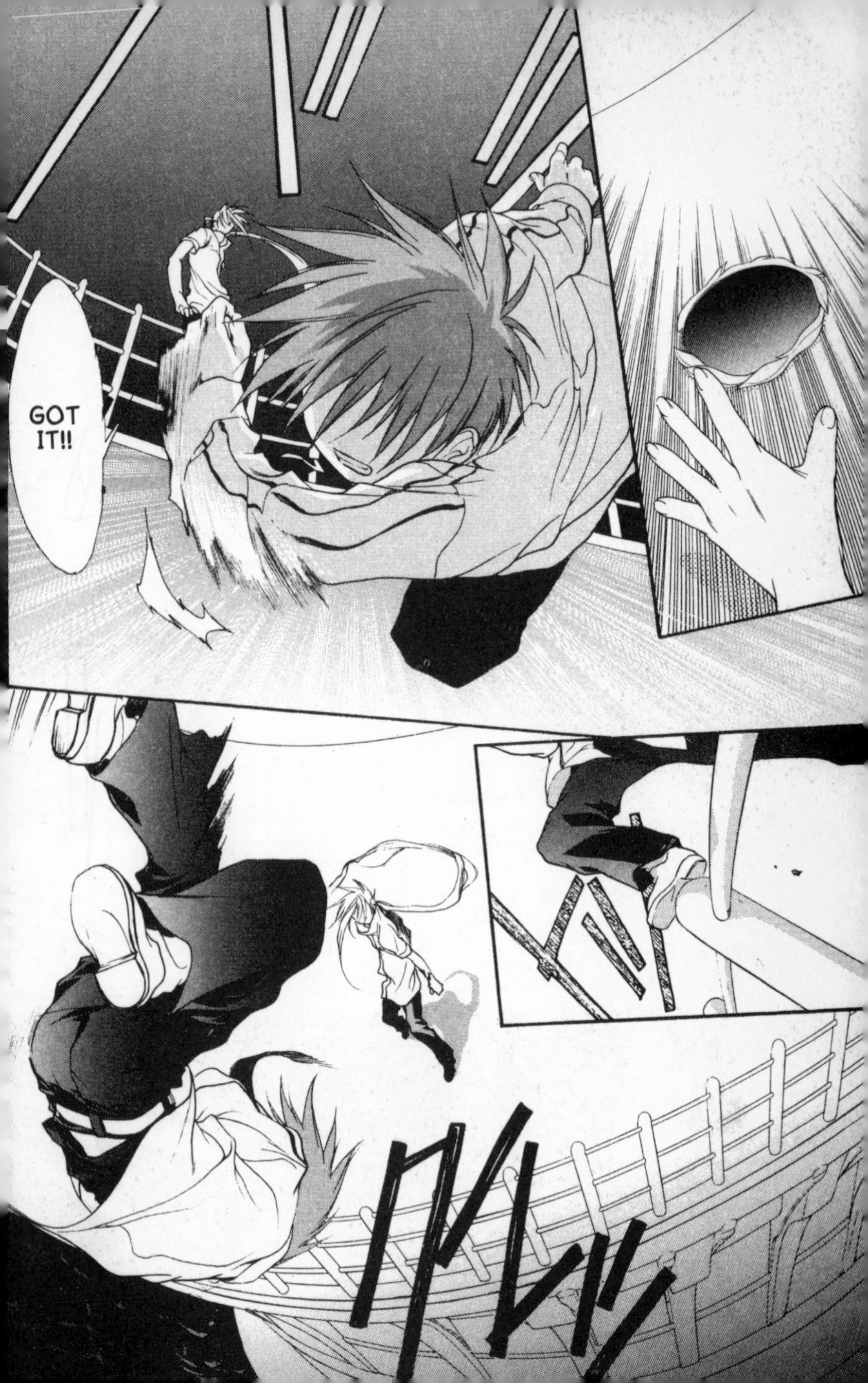
GOT IT!!

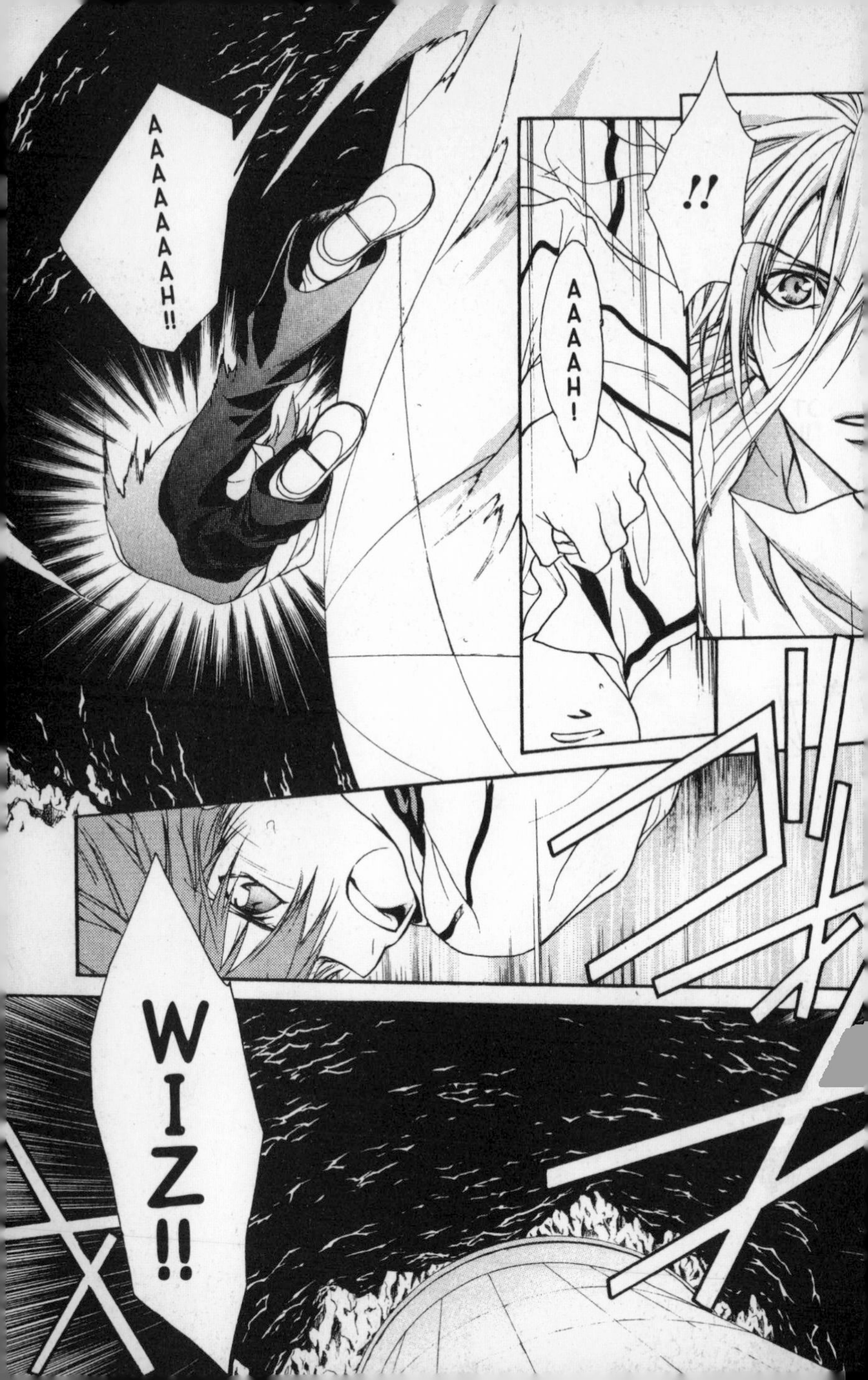
!!
AAAAAH!
AAAAAAAH!!
WIZ!!

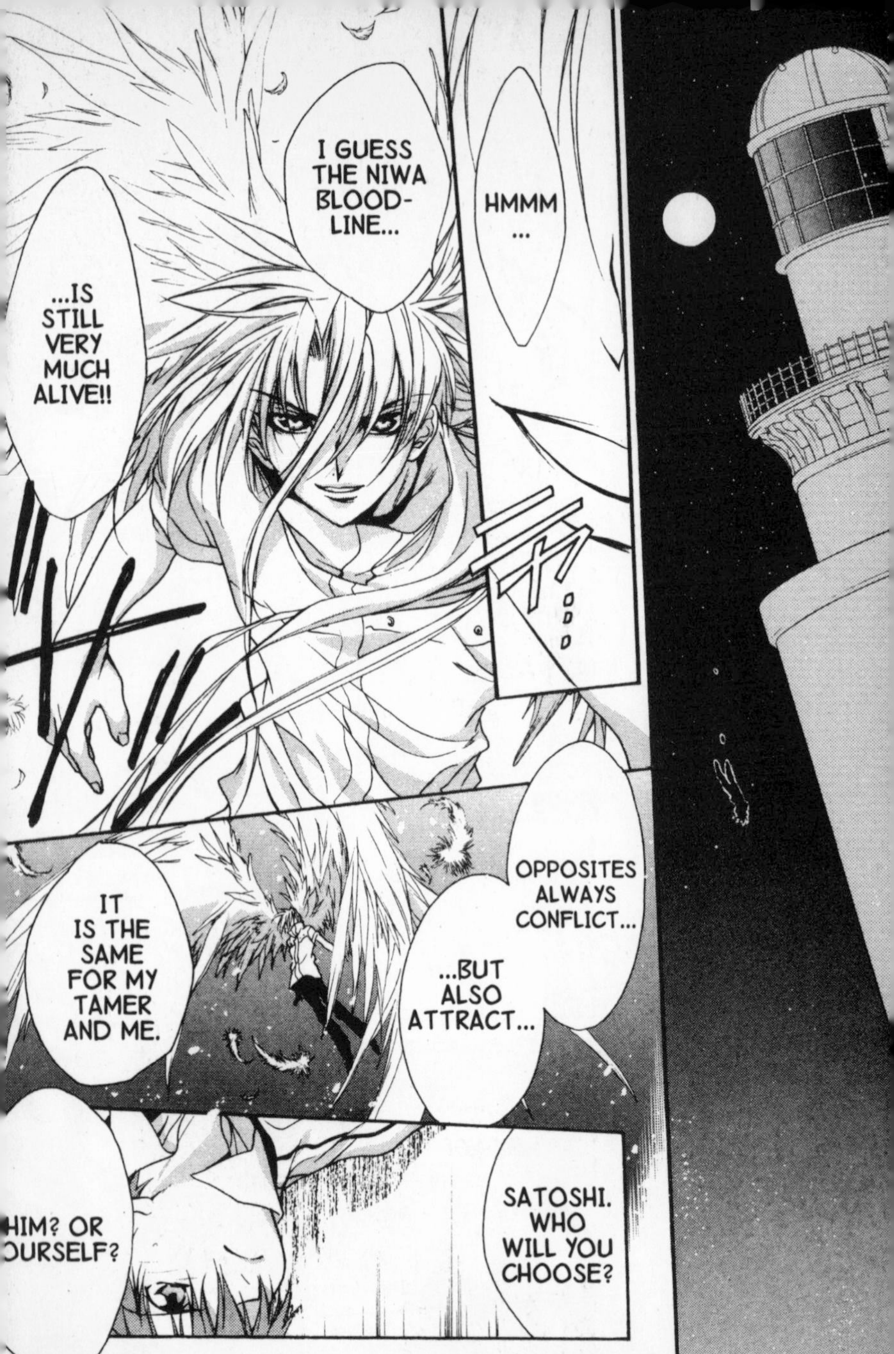
HMMM...
I GUESS THE NIWA BLOODLINE...
...IS STILL VERY MUCH ALIVE!!
OPPOSITES ALWAYS CONFLICT...
...BUT ALSO ATTRACT...
IT IS THE SAME FOR MY TAMER AND ME.
SATOSHI. WHO WILL YOU CHOOSE?
HIM? OR OURSELF?

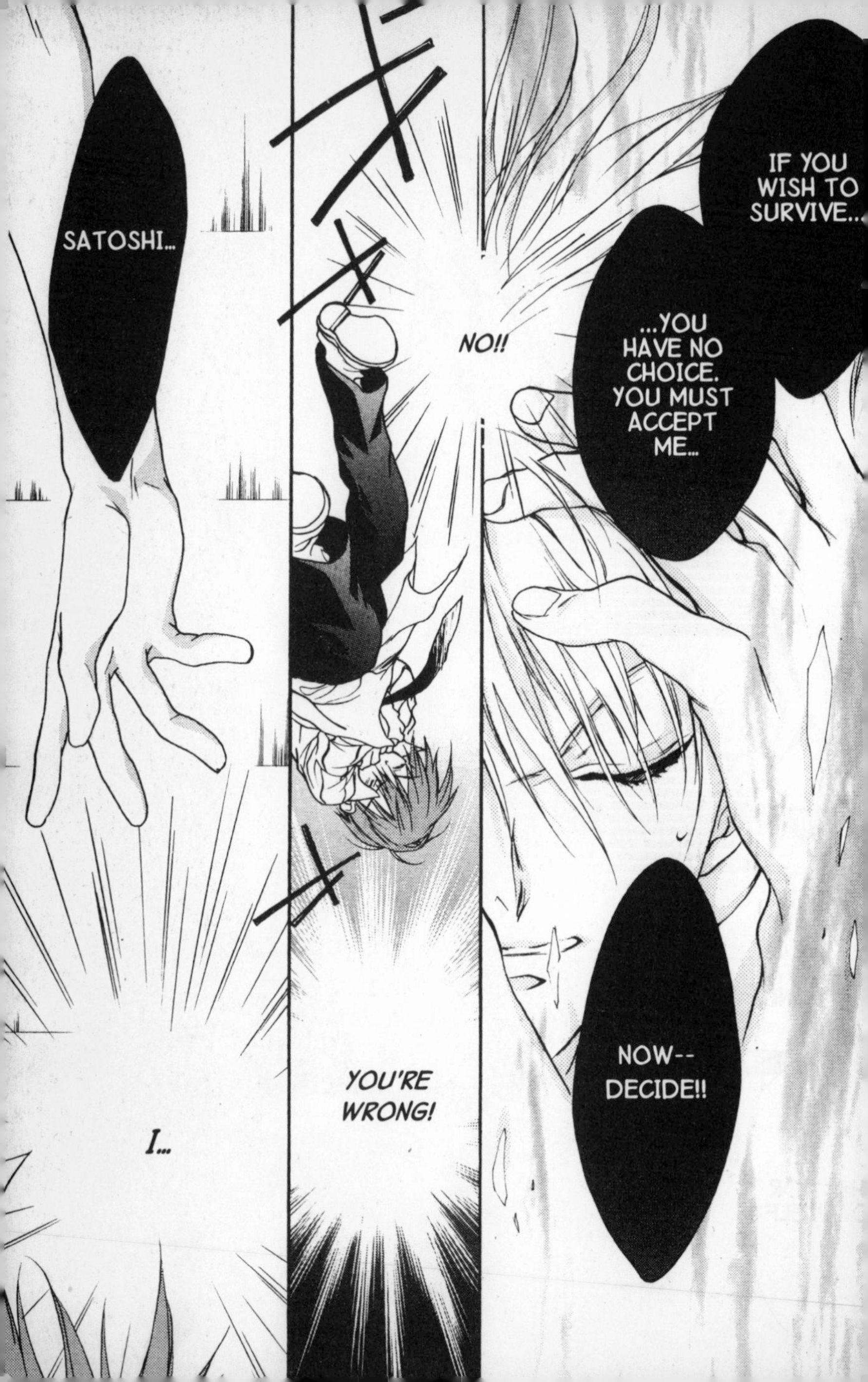
IF YOU WISH TO SURVIVE...
...YOU HAVE NO CHOICE. YOU MUST ACCEPT ME...
NOW-- DECIDE!!
NO!!
YOU'RE WRONG!
SATOSHI...
I...

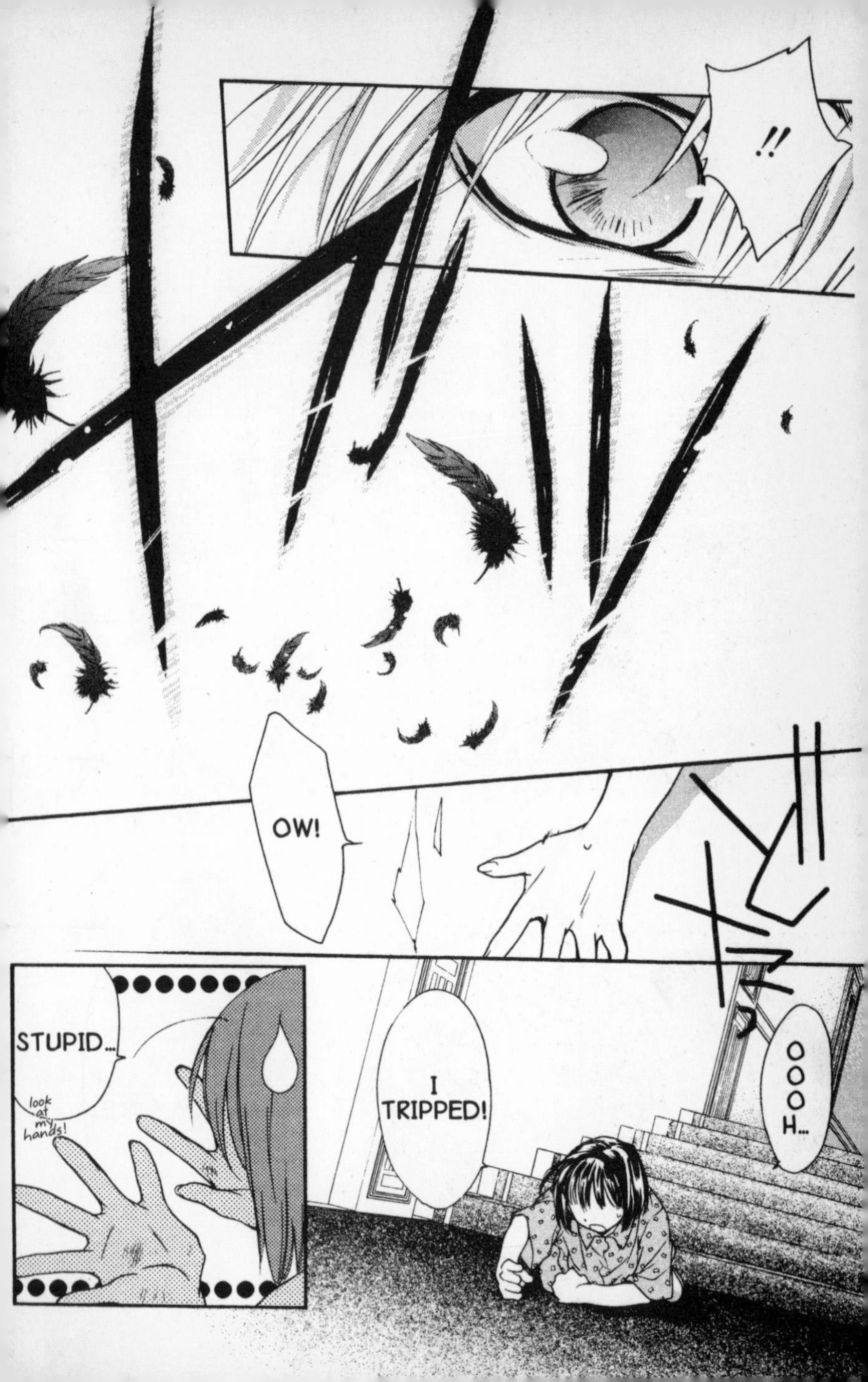
!!
OW!
OOOH...
I TRIPPED!
STUPID...
look at my hands!

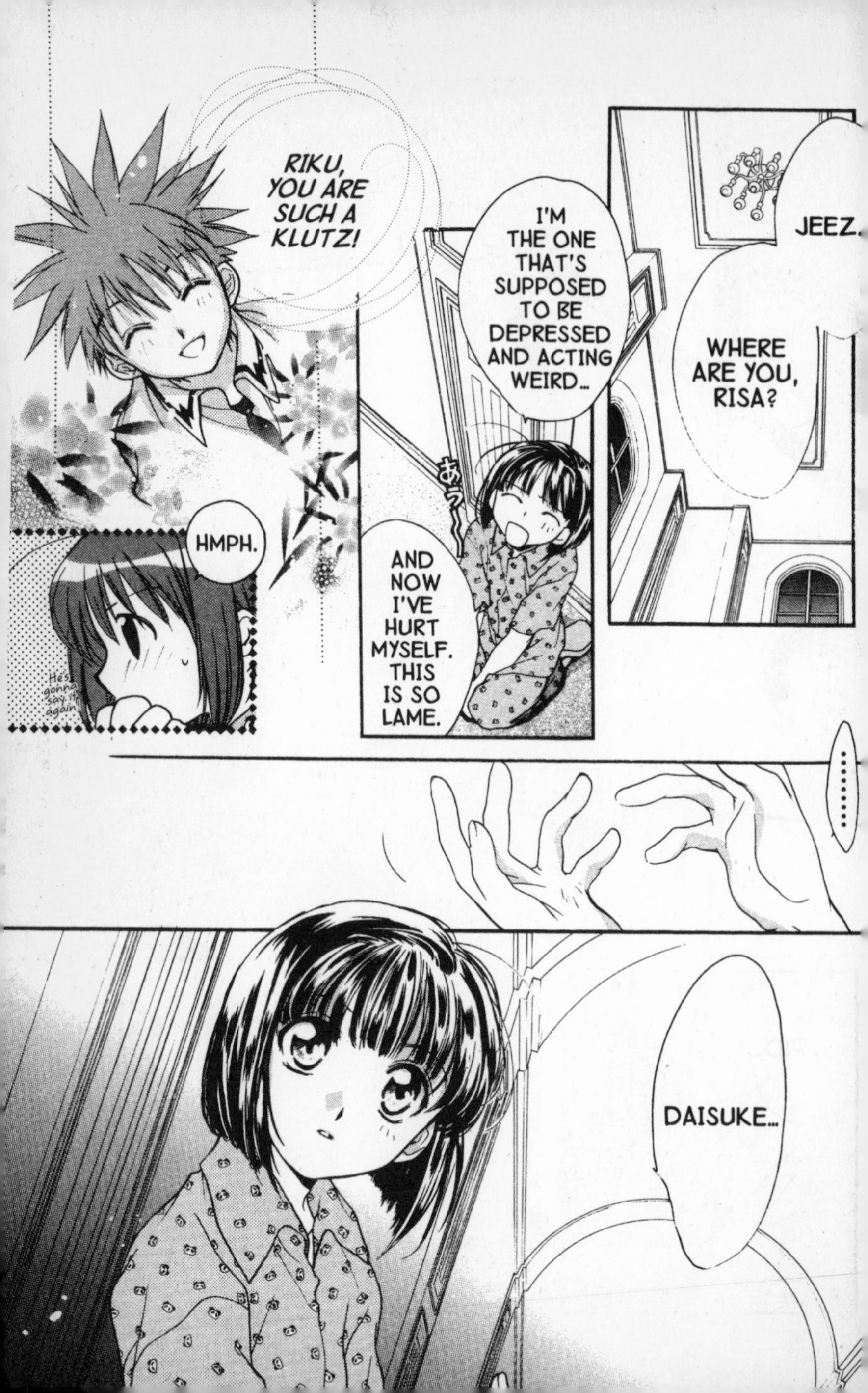
JEEZ.
WHERE ARE YOU, RISA?
I'M THE ONE THAT'S SUPPOSED TO BE DEPRESSED AND ACTING WEIRD...
あう～
AND NOW I'VE HURT MYSELF. THIS IS SO LAME.
RIKU, YOU ARE SUCH A KLUTZ!
HMPH.
He's gonna say it again!
......
DAISUKE...

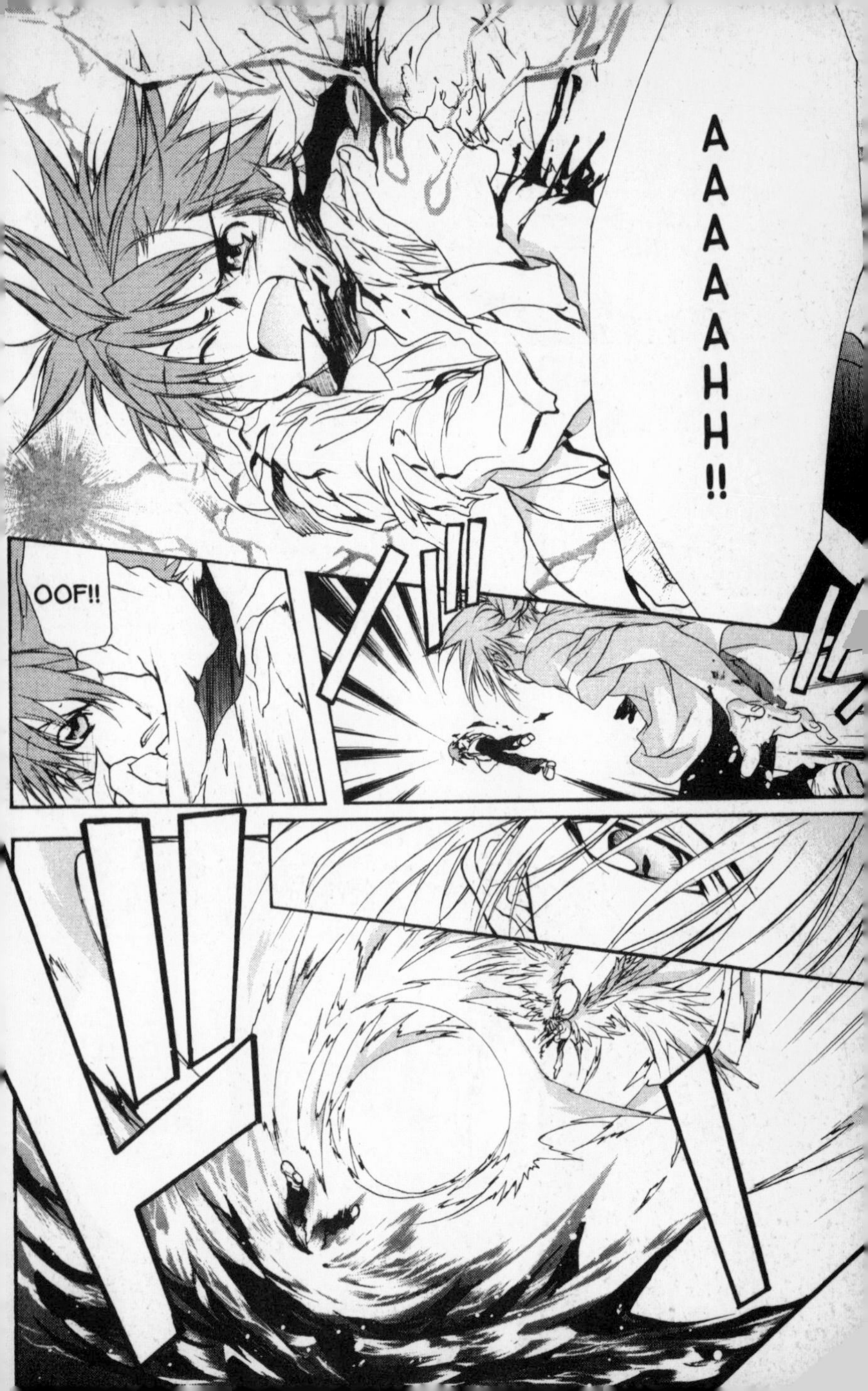
AAAAAHH!!
OOF!!

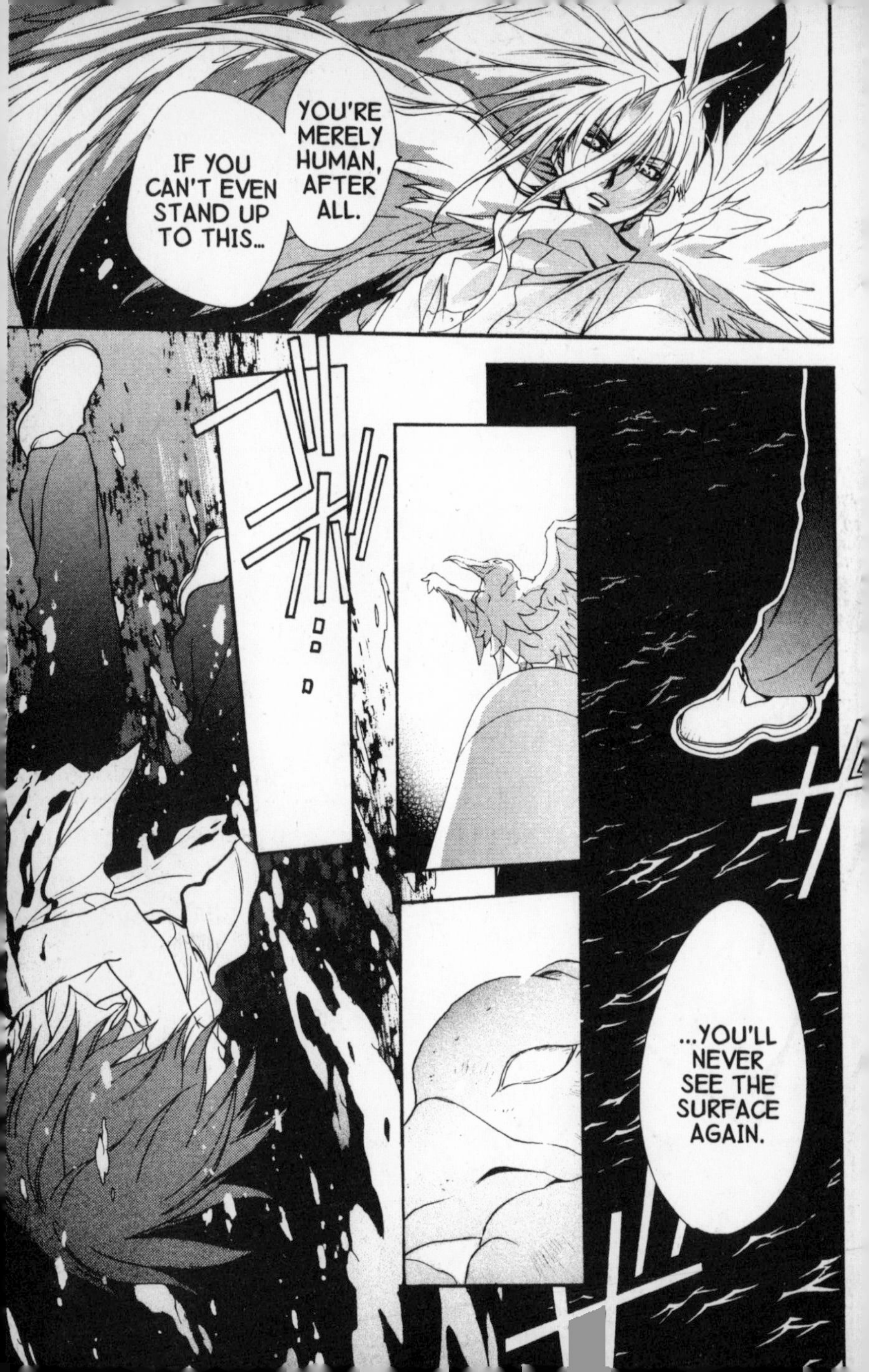
YOU'RE MERELY HUMAN, AFTER ALL.
IF YOU CAN'T EVEN STAND UP TO THIS...
...YOU'LL NEVER SEE THE SURFACE AGAIN.

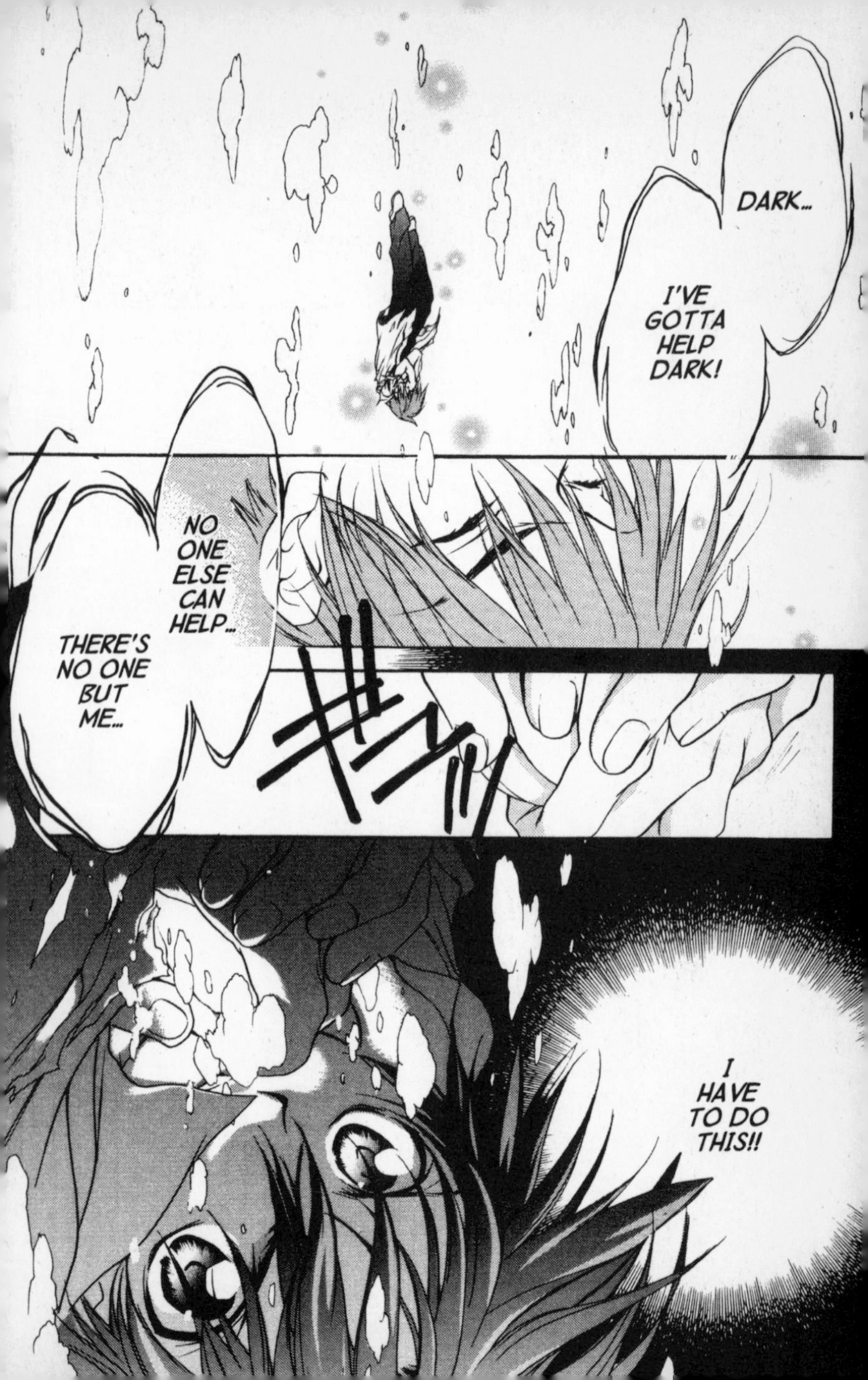
DARK...
I'VE GOTTA HELP DARK!
NO ONE ELSE CAN HELP...
THERE'S NO ONE BUT ME...
I HAVE TO DO THIS!!

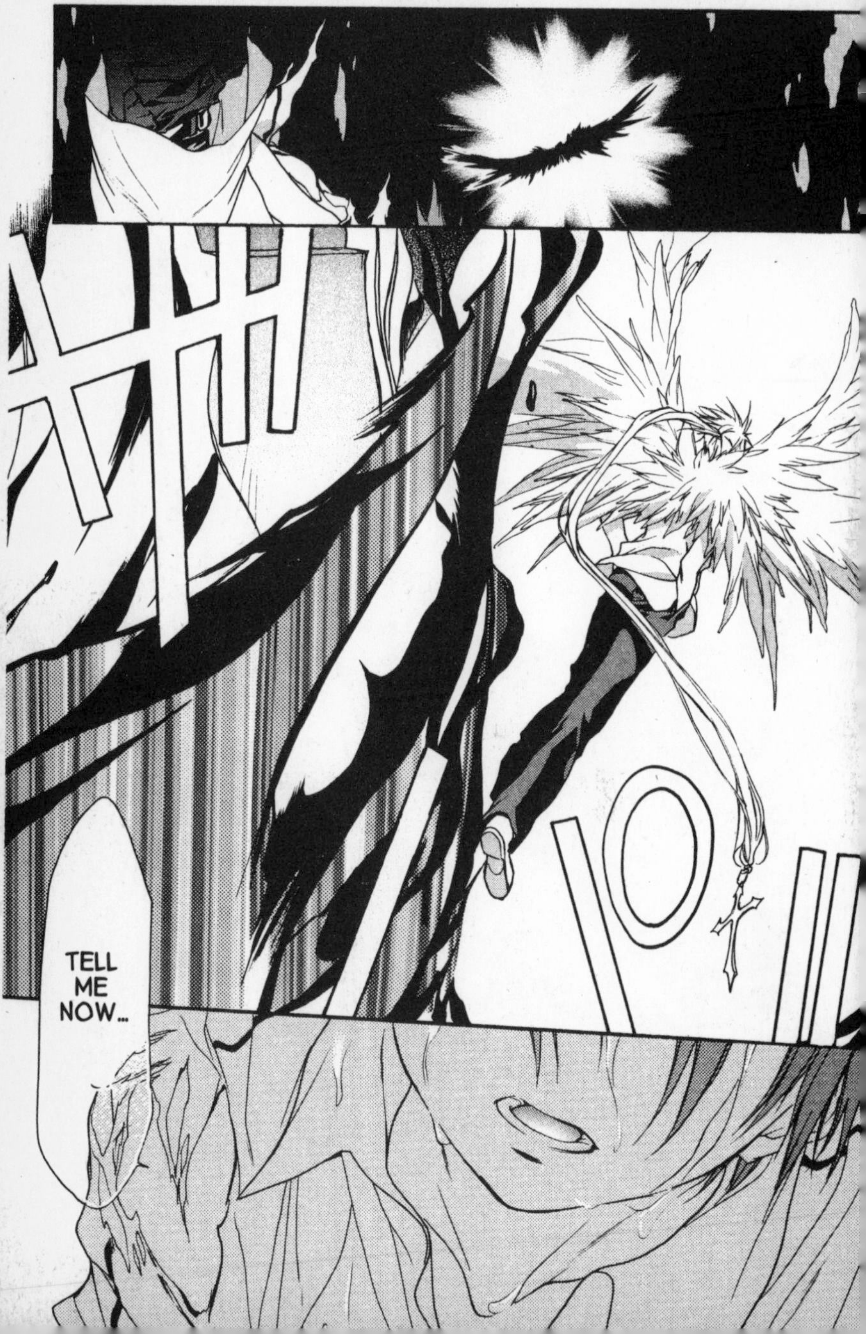
TELL ME NOW...

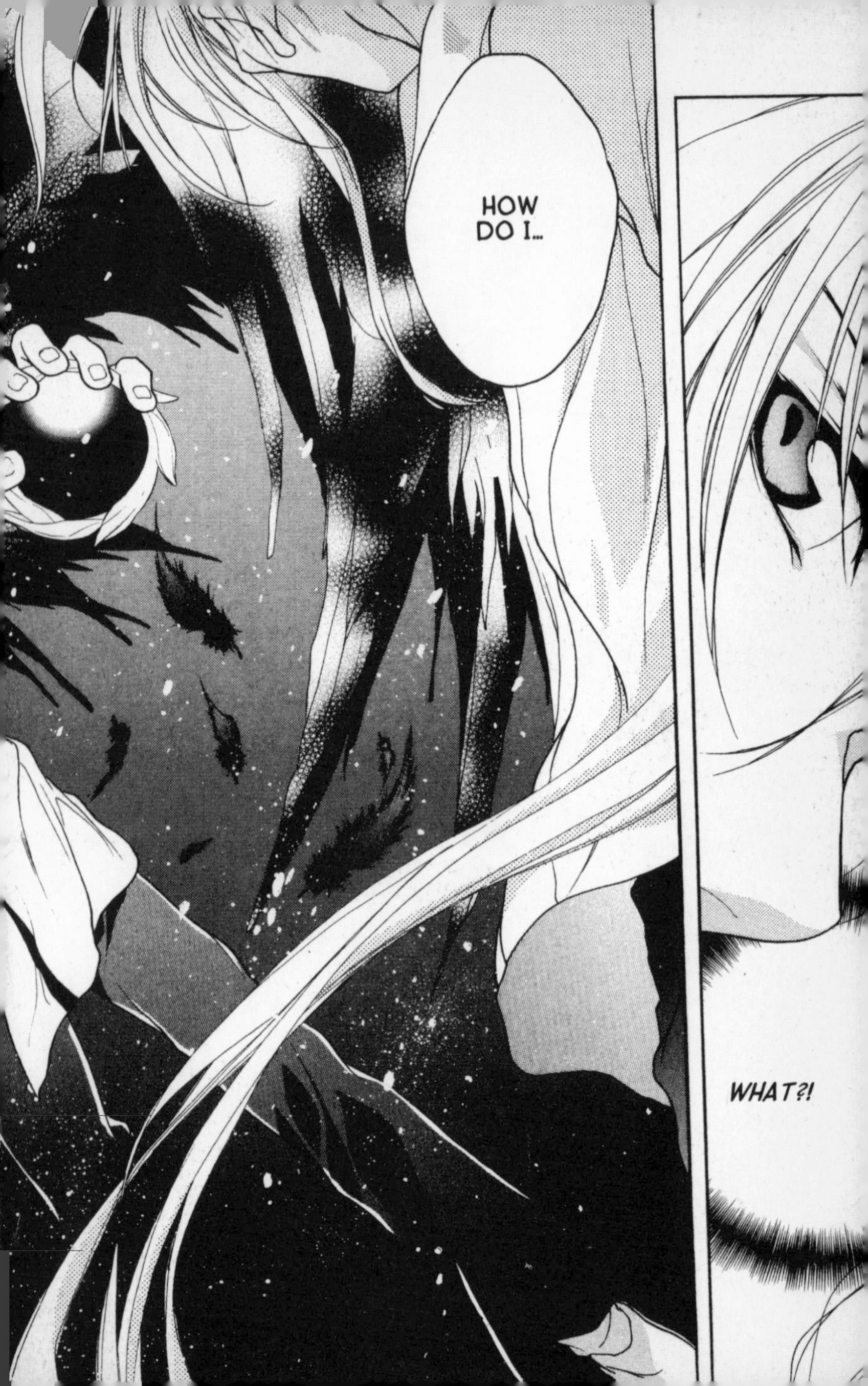
WHAT?!
HOW DO I...

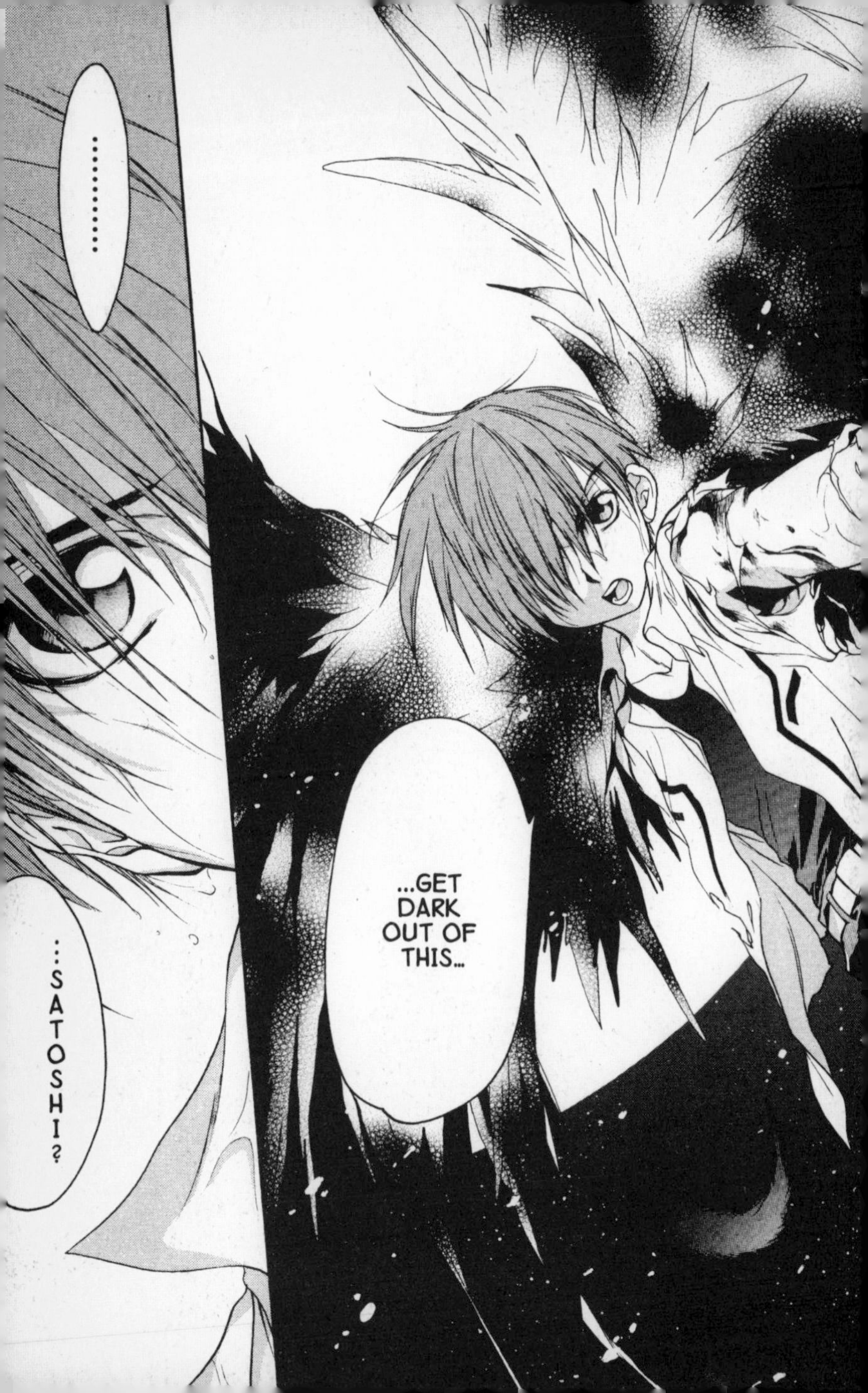
...GET DARK OUT OF THIS...
....
...SATOSHI?

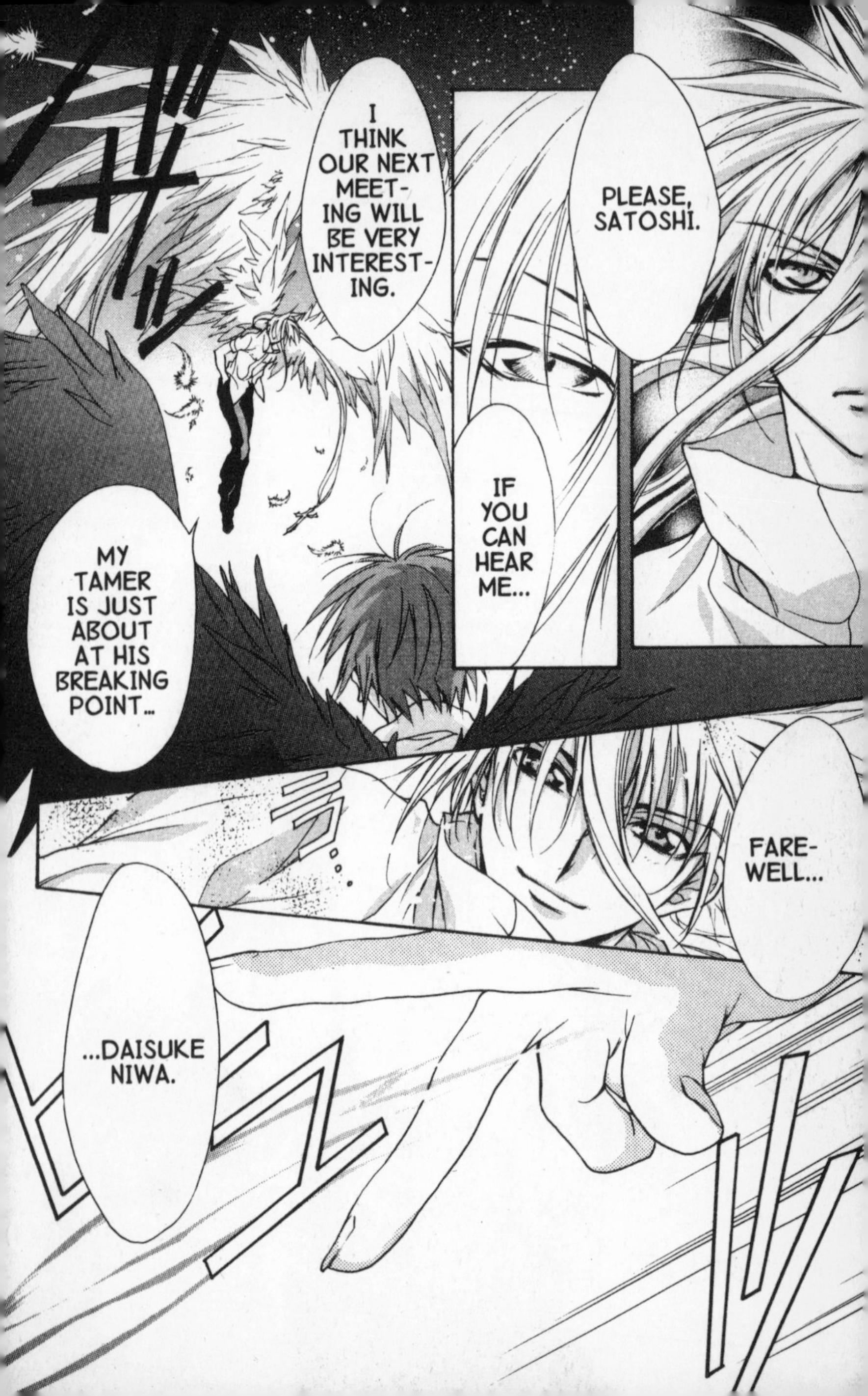
PLEASE, SATOSHI.
IF YOU CAN HEAR ME...
I THINK OUR NEXT MEET-ING WILL BE VERY INTEREST-ING.
MY TAMER IS JUST ABOUT AT HIS BREAKING POINT...
FARE-WELL...
...DAISUKE NIWA.

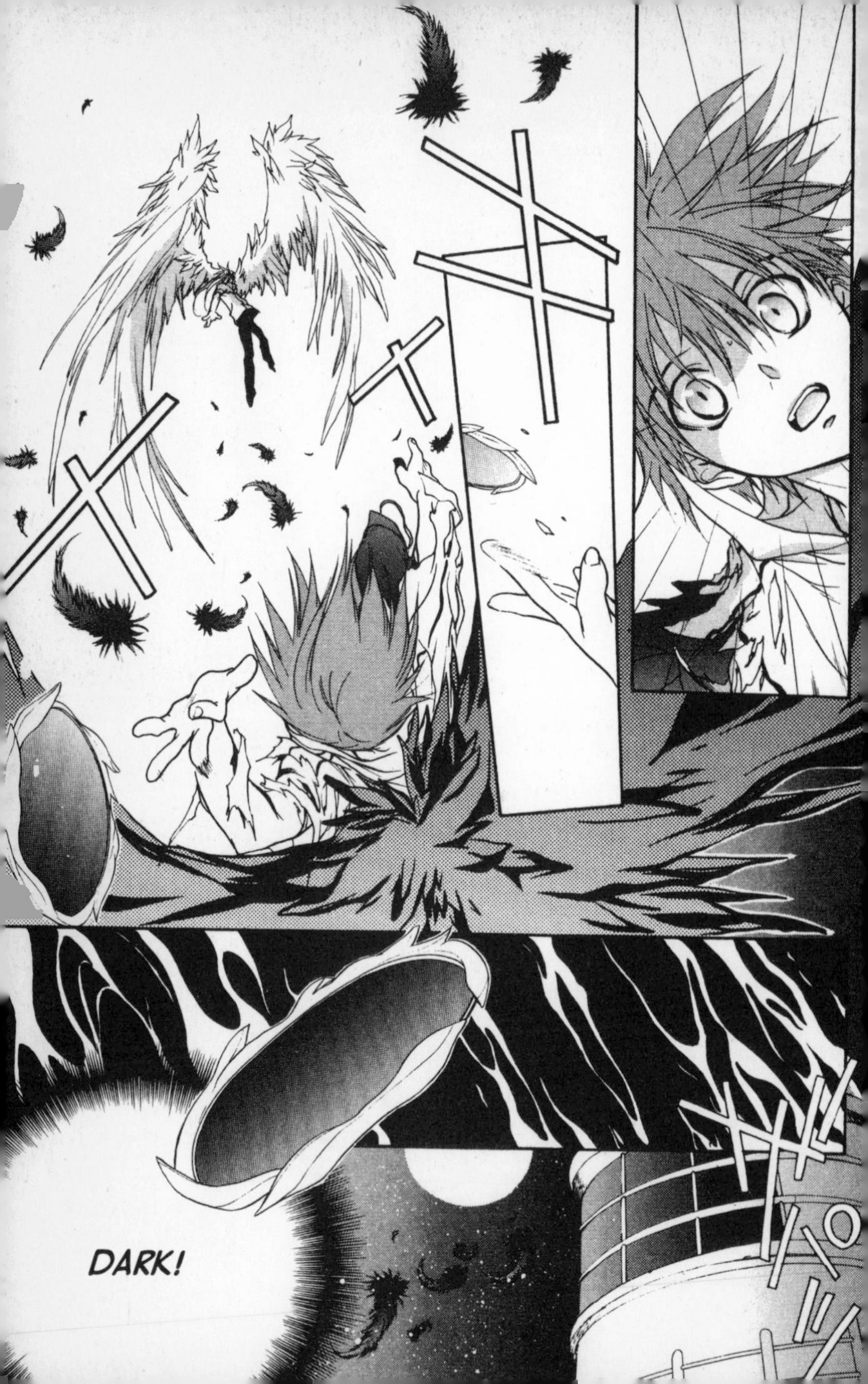
DARK!

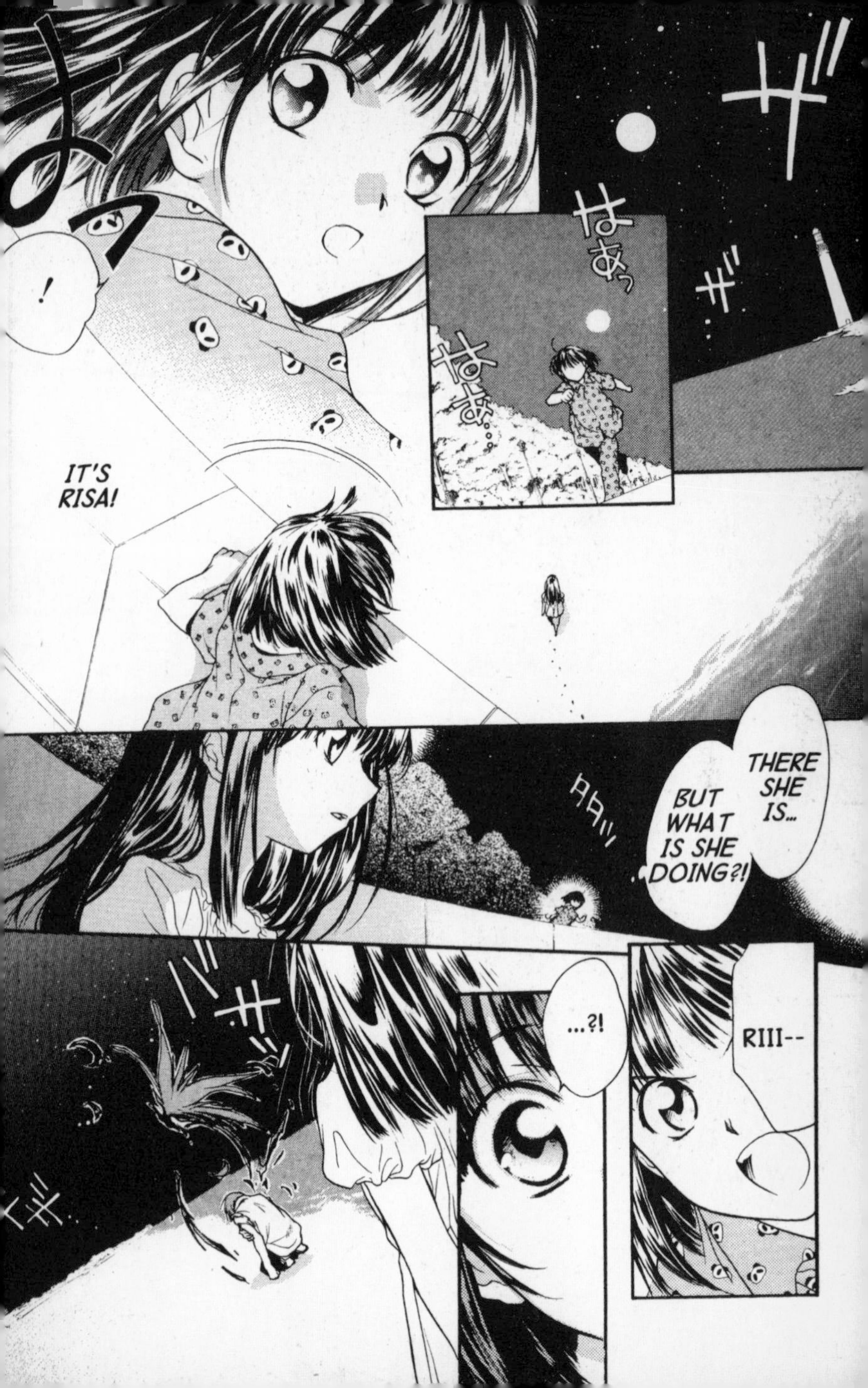
ザ
ザ…
はあっ
はあ…
あっ
!
IT'S RISA!
THERE SHE IS...
BUT WHAT IS SHE DOING?!
タタッ
RIII--
...?!
バサッ

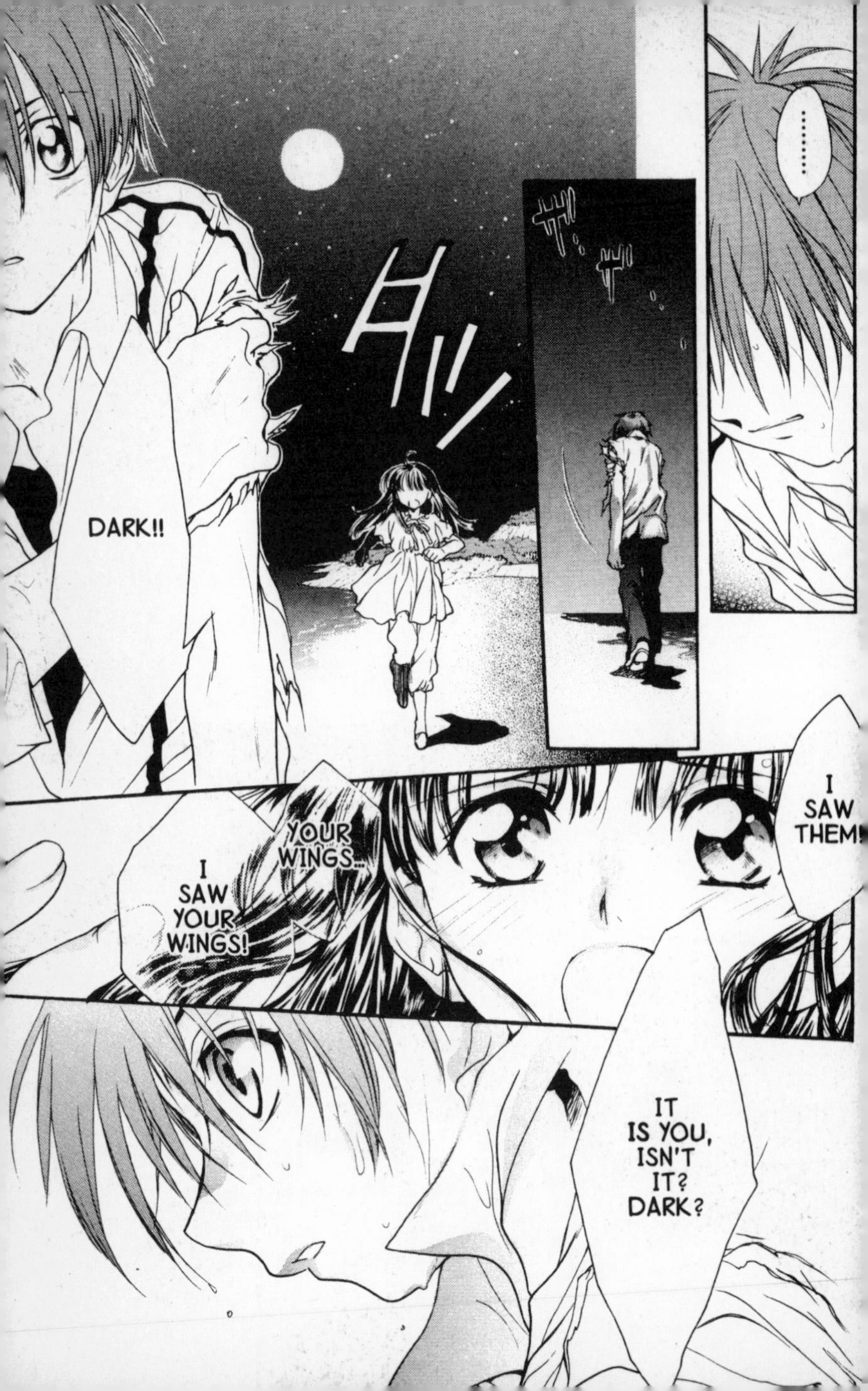
......
DARK!!
I SAW THEM!
YOUR WINGS...
I SAW YOUR WINGS!
IT IS YOU, ISN'T IT? DARK?

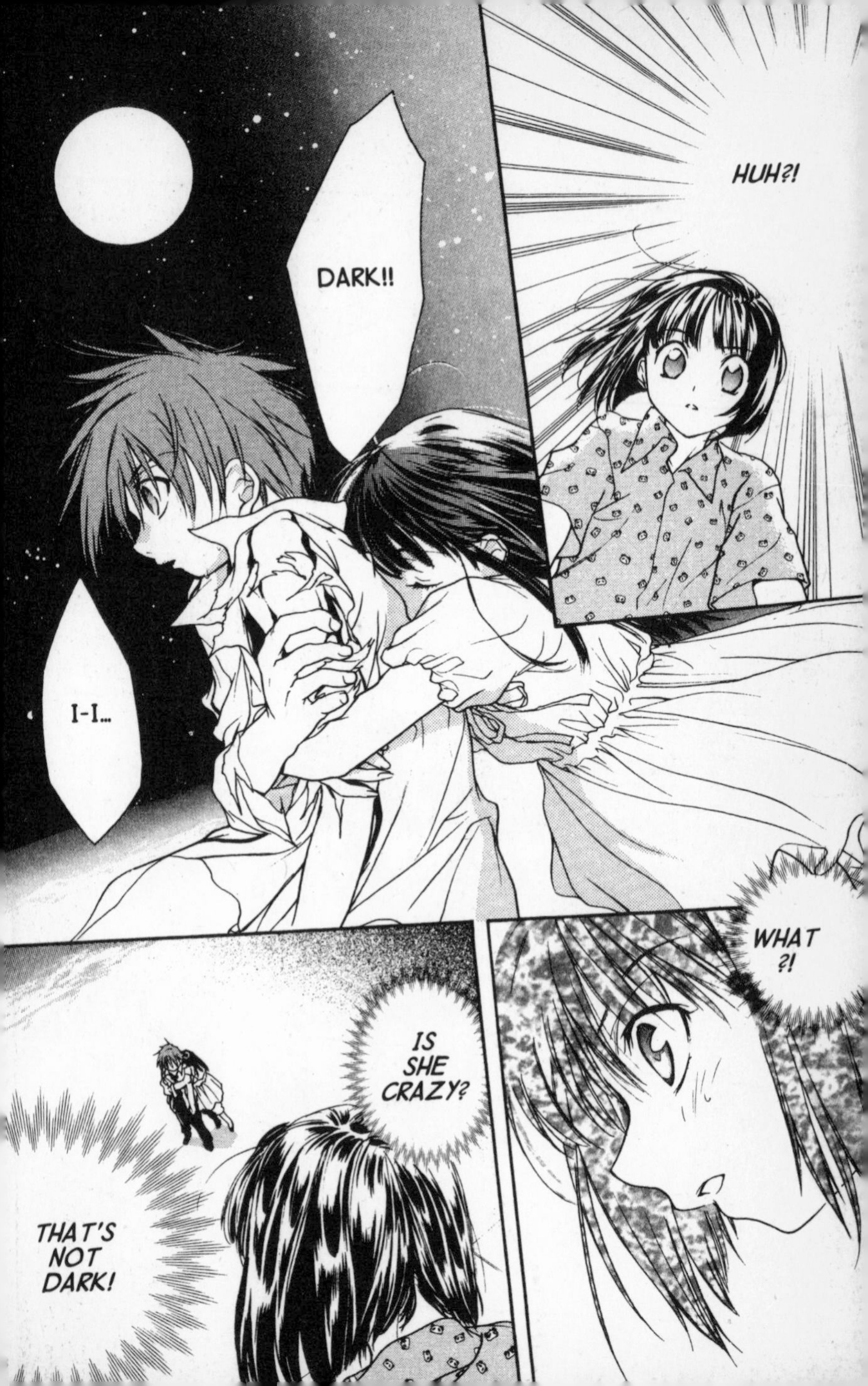
HUH?!
DARK!!
I-I...
WHAT ?!
IS SHE CRAZY?
THAT'S NOT DARK!

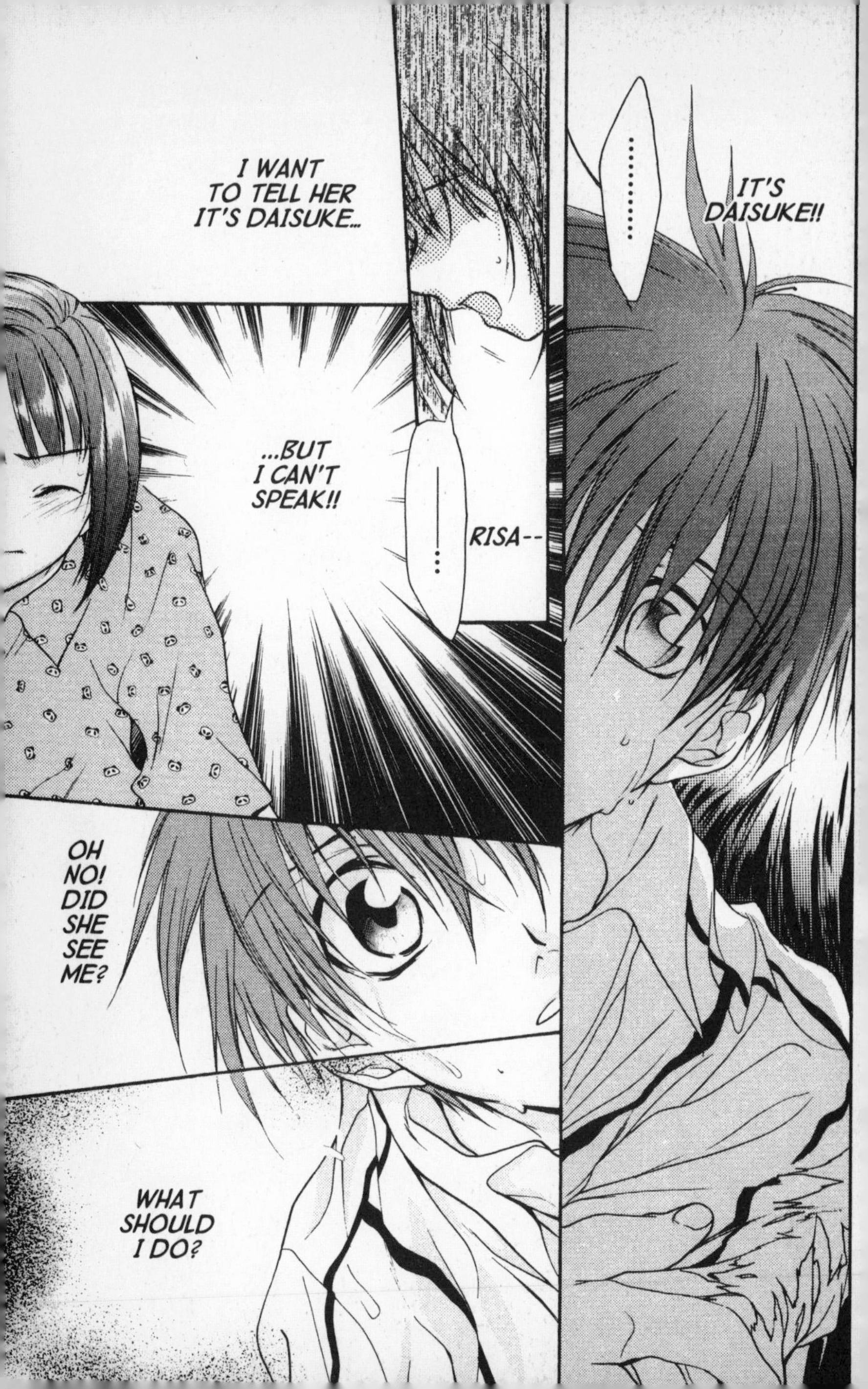
IT'S DAISUKE!!
......
I WANT TO TELL HER IT'S DAISUKE...
—...
RISA--
...BUT I CAN'T SPEAK!!
OH NO! DID SHE SEE ME?
WHAT SHOULD I DO?

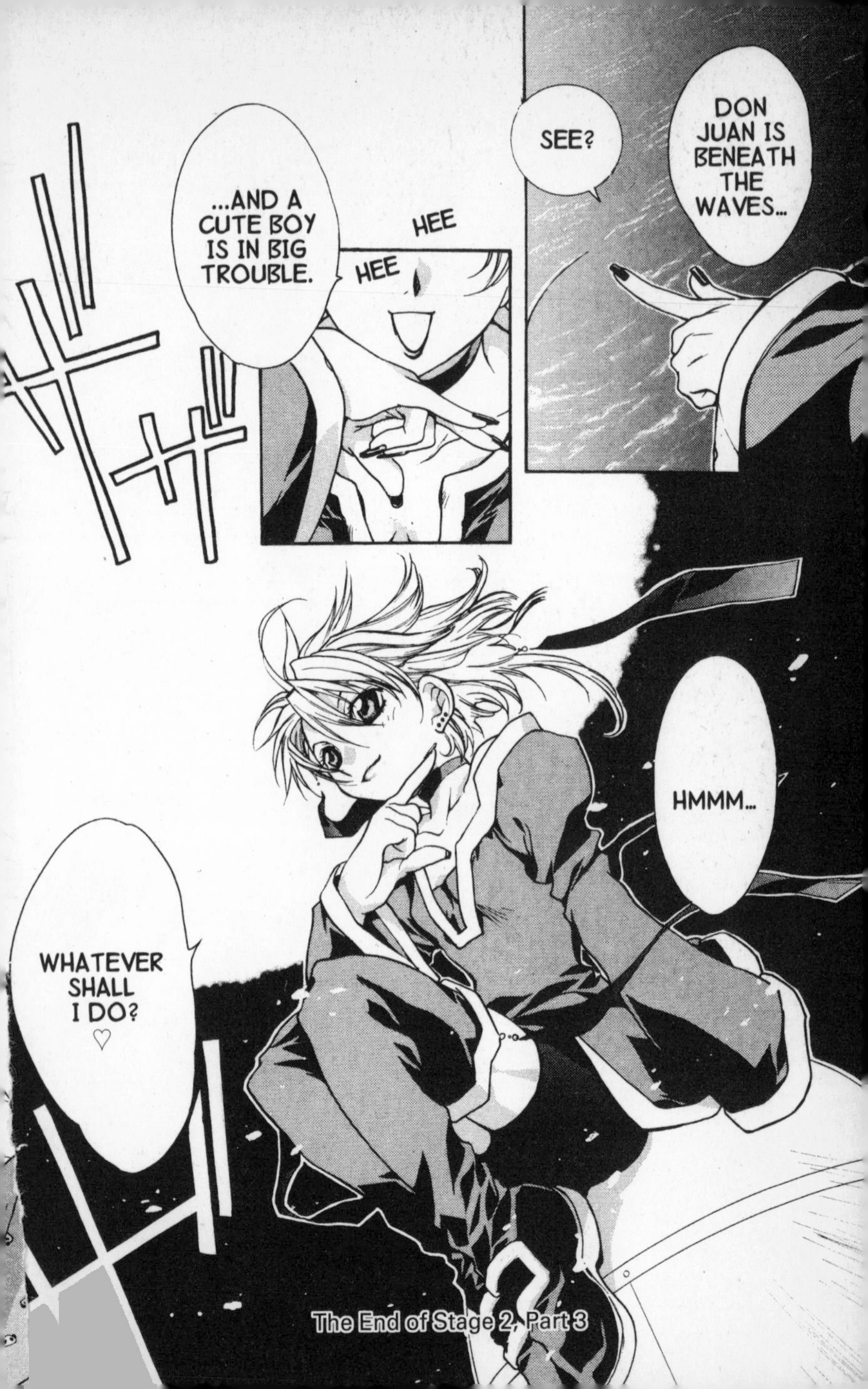
DON JUAN IS BENEATH THE WAVES...
SEE?
HEE HEE
...AND A CUTE BOY IS IN BIG TROUBLE.
HMMM...
WHATEVER SHALL I DO? ♡
The End of Stage 2, Part 3

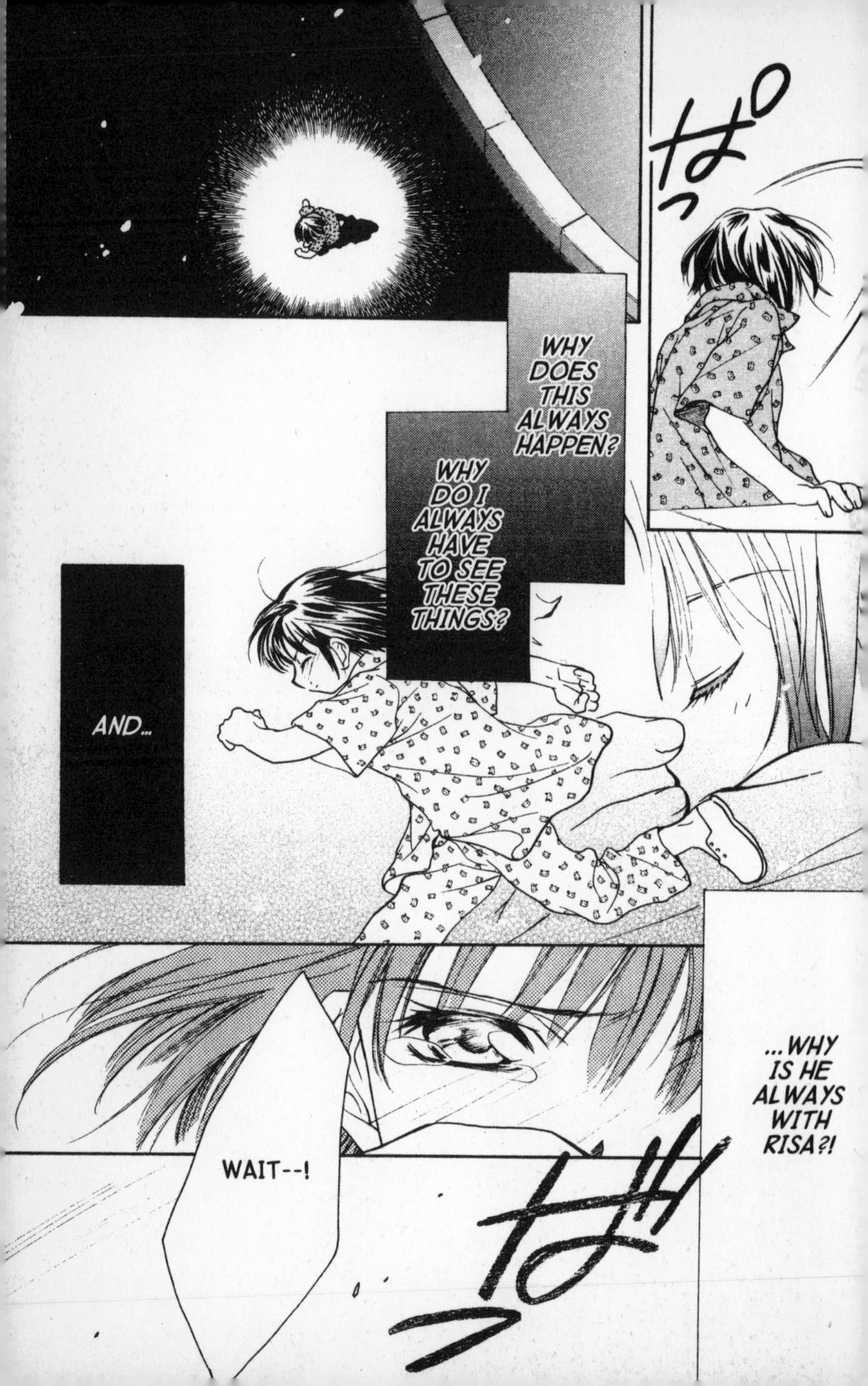
ぱっ
WHY DOES THIS ALWAYS HAPPEN?
WHY DO I ALWAYS HAVE TO SEE THESE THINGS?
AND...
...WHY IS HE ALWAYS WITH RISA?!
WAIT--!

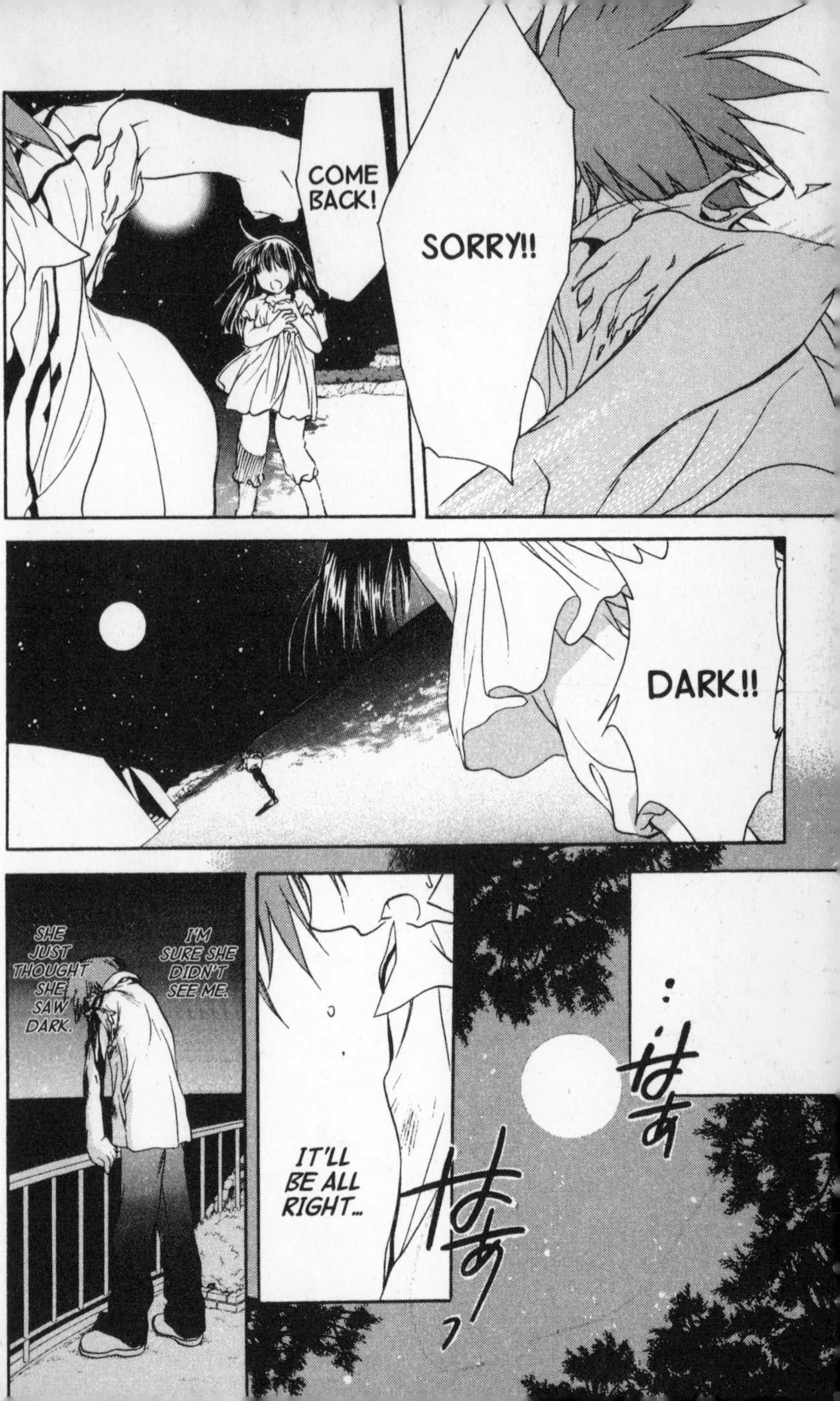
SORRY!!
COME BACK!
DARK!!
…はあ
はあっ
IT'LL BE ALL RIGHT…
I'M SURE SHE DIDN'T SEE ME.
SHE JUST THOUGHT SHE SAW DARK.

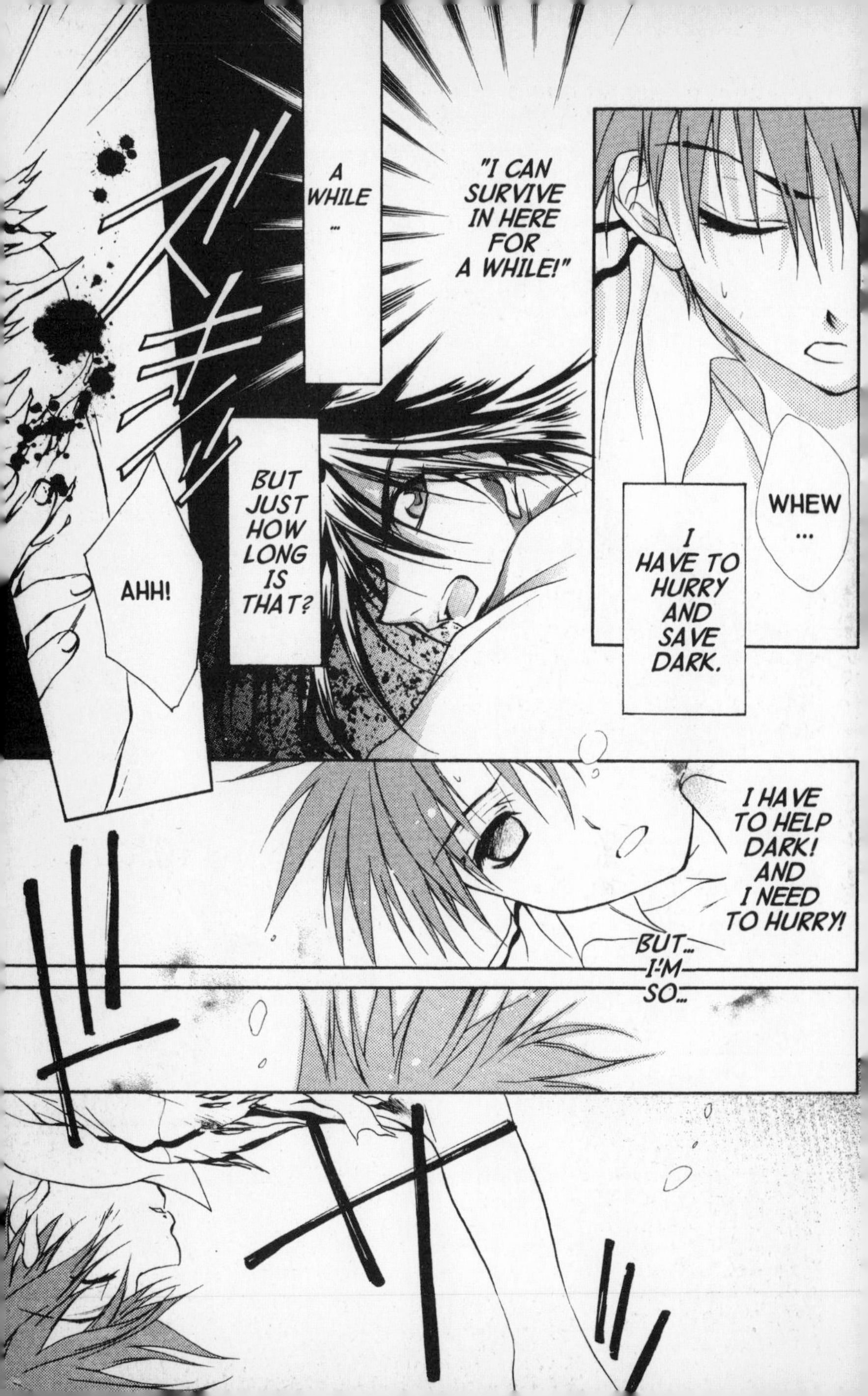
WHEW...
I HAVE TO HURRY AND SAVE DARK.
"I CAN SURVIVE IN HERE FOR A WHILE!"
A WHILE...
BUT JUST HOW LONG IS THAT?
AHH!
I HAVE TO HELP DARK! AND I NEED TO HURRY!
BUT... I'M SO...

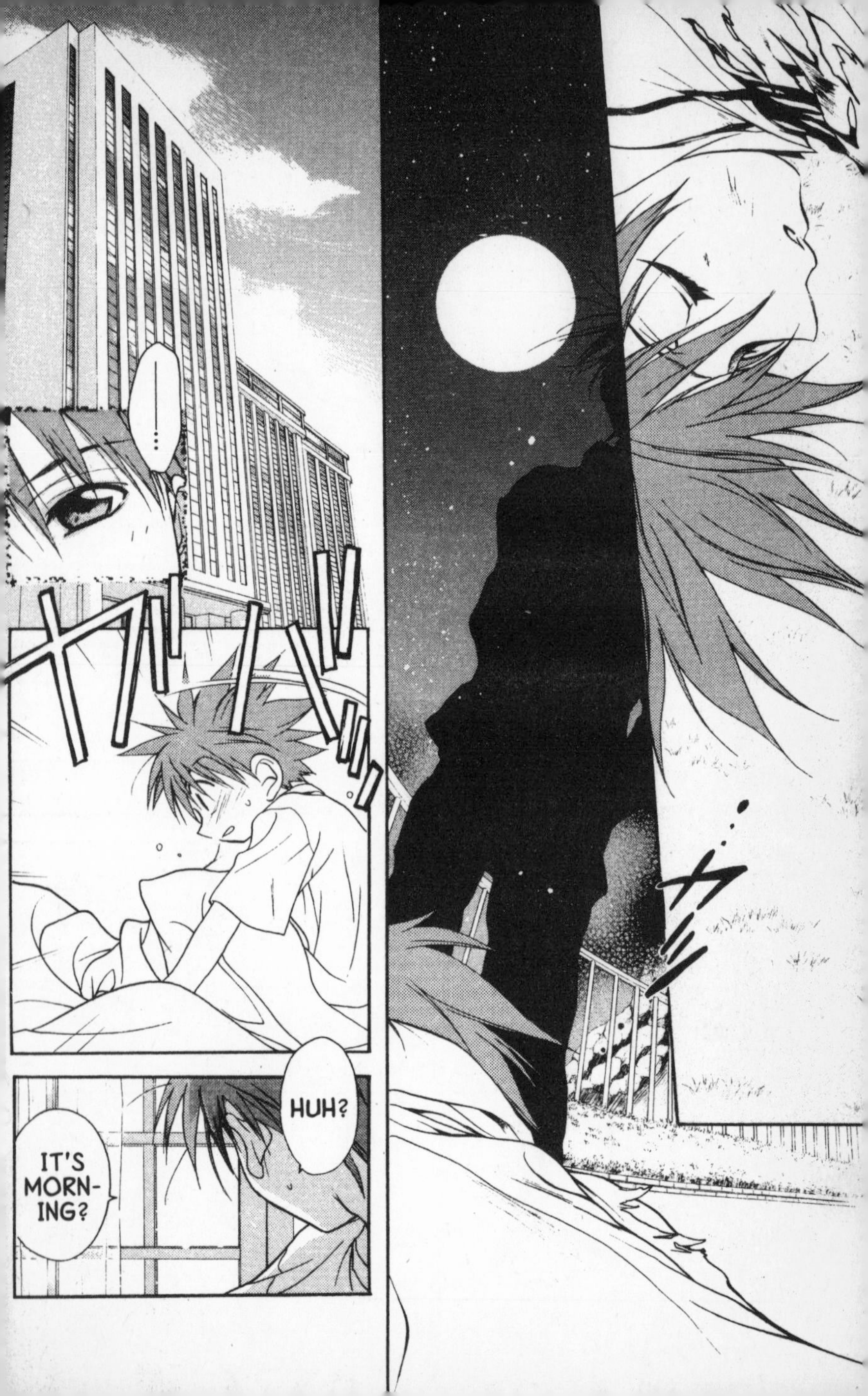
……
HUH?
IT'S MORNING-ING?

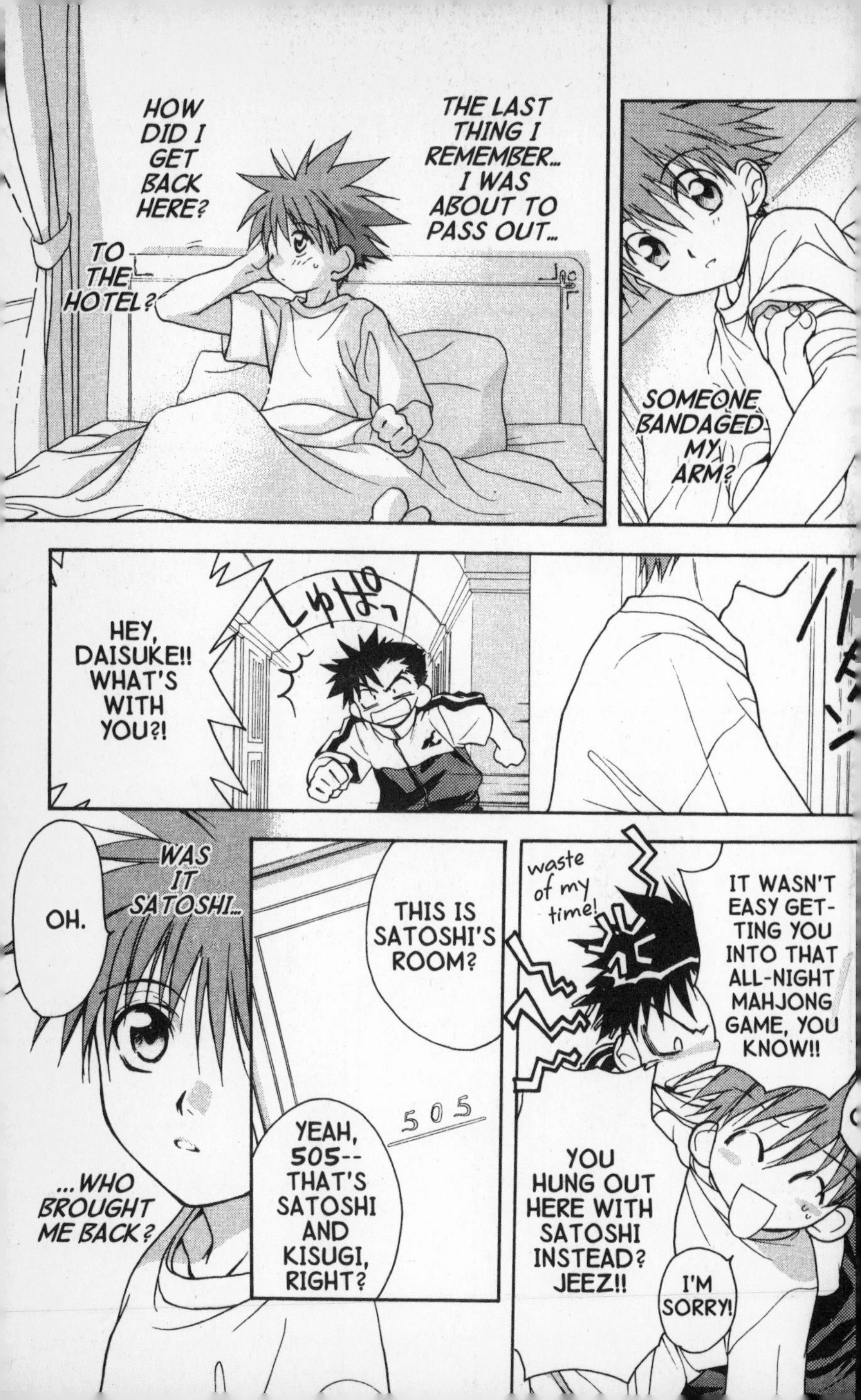
SOMEONE BANDAGED MY ARM?
THE LAST THING I REMEMBER... I WAS ABOUT TO PASS OUT...
HOW DID I GET BACK HERE?
TO THE HOTEL?
HEY, DAISUKE!! WHAT'S WITH YOU?!
IT WASN'T EASY GET-TING YOU INTO THAT ALL-NIGHT MAHJONG GAME, YOU KNOW!!
waste of my time!
YOU HUNG OUT HERE WITH SATOSHI INSTEAD? JEEZ!!
I'M SORRY!
THIS IS SATOSHI'S ROOM?
505
YEAH, 505-- THAT'S SATOSHI AND KISUGI, RIGHT?
WAS IT SATOSHI...
OH.
...WHO BROUGHT ME BACK?

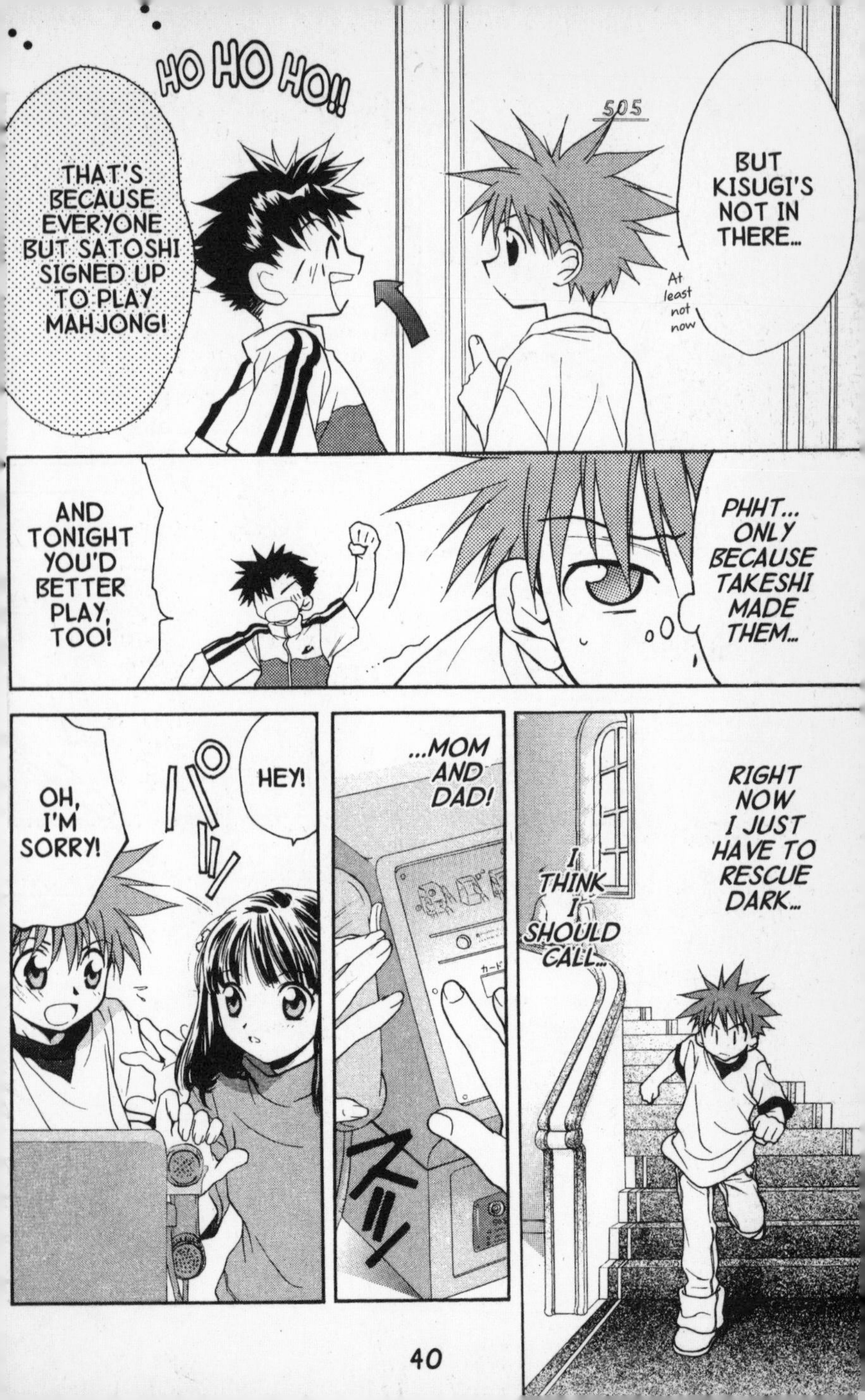
BUT KISUGI'S NOT IN THERE...
At least not now
HO HO HO!!
THAT'S BECAUSE EVERYONE BUT SATOSHI SIGNED UP TO PLAY MAHJONG!
505
PHHT... ONLY BECAUSE TAKESHI MADE THEM...
AND TONIGHT YOU'D BETTER PLAY, TOO!
RIGHT NOW I JUST HAVE TO RESCUE DARK...
I THINK I SHOULD CALL...
...MOM AND DAD!
HEY!
OH, I'M SORRY!

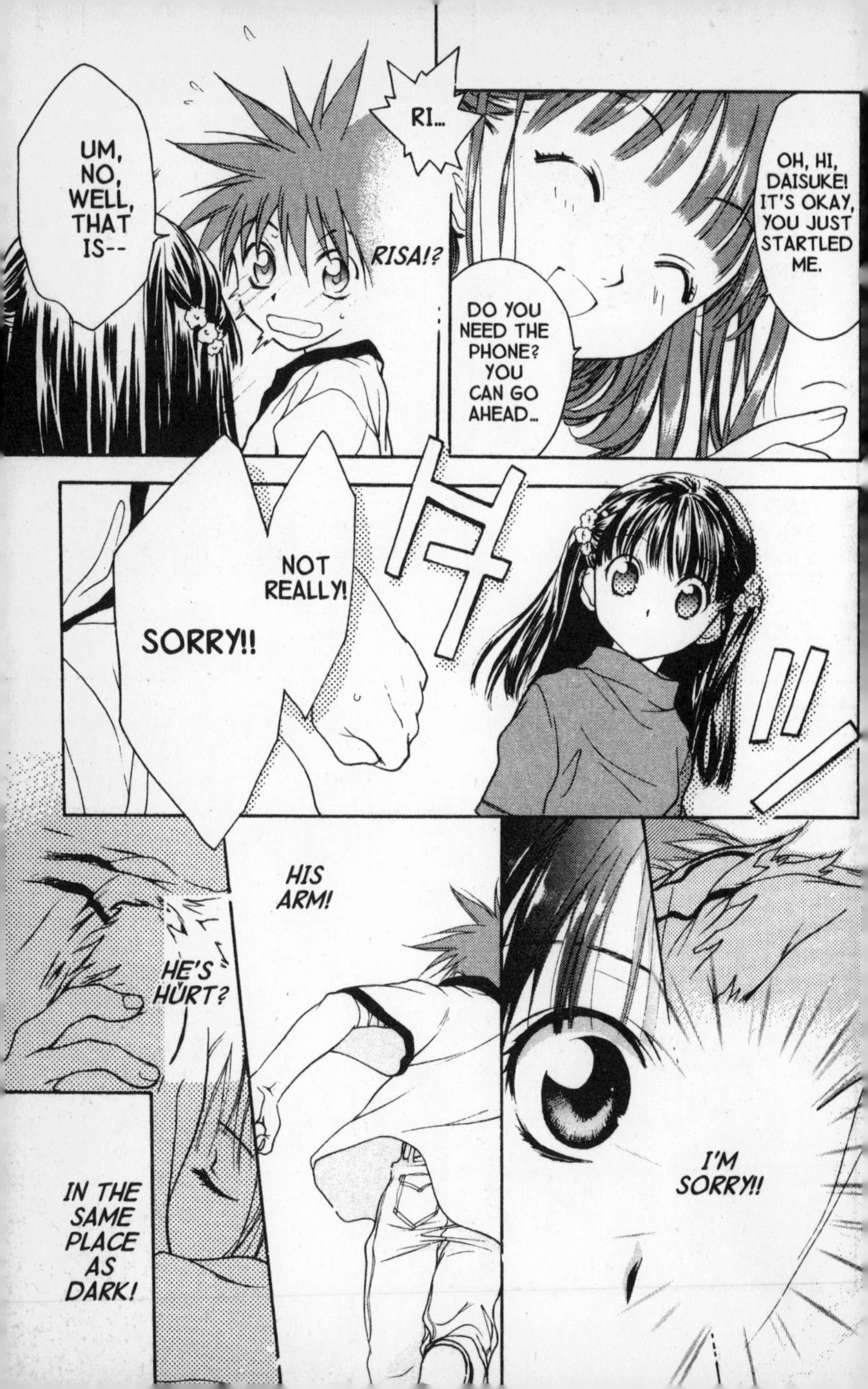
OH, HI, DAISUKE! IT'S OKAY, YOU JUST STARTLED ME.
DO YOU NEED THE PHONE? YOU CAN GO AHEAD...
RI...
RISA!?
UM, NO, WELL, THAT IS--
NOT REALLY!
SORRY!!
I'M SORRY!!
HIS ARM!
HE'S HURT?
IN THE SAME PLACE AS DARK!

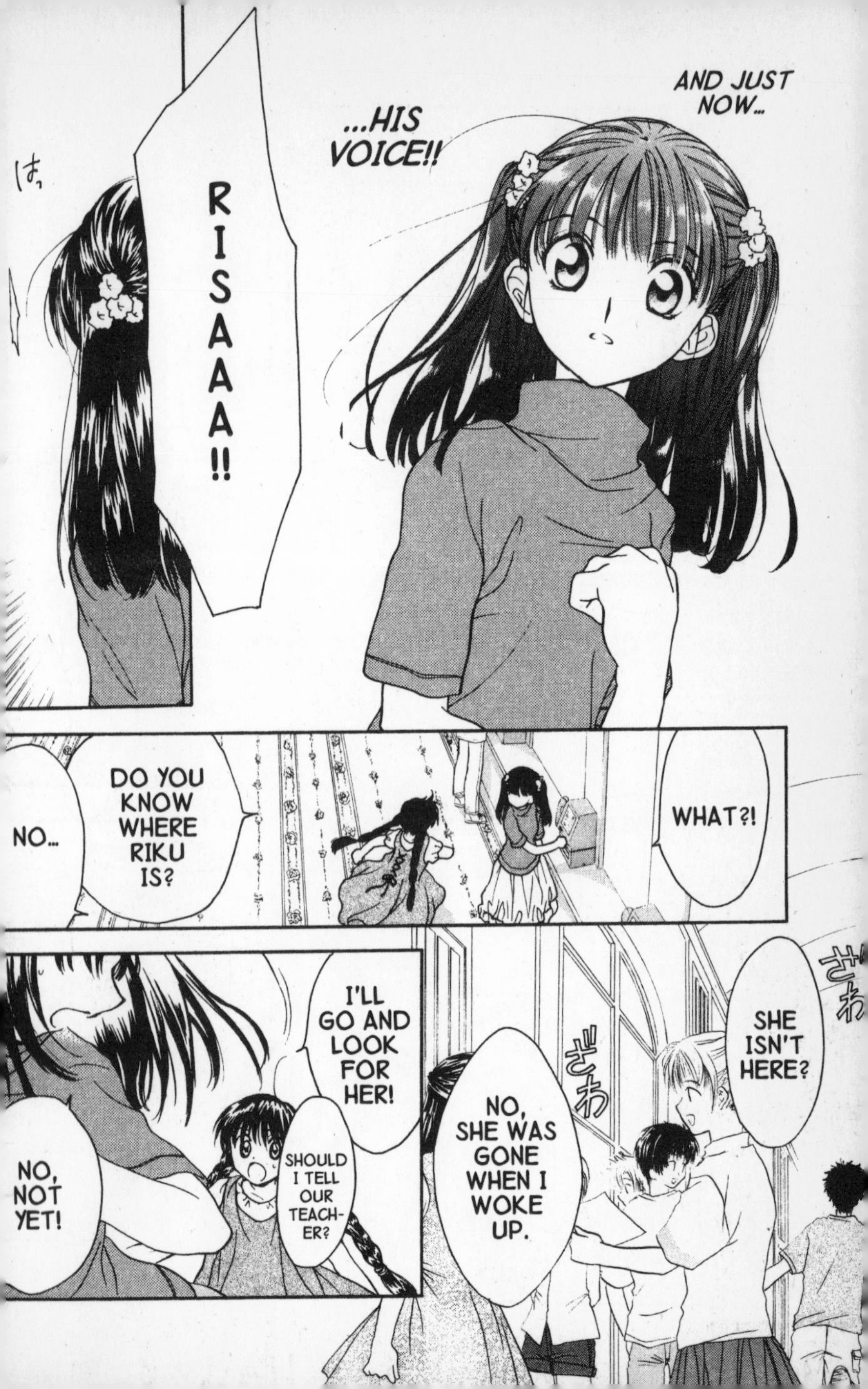
AND JUST NOW...
...HIS VOICE!!
RISAAAA!!
はっ
WHAT?!
DO YOU KNOW WHERE RIKU IS?
NO...
ざわ
ざわ
SHE ISN'T HERE?
NO, SHE WAS GONE WHEN I WOKE UP.
I'LL GO AND LOOK FOR HER!
SHOULD I TELL OUR TEACHER?
NO, NOT YET!

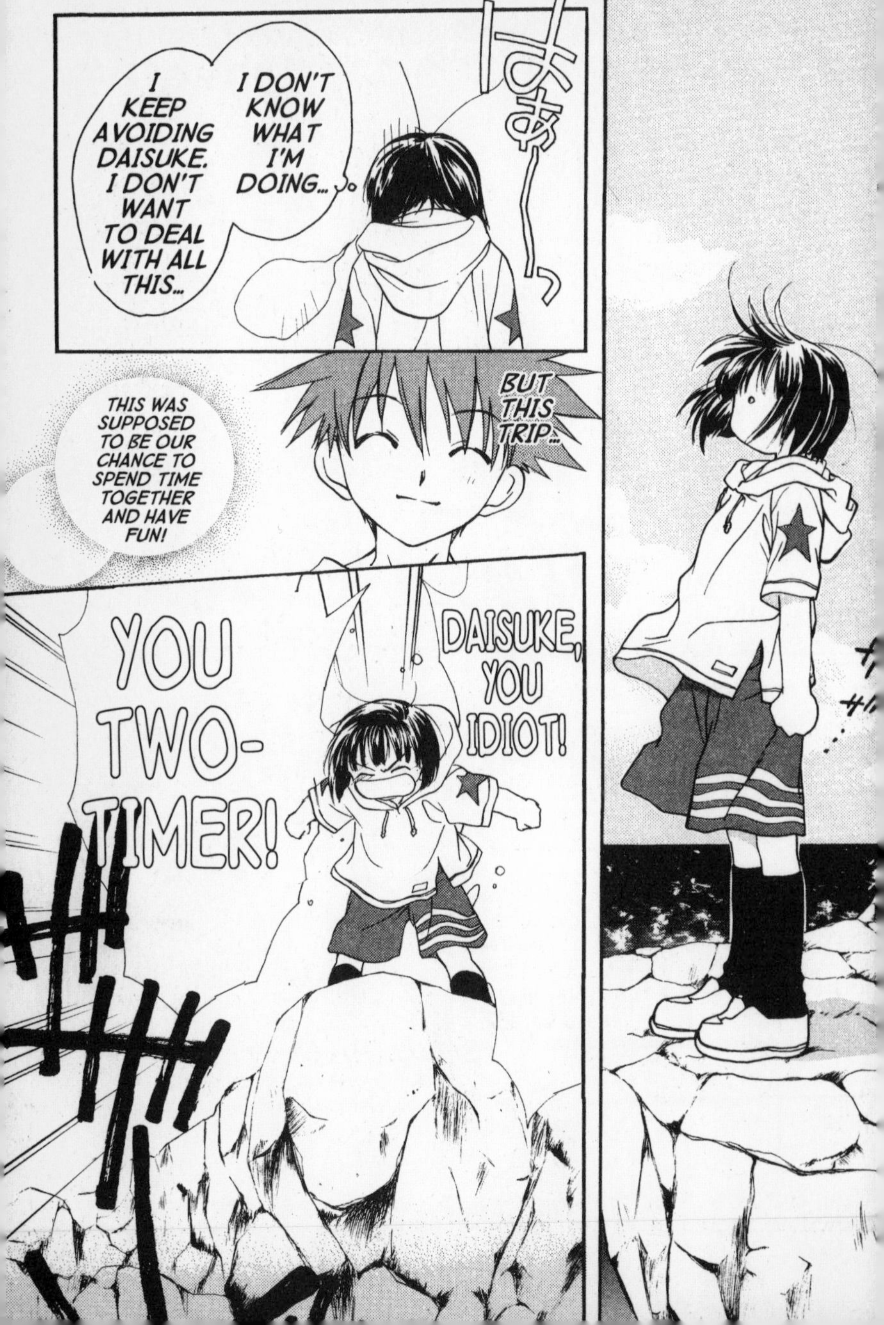
はぁ〜っ
I DON'T KNOW WHAT I'M DOING...
I KEEP AVOIDING DAISUKE. I DON'T WANT TO DEAL WITH ALL THIS...
BUT THIS TRIP...
THIS WAS SUPPOSED TO BE OUR CHANCE TO SPEND TIME TOGETHER AND HAVE FUN!
DAISUKE, YOU IDIOT!
YOU TWO-TIMER!

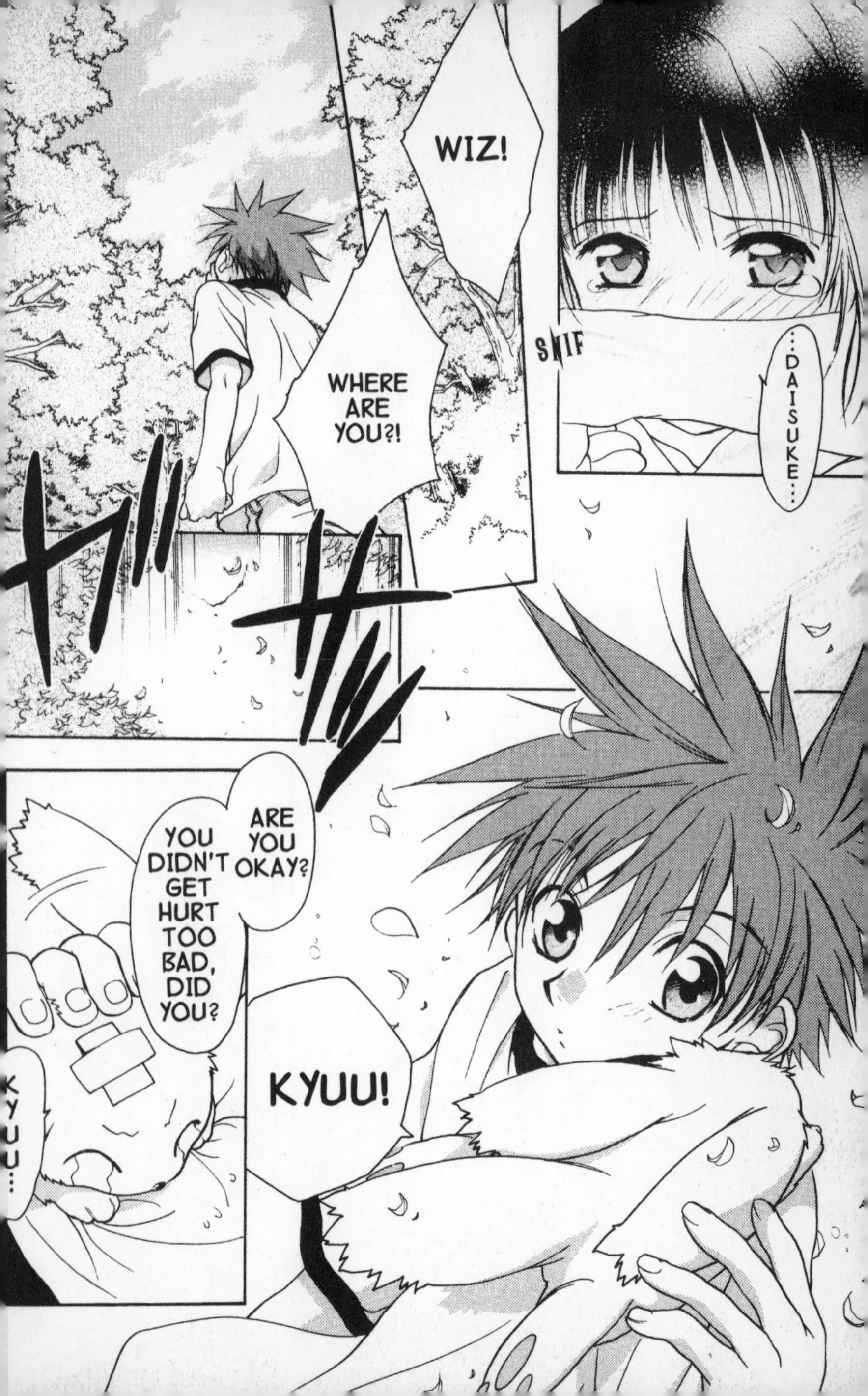

SNIF
...DAISUKE...
WIZ!
WHERE ARE YOU?!
ARE YOU OKAY?
YOU DIDN'T GET HURT TOO BAD, DID YOU?
KYUU!
KYUU...

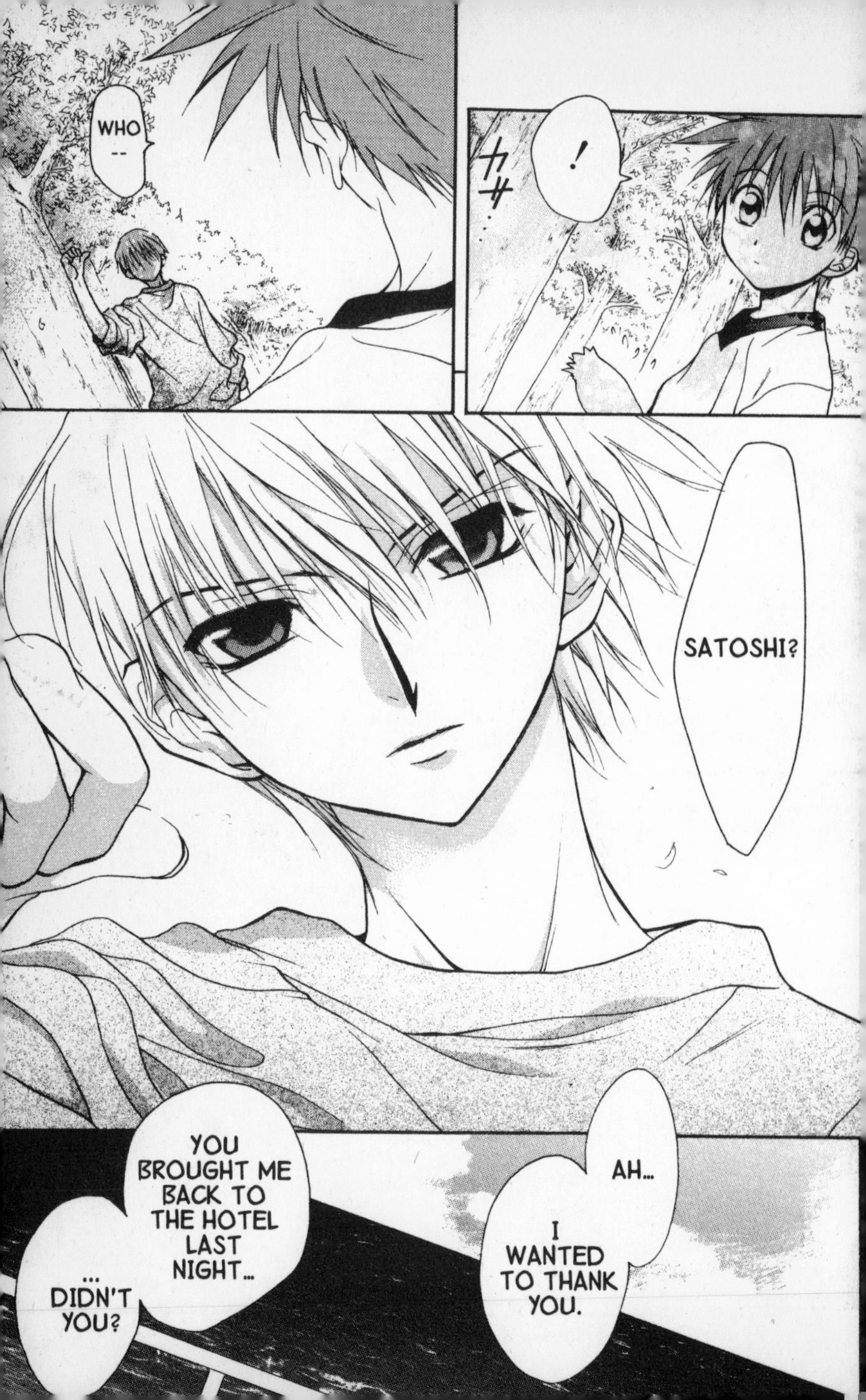
カサ…
!
WHO --
SATOSHI?
AH...
I WANTED TO THANK YOU.
YOU BROUGHT ME BACK TO THE HOTEL LAST NIGHT...
... DIDN'T YOU?

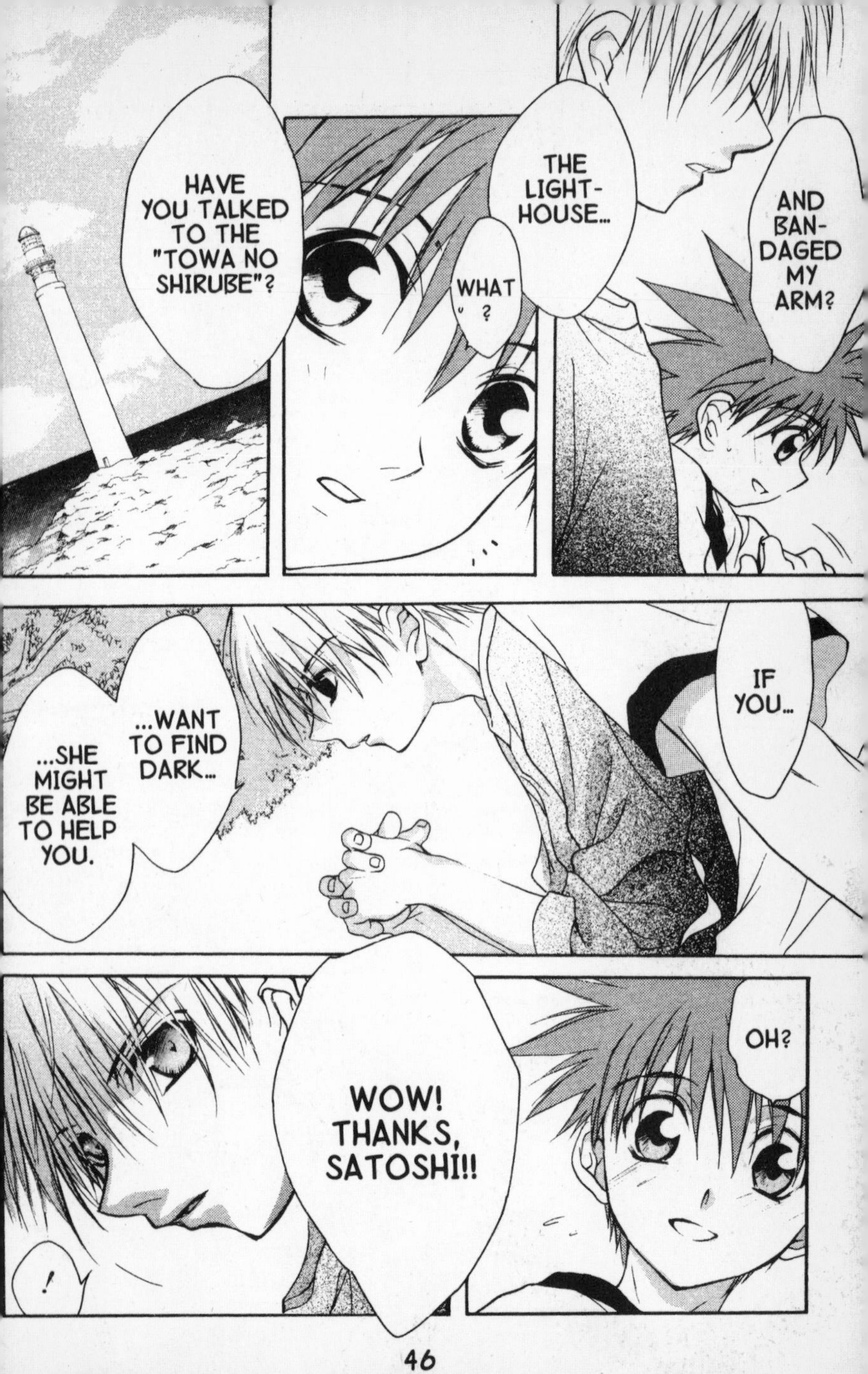
AND BAN-DAGED MY ARM?
THE LIGHT-HOUSE...
WHAT?
HAVE YOU TALKED TO THE "TOWA NO SHIRUBE"?
IF YOU...
...WANT TO FIND DARK...
...SHE MIGHT BE ABLE TO HELP YOU.
OH?
WOW! THANKS, SATOSHI!!
!

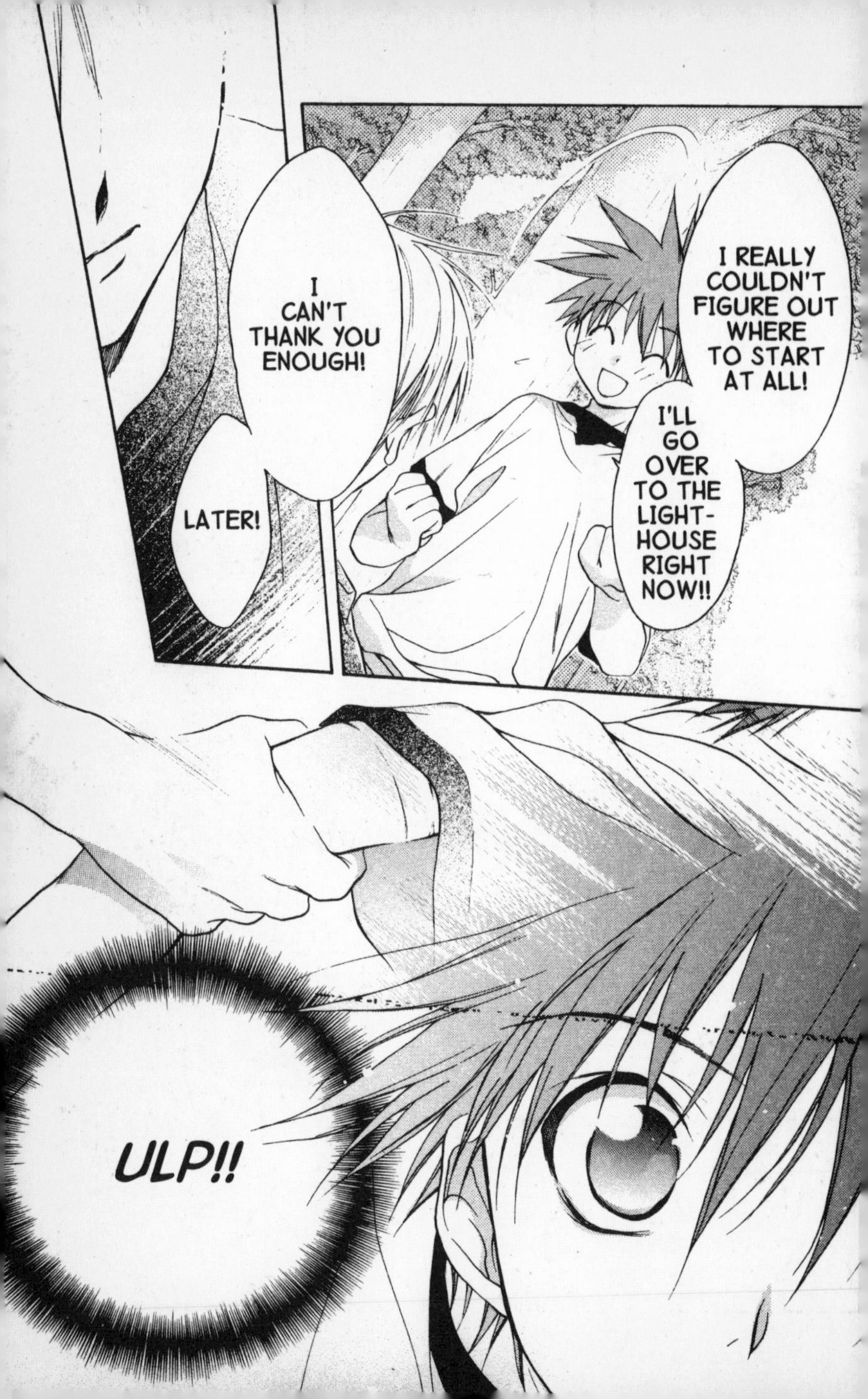
I REALLY COULDN'T FIGURE OUT WHERE TO START AT ALL!
I'LL GO OVER TO THE LIGHT-HOUSE RIGHT NOW!!
I CAN'T THANK YOU ENOUGH!
LATER!
ULP!!

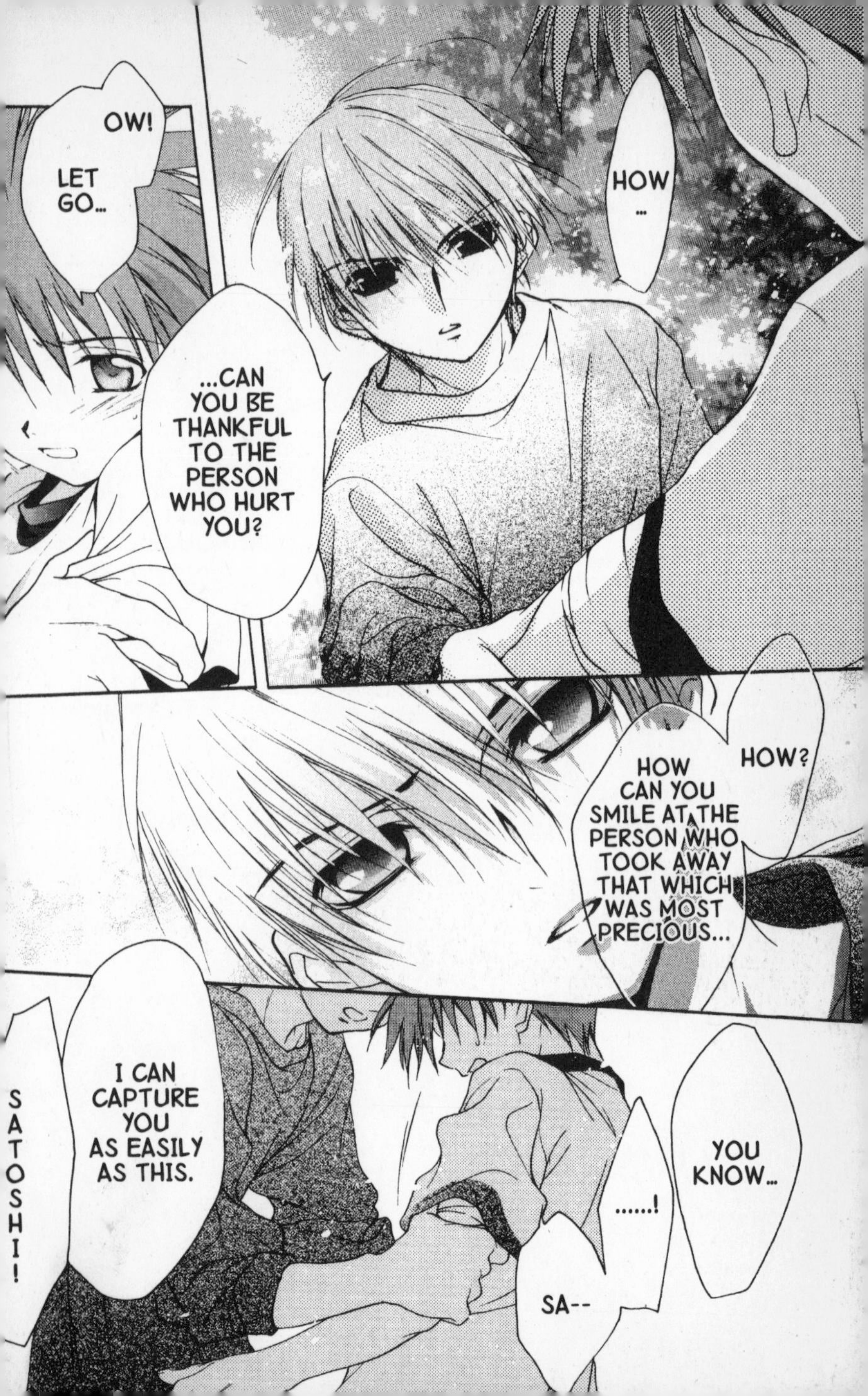
HOW...
...CAN YOU BE THANKFUL TO THE PERSON WHO HURT YOU?
OW!
LET GO...
HOW?
HOW CAN YOU SMILE AT THE PERSON WHO TOOK AWAY THAT WHICH WAS MOST PRECIOUS...
YOU KNOW...
......!
SA--
I CAN CAPTURE YOU AS EASILY AS THIS.
SATOSHI!

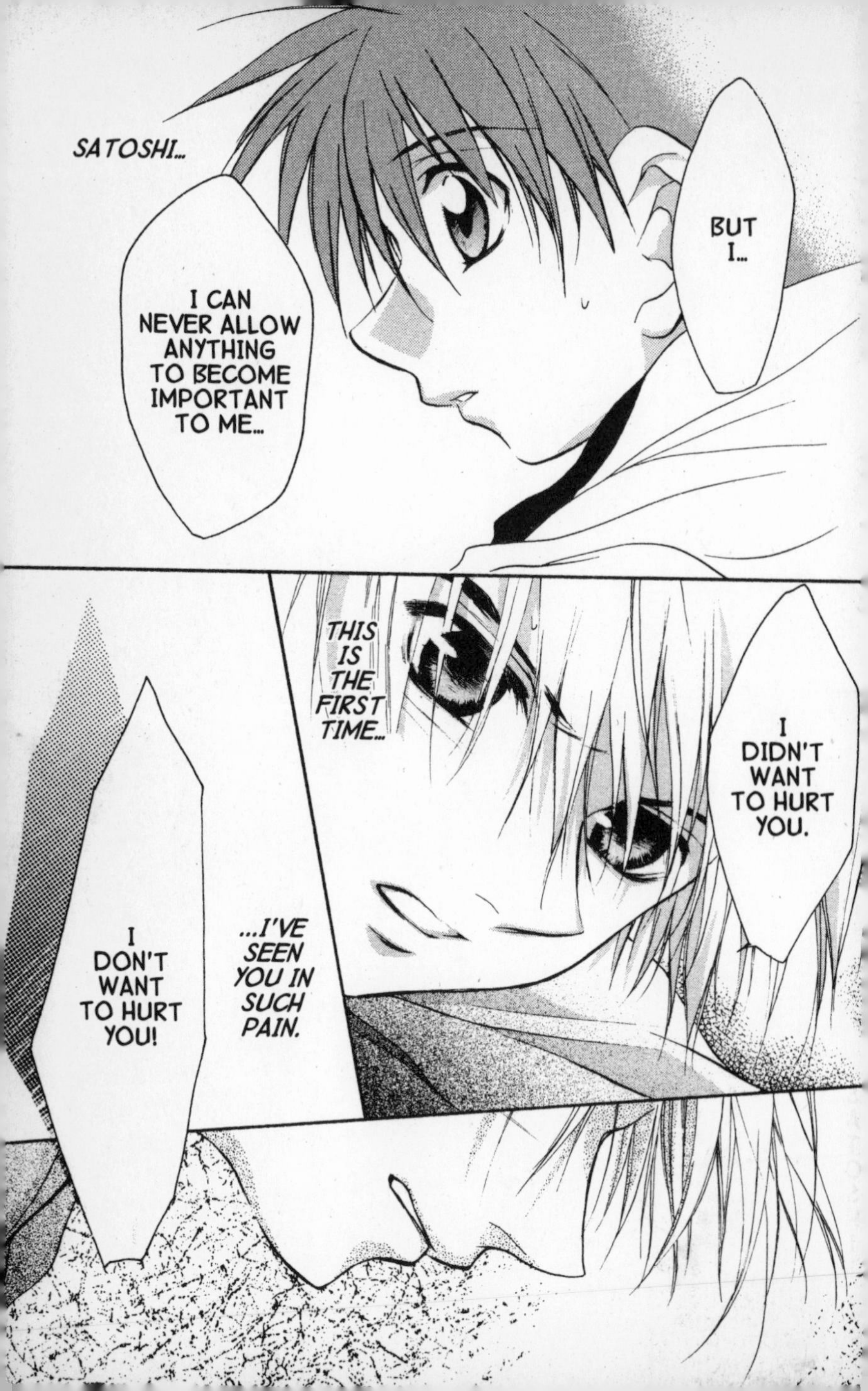
BUT I...
SATOSHI...
I CAN NEVER ALLOW ANYTHING TO BECOME IMPORTANT TO ME...
I DIDN'T WANT TO HURT YOU.
THIS IS THE FIRST TIME...
...I'VE SEEN YOU IN SUCH PAIN.
I DON'T WANT TO HURT YOU!

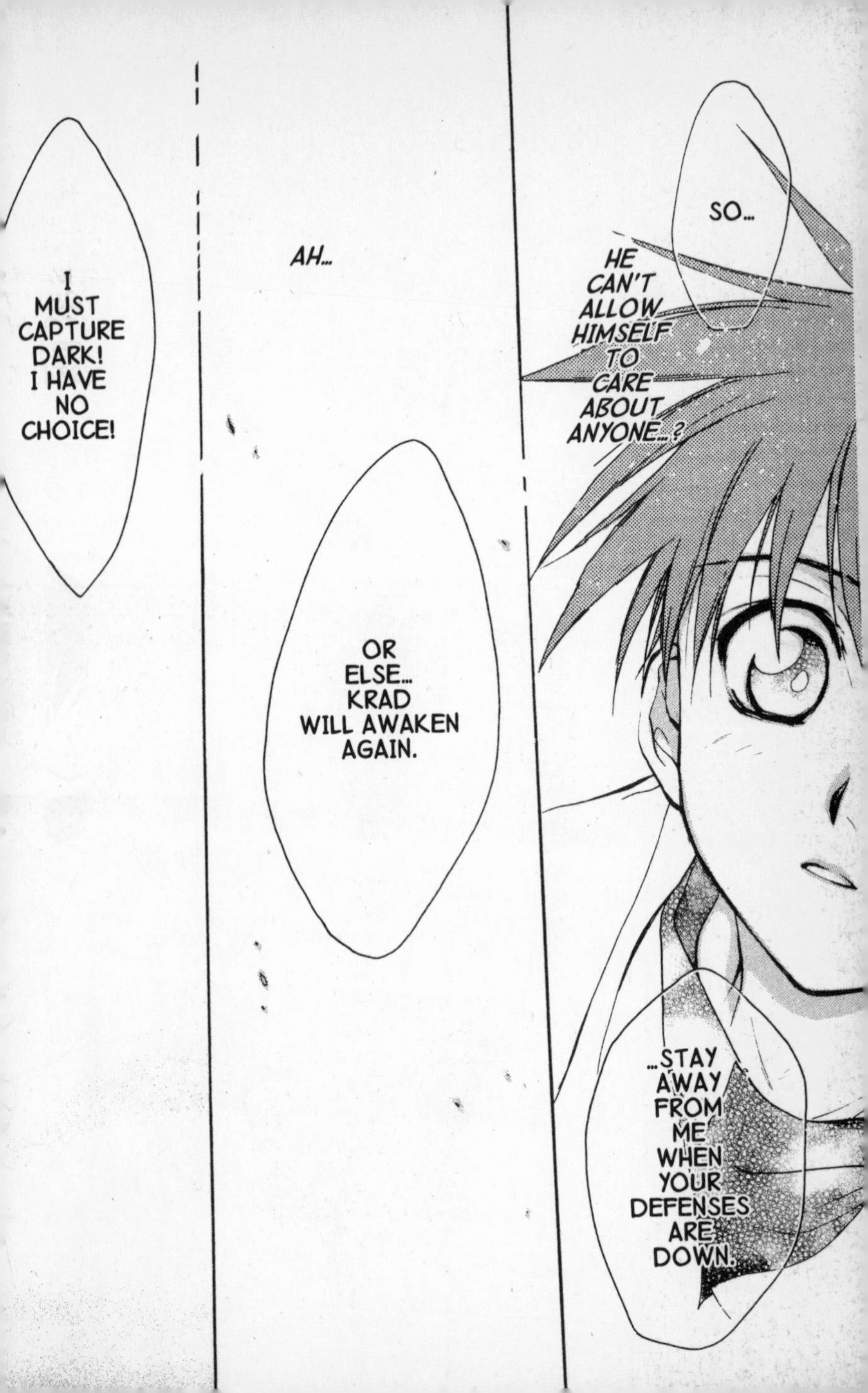
SO...
HE CAN'T ALLOW HIMSELF TO CARE ABOUT ANYONE...?
...STAY AWAY FROM ME WHEN YOUR DEFENSES ARE DOWN.
AH...
OR ELSE... KRAD WILL AWAKEN AGAIN.
I MUST CAPTURE DARK! I HAVE NO CHOICE!

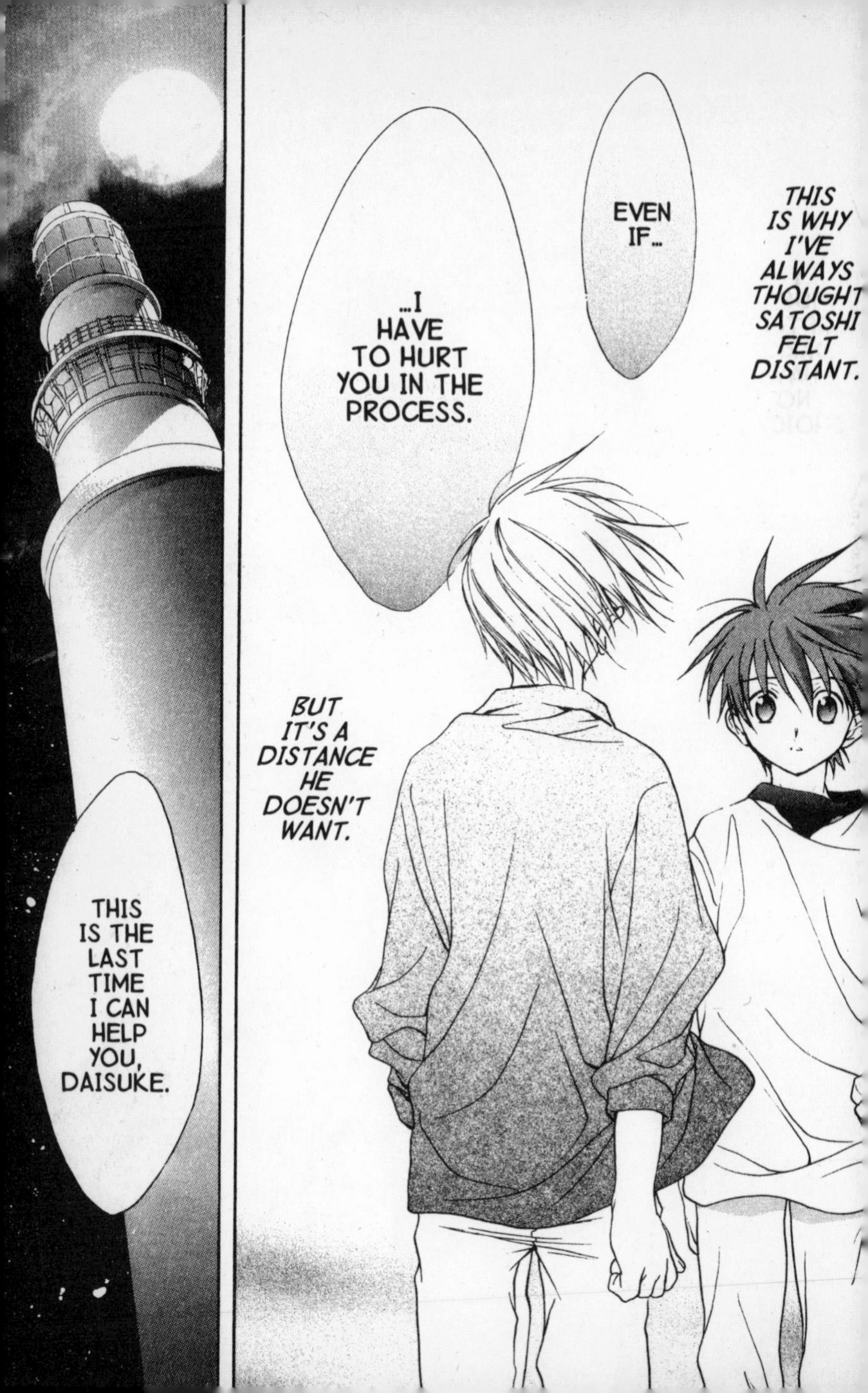
THIS IS WHY I'VE ALWAYS THOUGHT SATOSHI FELT DISTANT.
EVEN IF...
...I HAVE TO HURT YOU IN THE PROCESS.
BUT IT'S A DISTANCE HE DOESN'T WANT.
THIS IS THE LAST TIME I CAN HELP YOU, DAISUKE.

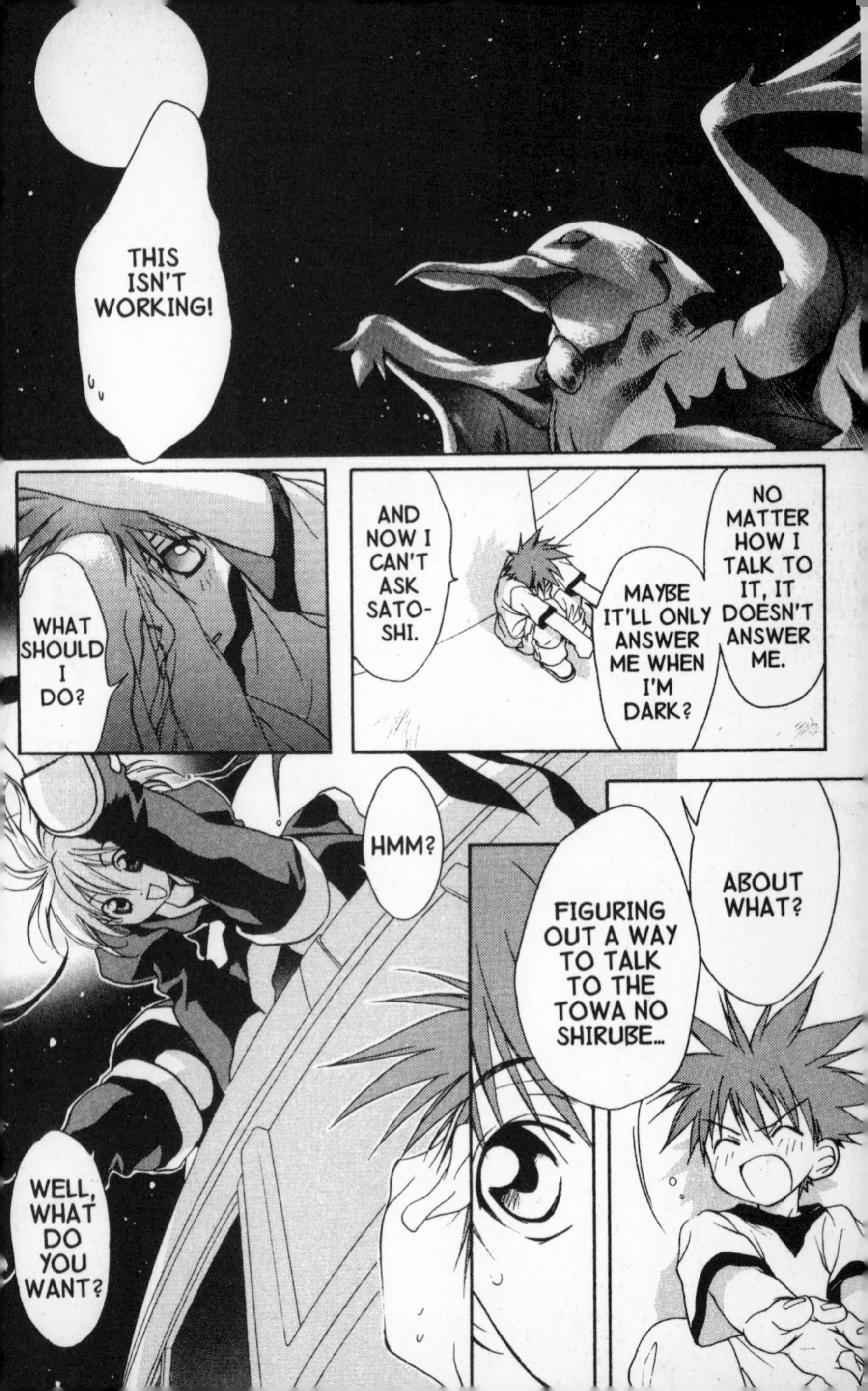
THIS ISN'T WORKING!
NO MATTER HOW I TALK TO IT, IT DOESN'T ANSWER ME.
MAYBE IT'LL ONLY ANSWER ME WHEN I'M DARK?
AND NOW I CAN'T ASK SATOSHI.
WHAT SHOULD I DO?
ABOUT WHAT?
FIGURING OUT A WAY TO TALK TO THE TOWA NO SHIRUBE...
HMM?
WELL, WHAT DO YOU WANT?

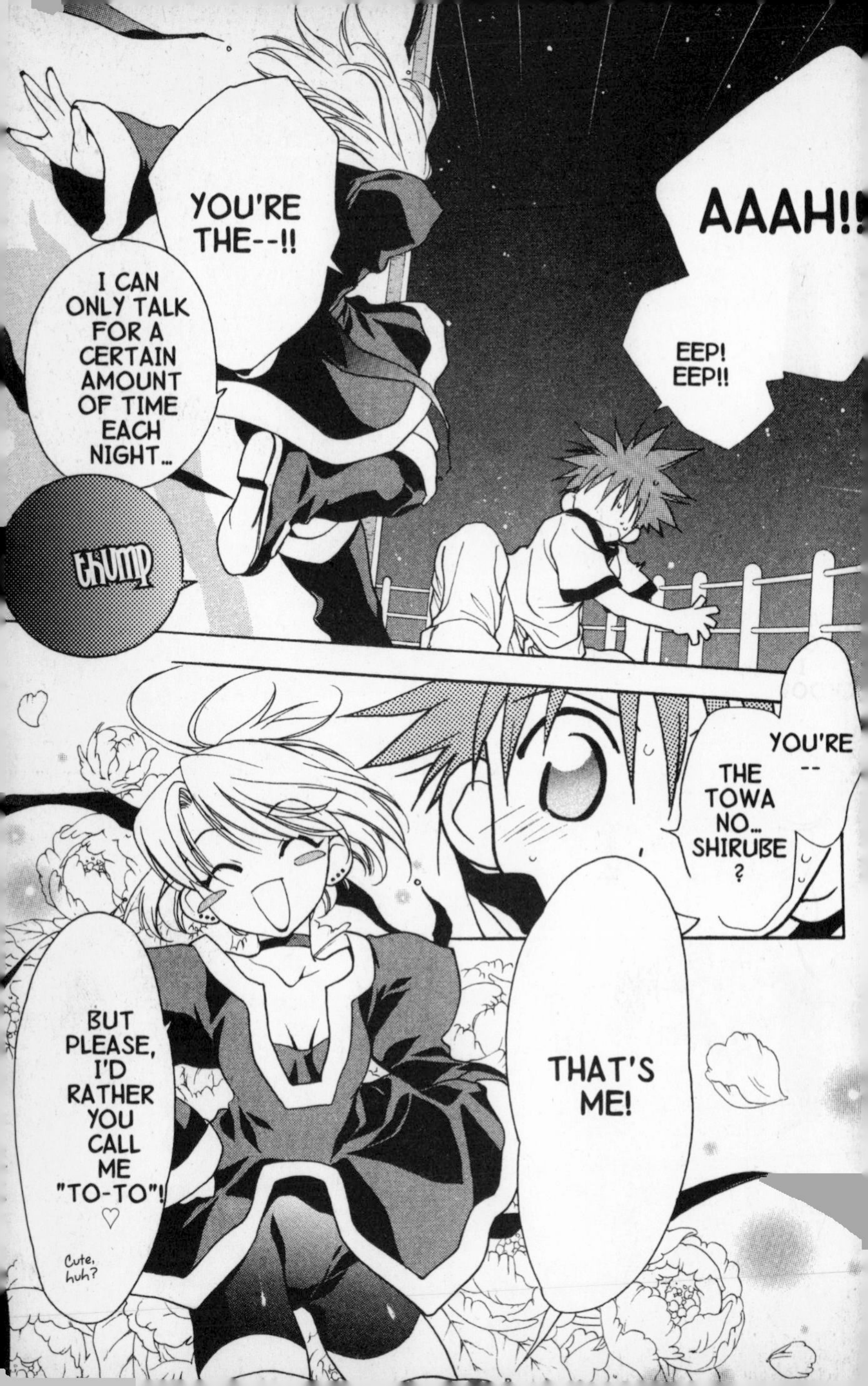
AAAH!!
EEP! EEP!!
YOU'RE THE--!!
I CAN ONLY TALK FOR A CERTAIN AMOUNT OF TIME EACH NIGHT...
THUMP
YOU'RE THE -- TOWA NO... SHIRUBE?
THAT'S ME!
BUT PLEASE, I'D RATHER YOU CALL ME "TO-TO"! ♡
Cute, huh?

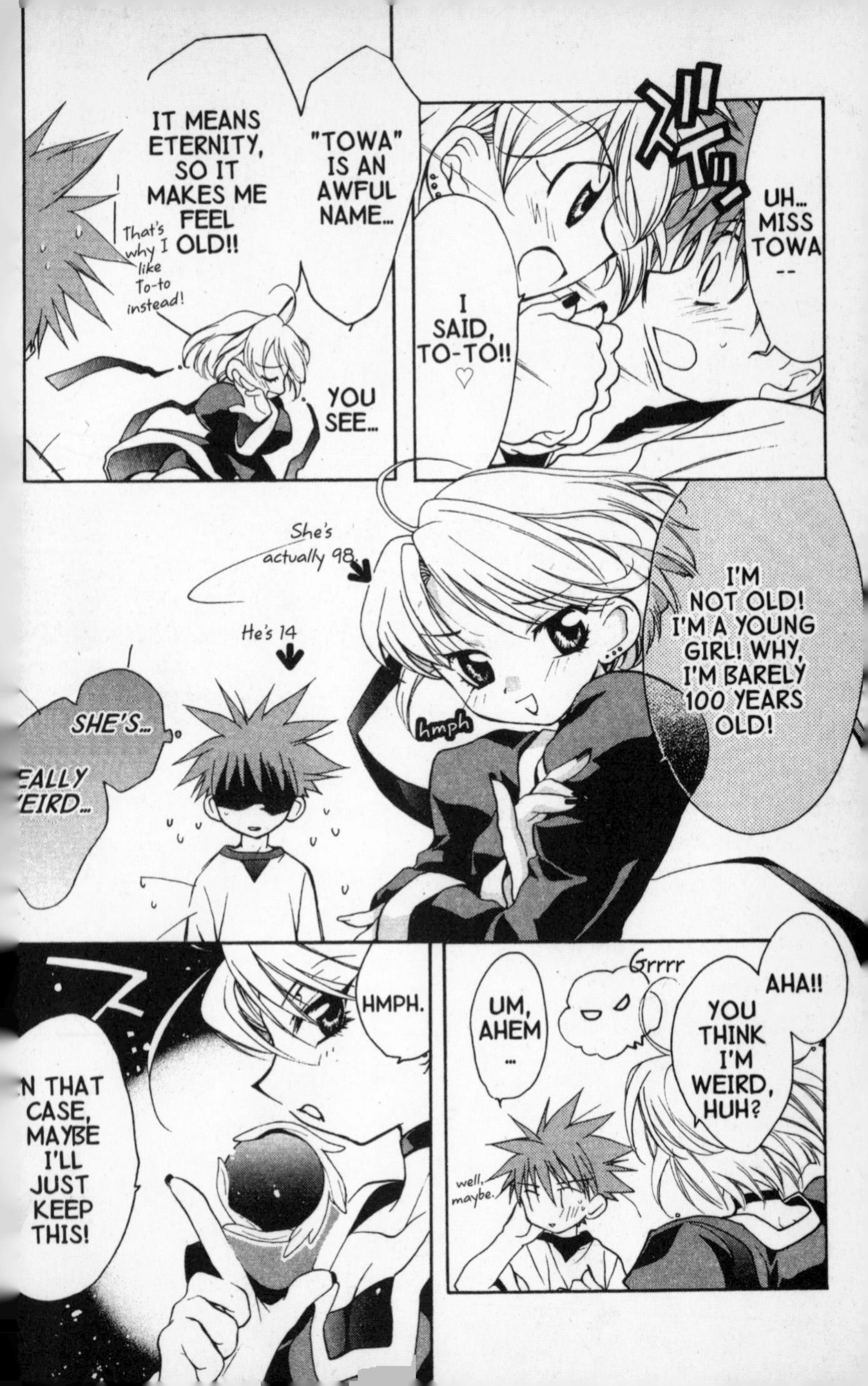
UH... MISS TOWA --
I SAID, TO-TO!! ♡
"TOWA" IS AN AWFUL NAME...
IT MEANS ETERNITY, SO IT MAKES ME FEEL OLD!!
That's why I like To-to instead!
YOU SEE...
I'M NOT OLD! I'M A YOUNG GIRL! WHY, I'M BARELY 100 YEARS OLD!
She's actually 98.
hmph
He's 14
SHE'S...
EALLY EIRD...
AHA!! YOU THINK I'M WEIRD, HUH?
Grrrr
UM, AHEM ...
well, maybe.
HMPH.
N THAT CASE, MAYBE I'LL JUST KEEP THIS!

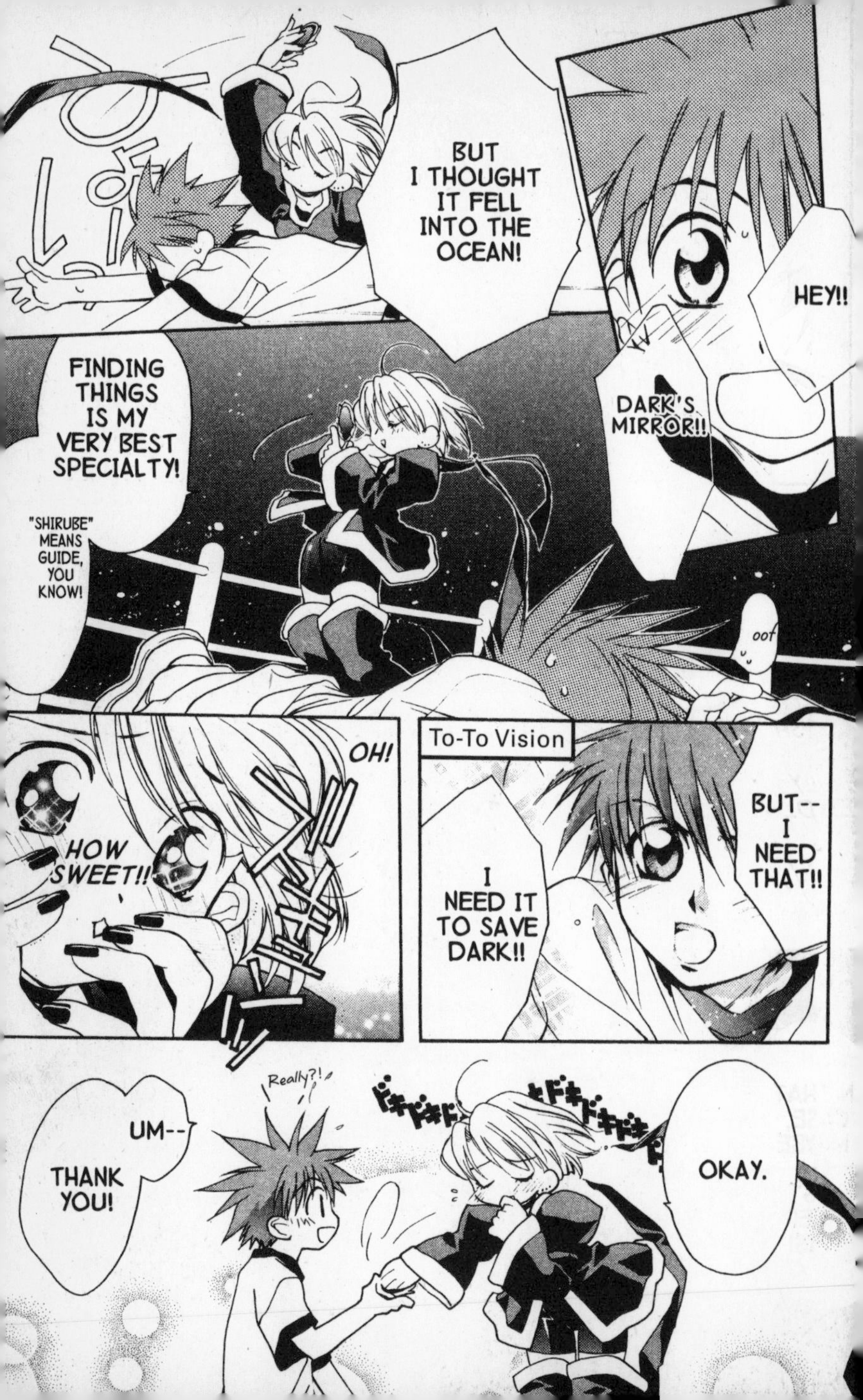
HEY!!
DARK'S MIRROR!!
BUT I THOUGHT IT FELL INTO THE OCEAN!
FINDING THINGS IS MY VERY BEST SPECIALTY!
"SHIRUBE" MEANS GUIDE, YOU KNOW!
oof
To-To Vision
BUT-- I NEED THAT!!
I NEED IT TO SAVE DARK!!
OH!
HOW SWEET!!
OKAY.
Really?!
UM--
THANK YOU!

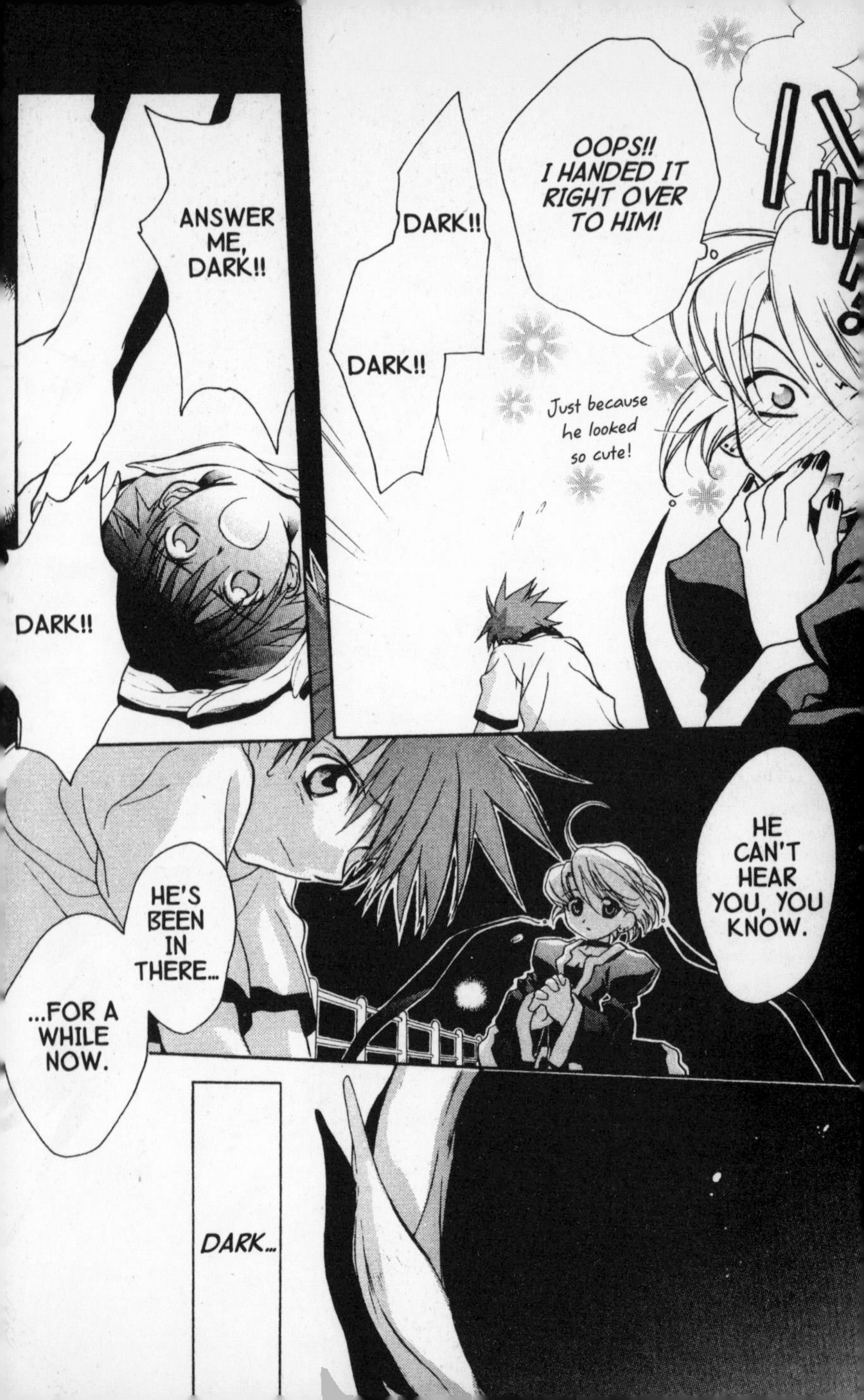
OOPS!! I HANDED IT RIGHT OVER TO HIM!
Just because he looked so cute!
DARK!!
DARK!!
ANSWER ME, DARK!!
DARK!!
HE CAN'T HEAR YOU, YOU KNOW.
HE'S BEEN IN THERE...
...FOR A WHILE NOW.
DARK...

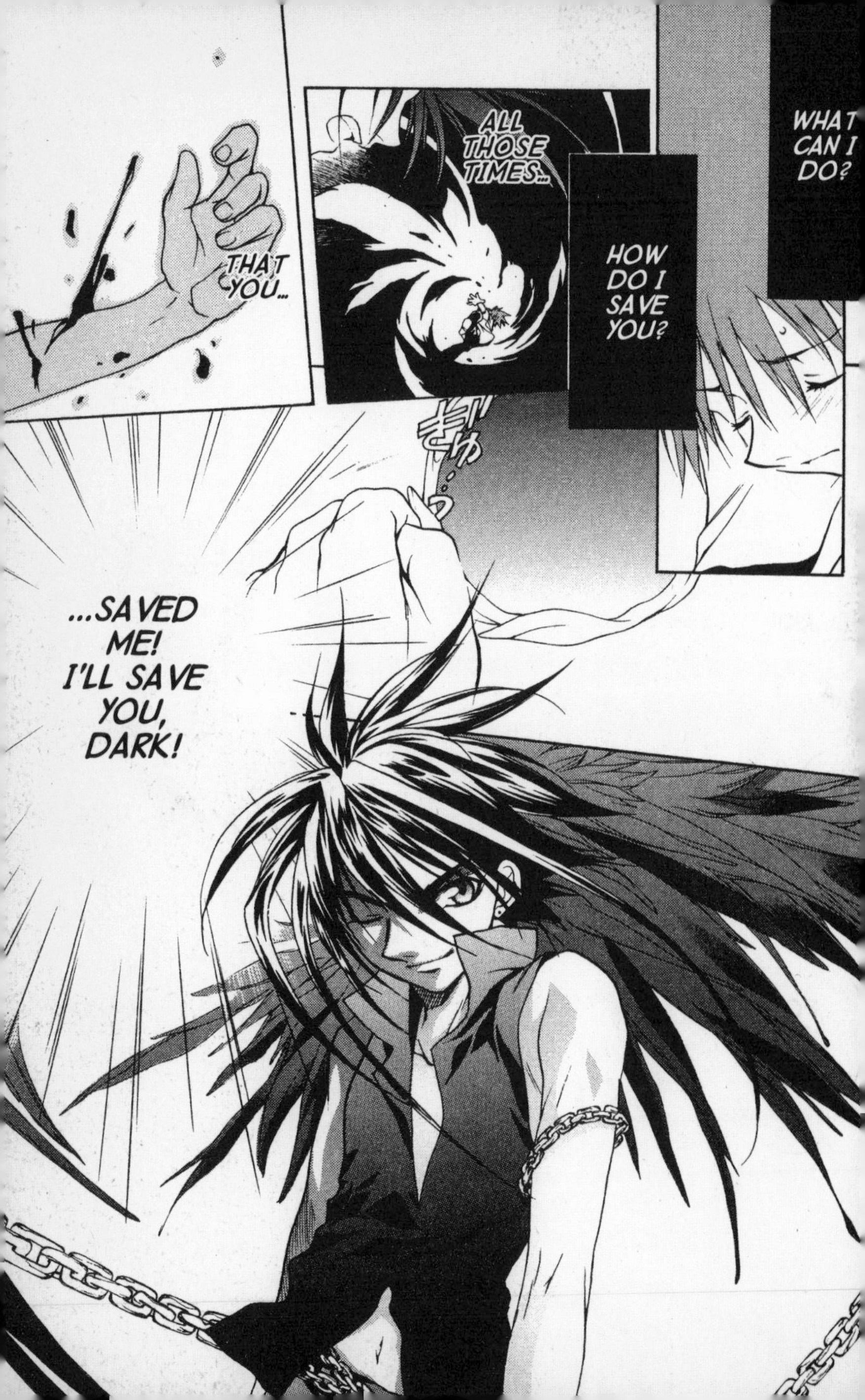
WHAT CAN I DO?
HOW DO I SAVE YOU?
ALL THOSE TIMES...
THAT YOU...
ぎゅ…っ
...SAVED ME! I'LL SAVE YOU, DARK!

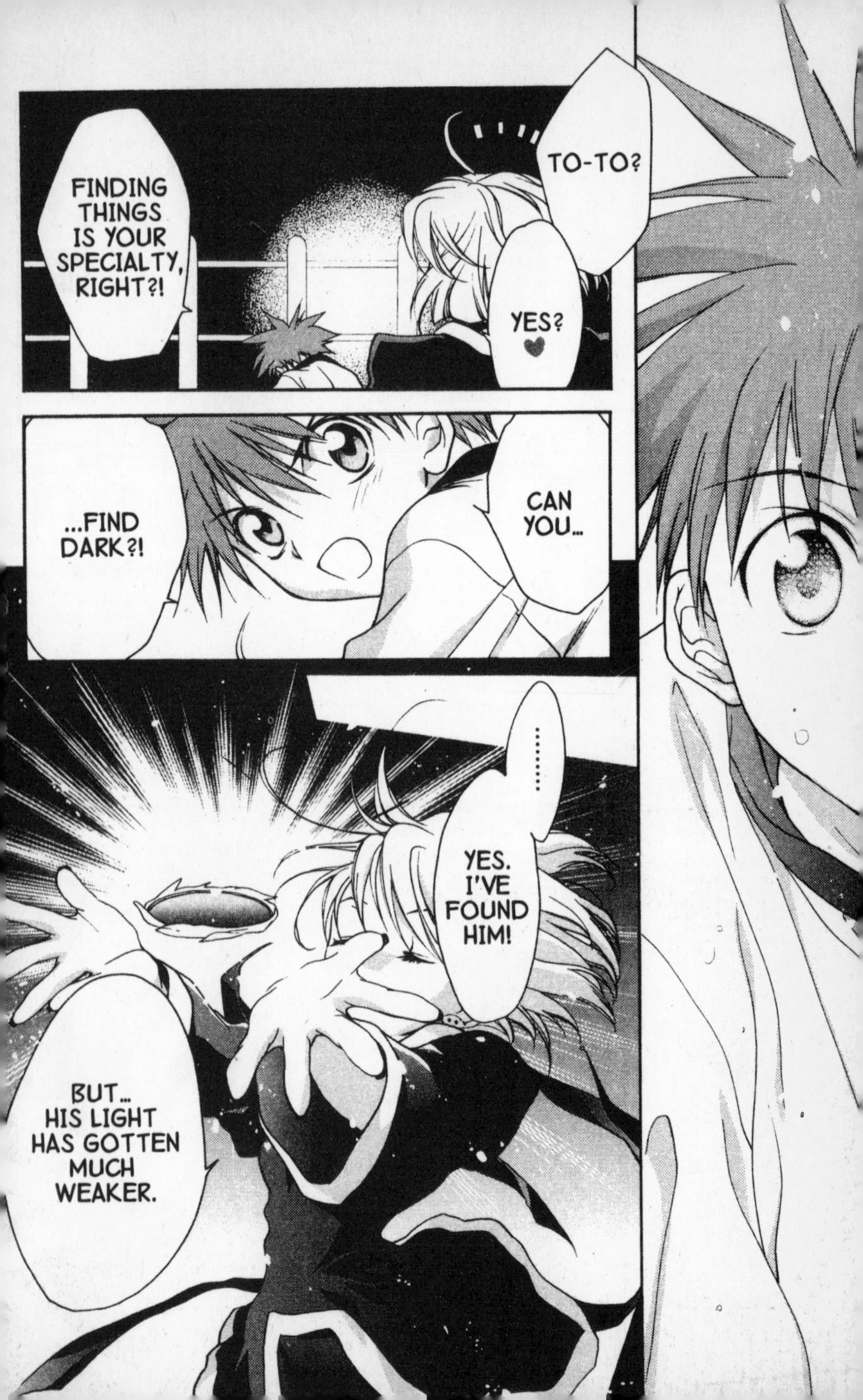
TO-TO?
YES? ♥
FINDING THINGS IS YOUR SPECIALTY, RIGHT?!
CAN YOU...
...FIND DARK?!
....
YES. I'VE FOUND HIM!
BUT... HIS LIGHT HAS GOTTEN MUCH WEAKER.

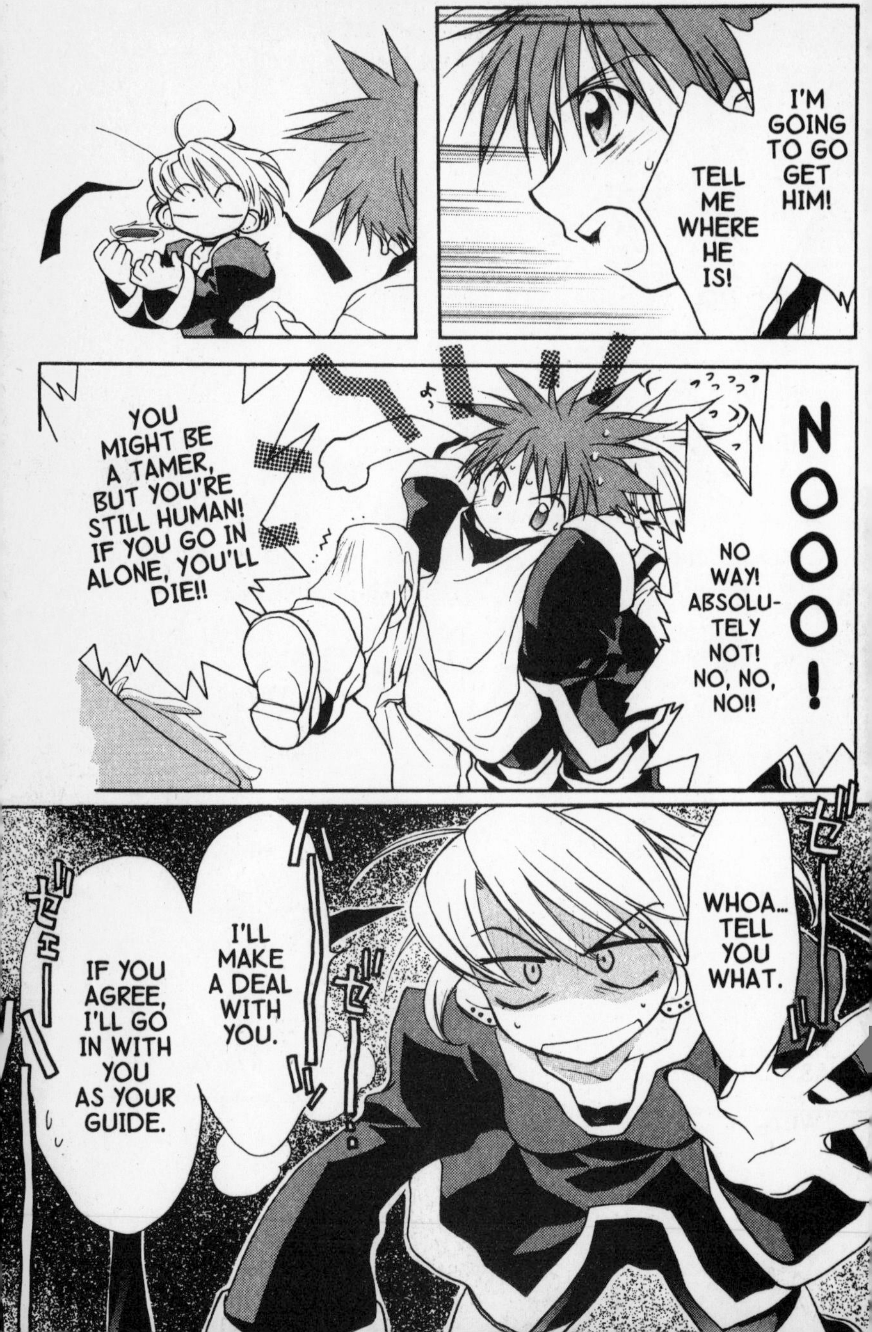
I'M GOING TO GO GET HIM!
TELL ME WHERE HE IS!
NOOOO!
NO WAY! ABSOLUTELY NOT! NO, NO, NO!!
YOU MIGHT BE A TAMER, BUT YOU'RE STILL HUMAN! IF YOU GO IN ALONE, YOU'LL DIE!!
WHOA... TELL YOU WHAT.
I'LL MAKE A DEAL WITH YOU.
IF YOU AGREE, I'LL GO IN WITH YOU AS YOUR GUIDE.

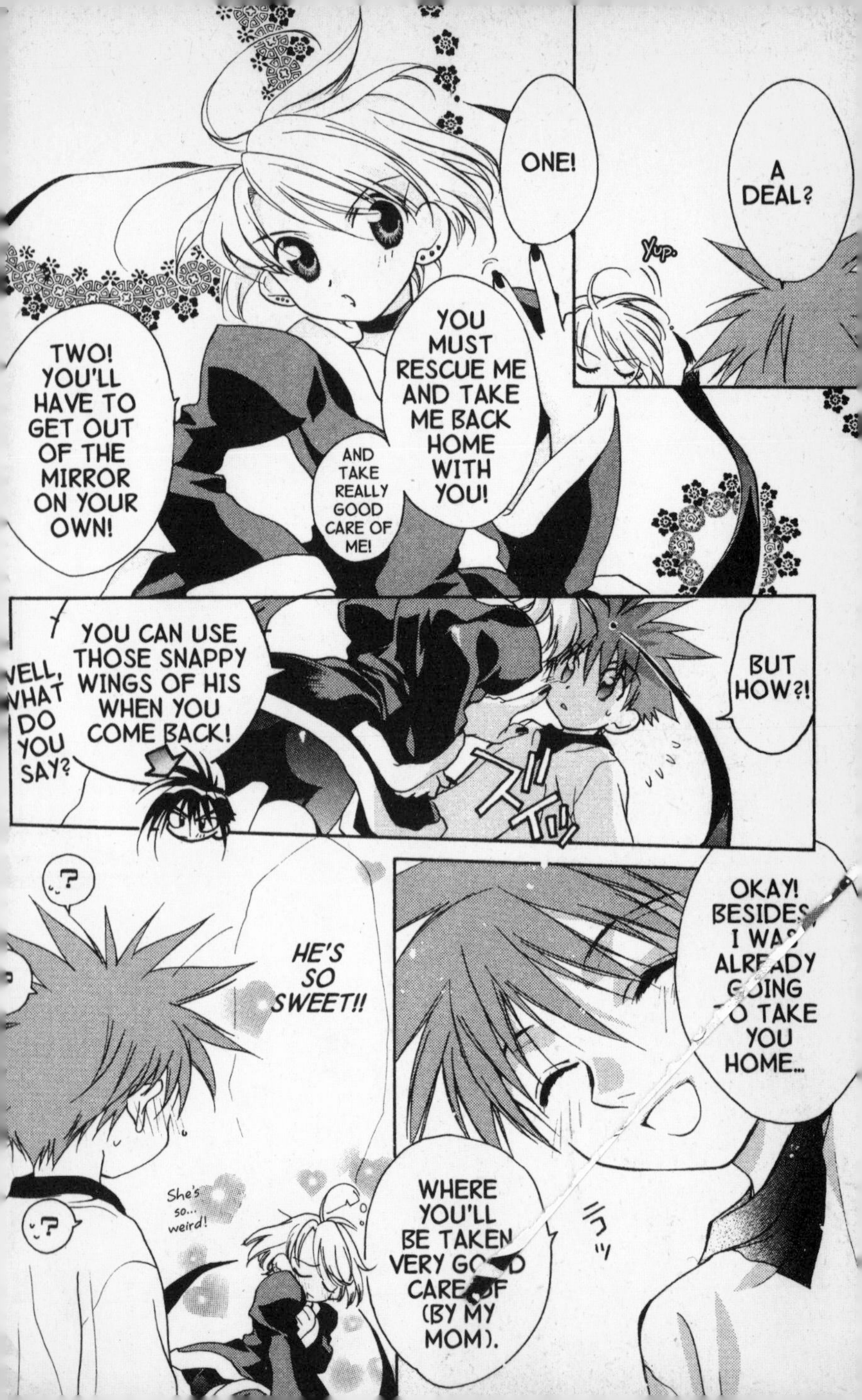
A DEAL?
Yup.
ONE!
YOU MUST RESCUE ME AND TAKE ME BACK HOME WITH YOU!
AND TAKE REALLY GOOD CARE OF ME!
TWO! YOU'LL HAVE TO GET OUT OF THE MIRROR ON YOUR OWN!
BUT HOW?!
YOU CAN USE THOSE SNAPPY WINGS OF HIS WHEN YOU COME BACK!
WELL, WHAT DO YOU SAY?
OKAY! BESIDES, I WAS ALREADY GOING TO TAKE YOU HOME...
ニコッ
WHERE YOU'LL BE TAKEN VERY GOOD CARE OF (BY MY MOM).
HE'S SO SWEET!!
?
She's so... weird!
?

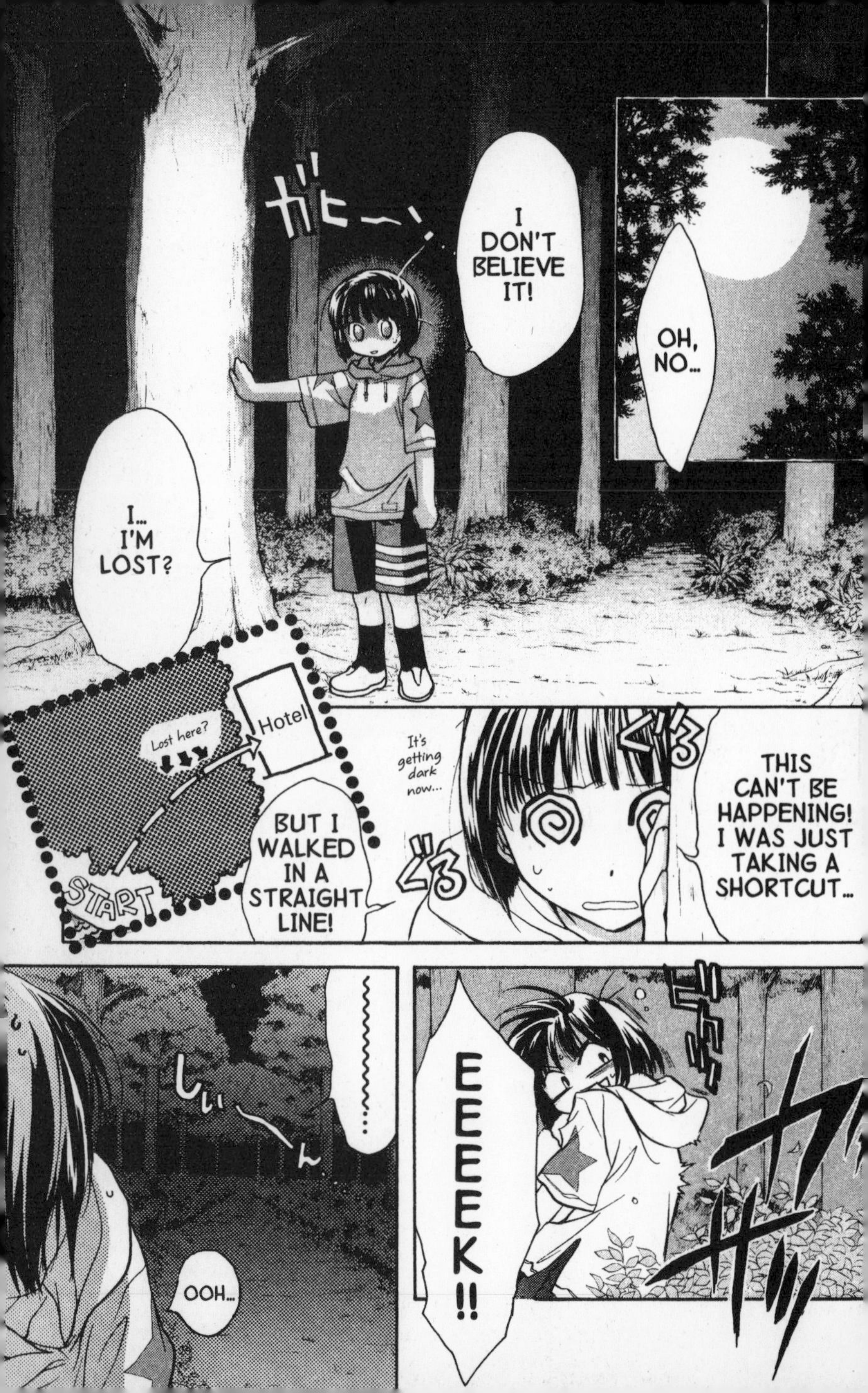
OH, NO...
ガビ〜ン
I DON'T BELIEVE IT!
I... I'M LOST?
THIS CAN'T BE HAPPENING! I WAS JUST TAKING A SHORTCUT...
ぐる
ぐる
It's getting dark now...
BUT I WALKED IN A STRAIGHT LINE!
Hotel
Lost here?
START
EEEEEK!!
......
しい〜ん
OOH...

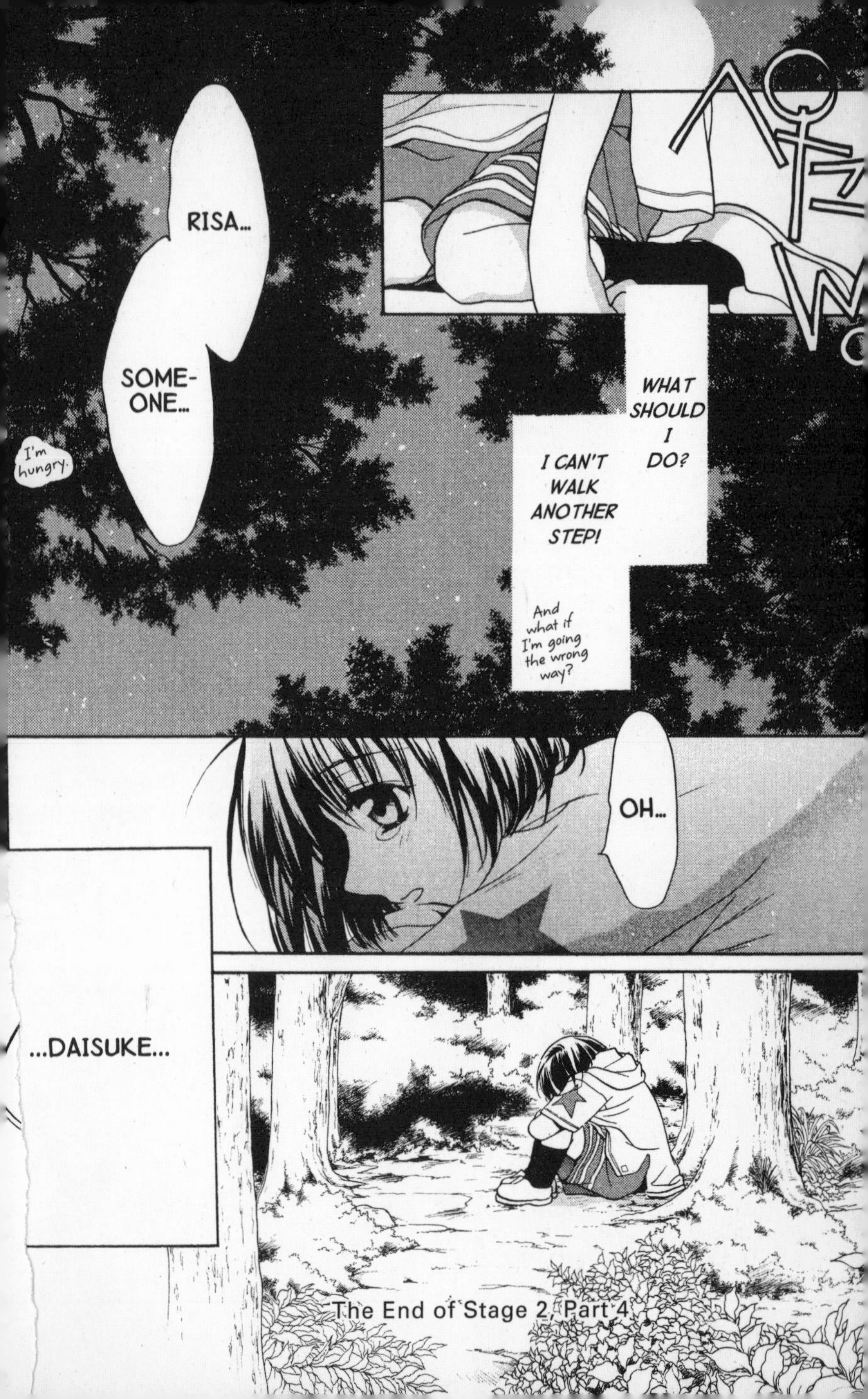
WHAT SHOULD I DO?
I CAN'T WALK ANOTHER STEP!
And what if I'm going the wrong way?
RISA...
SOME-ONE...
I'm hungry.
OH...
...DAISUKE...
The End of Stage 2, Part 4

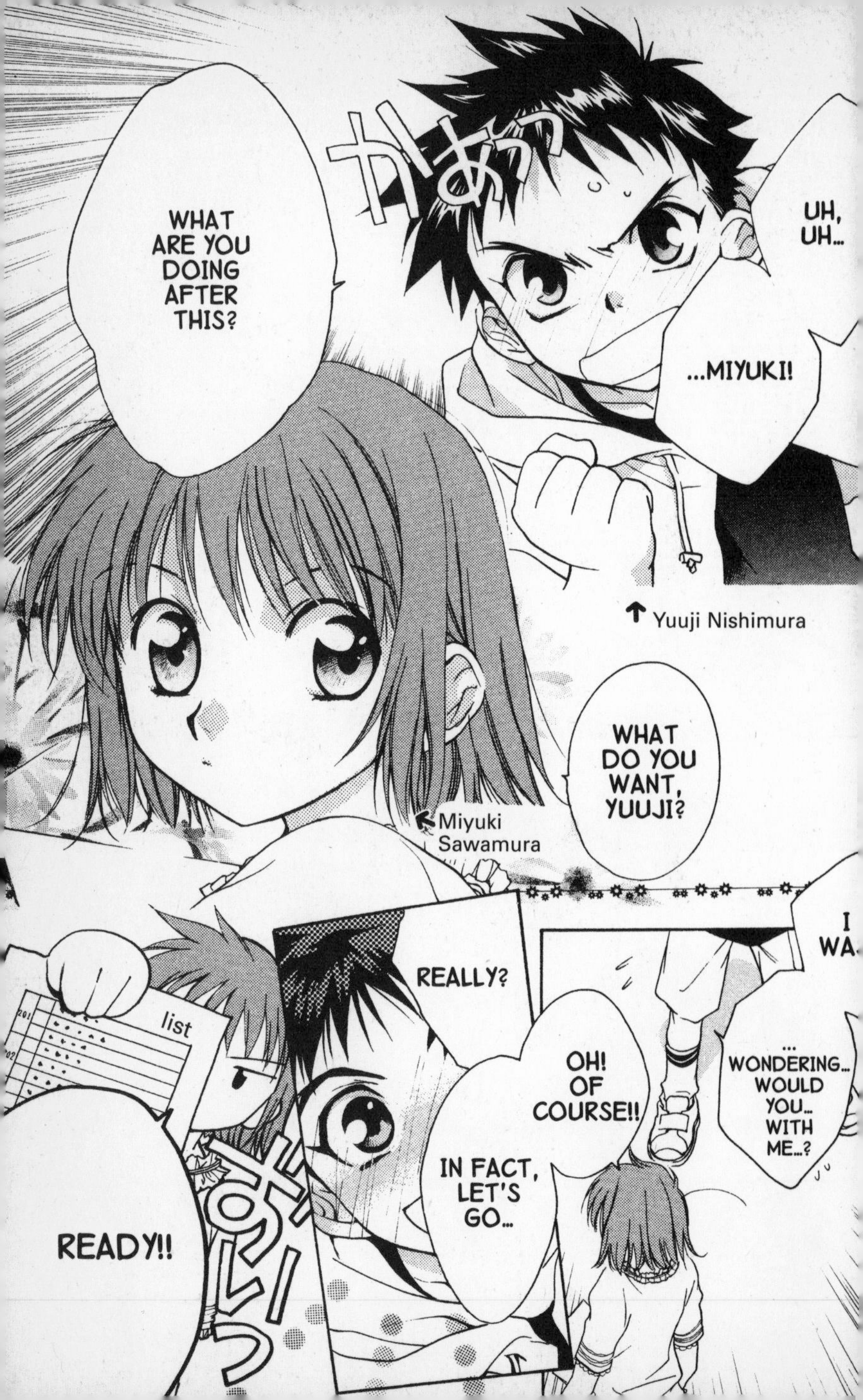
UH, UH...
かぁっ
...MIYUKI!
Yuuji Nishimura
WHAT DO YOU WANT, YUUJI?
Miyuki Sawamura
WHAT ARE YOU DOING AFTER THIS?
I WA...
...WONDERING... WOULD YOU... WITH ME...?
REALLY?
OH! OF COURSE!!
IN FACT, LET'S GO...
ずいっ
list
READY!!

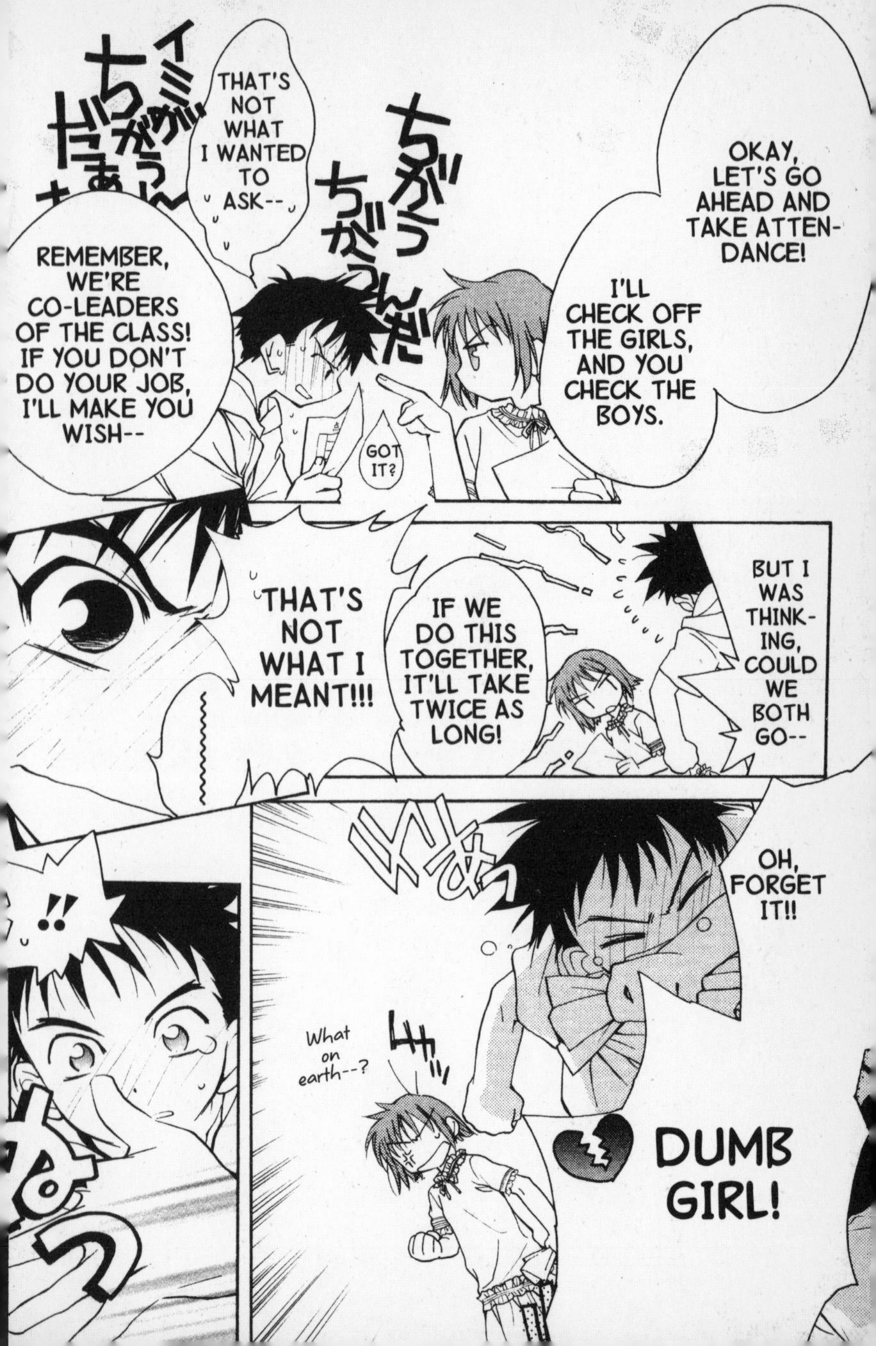
OKAY, LET'S GO AHEAD AND TAKE ATTEN-DANCE!
I'LL CHECK OFF THE GIRLS, AND YOU CHECK THE BOYS.
GOT IT?
ちがうちがうんだ
THAT'S NOT WHAT I WANTED TO ASK--
REMEMBER, WE'RE CO-LEADERS OF THE CLASS! IF YOU DON'T DO YOUR JOB, I'LL MAKE YOU WISH--
BUT I WAS THINK-ING, COULD WE BOTH GO--
IF WE DO THIS TOGETHER, IT'LL TAKE TWICE AS LONG!
THAT'S NOT WHAT I MEANT!!!
OH, FORGET IT!!
What on earth--?
DUMB GIRL!
!!

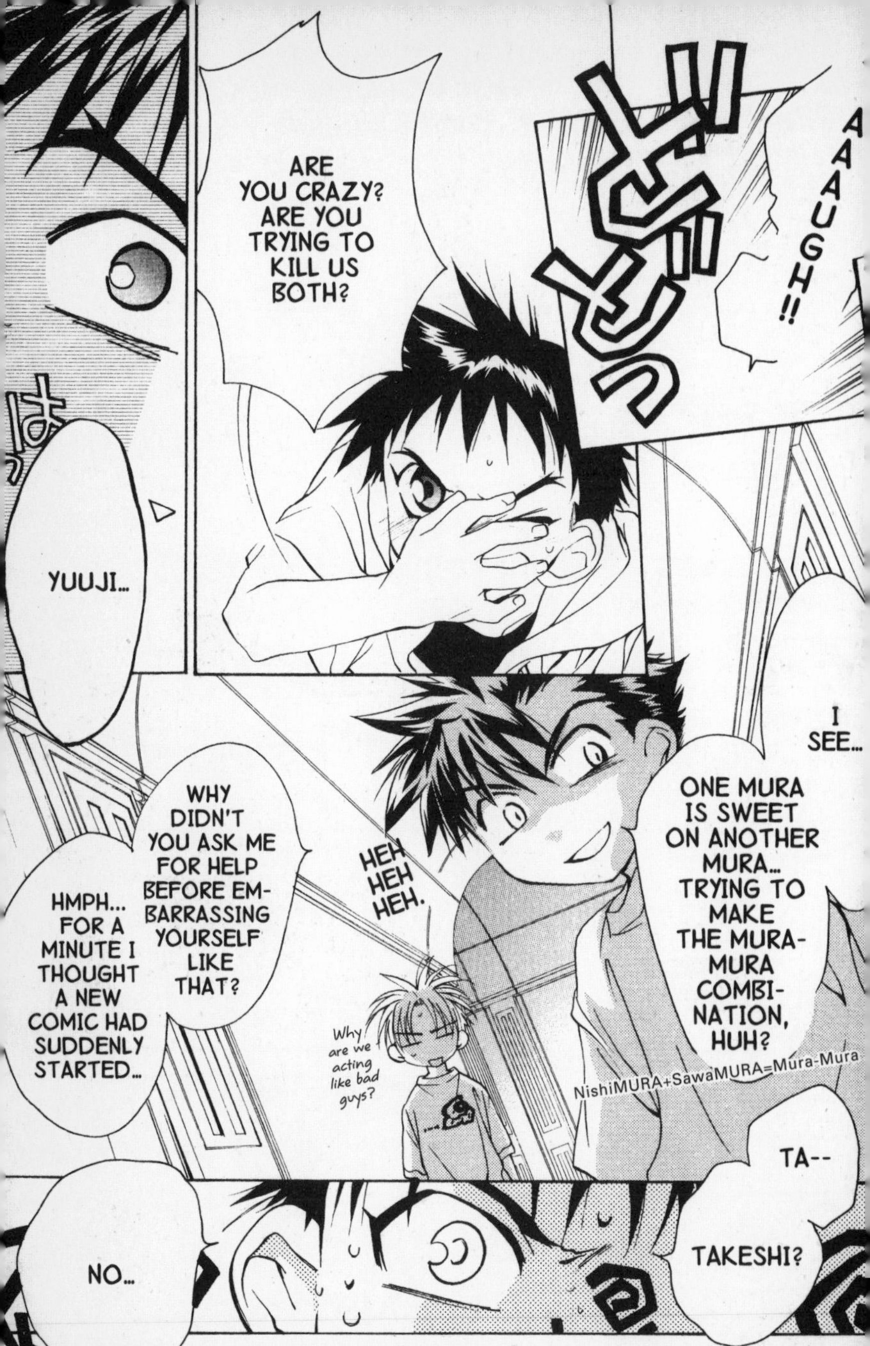
AAAUGH!!
ARE YOU CRAZY? ARE YOU TRYING TO KILL US BOTH?
は
YUUJI...
I SEE...
ONE MURA IS SWEET ON ANOTHER MURA... TRYING TO MAKE THE MURA-MURA COMBI-NATION, HUH?
NishiMURA+SawaMURA=Mura-Mura
HEH HEH HEH.
WHY DIDN'T YOU ASK ME FOR HELP BEFORE EM-BARRASSING YOURSELF LIKE THAT?
HMPH... FOR A MINUTE I THOUGHT A NEW COMIC HAD SUDDENLY STARTED...
Why are we acting like bad guys?
TA--
TAKESHI?
NO...

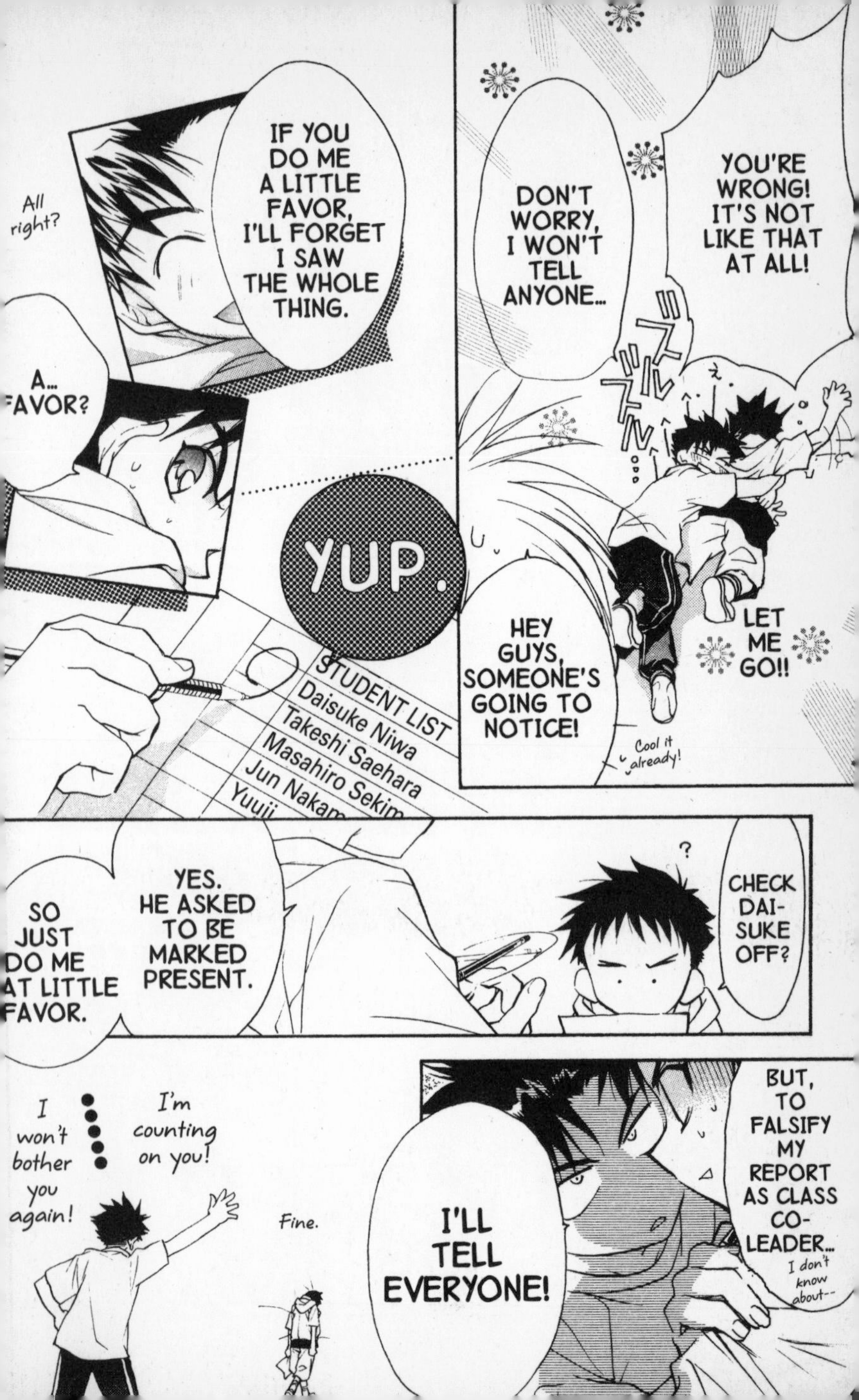
YOU'RE WRONG! IT'S NOT LIKE THAT AT ALL!
DON'T WORRY, I WON'T TELL ANYONE...
LET ME GO!!
HEY GUYS, SOMEONE'S GOING TO NOTICE!
Cool it already!
IF YOU DO ME A LITTLE FAVOR, I'LL FORGET I SAW THE WHOLE THING.
All right?
A... FAVOR?
YUP.
STUDENT LIST
Daisuke Niwa
Takeshi Saehara
Masahiro Sekim
Jun Nakam
Yuuji
CHECK DAI-SUKE OFF?
YES. HE ASKED TO BE MARKED PRESENT.
SO JUST DO ME AT LITTLE FAVOR.
BUT, TO FALSIFY MY REPORT AS CLASS CO-LEADER...
I don't know about--
I'LL TELL EVERYONE!
Fine.
I'm counting on you!
I won't bother you again!

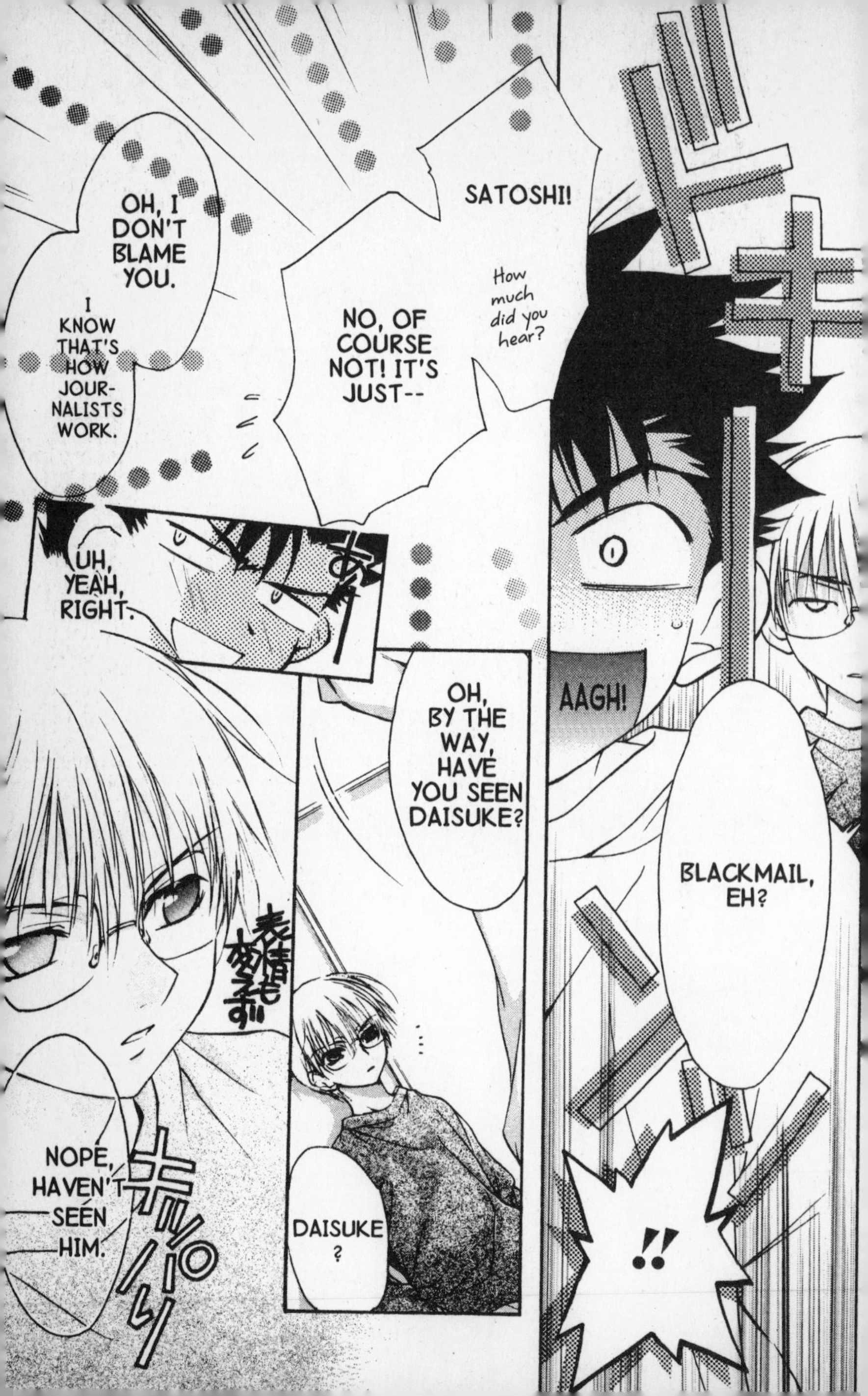

ドキ
BLACKMAIL, EH?
!!
AAGH!
SATOSHI!
How much did you hear?
NO, OF COURSE NOT! IT'S JUST--
OH, I DON'T BLAME YOU.
I KNOW THAT'S HOW JOURNALISTS WORK.
UH, YEAH, RIGHT.
OH, BY THE WAY, HAVE YOU SEEN DAISUKE?
...
DAISUKE?
表情も変えず
NOPE, HAVEN'T SEEN HIM.
キッパリ

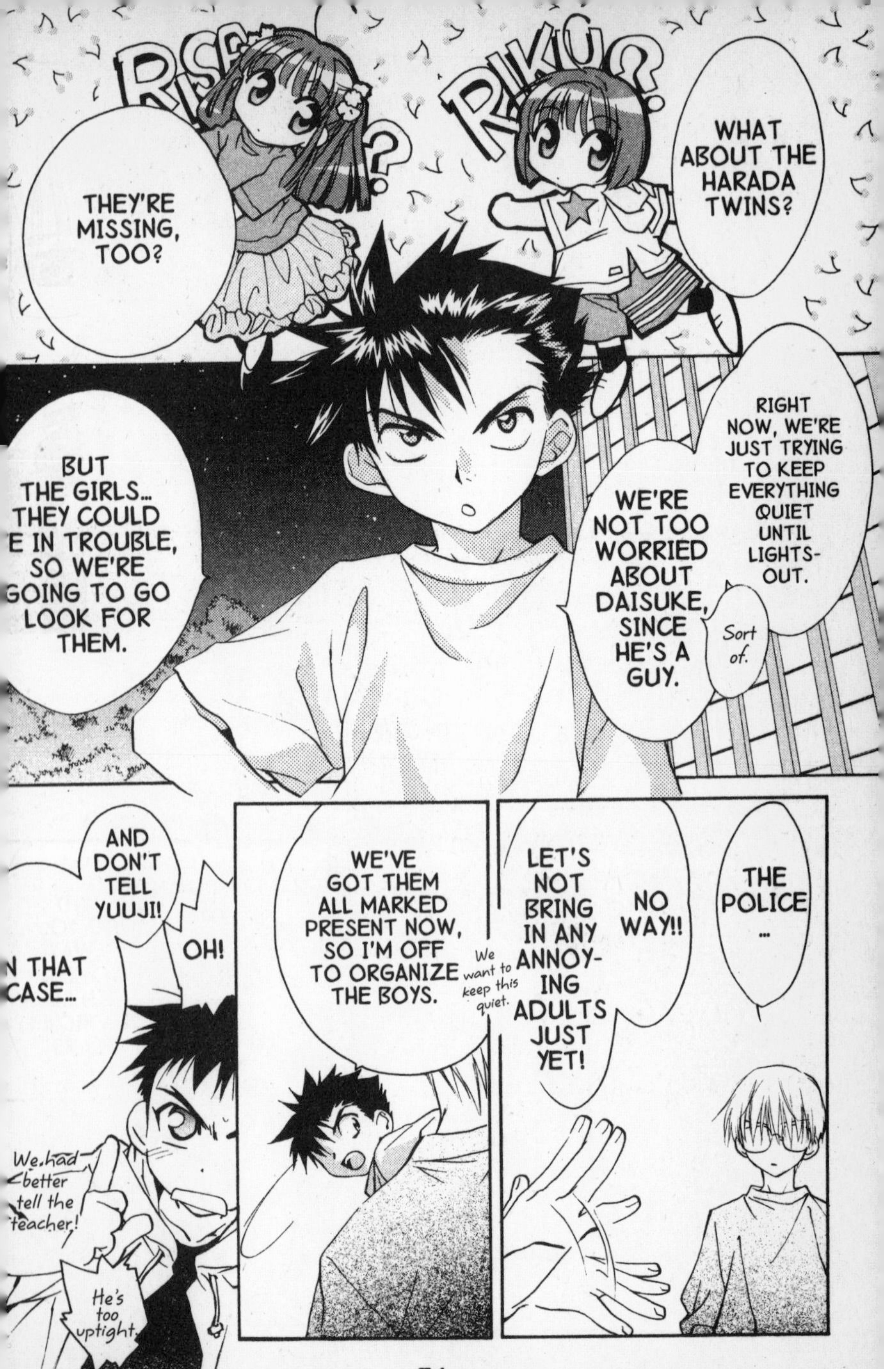
RIKU??
RISA??
WHAT ABOUT THE HARADA TWINS?
THEY'RE MISSING, TOO?
RIGHT NOW, WE'RE JUST TRYING TO KEEP EVERYTHING QUIET UNTIL LIGHTS-OUT.
WE'RE NOT TOO WORRIED ABOUT DAISUKE, SINCE HE'S A GUY.
Sort of.
BUT THE GIRLS... THEY COULD E IN TROUBLE, SO WE'RE GOING TO GO LOOK FOR THEM.
THE POLICE ...
NO WAY!!
LET'S NOT BRING IN ANY ANNOY-ING ADULTS JUST YET!
We want to keep this quiet.
WE'VE GOT THEM ALL MARKED PRESENT NOW, SO I'M OFF TO ORGANIZE THE BOYS.
OH!
N THAT CASE...
AND DON'T TELL YUUJI!
We had better tell the teacher!
He's too uptight.

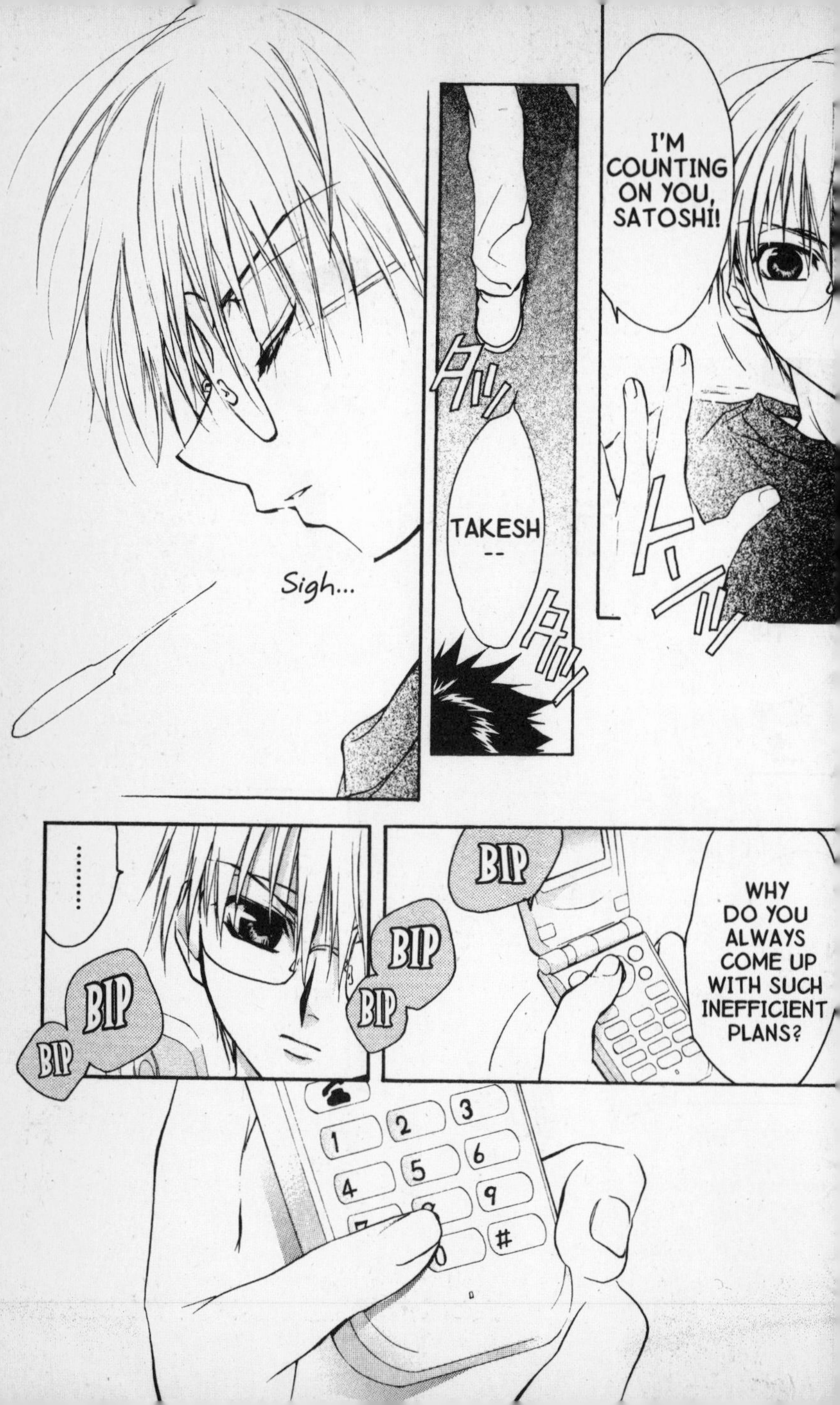
I'M COUNTING ON YOU, SATOSHI!
TAKESH --
Sigh...
WHY DO YOU ALWAYS COME UP WITH SUCH INEFFICIENT PLANS?
BIP
BIP
BIP
......
BIP
BIP

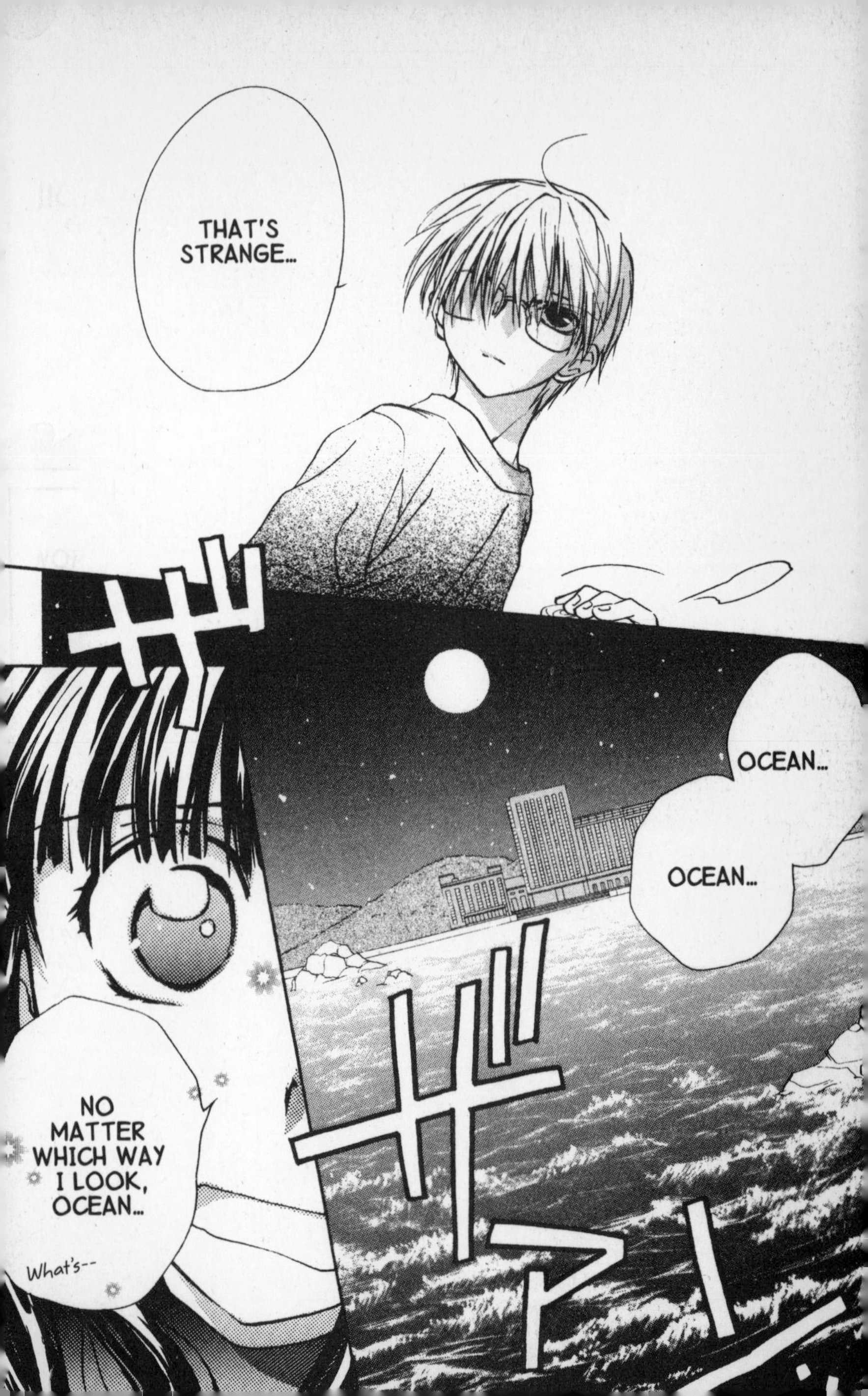
THAT'S STRANGE...
OCEAN...
OCEAN...
NO MATTER WHICH WAY I LOOK, OCEAN...
What's--

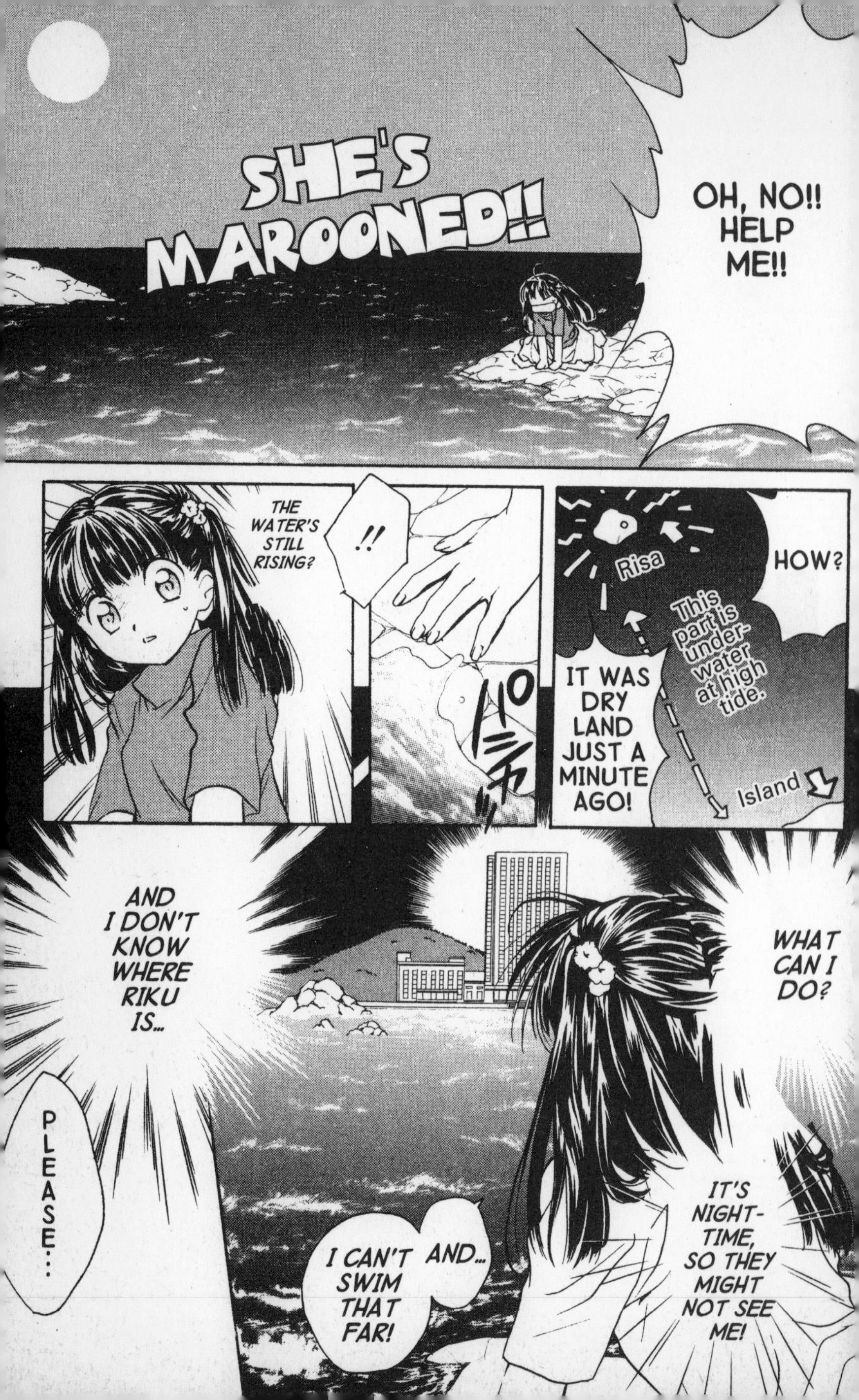

OH, NO!! HELP ME!!
SHE'S MAROONED!!
HOW?
Risa
This part is underwater at high tide.
IT WAS DRY LAND JUST A MINUTE AGO!
Island
!!
THE WATER'S STILL RISING?
WHAT CAN I DO?
AND I DON'T KNOW WHERE RIKU IS...
IT'S NIGHT-TIME, SO THEY MIGHT NOT SEE ME!
AND...
I CAN'T SWIM THAT FAR!
PLEASE...

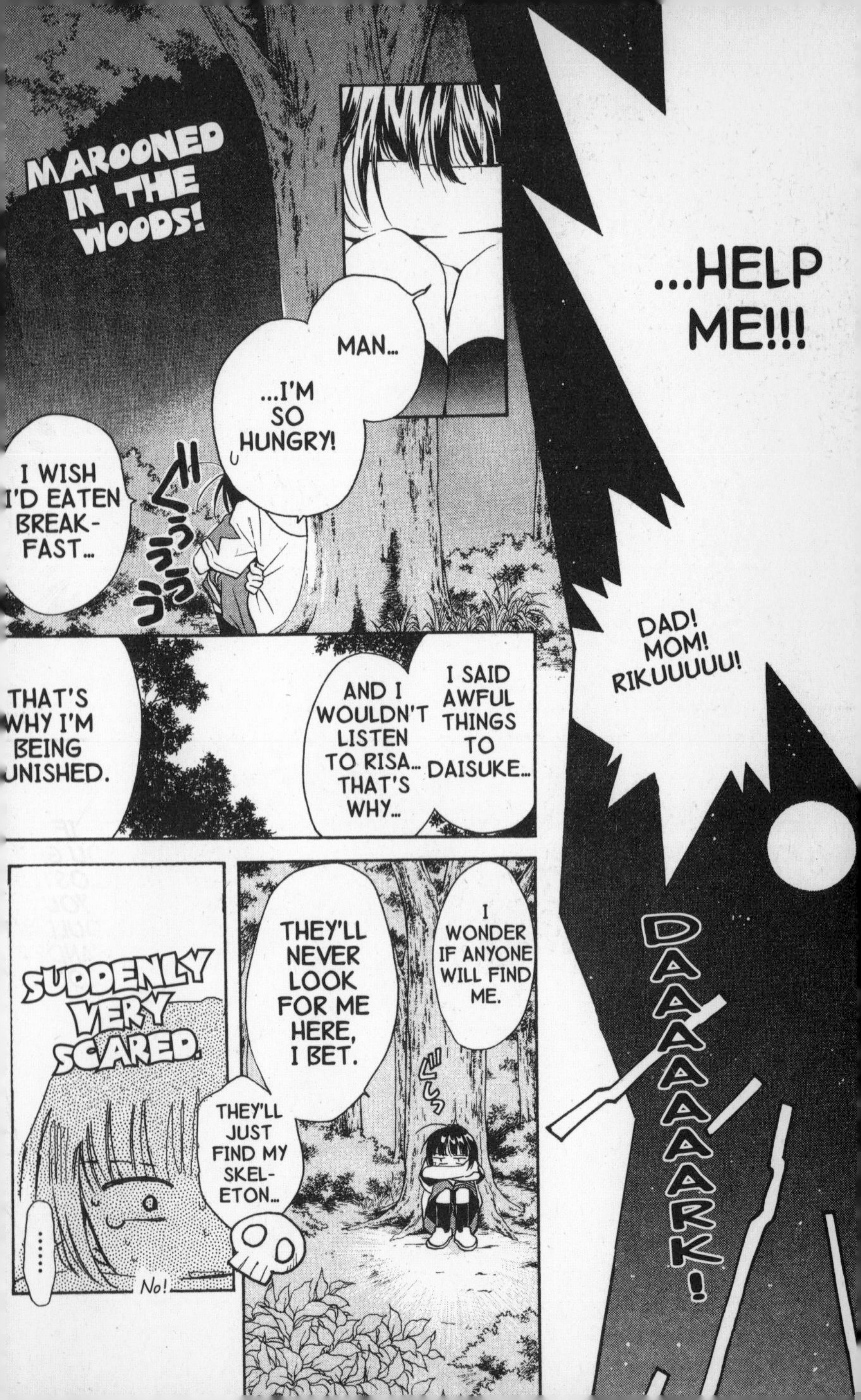
...HELP ME!!!
DAD! MOM! RIKUUUUU!
DAAAAAAARK!
MAROONED IN THE WOODS!
MAN...
...I'M SO HUNGRY!
I WISH I'D EATEN BREAK-FAST...
I SAID AWFUL THINGS TO DAISUKE...
AND I WOULDN'T LISTEN TO RISA... THAT'S WHY...
THAT'S WHY I'M BEING UNISHED.
I WONDER IF ANYONE WILL FIND ME.
THEY'LL NEVER LOOK FOR ME HERE, I BET.
THEY'LL JUST FIND MY SKEL-ETON...
SUDDENLY VERY SCARED.
......
No!

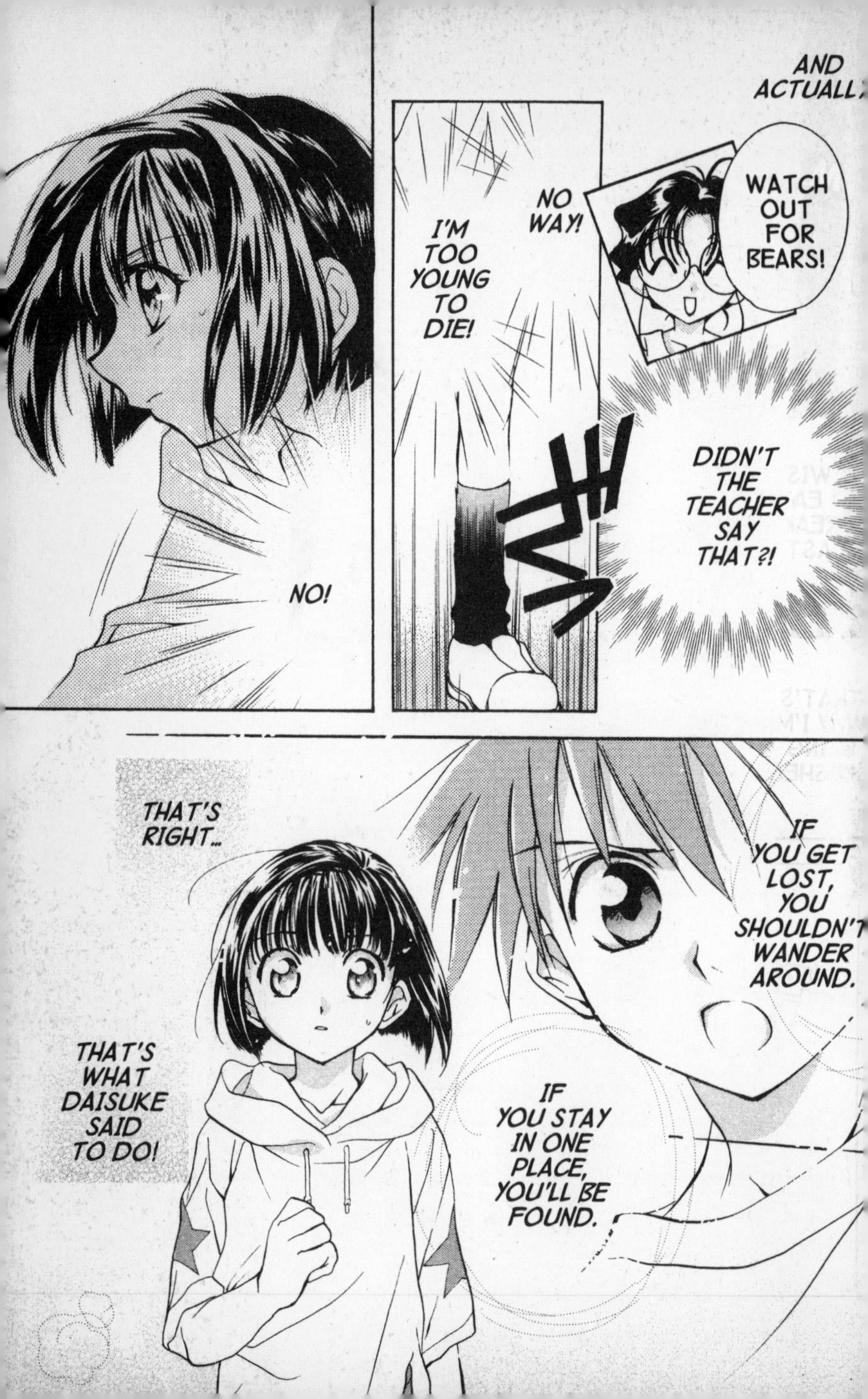
AND ACTUALL
WATCH OUT FOR BEARS!
DIDN'T THE TEACHER SAY THAT?!
NO WAY!
I'M TOO YOUNG TO DIE!
NO!
IF YOU GET LOST, YOU SHOULDN'T WANDER AROUND.
IF YOU STAY IN ONE PLACE, YOU'LL BE FOUND.
THAT'S RIGHT...
THAT'S WHAT DAISUKE SAID TO DO!

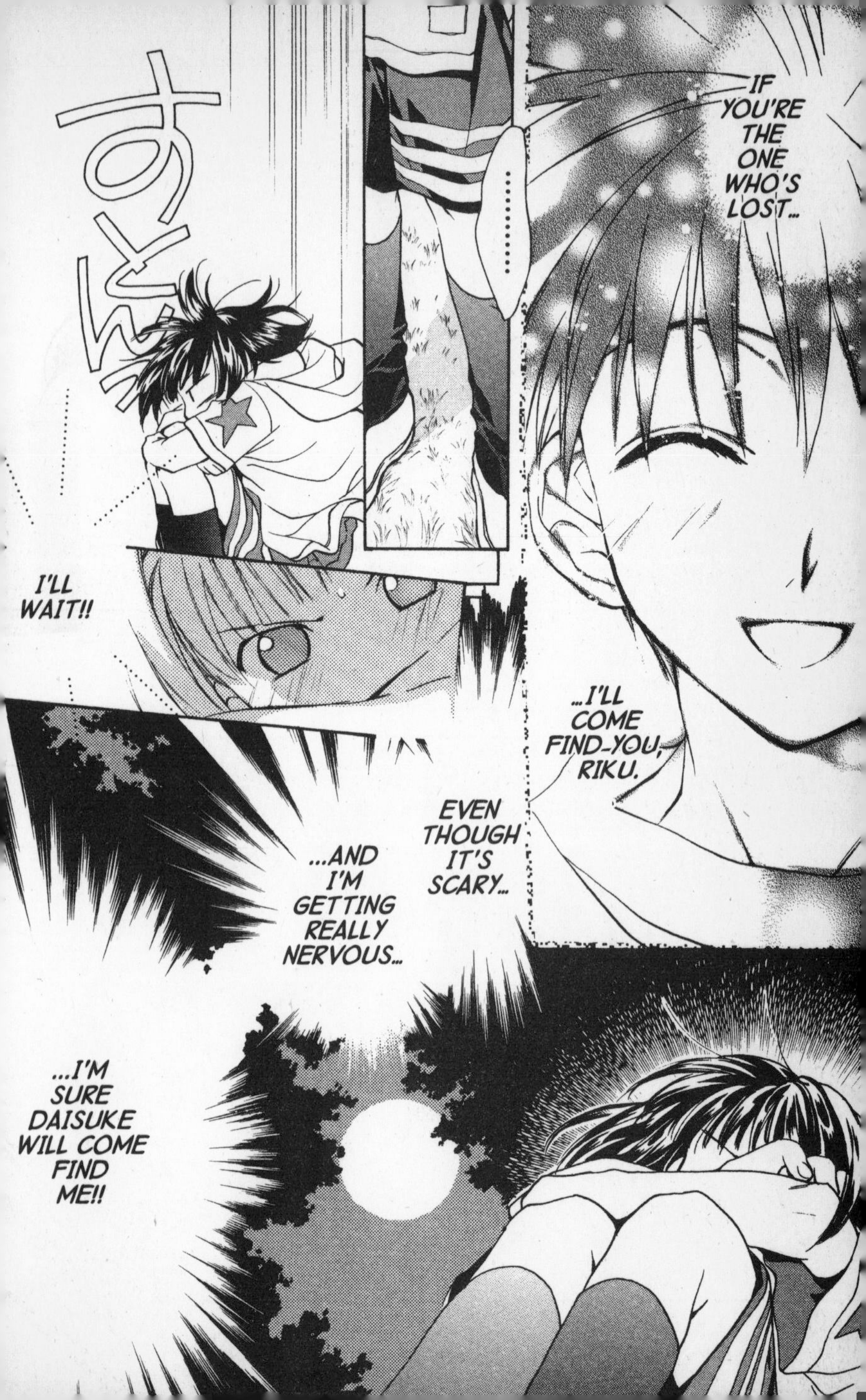

IF YOU'RE THE ONE WHO'S LOST...
...I'LL COME FIND-YOU, RIKU.
......
I'LL WAIT!!
EVEN THOUGH IT'S SCARY...
...AND I'M GETTING REALLY NERVOUS...
...I'M SURE DAISUKE WILL COME FIND ME!!

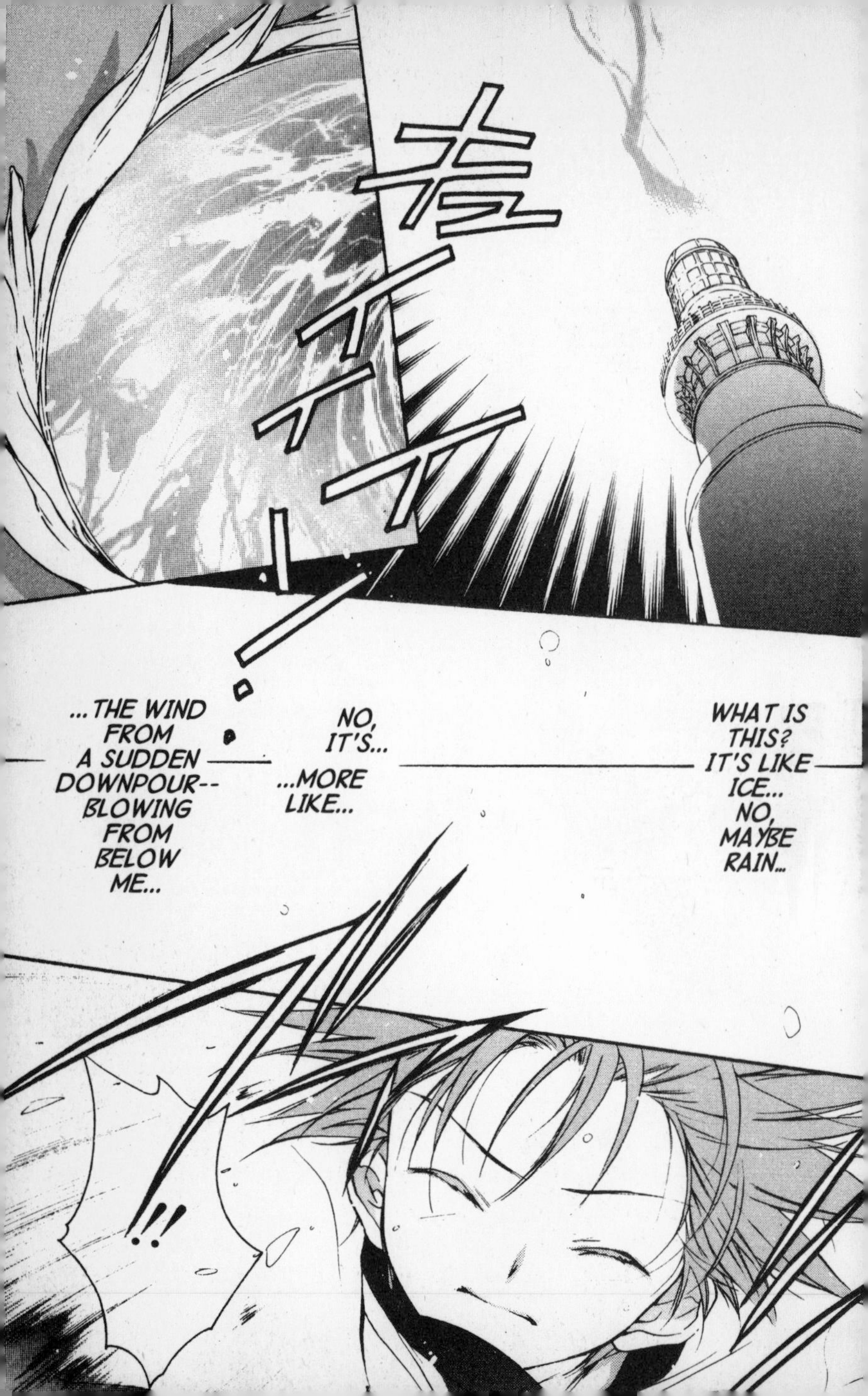
WHAT IS THIS? IT'S LIKE ICE... NO, MAYBE RAIN...
NO, IT'S...
...MORE LIKE...
...THE WIND FROM A SUDDEN DOWNPOUR-- BLOWING FROM BELOW ME...
!!

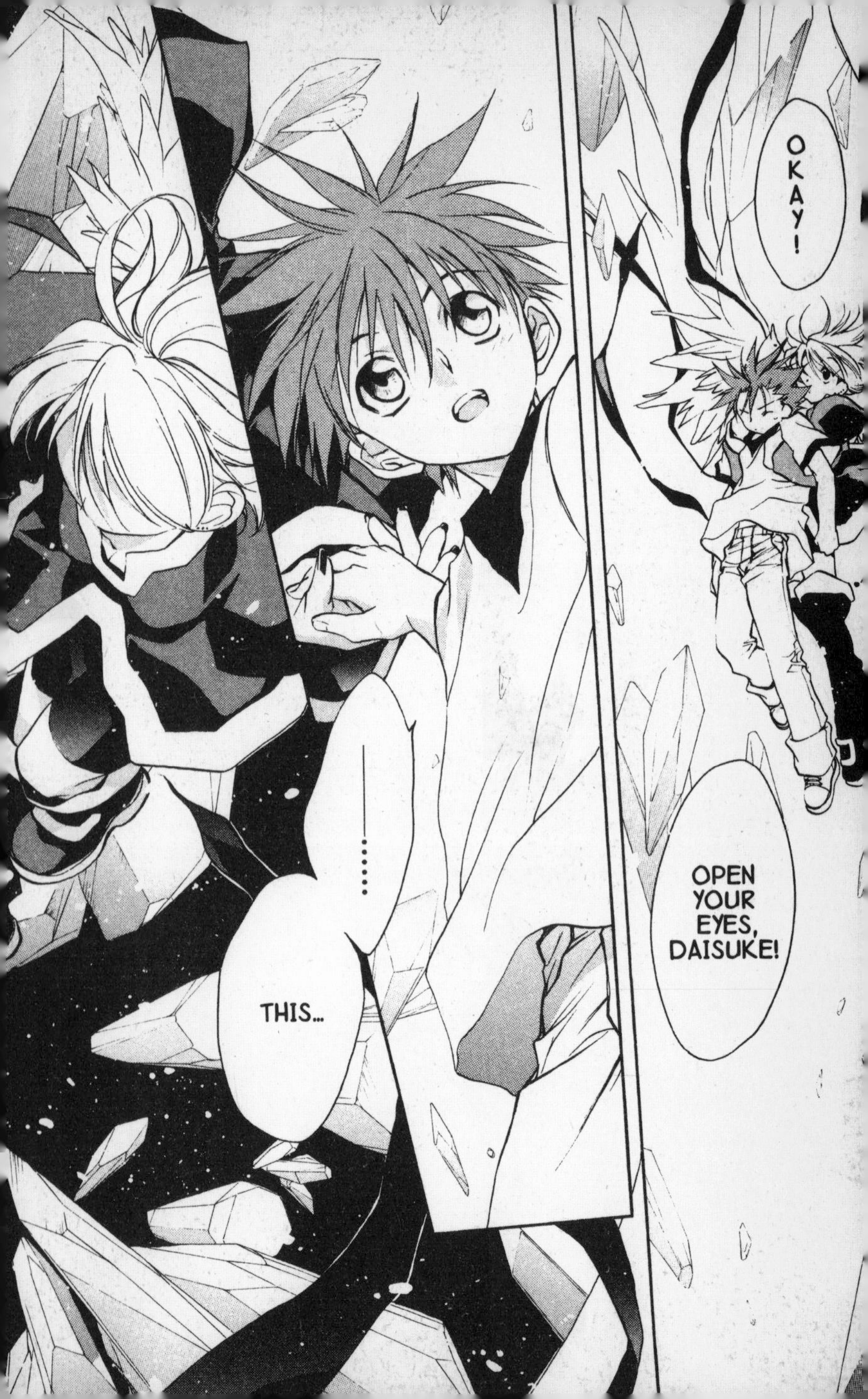
OKAY!
OPEN YOUR EYES, DAISUKE!
......
THIS...

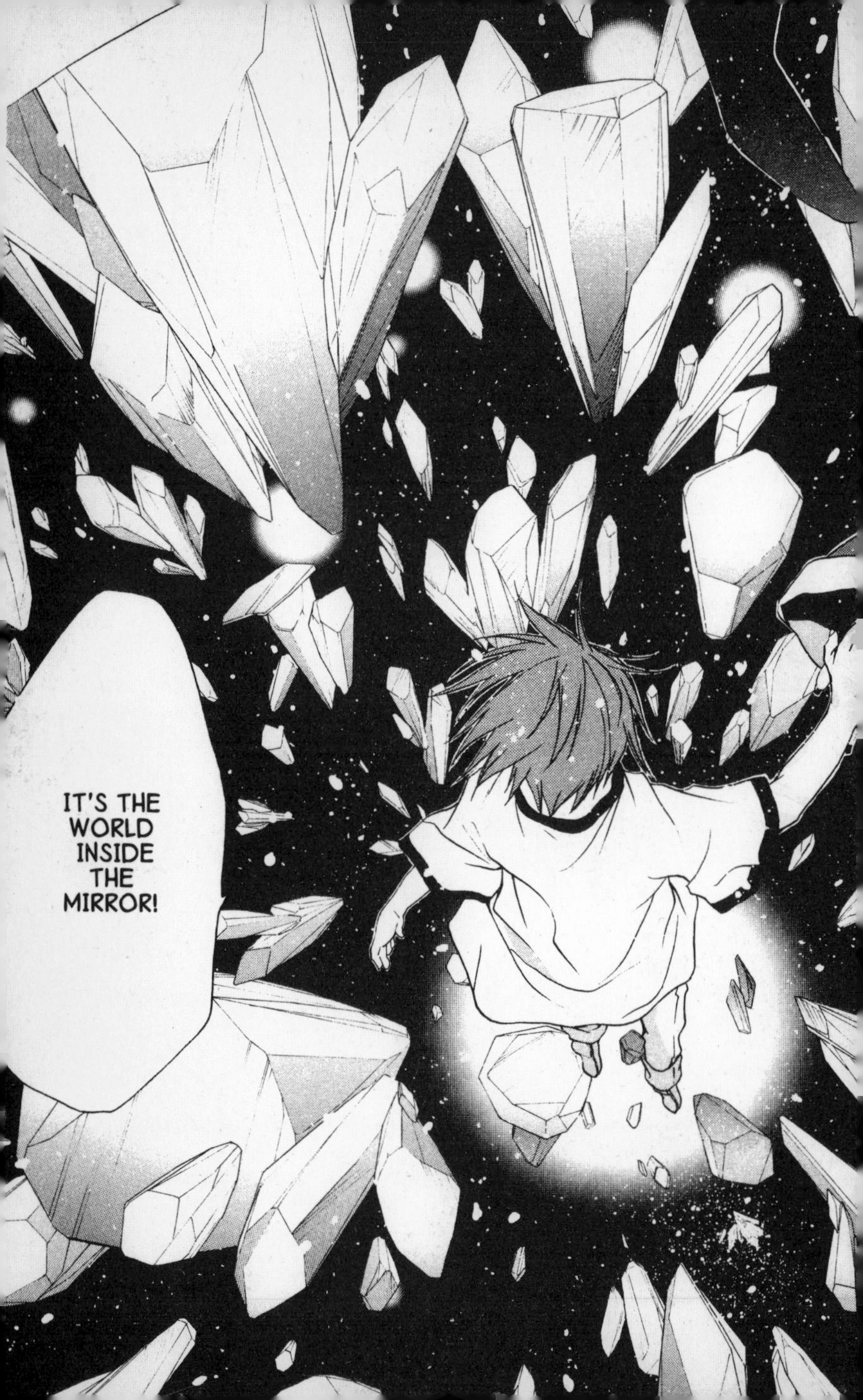
IT'S THE WORLD INSIDE THE MIRROR!

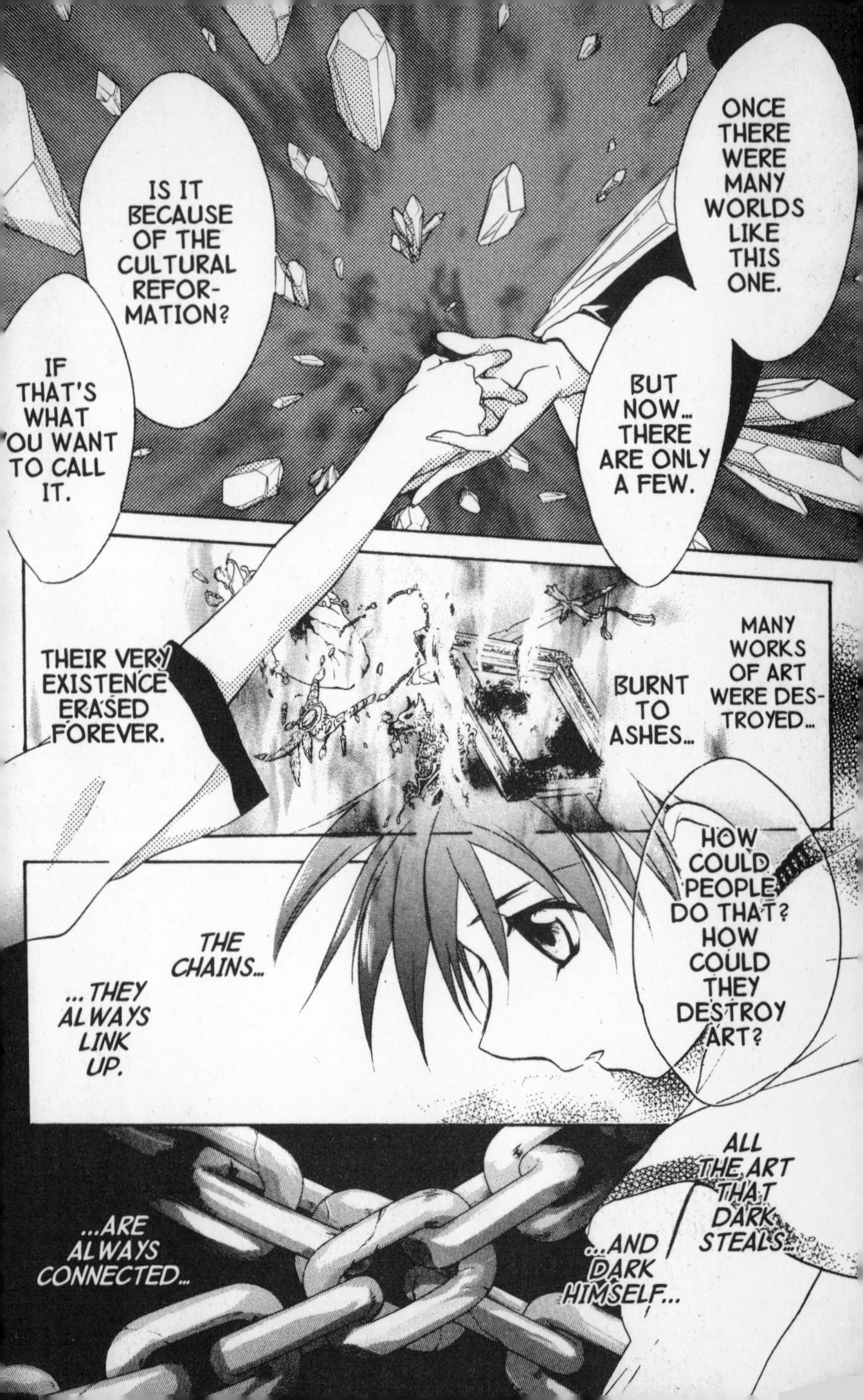
ONCE THERE WERE MANY WORLDS LIKE THIS ONE.
BUT NOW... THERE ARE ONLY A FEW.
IS IT BECAUSE OF THE CULTURAL REFOR-MATION?
IF THAT'S WHAT OU WANT TO CALL IT.
MANY WORKS OF ART WERE DES-TROYED...
BURNT TO ASHES...
THEIR VERY EXISTENCE ERASED FOREVER.
HOW COULD PEOPLE DO THAT? HOW COULD THEY DESTROY ART?
THE CHAINS...
...THEY ALWAYS LINK UP.
ALL THE ART THAT DARK STEALS...
...AND DARK HIMSELF...
...ARE ALWAYS CONNECTED...

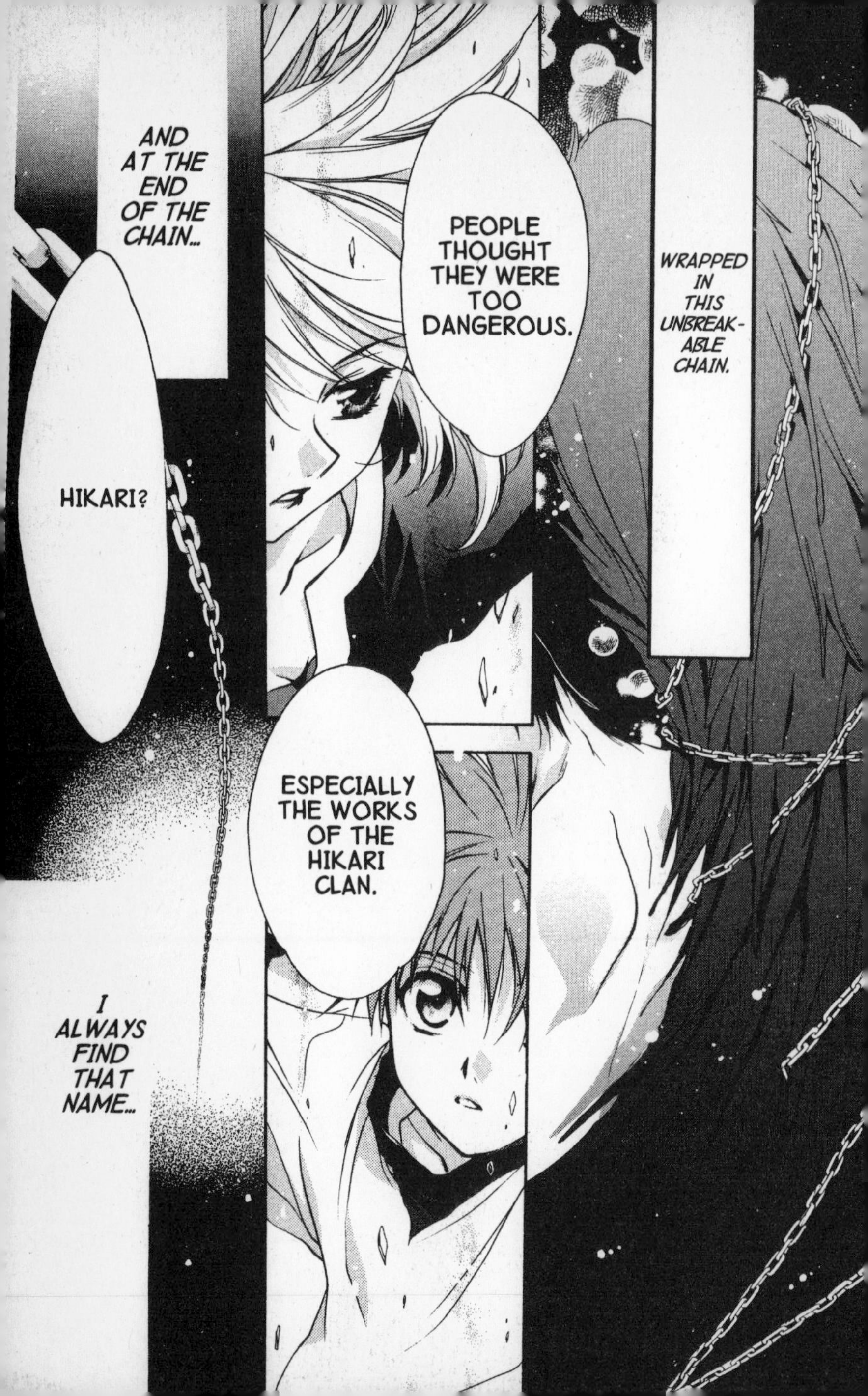
WRAPPED IN THIS UNBREAK-ABLE CHAIN.
PEOPLE THOUGHT THEY WERE TOO DANGEROUS.
ESPECIALLY THE WORKS OF THE HIKARI CLAN.
AND AT THE END OF THE CHAIN...
HIKARI?
I ALWAYS FIND THAT NAME...

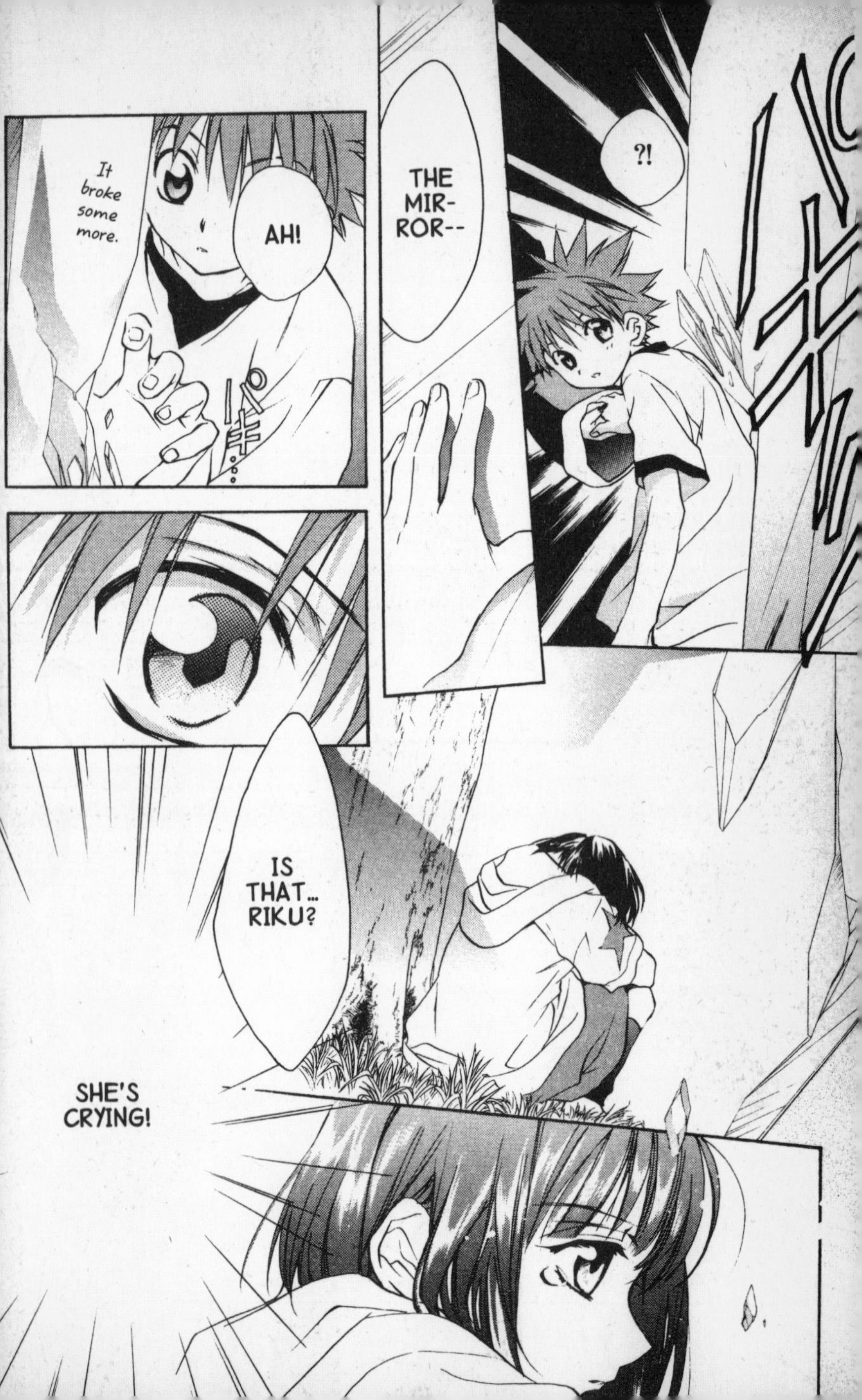
?!
THE MIR-ROR--
AH!
It broke some more.
IS THAT... RIKU?
SHE'S CRYING!

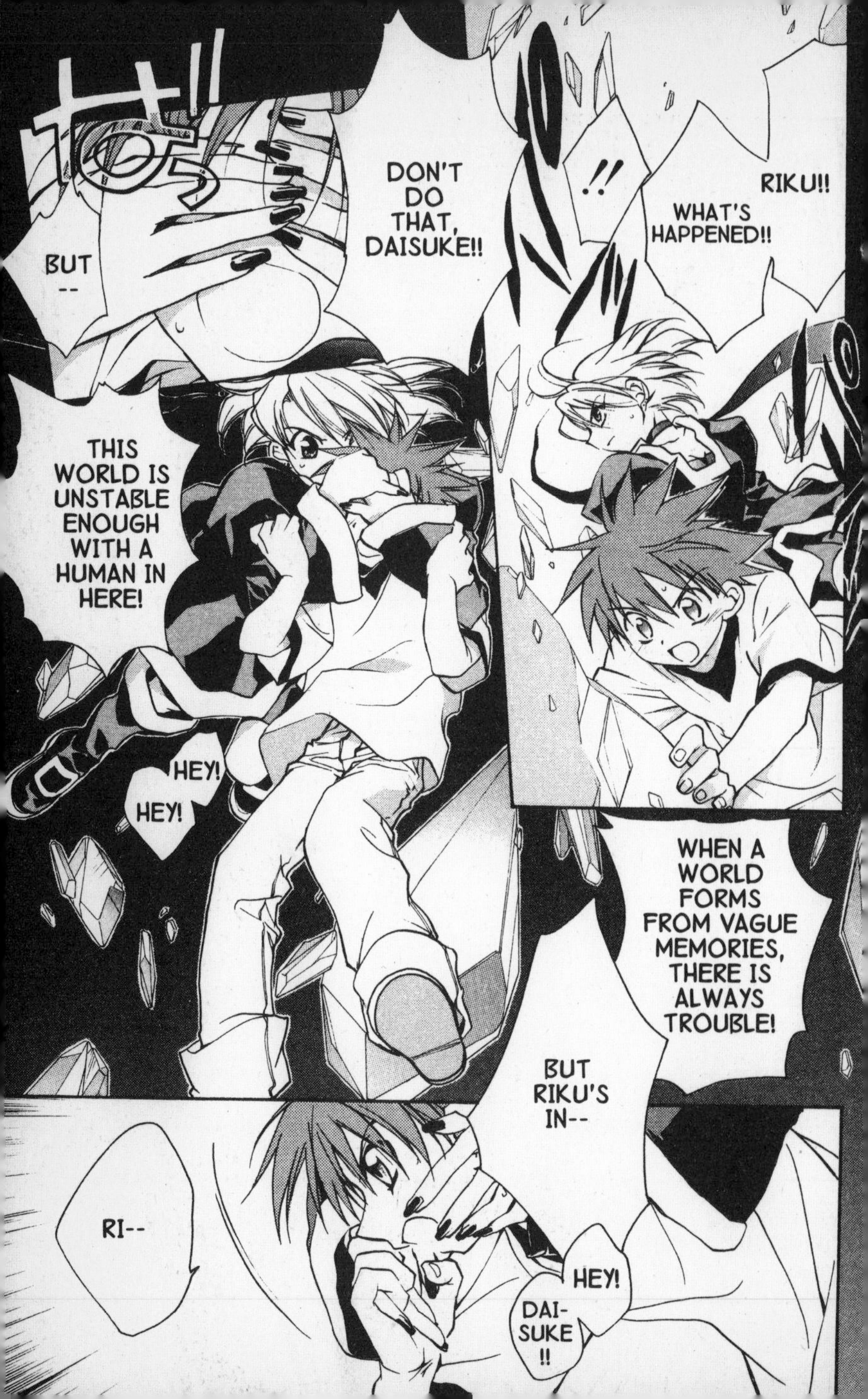
RIKU!!
WHAT'S HAPPENED!!
!!
DON'T DO THAT, DAISUKE!!
BUT --
THIS WORLD IS UNSTABLE ENOUGH WITH A HUMAN IN HERE!
HEY!
HEY!
WHEN A WORLD FORMS FROM VAGUE MEMORIES, THERE IS ALWAYS TROUBLE!
BUT RIKU'S IN--
HEY!
DAI-SUKE!!
RI--

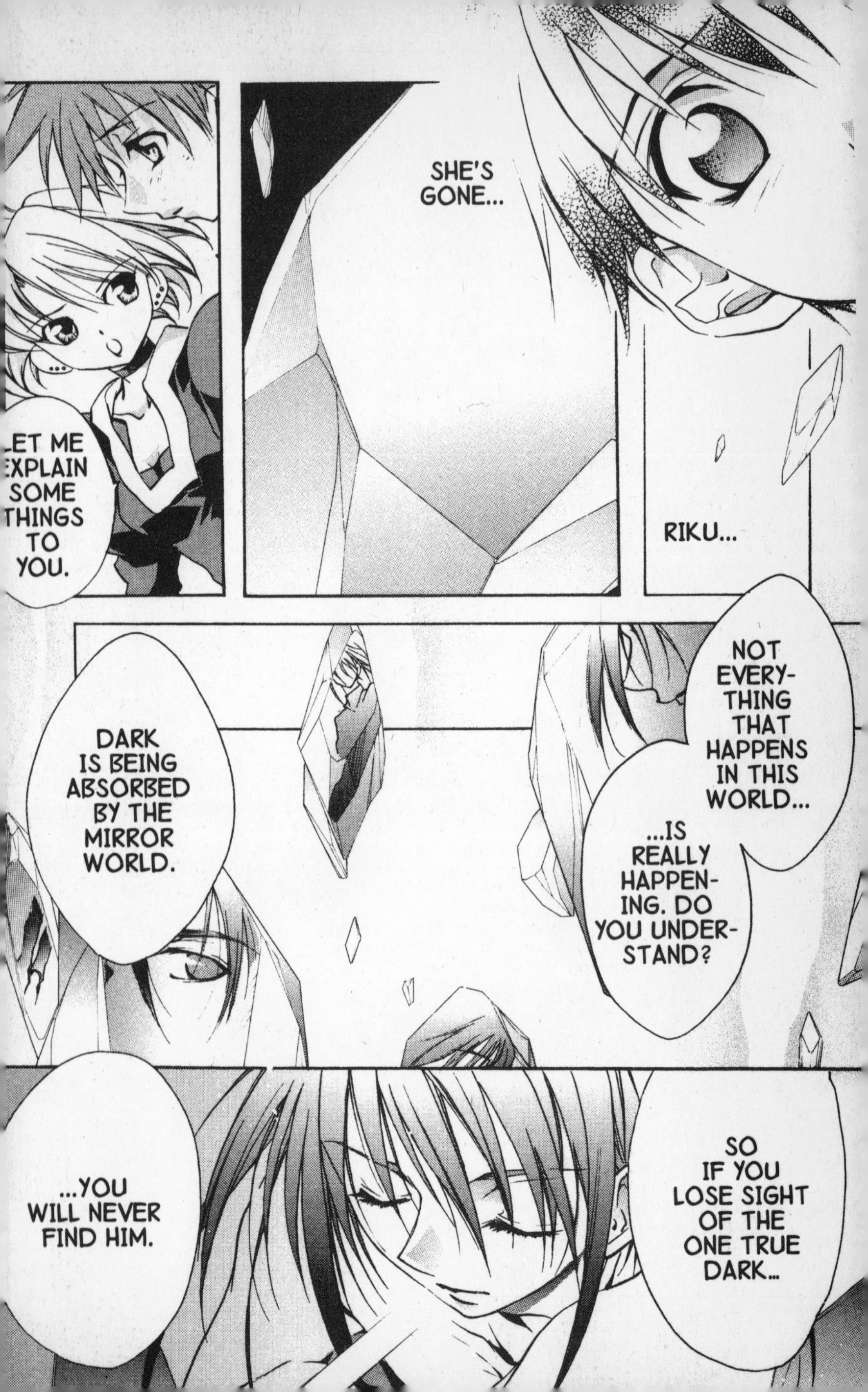
RIKU...
SHE'S GONE...
LET ME EXPLAIN SOME THINGS TO YOU.
NOT EVERY-THING THAT HAPPENS IN THIS WORLD...
...IS REALLY HAPPEN-ING. DO YOU UNDER-STAND?
DARK IS BEING ABSORBED BY THE MIRROR WORLD.
SO IF YOU LOSE SIGHT OF THE ONE TRUE DARK...
...YOU WILL NEVER FIND HIM.

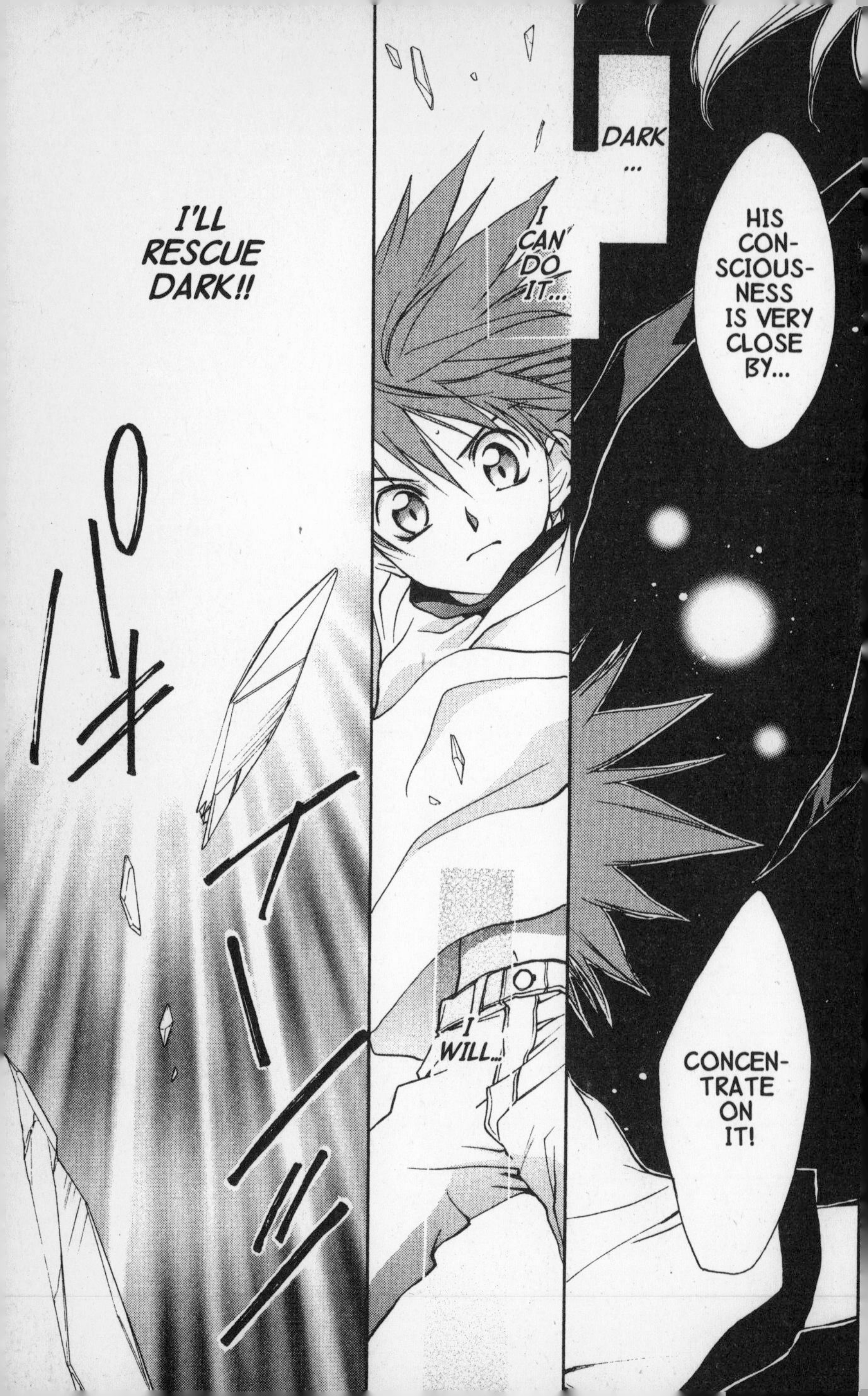
DARK...
HIS CONSCIOUSNESS IS VERY CLOSE BY...
CONCENTRATE ON IT!
I CAN DO IT...
I WILL...
I'LL RESCUE DARK!!
パキーン

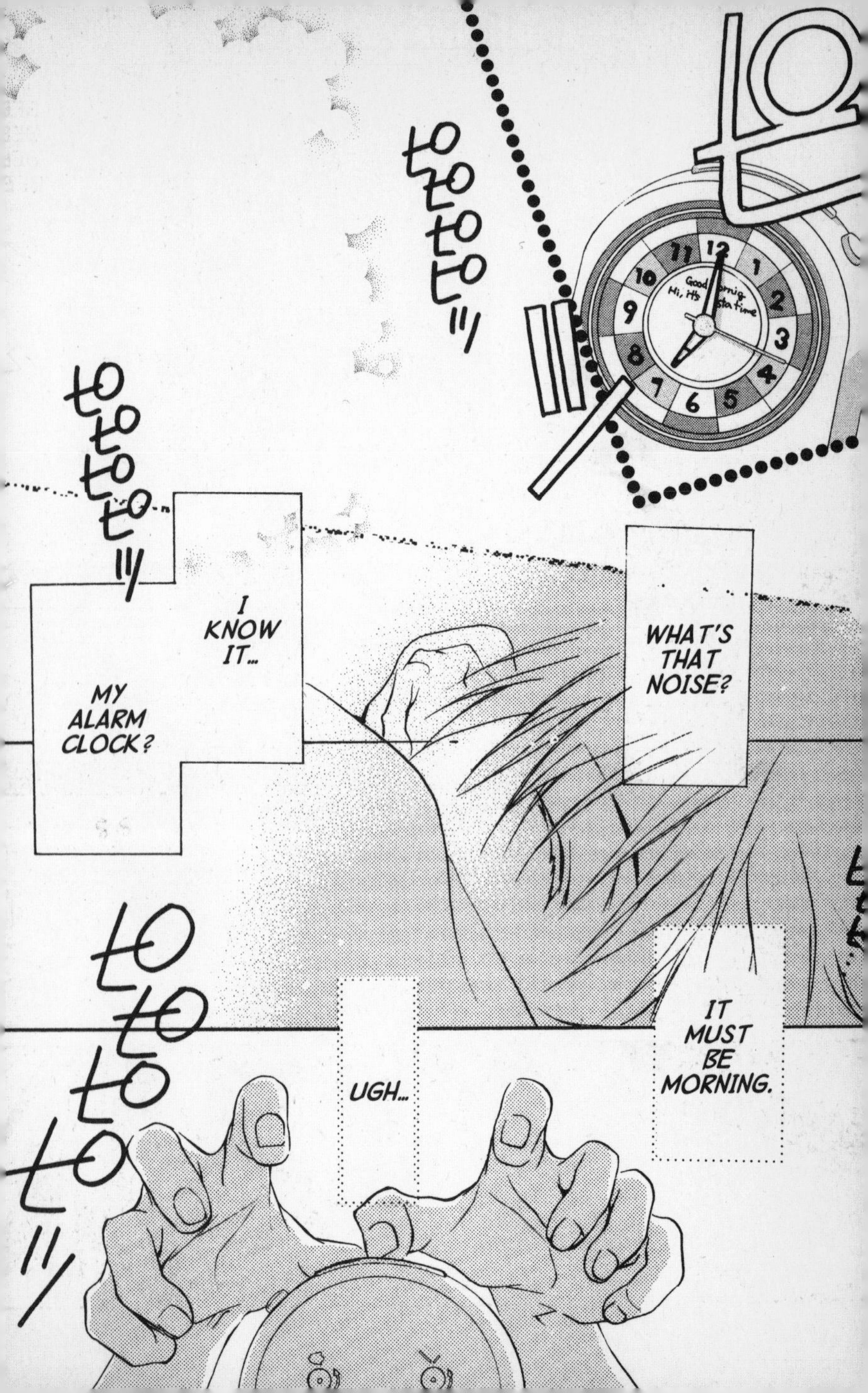
ピピピピピッ
ピピピピピッ
WHAT'S THAT NOISE?
I KNOW IT...
MY ALARM CLOCK?
IT MUST BE MORNING.
UGH...
ピピピピピッ

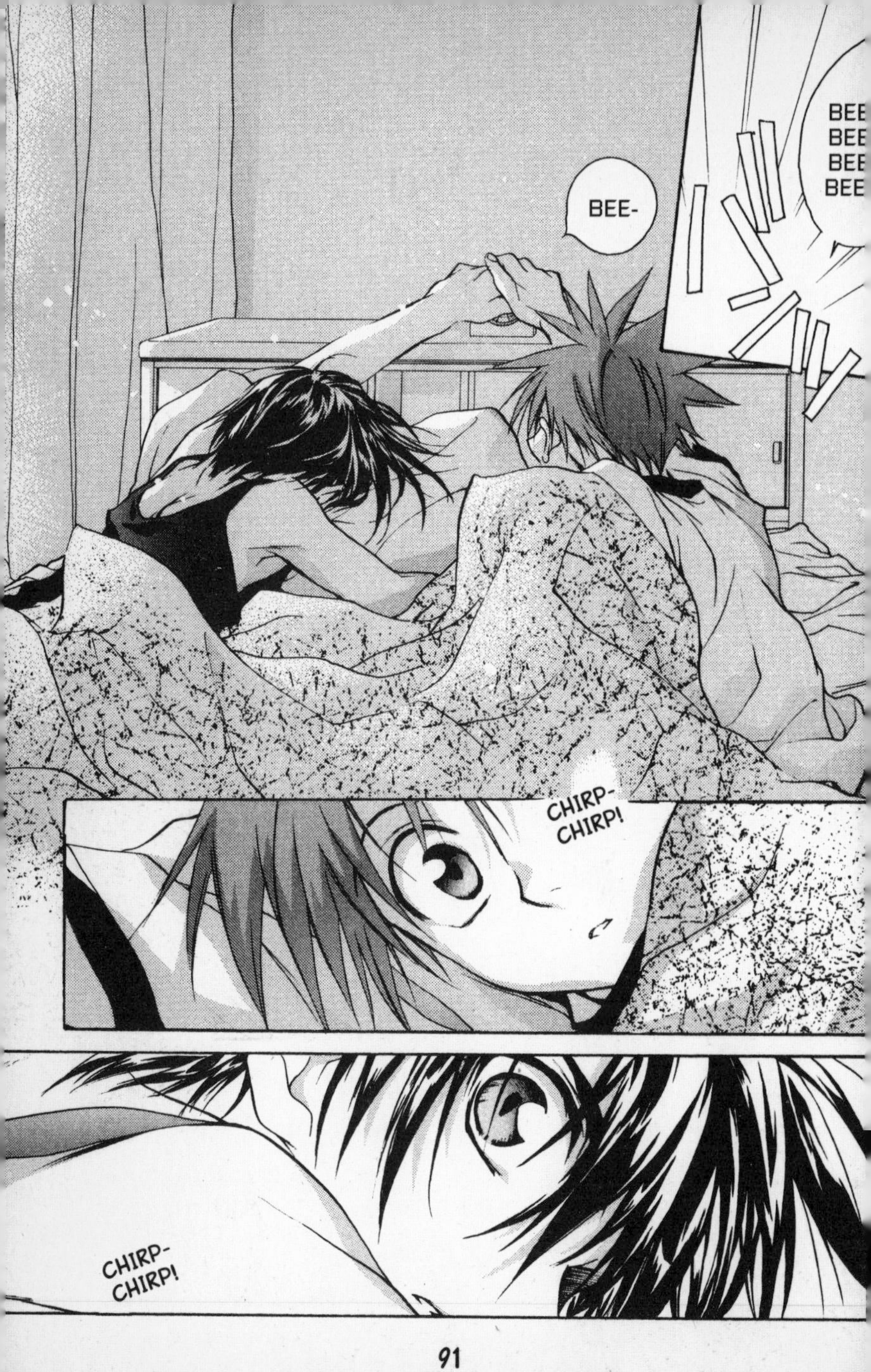
BEE
BEE
BEE
BEE
BEE-
CHIRP-CHIRP!
CHIRP-CHIRP!

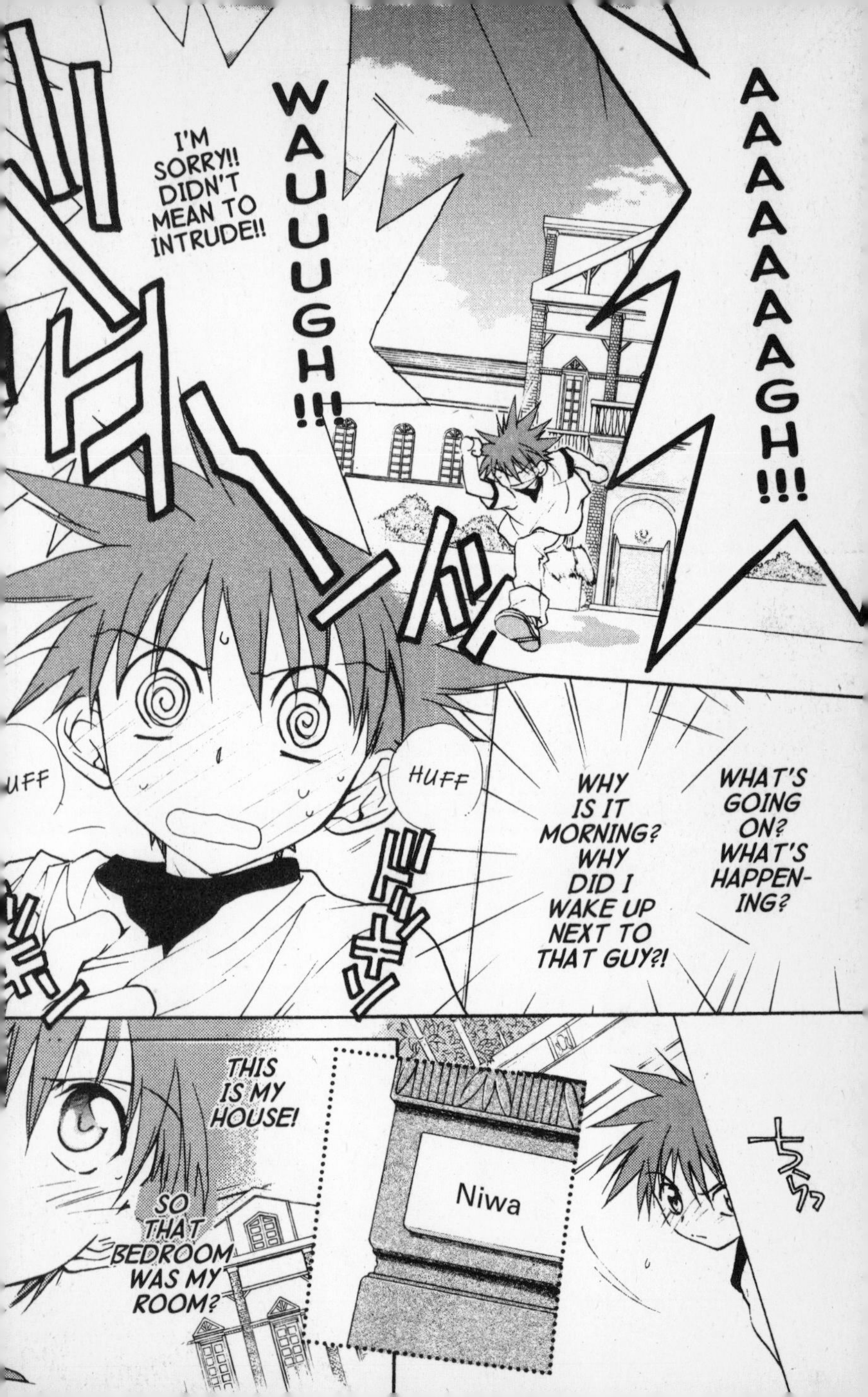
AAAAAAAAGH!!!
WAUUUGH!!!
I'M SORRY!! DIDN'T MEAN TO INTRUDE!!
WHAT'S GOING ON? WHAT'S HAPPEN-ING?
WHY IS IT MORNING? WHY DID I WAKE UP NEXT TO THAT GUY?!
HUFF
UFF
Niwa
THIS IS MY HOUSE!
SO THAT BEDROOM WAS MY ROOM?

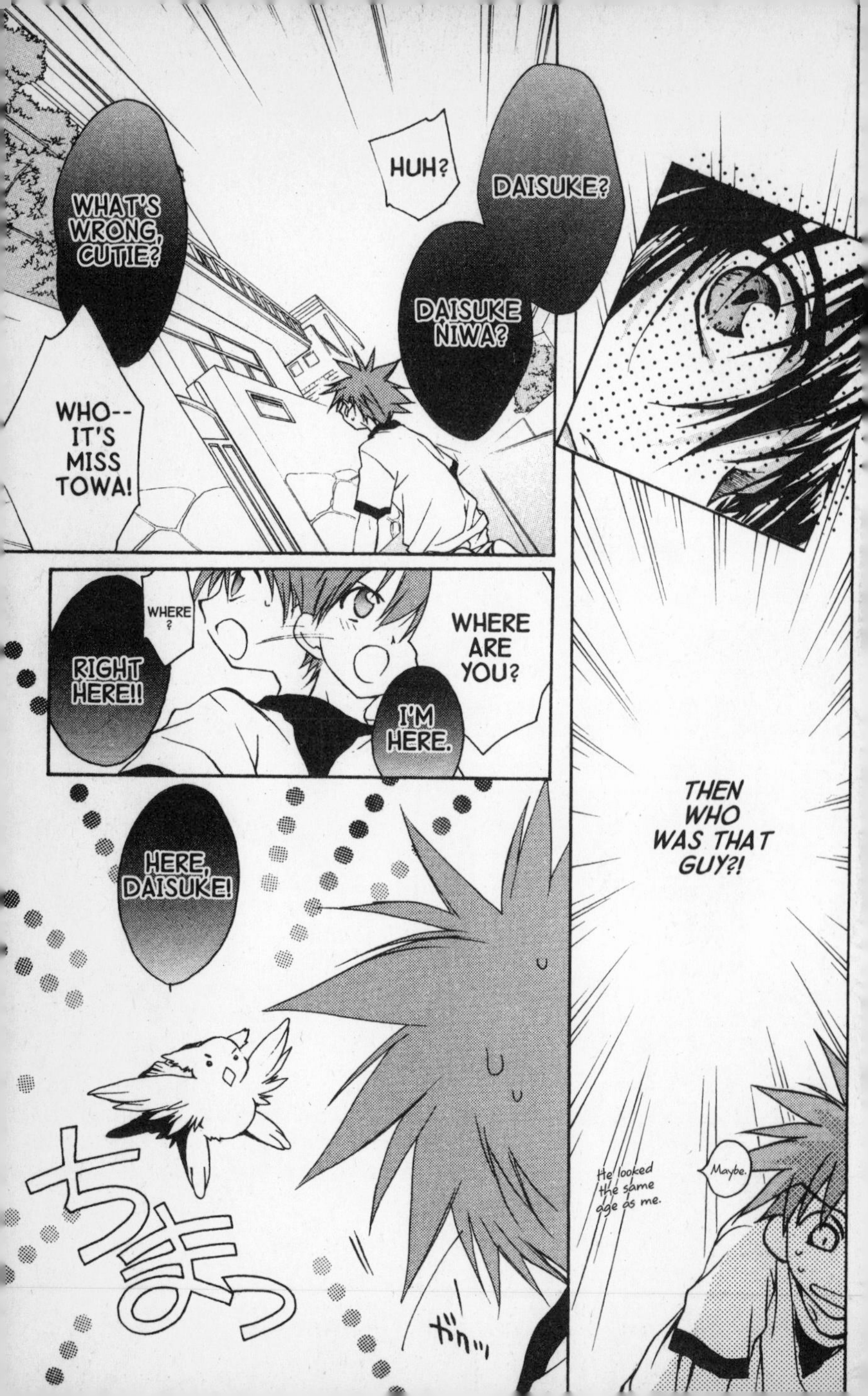
DAISUKE?
HUH?
DAISUKE NIWA?
WHAT'S WRONG, CUTIE?
WHO-- IT'S MISS TOWA!
WHERE ARE YOU?
I'M HERE.
WHERE?
RIGHT HERE!!
HERE, DAISUKE!
ちまっ
ガクッ
THEN WHO WAS THAT GUY?!
Maybe.
He looked the same age as me.

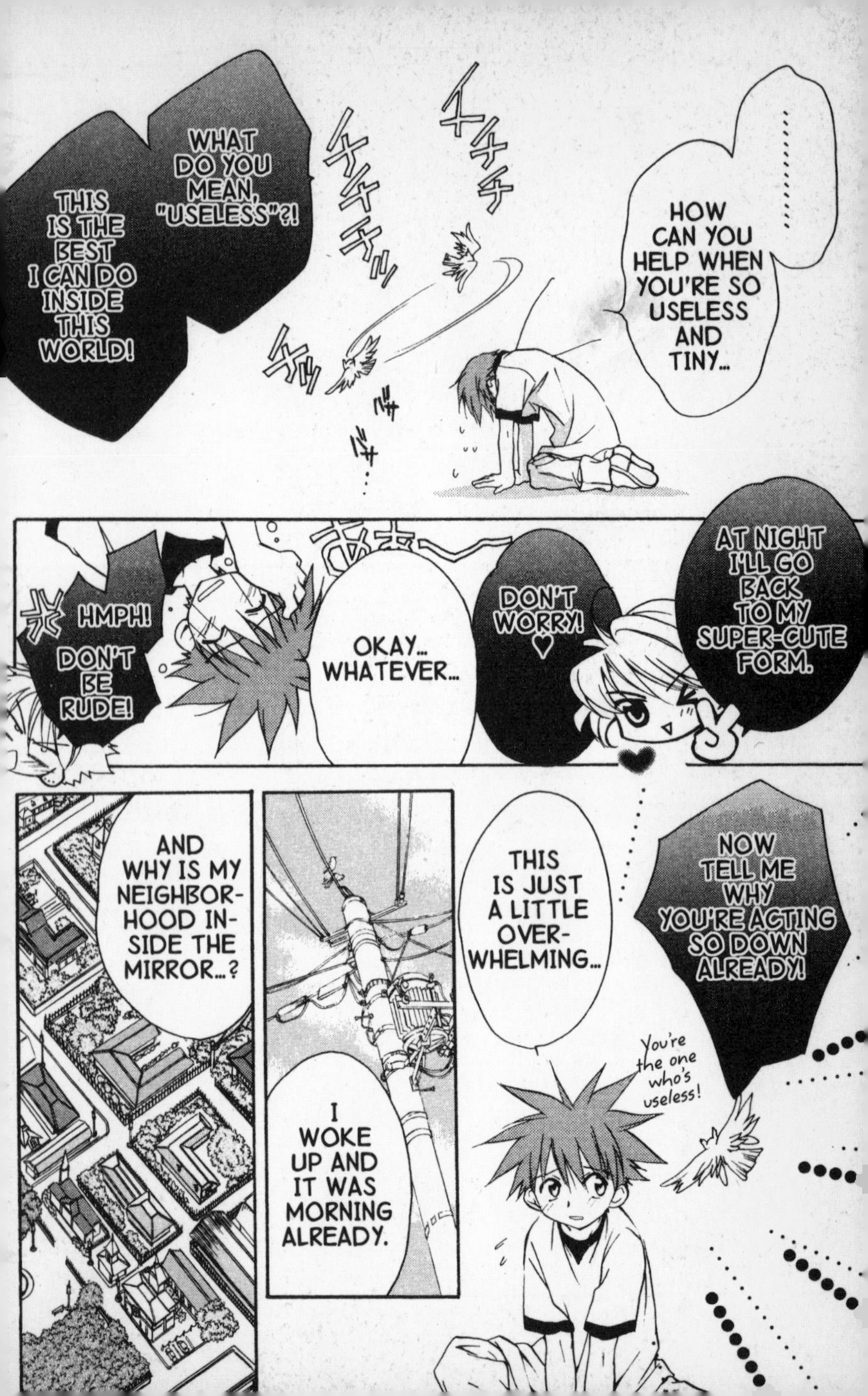

......
HOW CAN YOU HELP WHEN YOU'RE SO USELESS AND TINY...
WHAT DO YOU MEAN, "USELESS"?!
THIS IS THE BEST I CAN DO INSIDE THIS WORLD!
AT NIGHT I'LL GO BACK TO MY SUPER-CUTE FORM.
DON'T WORRY! ♥
OKAY... WHATEVER...
HMPH! DON'T BE RUDE!
NOW TELL ME WHY YOU'RE ACTING SO DOWN ALREADY!
You're the one who's useless!
THIS IS JUST A LITTLE OVERWHELMING...
I WOKE UP AND IT WAS MORNING ALREADY.
AND WHY IS MY NEIGHBORHOOD INSIDE THE MIRROR...?

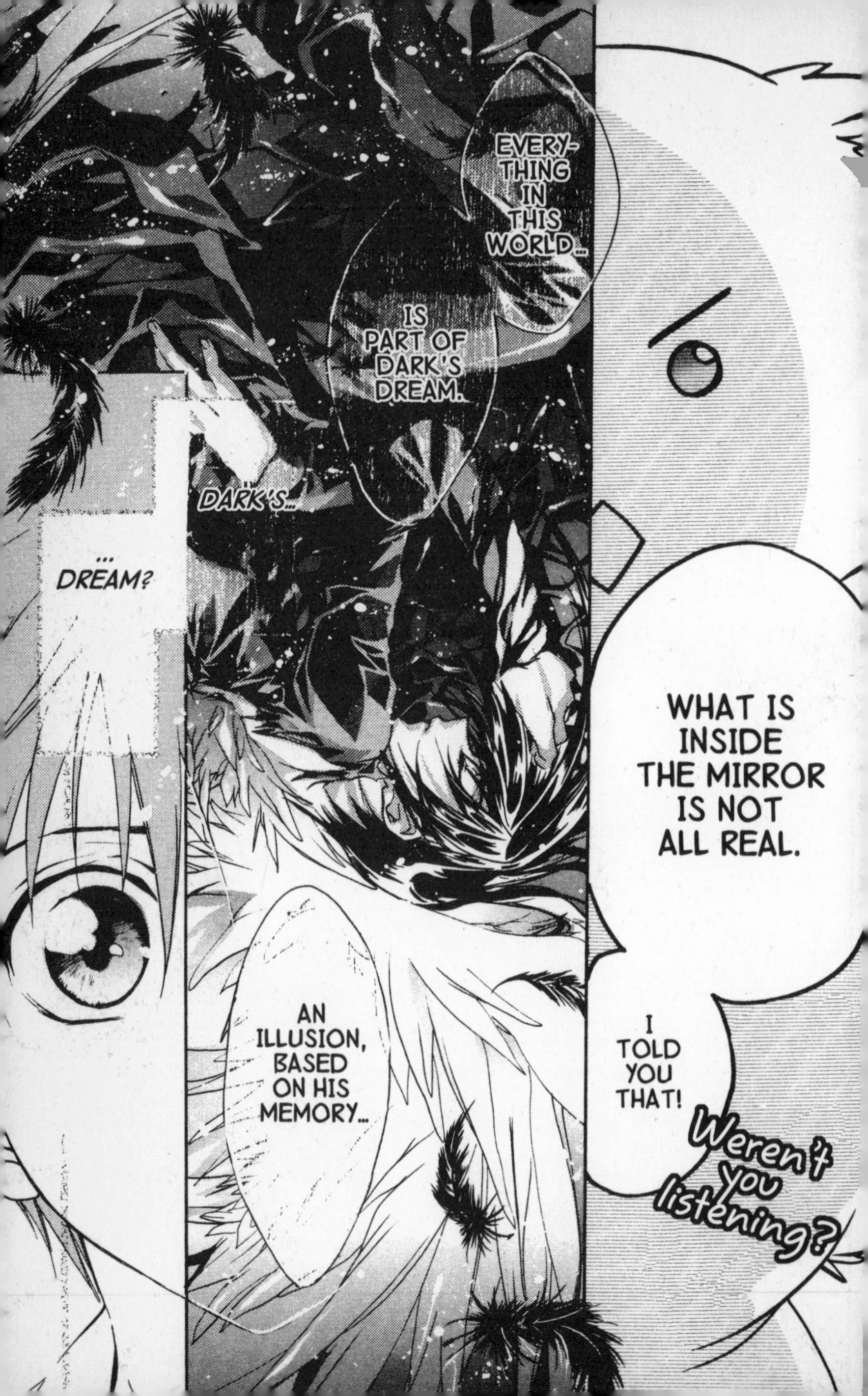
WHAT IS INSIDE THE MIRROR IS NOT ALL REAL.
I TOLD YOU THAT!
Weren't you listening?
EVERYTHING IN THIS WORLD...
IS PART OF DARK'S DREAM.
DARK'S...
...DREAM?
AN ILLUSION, BASED ON HIS MEMORY...

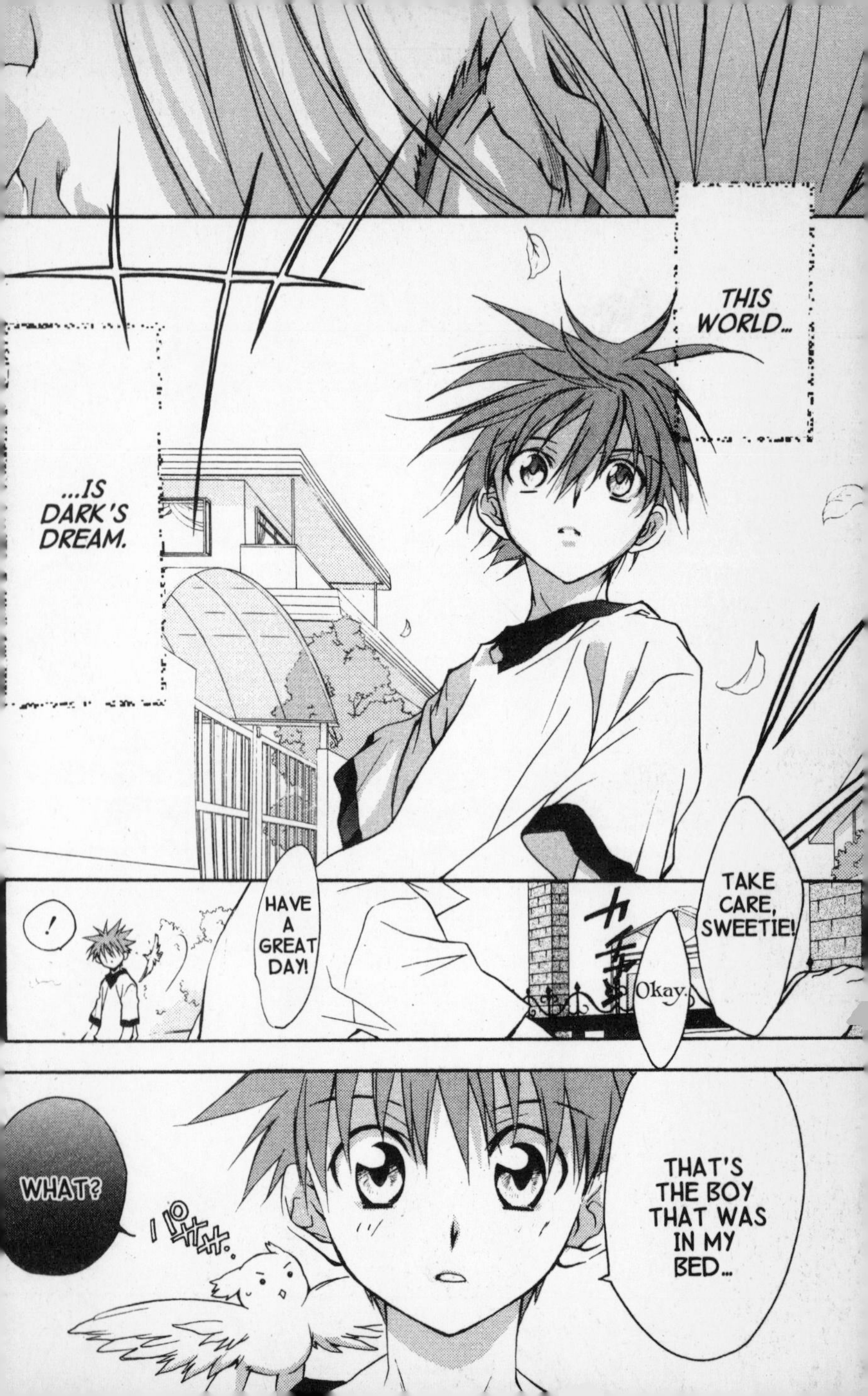
THIS WORLD...
...IS DARK'S DREAM.
TAKE CARE, SWEETIE!
Okay.
HAVE A GREAT DAY!
!
THAT'S THE BOY THAT WAS IN MY BED...
WHAT?

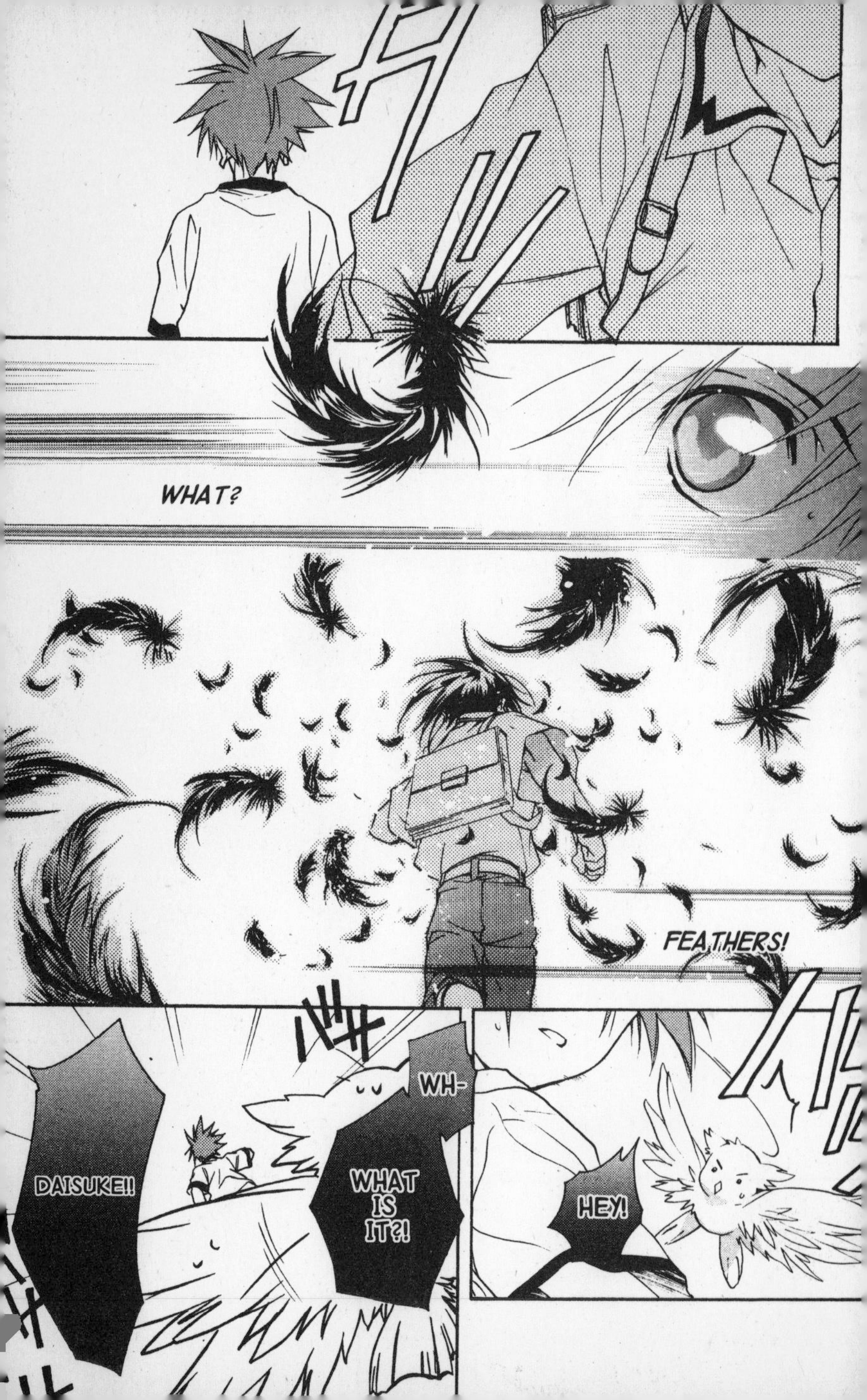
WHAT?
FEATHERS!
HEY!
WH-
WHAT IS IT?!
DAISUKE!!

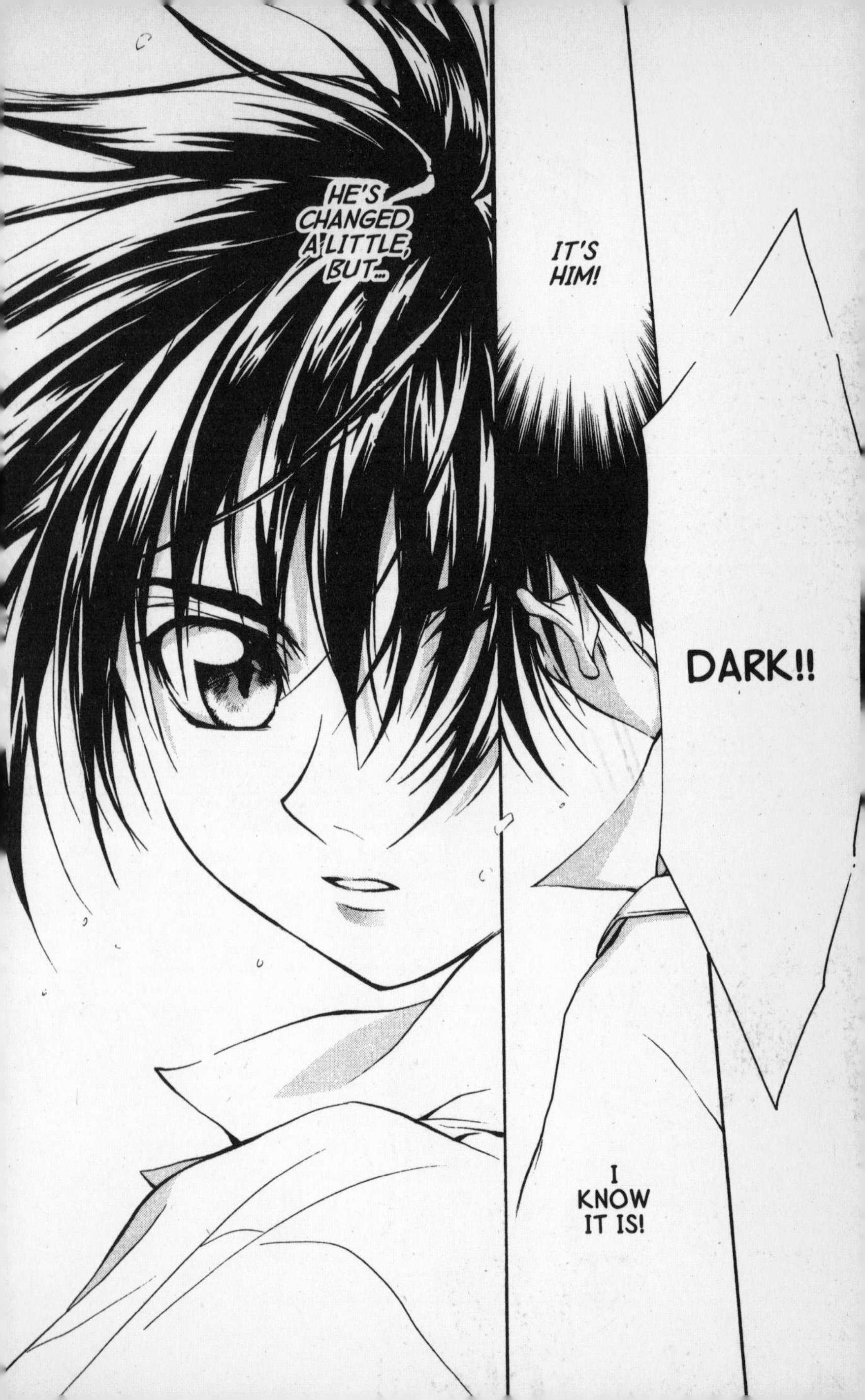
HE'S CHANGED A LITTLE, BUT...
IT'S HIM!
DARK!!
I KNOW IT IS!

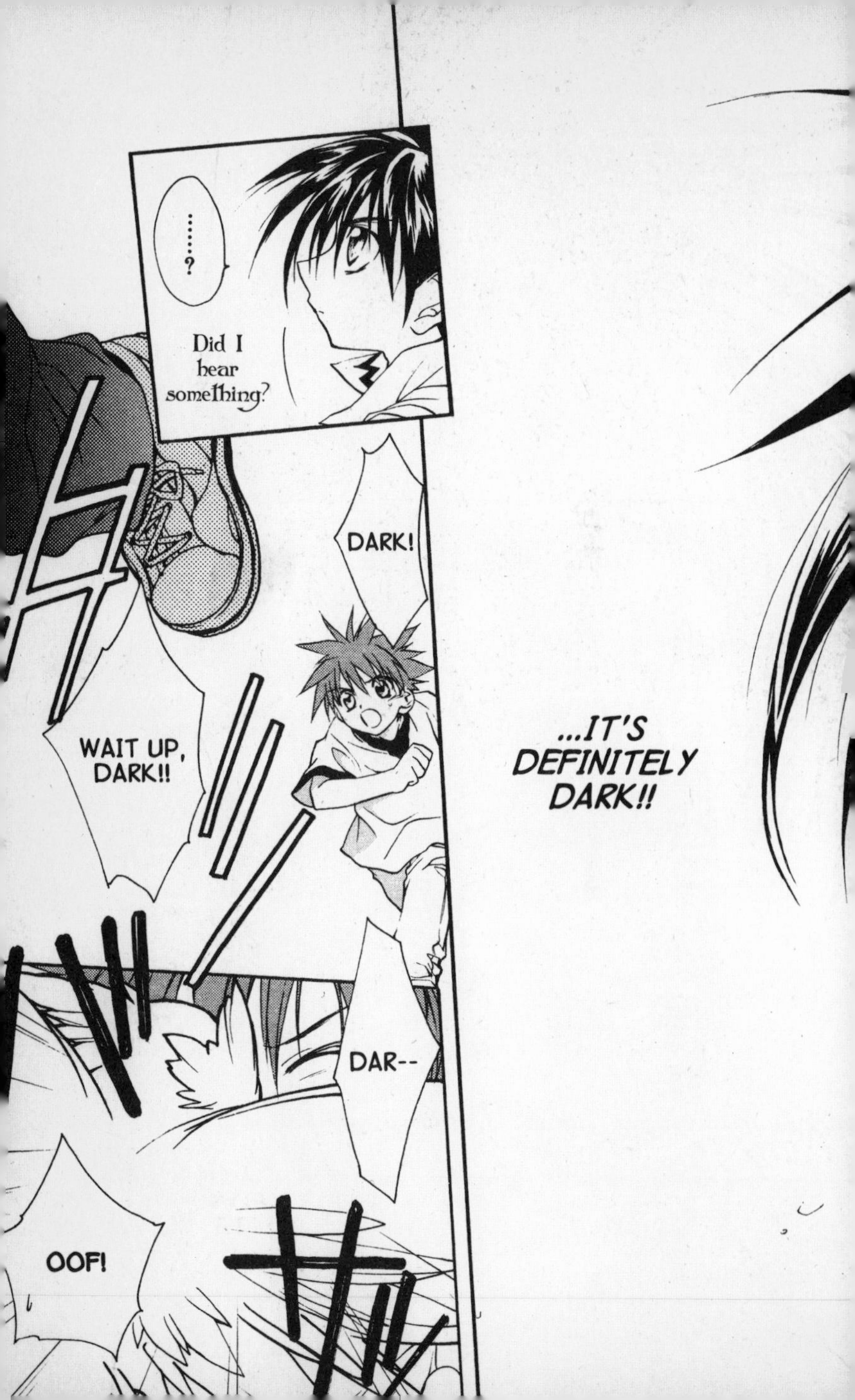
...IT'S DEFINITELY DARK!!
......?
Did I hear something?
DARK!
WAIT UP, DARK!!
DAR--
OOF!

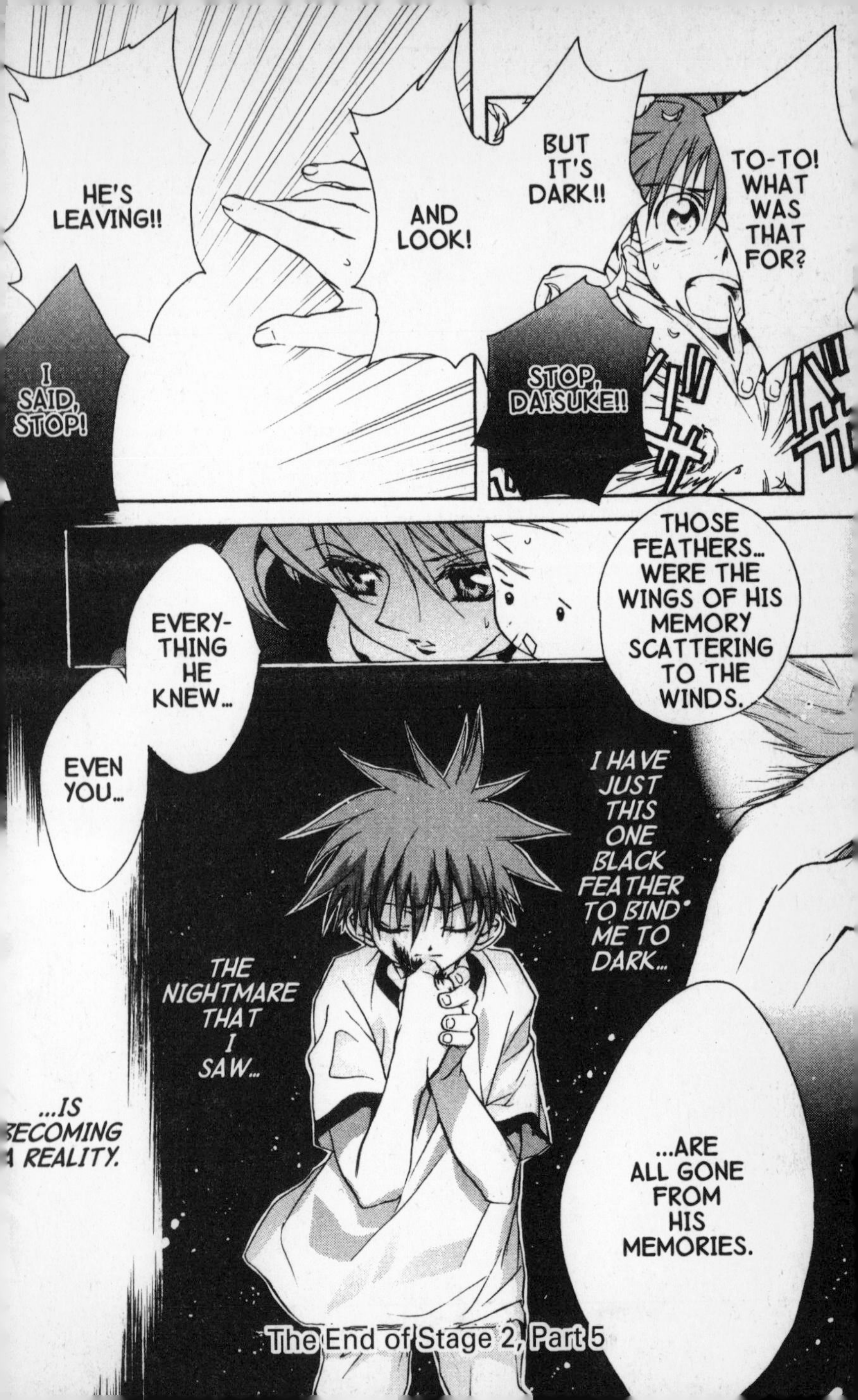
TO-TO! WHAT WAS THAT FOR?
BUT IT'S DARK!!
STOP, DAISUKE!!
AND LOOK!
HE'S LEAVING!!
I SAID, STOP!
THOSE FEATHERS... WERE THE WINGS OF HIS MEMORY SCATTERING TO THE WINDS.
EVERY-THING HE KNEW...
EVEN YOU...
I HAVE JUST THIS ONE BLACK FEATHER TO BIND ME TO DARK...
...ARE ALL GONE FROM HIS MEMORIES.
THE NIGHTMARE THAT I SAW...
...IS BECOMING A REALITY.
The End of Stage 2, Part 5

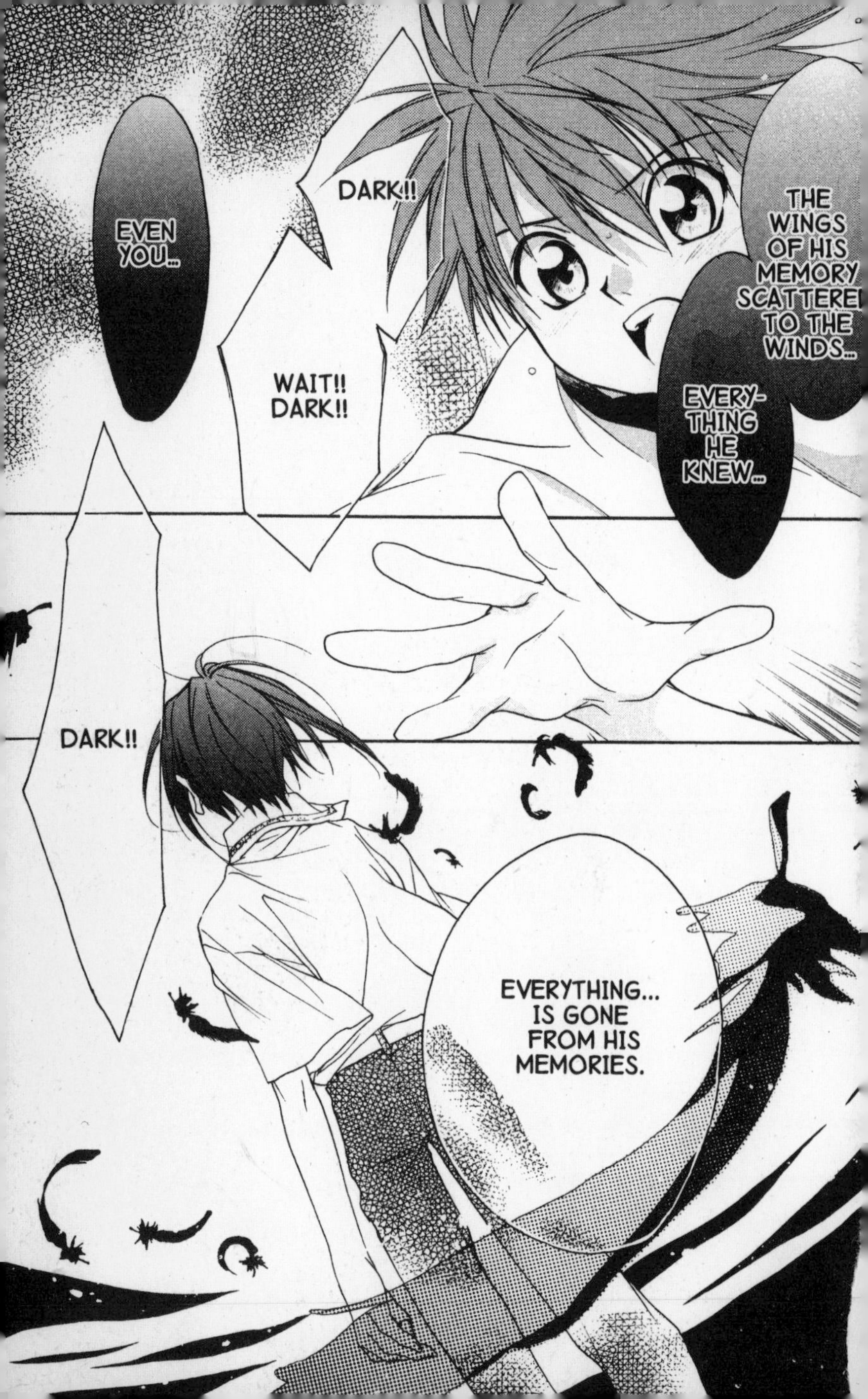
THE WINGS OF HIS MEMORY SCATTERE TO THE WINDS...
EVERY-THING HE KNEW...
DARK!!
WAIT!! DARK!!
EVEN YOU...
DARK!!
EVERYTHING... IS GONE FROM HIS MEMORIES.

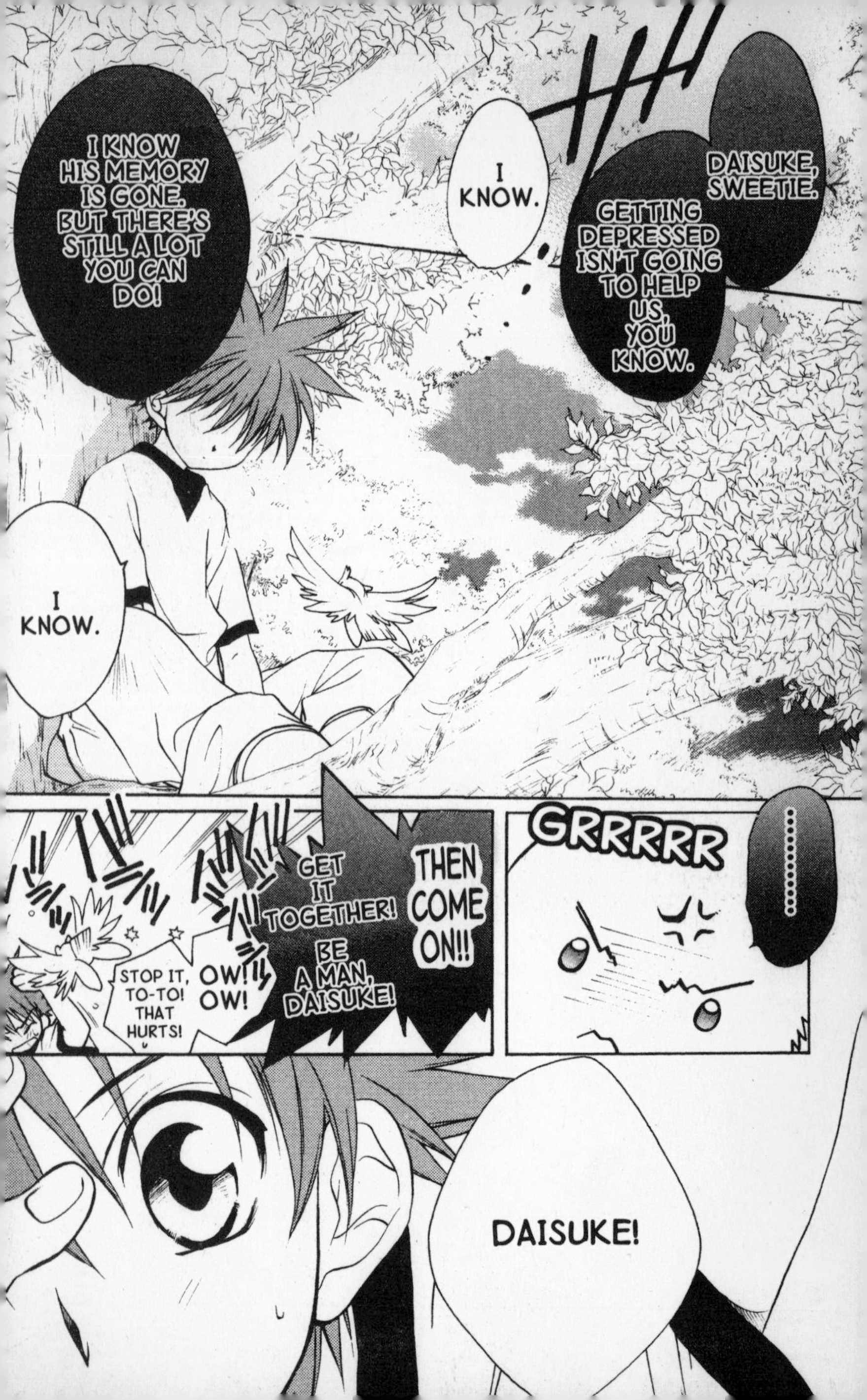
DAISUKE, SWEETIE.
GETTING DEPRESSED ISN'T GOING TO HELP US, YOU KNOW.
I KNOW.
I KNOW HIS MEMORY IS GONE. BUT THERE'S STILL A LOT YOU CAN DO!
I KNOW.
....
GRRRRR
THEN COME ON!!
GET IT TOGETHER!
BE A MAN, DAISUKE!
OW! OW!
STOP IT, TO-TO! THAT HURTS!
DAISUKE!

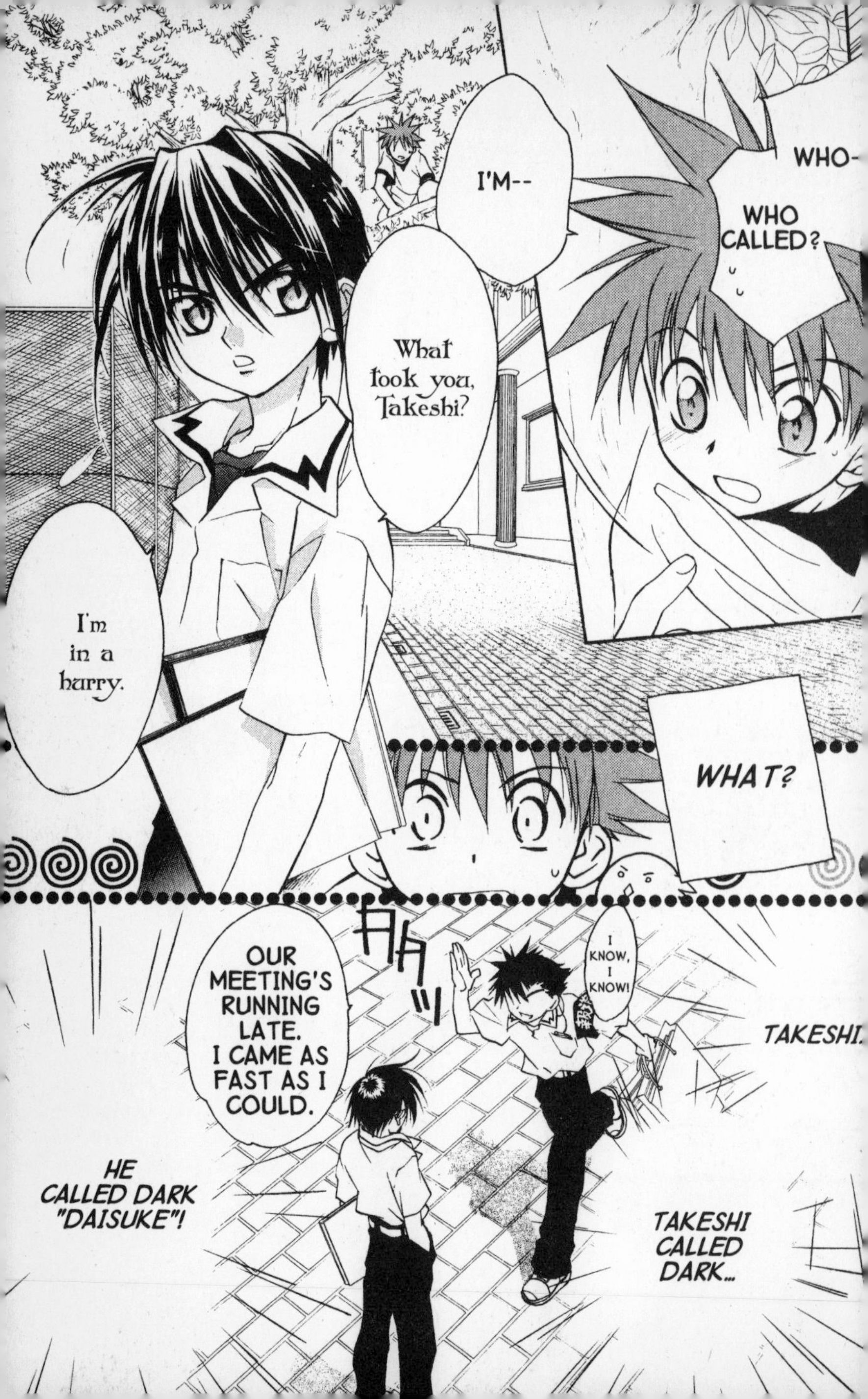
WHO-
WHO CALLED?
I'M--
What took you, Takeshi?
I'm in a hurry.
WHAT?
TAKESHI.
I KNOW, I KNOW!
OUR MEETING'S RUNNING LATE. I CAME AS FAST AS I COULD.
TAKESHI CALLED DARK...
HE CALLED DARK "DAISUKE"!

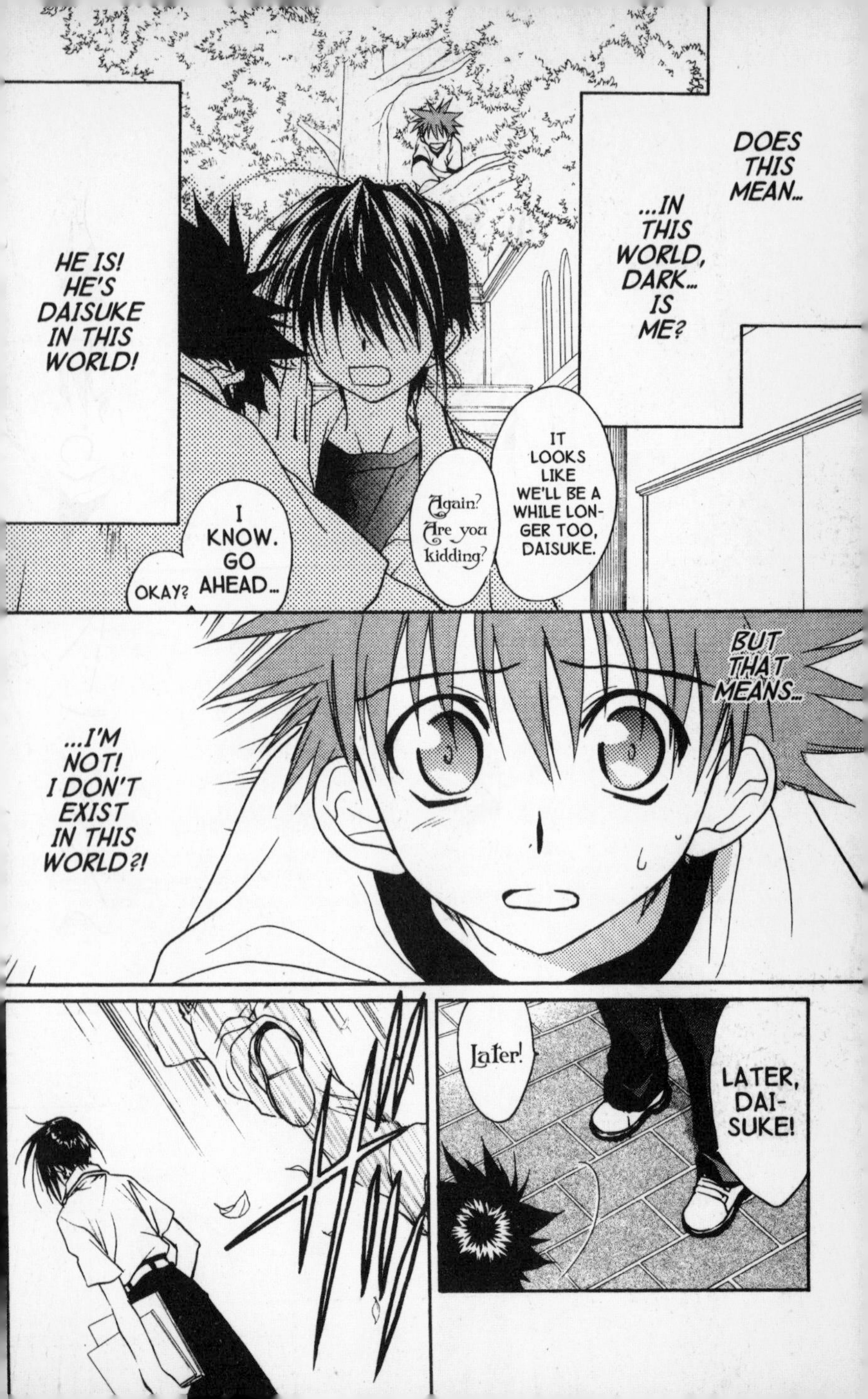
DOES THIS MEAN...
...IN THIS WORLD, DARK... IS ME?
HE IS! HE'S DAISUKE IN THIS WORLD!
IT LOOKS LIKE WE'LL BE A WHILE LONGER TOO, DAISUKE.
Again? Are you kidding?
I KNOW. GO AHEAD...
OKAY?
BUT THAT MEANS...
...I'M NOT! I DON'T EXIST IN THIS WORLD?!
LATER, DAISUKE!
Later!

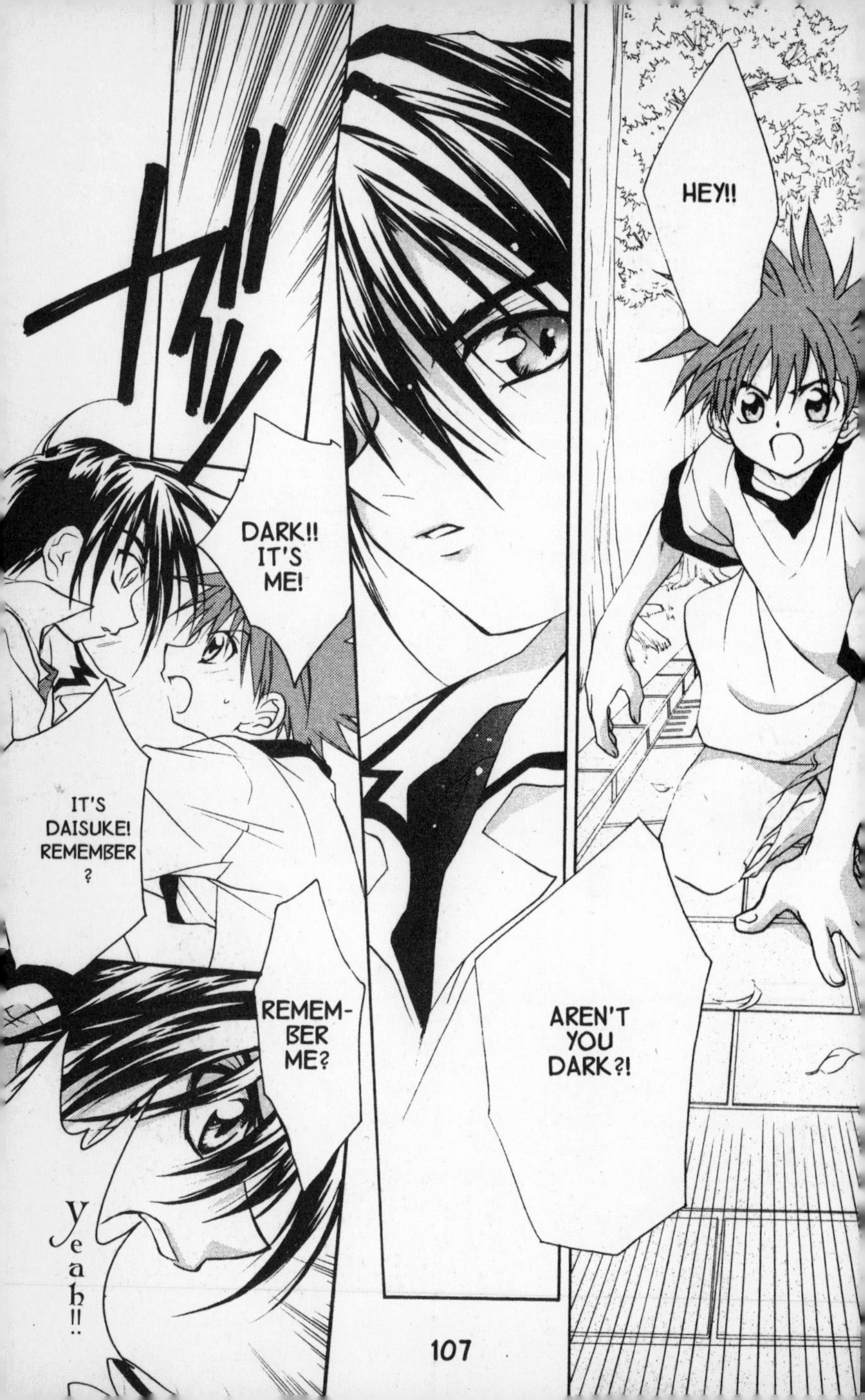
HEY!!
AREN'T YOU DARK?!
DARK!! IT'S ME!
IT'S DAISUKE! REMEMBER?
REMEMBER ME?
yeah!!

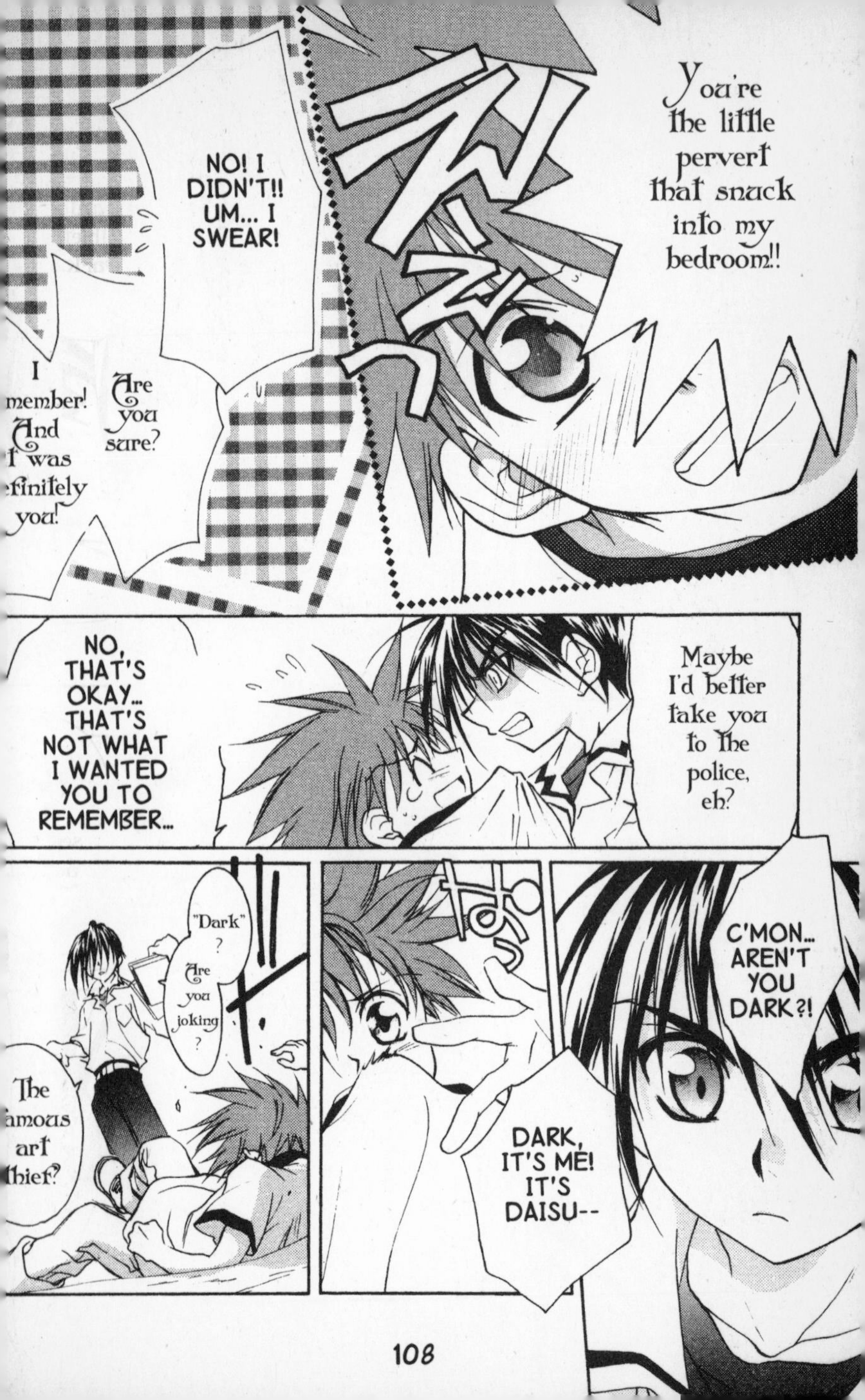
You're the little pervert that snuck into my bedroom!!
NO! I DIDN'T!! UM... I SWEAR!
Are you sure?
I member! And t was efinitely you!
Maybe I'd better take you to the police, eh?
NO, THAT'S OKAY... THAT'S NOT WHAT I WANTED YOU TO REMEMBER...
C'MON... AREN'T YOU DARK?!
DARK, IT'S ME! IT'S DAISU--
"Dark"? Are you joking?
The amous art hief?

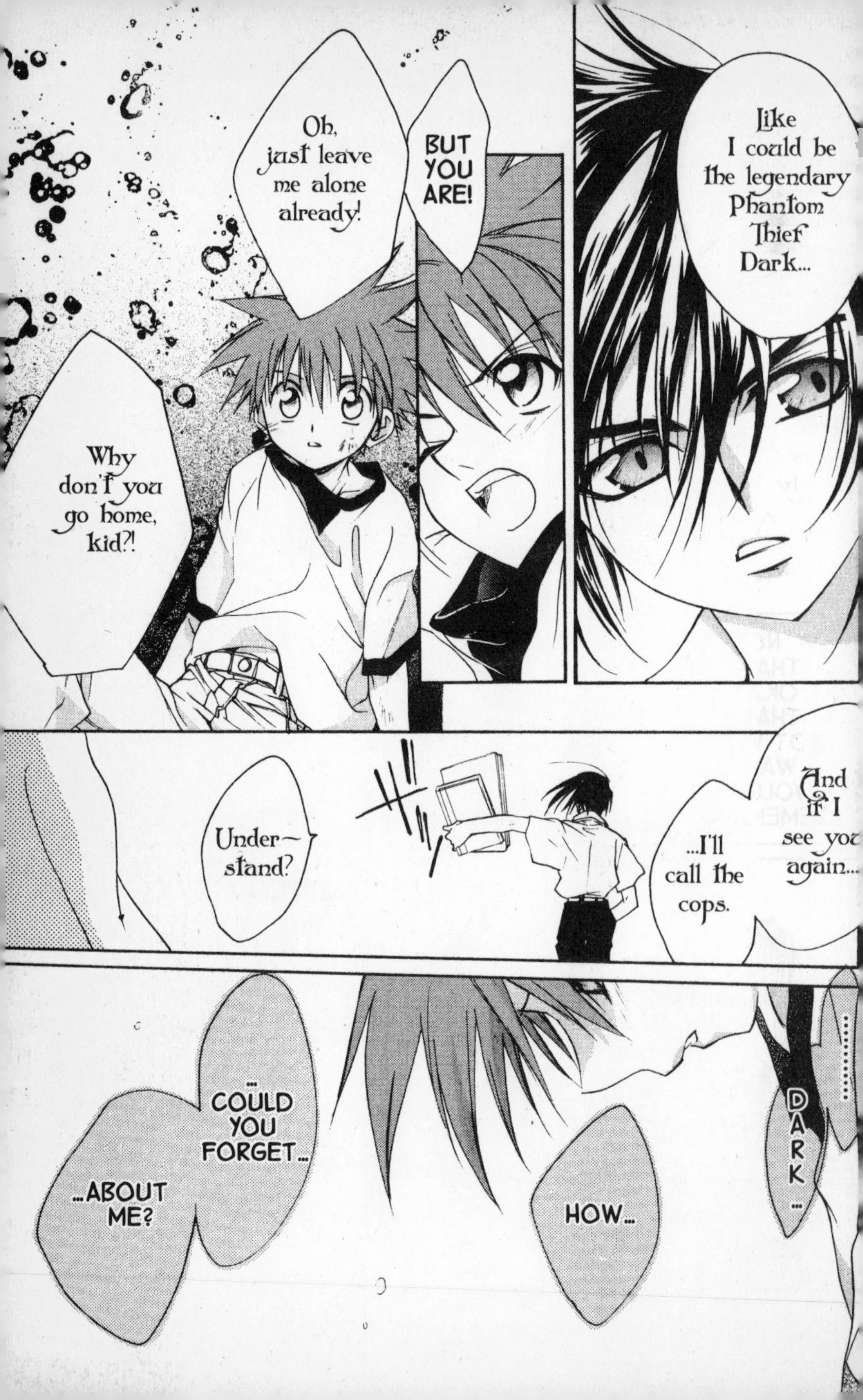
Like I could be the legendary Phantom Thief Dark...
BUT YOU ARE!
Oh, just leave me alone already!
Why don't you go home, kid?!
And if I see you again...
...I'll call the cops.
Under-stand?
......
DARK...
HOW...
...COULD YOU FORGET...
...ABOUT ME?

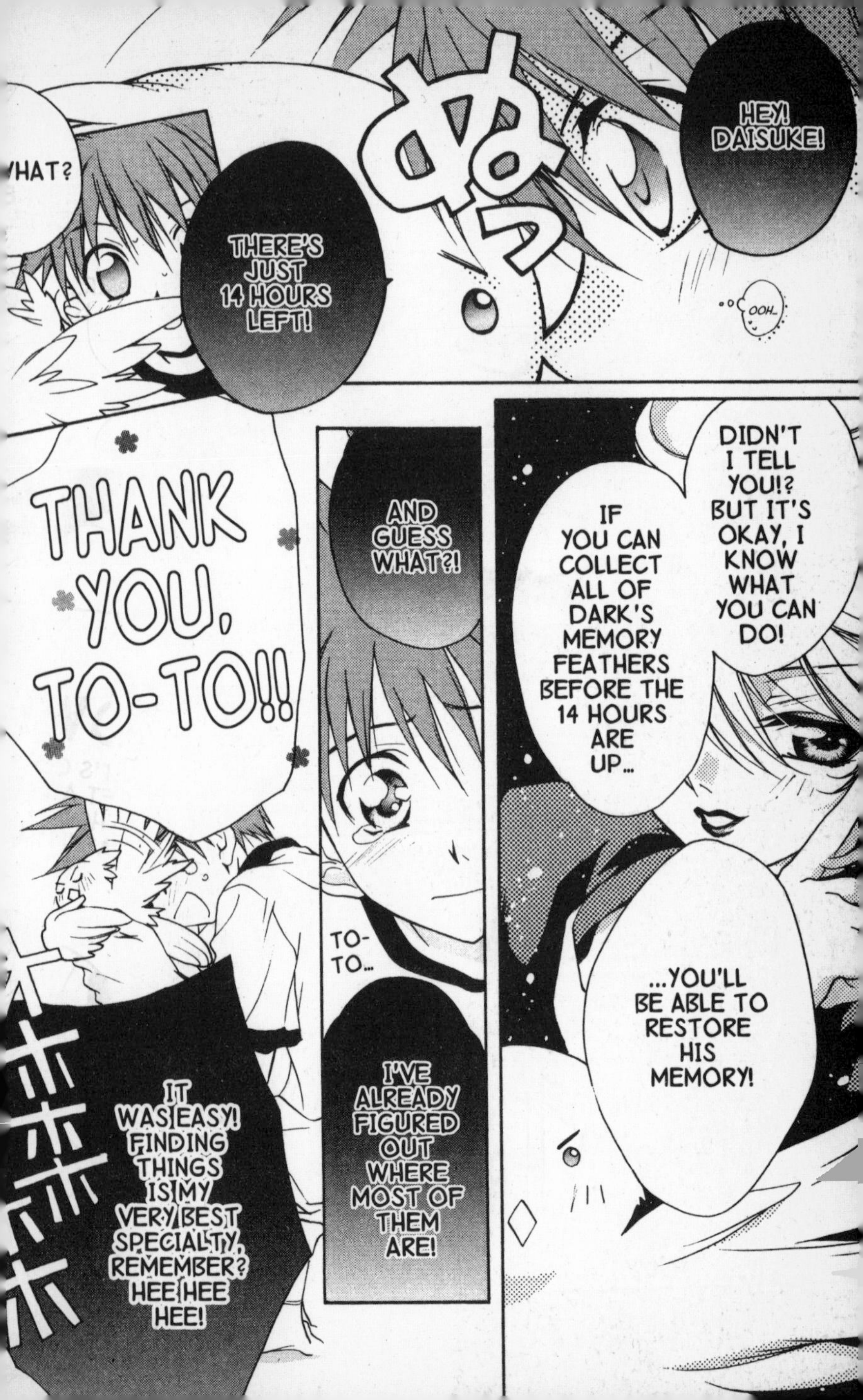
HEY! DAISUKE!
ぬっ
OOH...
THERE'S JUST 14 HOURS LEFT!
HAT?
DIDN'T I TELL YOU!? BUT IT'S OKAY, I KNOW WHAT YOU CAN DO!
IF YOU CAN COLLECT ALL OF DARK'S MEMORY FEATHERS BEFORE THE 14 HOURS ARE UP...
...YOU'LL BE ABLE TO RESTORE HIS MEMORY!
AND GUESS WHAT?!
TO-TO...
I'VE ALREADY FIGURED OUT WHERE MOST OF THEM ARE!
THANK YOU, TO-TO!!
IT WAS EASY! FINDING THINGS IS MY VERY BEST SPECIALTY, REMEMBER? HEE HEE HEE!
ホホホホ

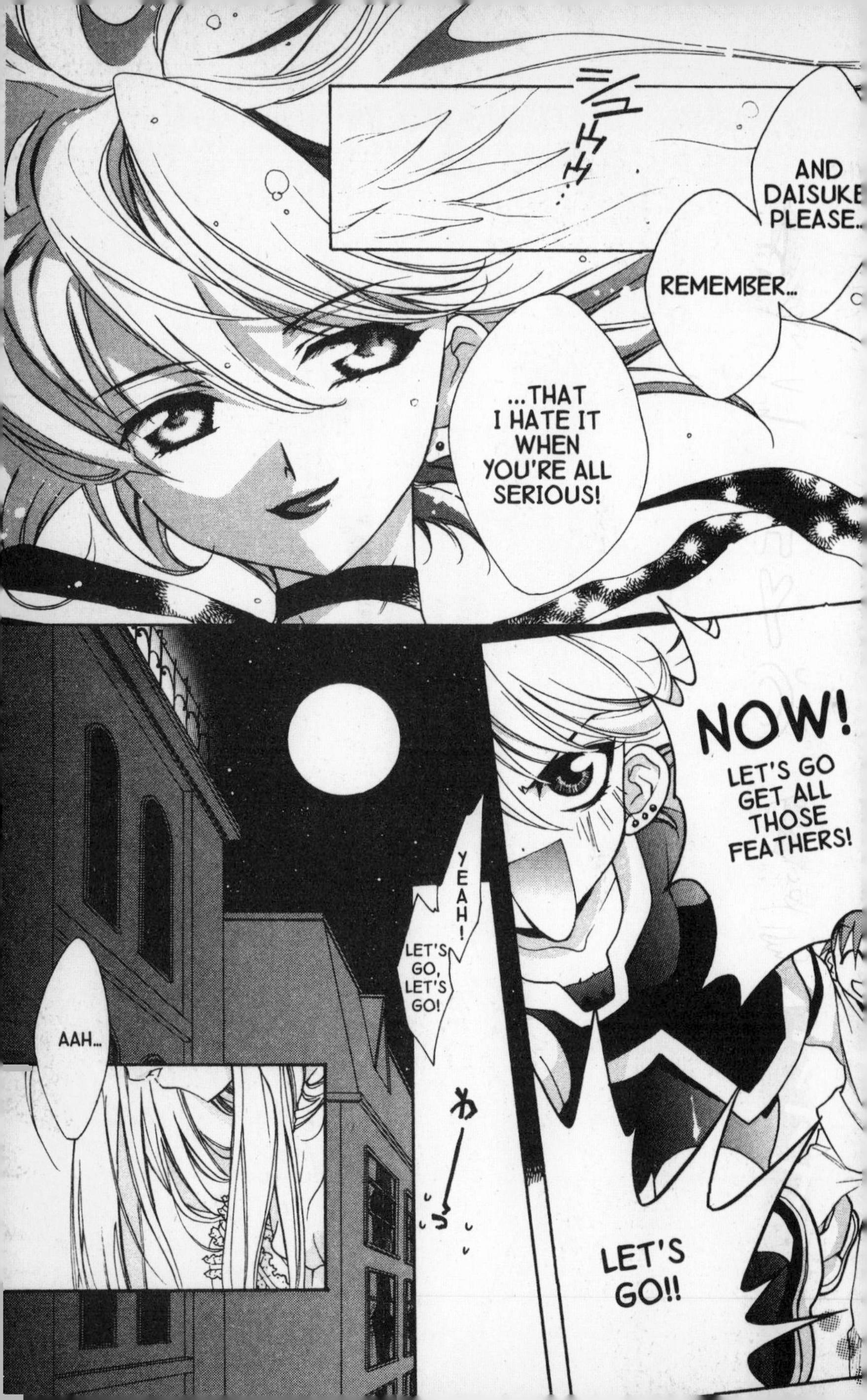
AND DAISUKE PLEASE...
REMEMBER...
...THAT I HATE IT WHEN YOU'RE ALL SERIOUS!
NOW!
LET'S GO GET ALL THOSE FEATHERS!
YEAH!
LET'S GO, LET'S GO!
LET'S GO!!
AAH...

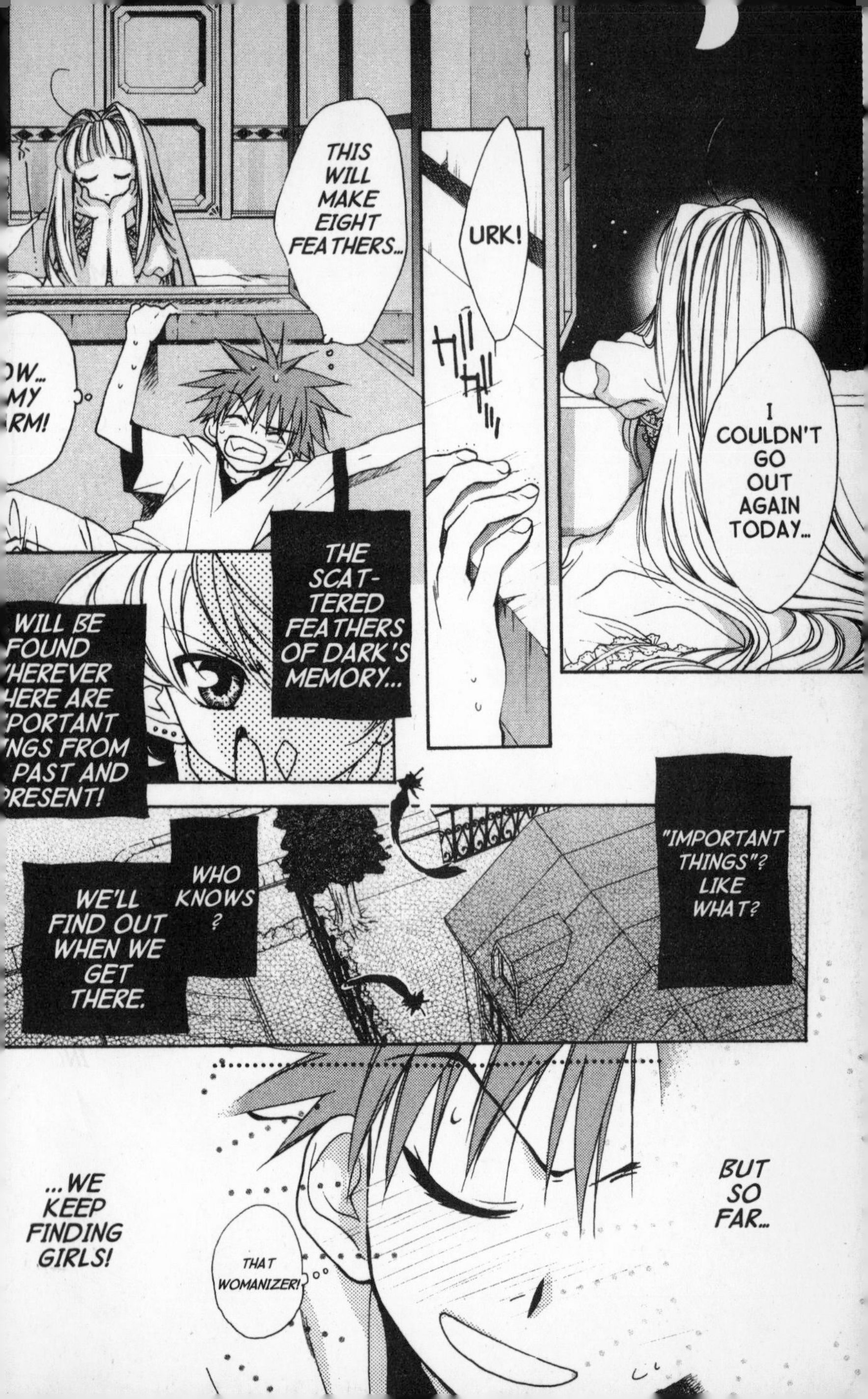
I COULDN'T GO OUT AGAIN TODAY...
URK!
THIS WILL MAKE EIGHT FEATHERS...
OW... MY RM!
THE SCATTERED FEATHERS OF DARK'S MEMORY...
WILL BE FOUND HEREVER HERE ARE PORTANT NGS FROM PAST AND RESENT!
"IMPORTANT THINGS"? LIKE WHAT?
WHO KNOWS?
WE'LL FIND OUT WHEN WE GET THERE.
BUT SO FAR...
THAT WOMANIZER!
...WE KEEP FINDING GIRLS!

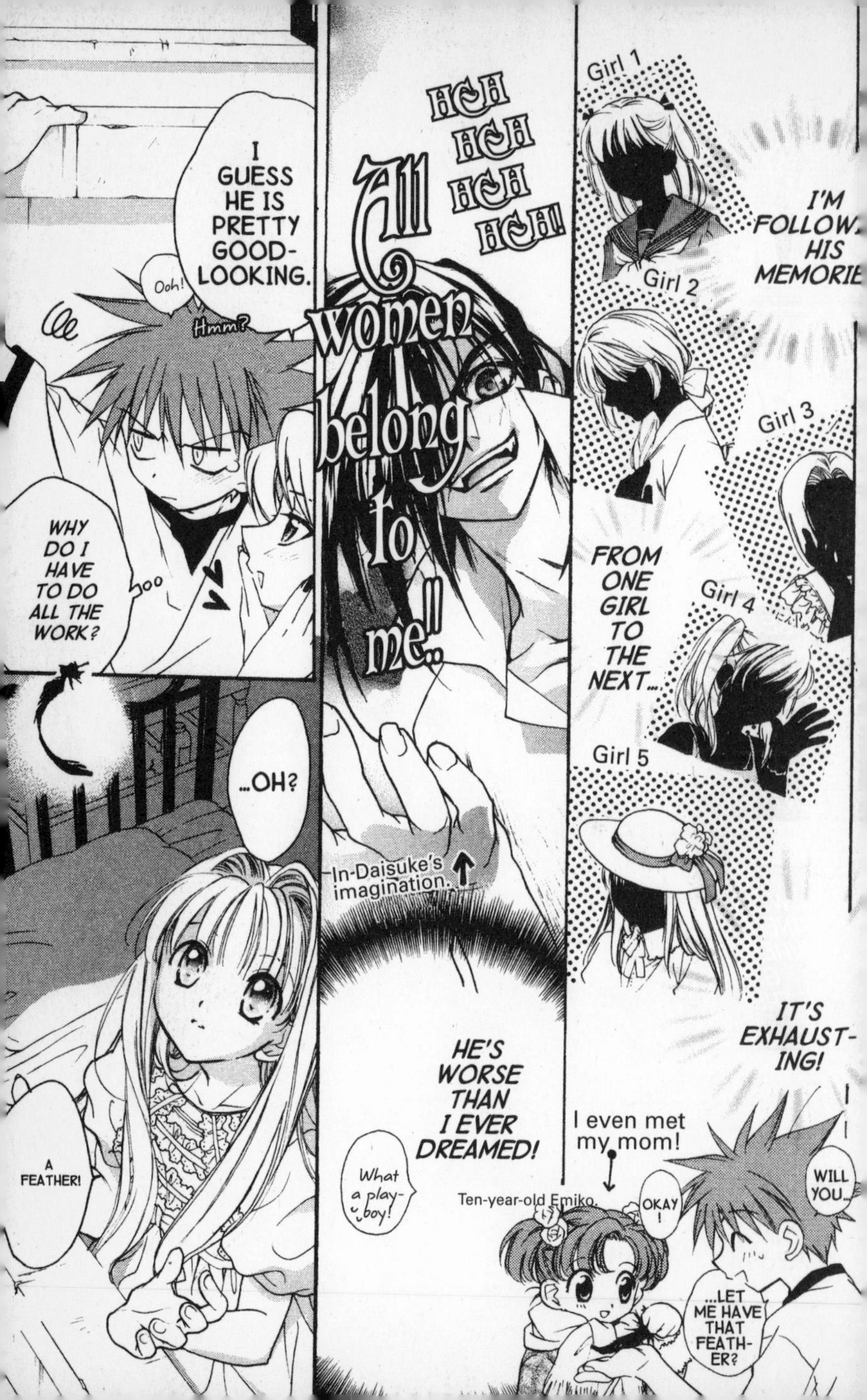
Girl 1
I'M FOLLOW
HIS MEMORIE
Girl 2
Girl 3
FROM ONE GIRL TO THE NEXT...
Girl 4
Girl 5
IT'S EXHAUSTING!
WILL YOU...
I even met my mom!
OKAY!
...LET ME HAVE THAT FEATHER?
Ten-year-old Emiko.
HCH HCH HCH HCH!
"All women belong to me"...
In-Daisuke's imagination.
HE'S WORSE THAN I EVER DREAMED!
What a play-boy!
I GUESS HE IS PRETTY GOOD-LOOKING.
Ooh!
Hmm?
WHY DO I HAVE TO DO ALL THE WORK?
...OH?
A FEATHER!

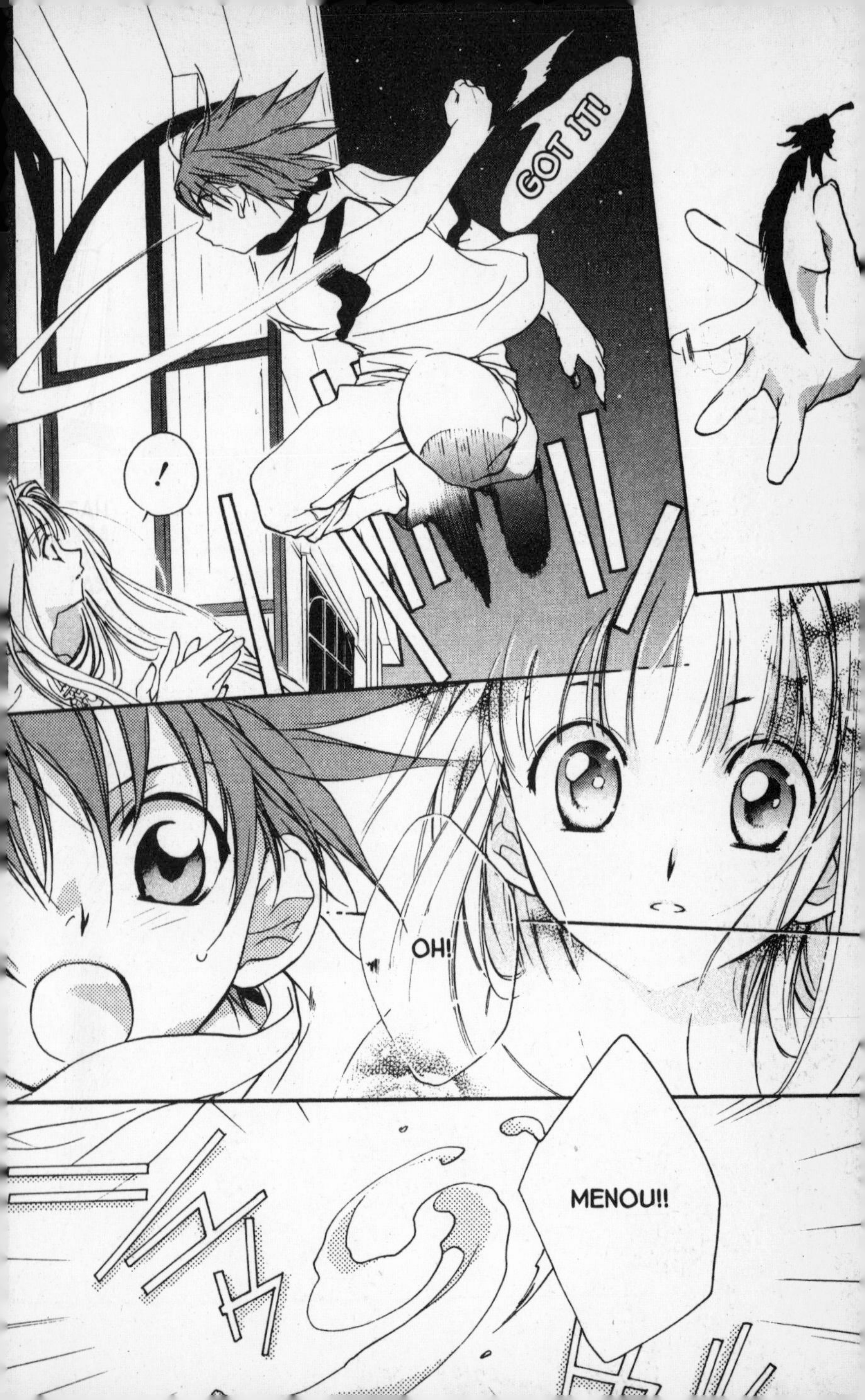
GOT IT!
!
OH!
MENOU!!

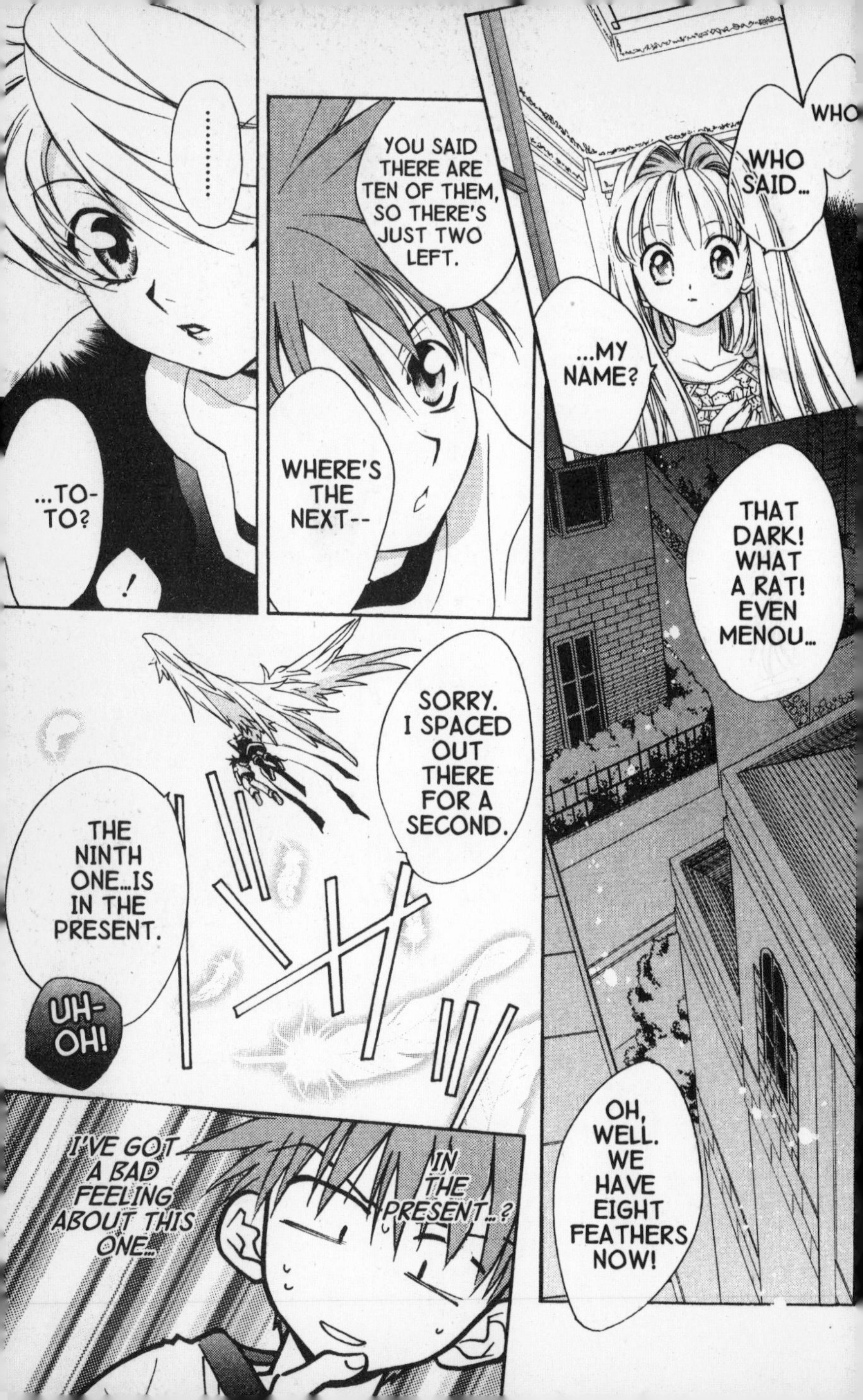
WHO
WHO SAID...
...MY NAME?
THAT DARK! WHAT A RAT! EVEN MENOU...
OH, WELL. WE HAVE EIGHT FEATHERS NOW!
YOU SAID THERE ARE TEN OF THEM, SO THERE'S JUST TWO LEFT.
WHERE'S THE NEXT--
....
...TO-TO?
!
SORRY. I SPACED OUT THERE FOR A SECOND.
THE NINTH ONE...IS IN THE PRESENT.
UH-OH!
IN THE PRESENT...?
I'VE GOT A BAD FEELING ABOUT THIS ONE...

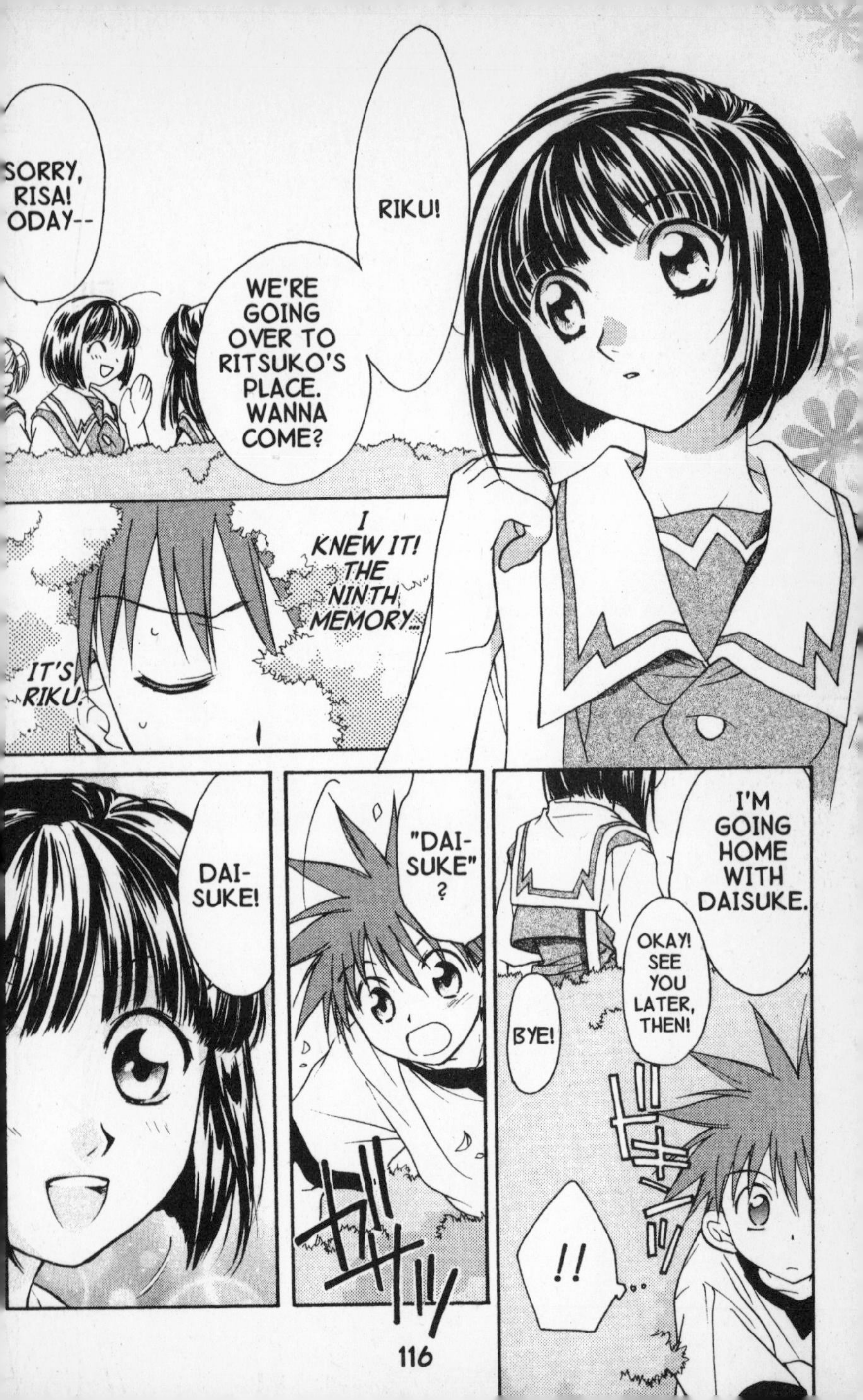
RIKU!
WE'RE GOING OVER TO RITSUKO'S PLACE. WANNA COME?
SORRY, RISA! ODAY--
I KNEW IT! THE NINTH MEMORY...
IT'S RIKU.
I'M GOING HOME WITH DAISUKE.
OKAY! SEE YOU LATER, THEN!
BYE!
!!
"DAI-SUKE"?
DAI-SUKE!

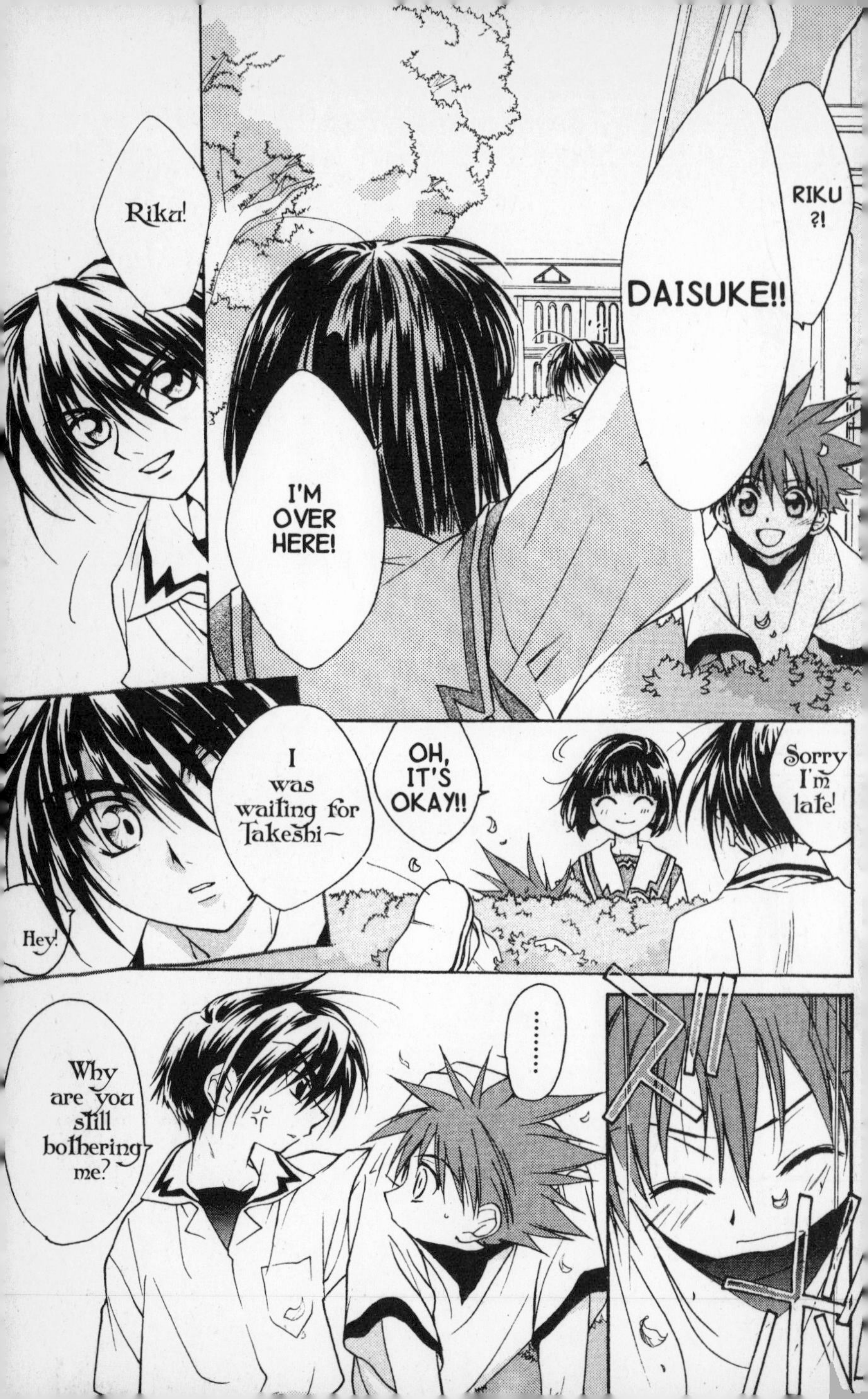
RIKU ?!
DAISUKE!!
I'M OVER HERE!
Riku!
Sorry I'm late!
OH, IT'S OKAY!!
I was waiting for Takeshi~
Hey!
......
Why are you still bothering me?

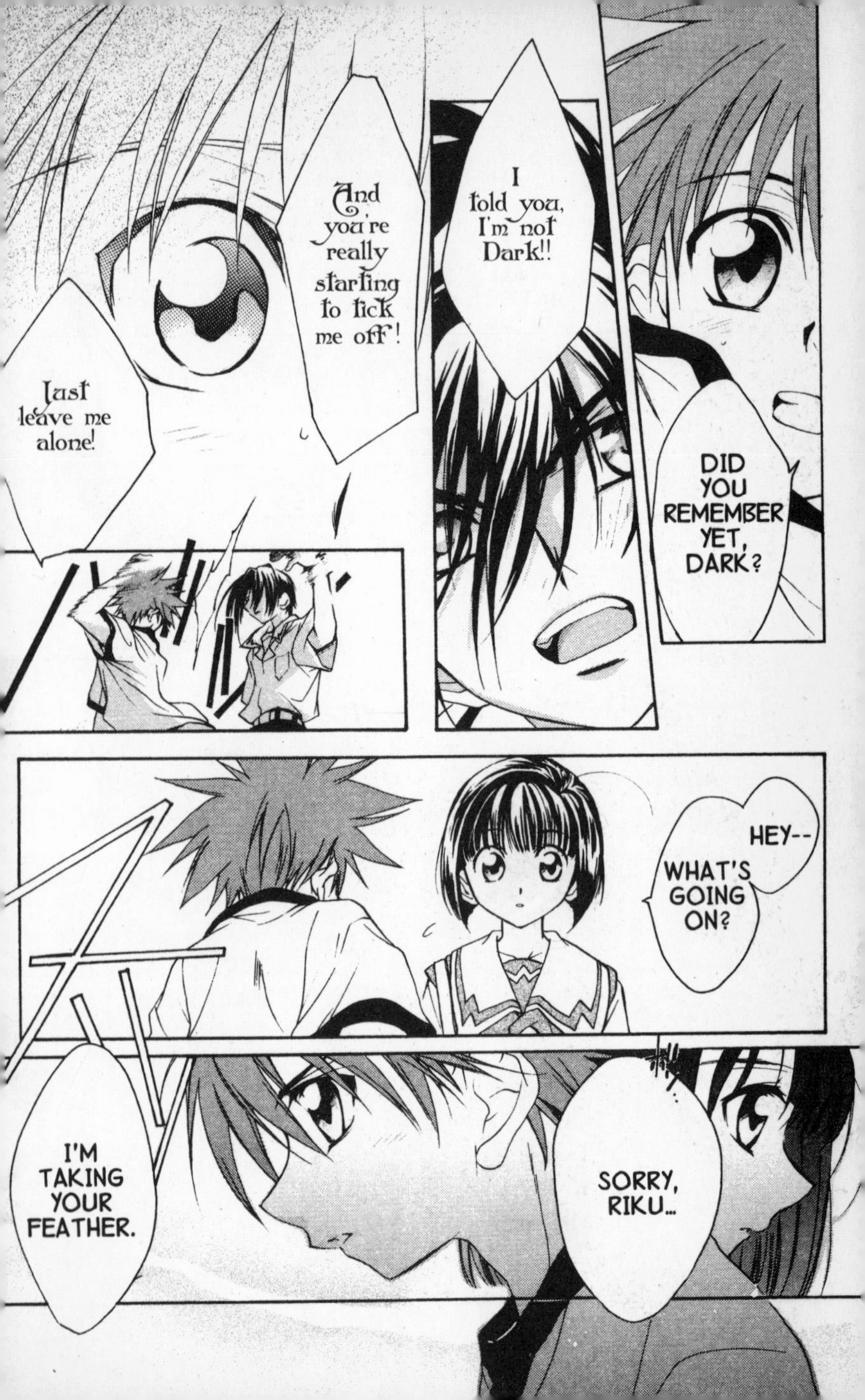
DID YOU REMEMBER YET, DARK?
I told you, I'm not Dark!!
And you're really starting to tick me off!
Just leave me alone!
HEY-- WHAT'S GOING ON?
SORRY, RIKU...
I'M TAKING YOUR FEATHER.

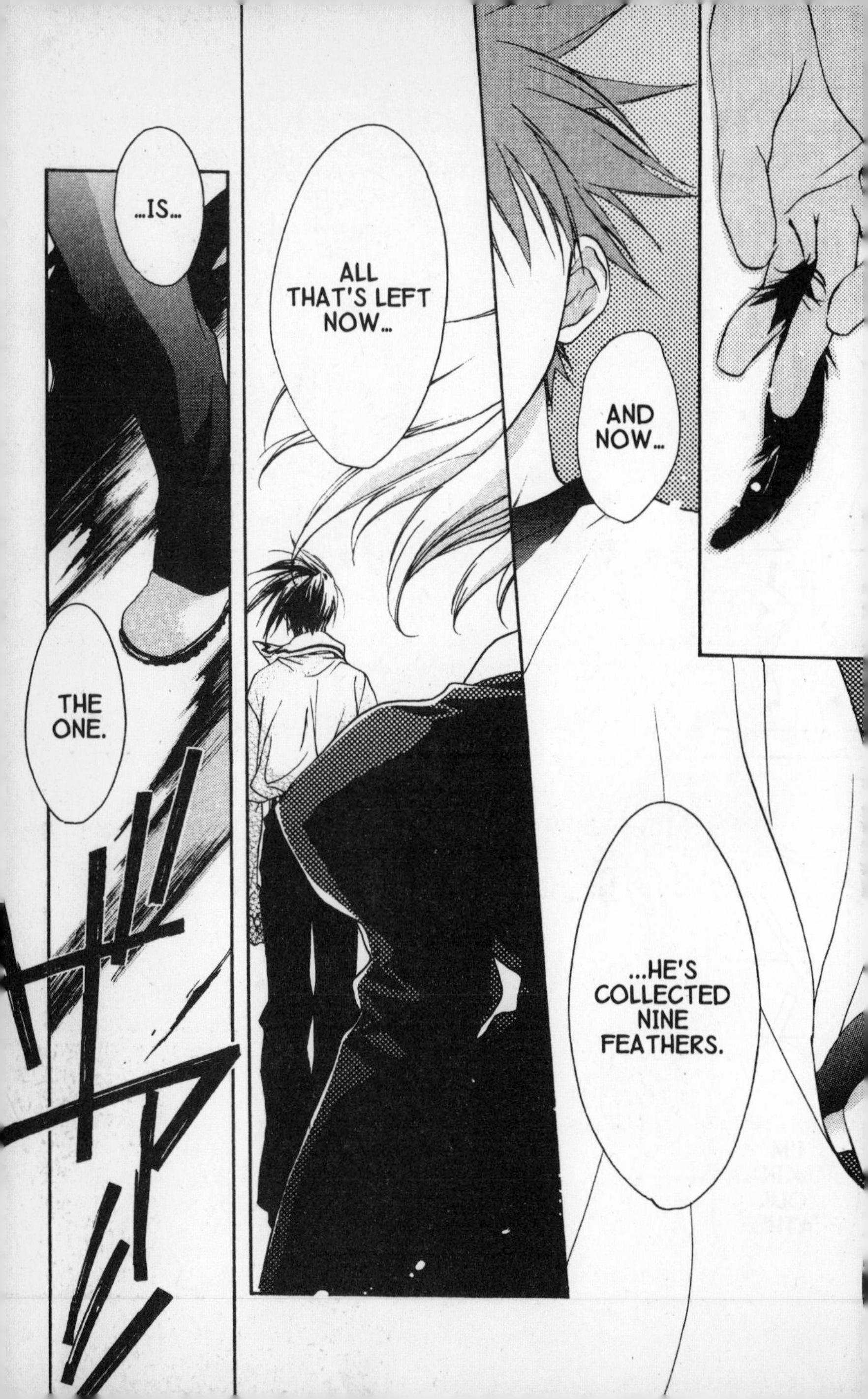
AND NOW...
...HE'S COLLECTED NINE FEATHERS.
ALL THAT'S LEFT NOW...
...IS...
THE ONE.

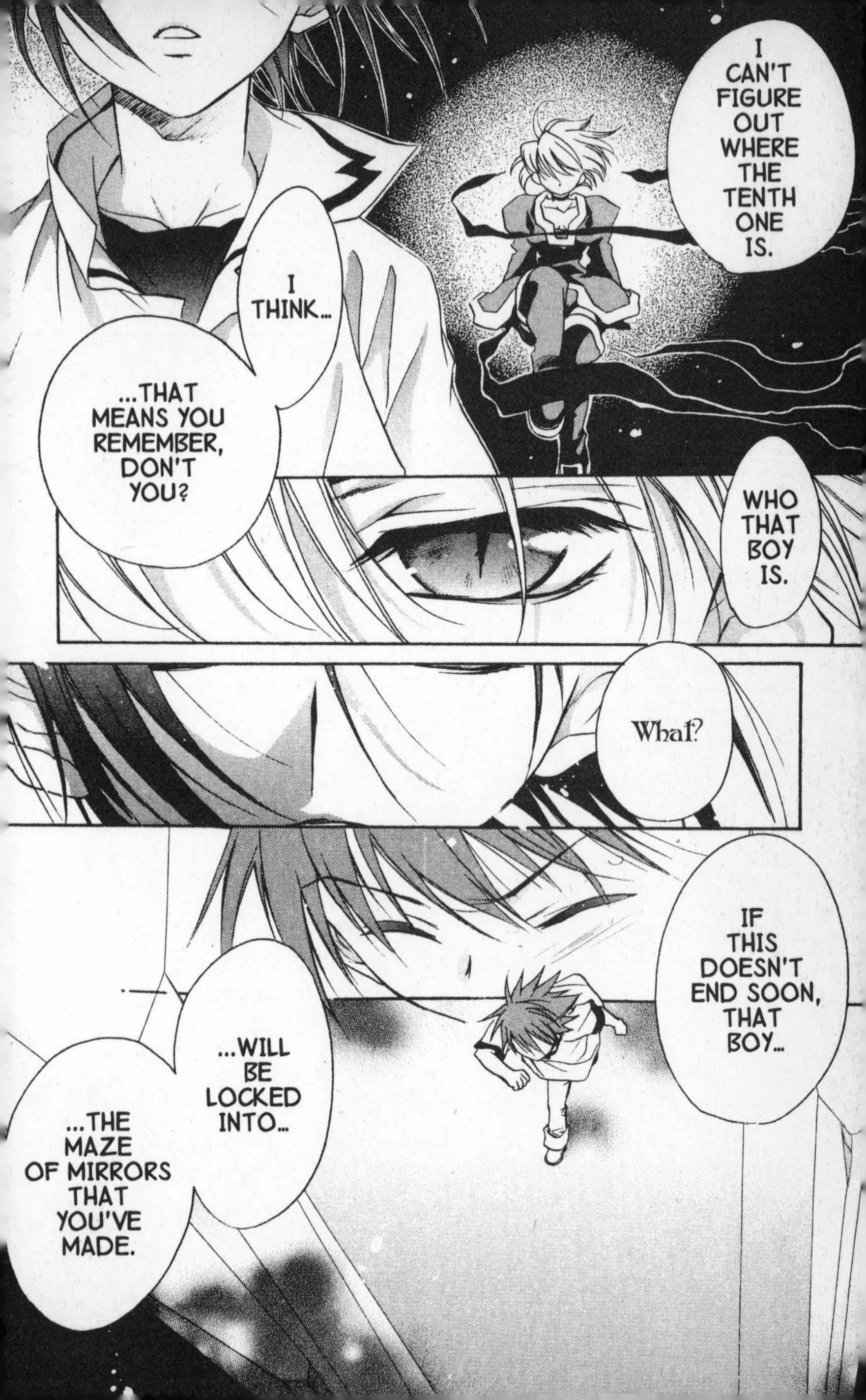
I CAN'T FIGURE OUT WHERE THE TENTH ONE IS.
WHO THAT BOY IS.
I THINK...
...THAT MEANS YOU REMEMBER, DON'T YOU?
What?
IF THIS DOESN'T END SOON, THAT BOY...
...WILL BE LOCKED INTO...
...THE MAZE OF MIRRORS THAT YOU'VE MADE.

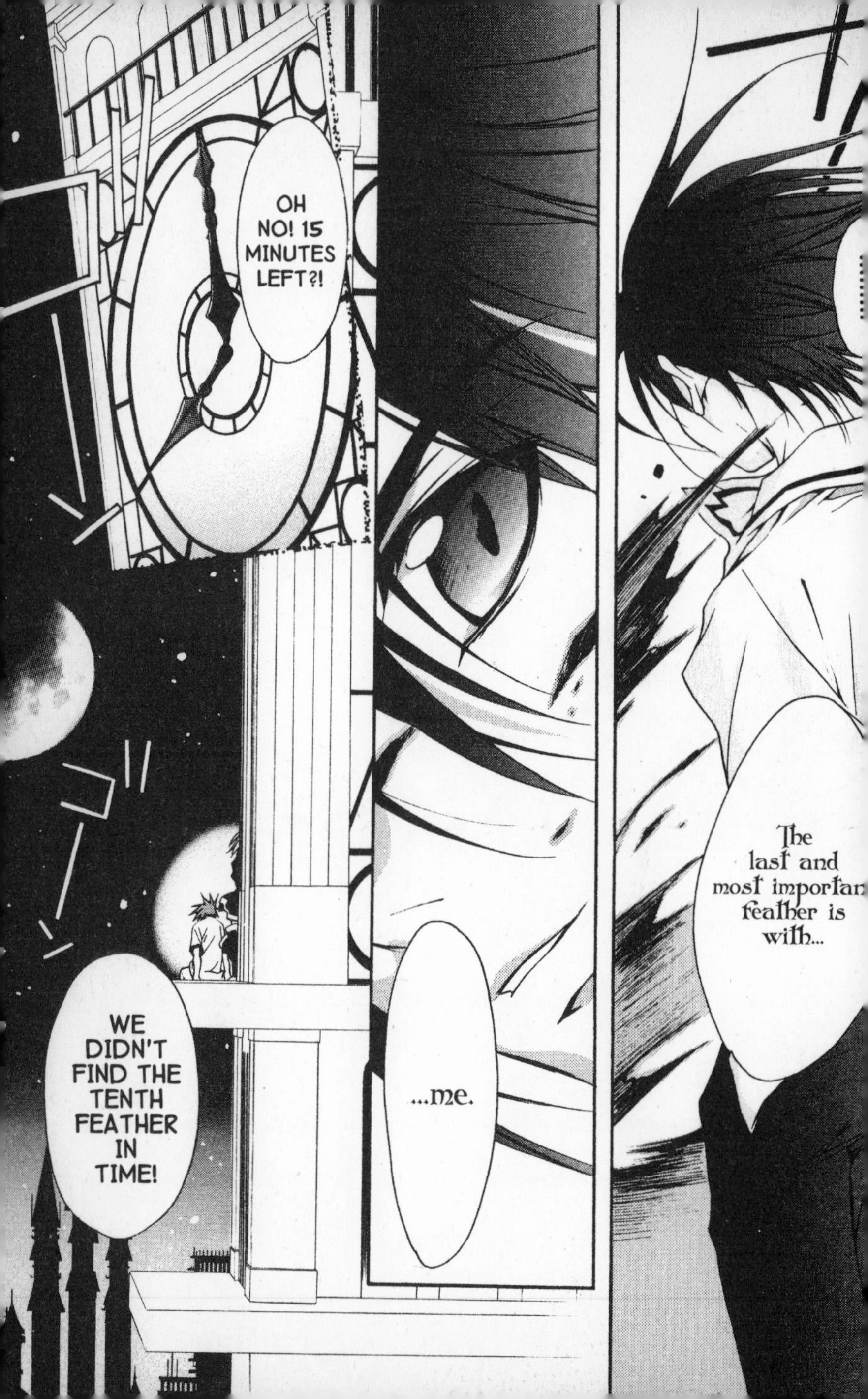
The last and most importan feather is with...
...me.
OH NO! 15 MINUTES LEFT?!
WE DIDN'T FIND THE TENTH FEATHER IN TIME!

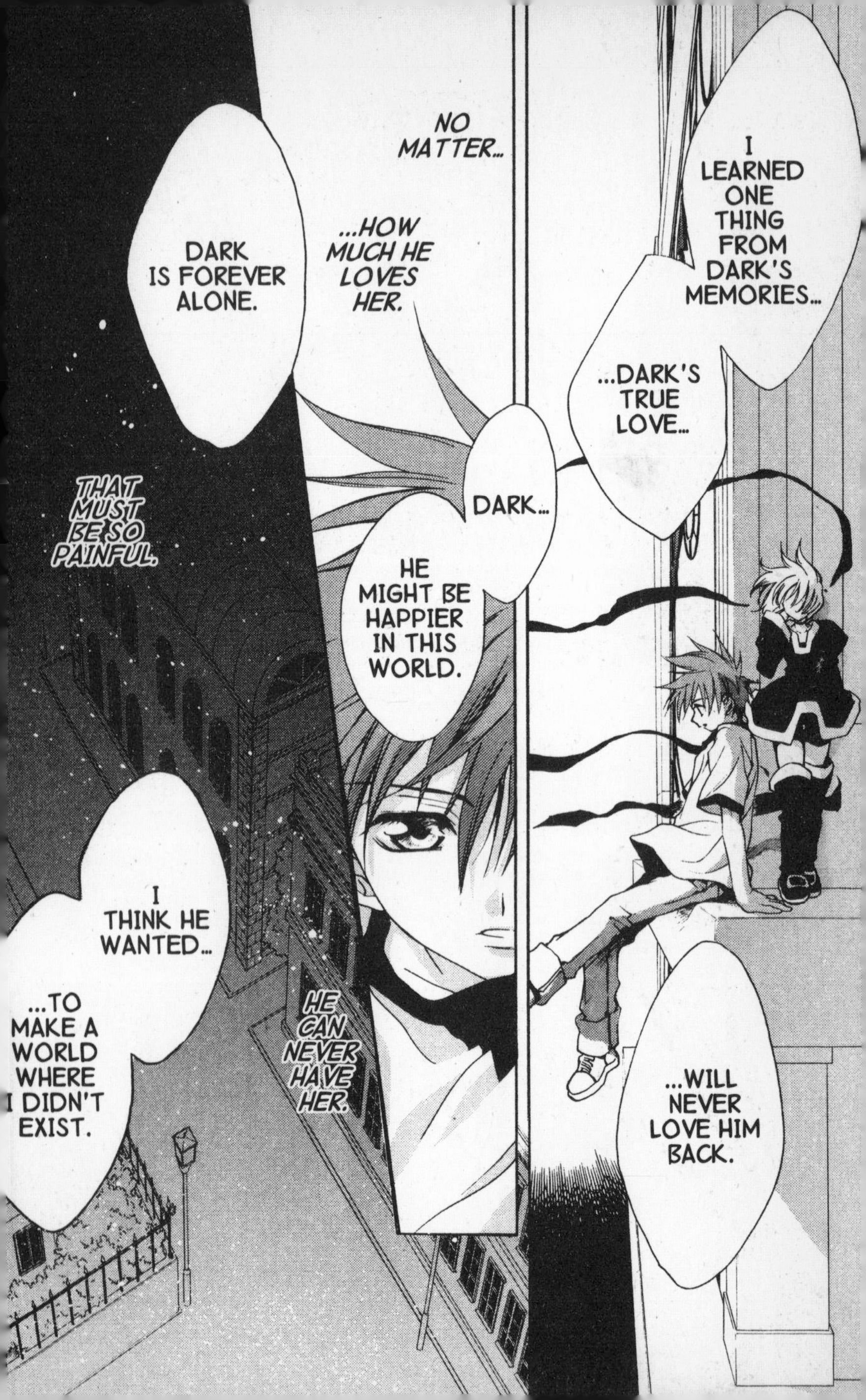
I LEARNED ONE THING FROM DARK'S MEMORIES...
...DARK'S TRUE LOVE...
...WILL NEVER LOVE HIM BACK.
NO MATTER...
...HOW MUCH HE LOVES HER.
DARK...
HE MIGHT BE HAPPIER IN THIS WORLD.
HE CAN NEVER HAVE HER.
DARK IS FOREVER ALONE.
THAT MUST BE SO PAINFUL.
I THINK HE WANTED...
...TO MAKE A WORLD WHERE I DIDN'T EXIST.

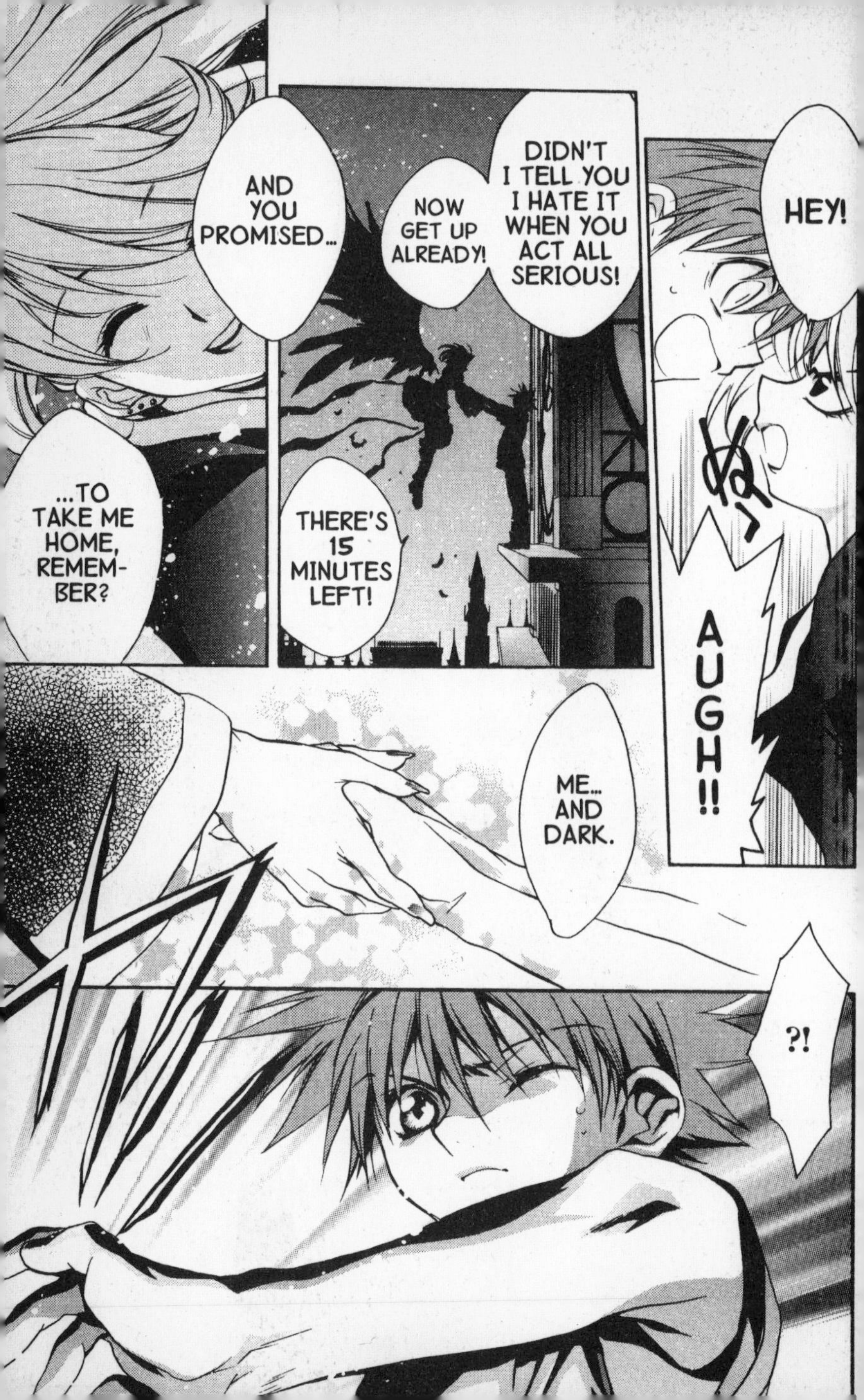
HEY!
AUGH!!
DIDN'T I TELL YOU I HATE IT WHEN YOU ACT ALL SERIOUS!
NOW GET UP ALREADY!
THERE'S 15 MINUTES LEFT!
AND YOU PROMISED...
...TO TAKE ME HOME, REMEM-BER?
ME... AND DARK.
?!

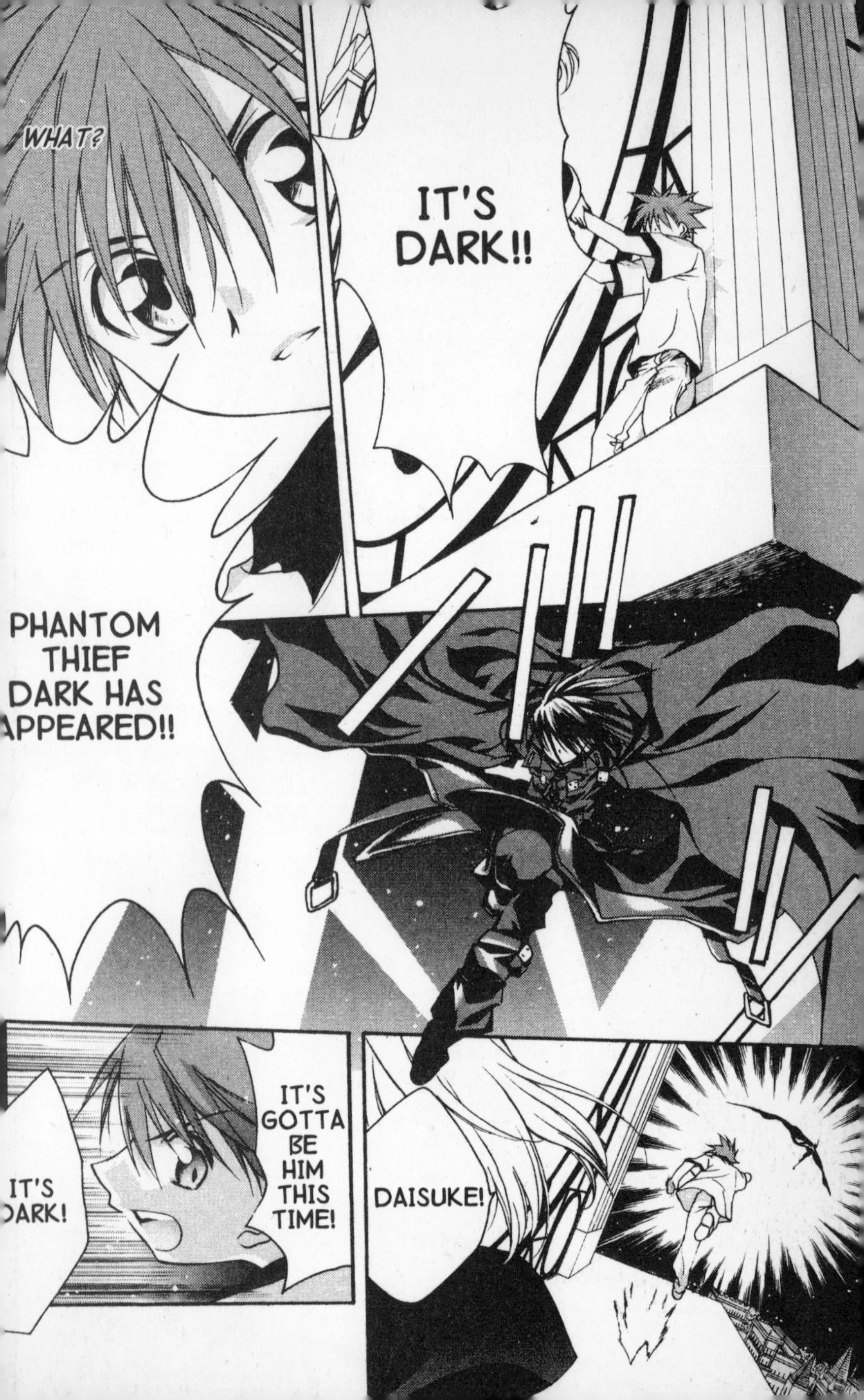
IT'S DARK!!
WHAT?
PHANTOM THIEF DARK HAS APPEARED!!
DAISUKE!
IT'S GOTTA BE HIM THIS TIME!
IT'S DARK!

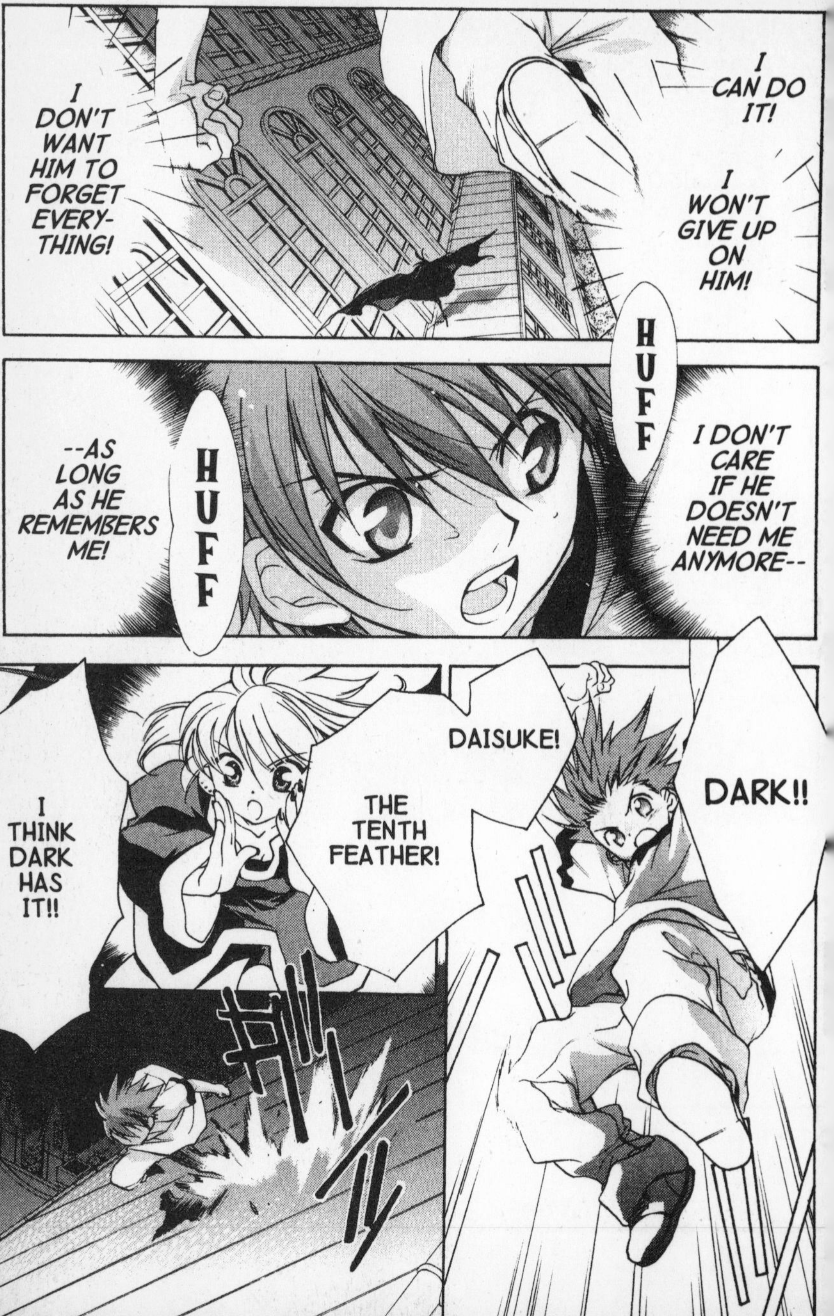
I CAN DO IT!
I WON'T GIVE UP ON HIM!
I DON'T WANT HIM TO FORGET EVERY-THING!
HUFF
I DON'T CARE IF HE DOESN'T NEED ME ANYMORE--
HUFF
--AS LONG AS HE REMEMBERS ME!
DARK!!
DAISUKE!
THE TENTH FEATHER!
I THINK DARK HAS IT!!

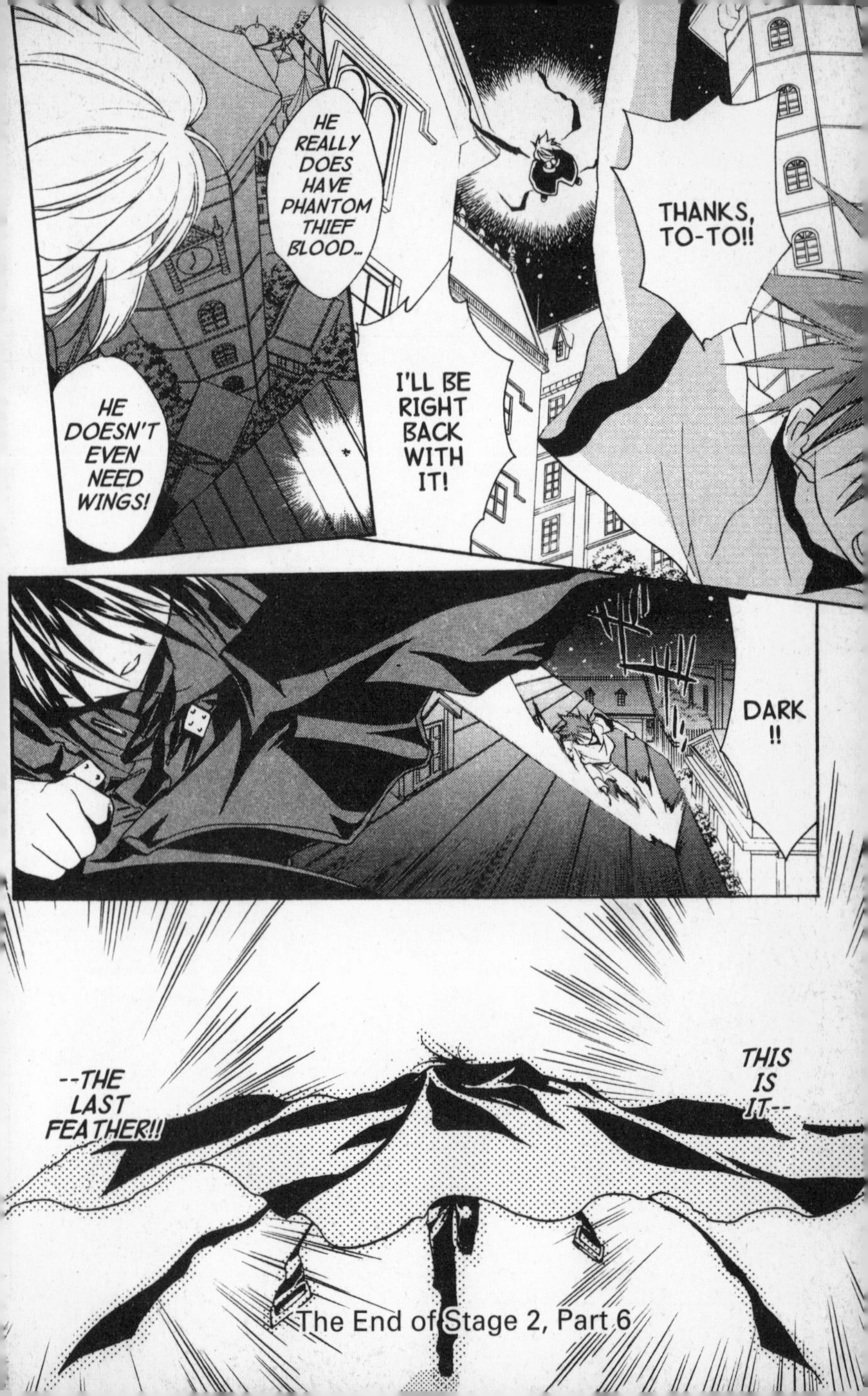
THANKS, TO-TO!!
I'LL BE RIGHT BACK WITH IT!
HE REALLY DOES HAVE PHANTOM THIEF BLOOD...
HE DOESN'T EVEN NEED WINGS!
DARK!!
THIS IS IT--
--THE LAST FEATHER!!
The End of Stage 2, Part 6

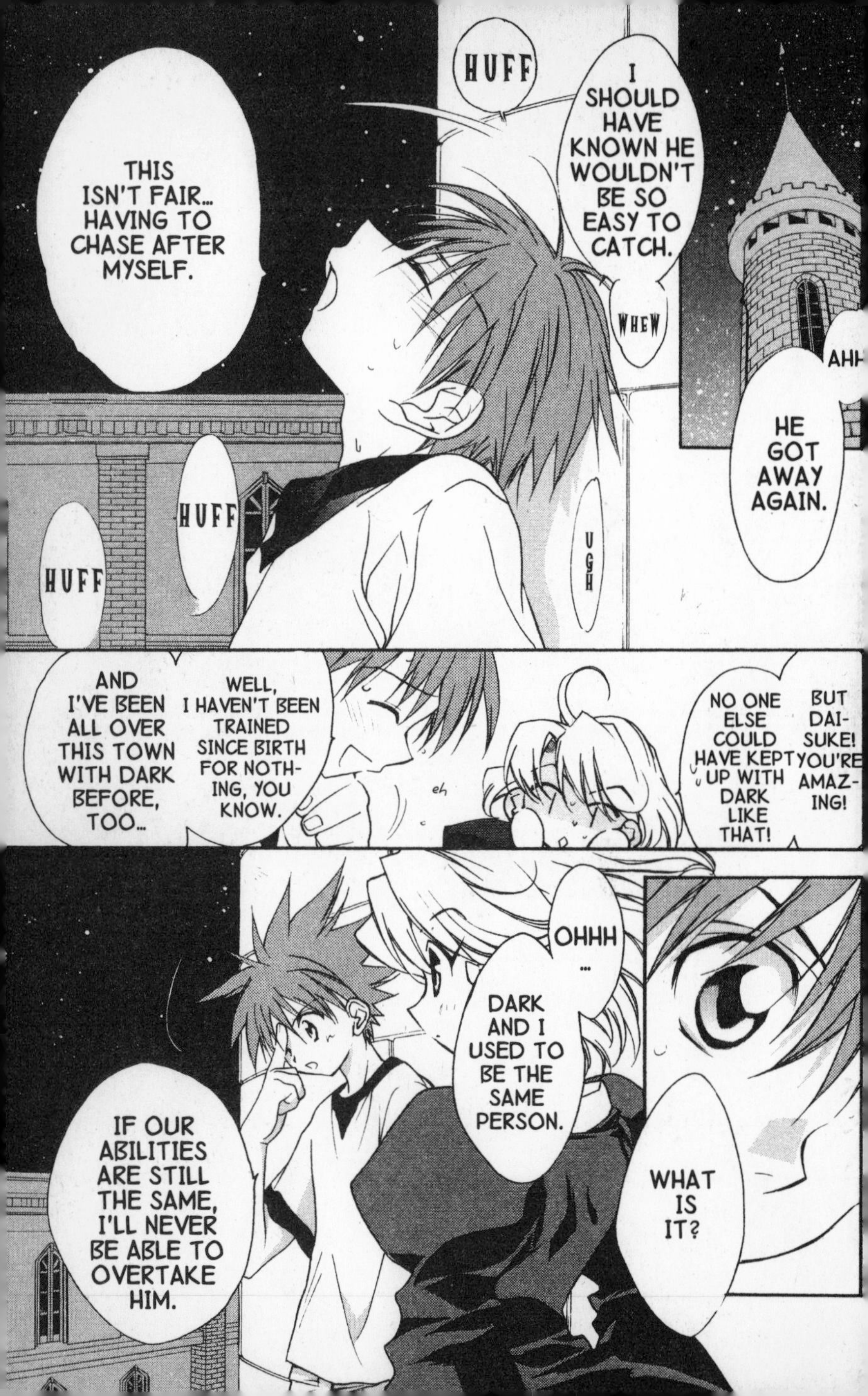
AHH
HE GOT AWAY AGAIN.
HUFF
I SHOULD HAVE KNOWN HE WOULDN'T BE SO EASY TO CATCH.
WHEW
UGH
HUFF
HUFF
THIS ISN'T FAIR... HAVING TO CHASE AFTER MYSELF.
BUT DAI-SUKE! YOU'RE AMAZ-ING!
NO ONE ELSE COULD HAVE KEPT UP WITH DARK LIKE THAT!
eh
WELL, I HAVEN'T BEEN TRAINED SINCE BIRTH FOR NOTH-ING, YOU KNOW.
AND I'VE BEEN ALL OVER THIS TOWN WITH DARK BEFORE, TOO...
WHAT IS IT?
OHHH...
DARK AND I USED TO BE THE SAME PERSON.
IF OUR ABILITIES ARE STILL THE SAME, I'LL NEVER BE ABLE TO OVERTAKE HIM.

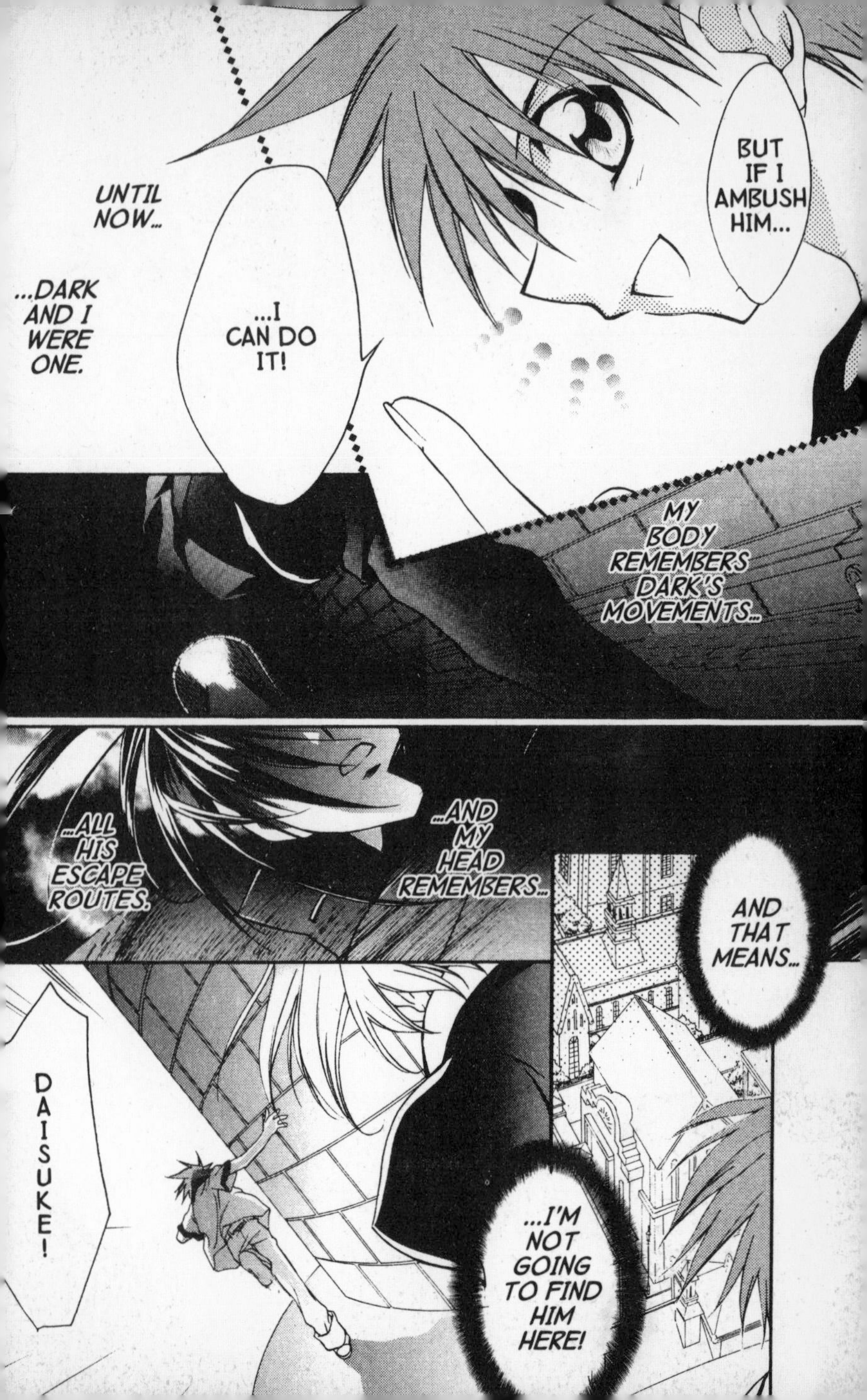
BUT IF I AMBUSH HIM...
...I CAN DO IT!
UNTIL NOW...
...DARK AND I WERE ONE.
MY BODY REMEMBERS DARK'S MOVEMENTS...
...AND MY HEAD REMEMBERS...
...ALL HIS ESCAPE ROUTES.
AND THAT MEANS...
...I'M NOT GOING TO FIND HIM HERE!
DAISUKE!

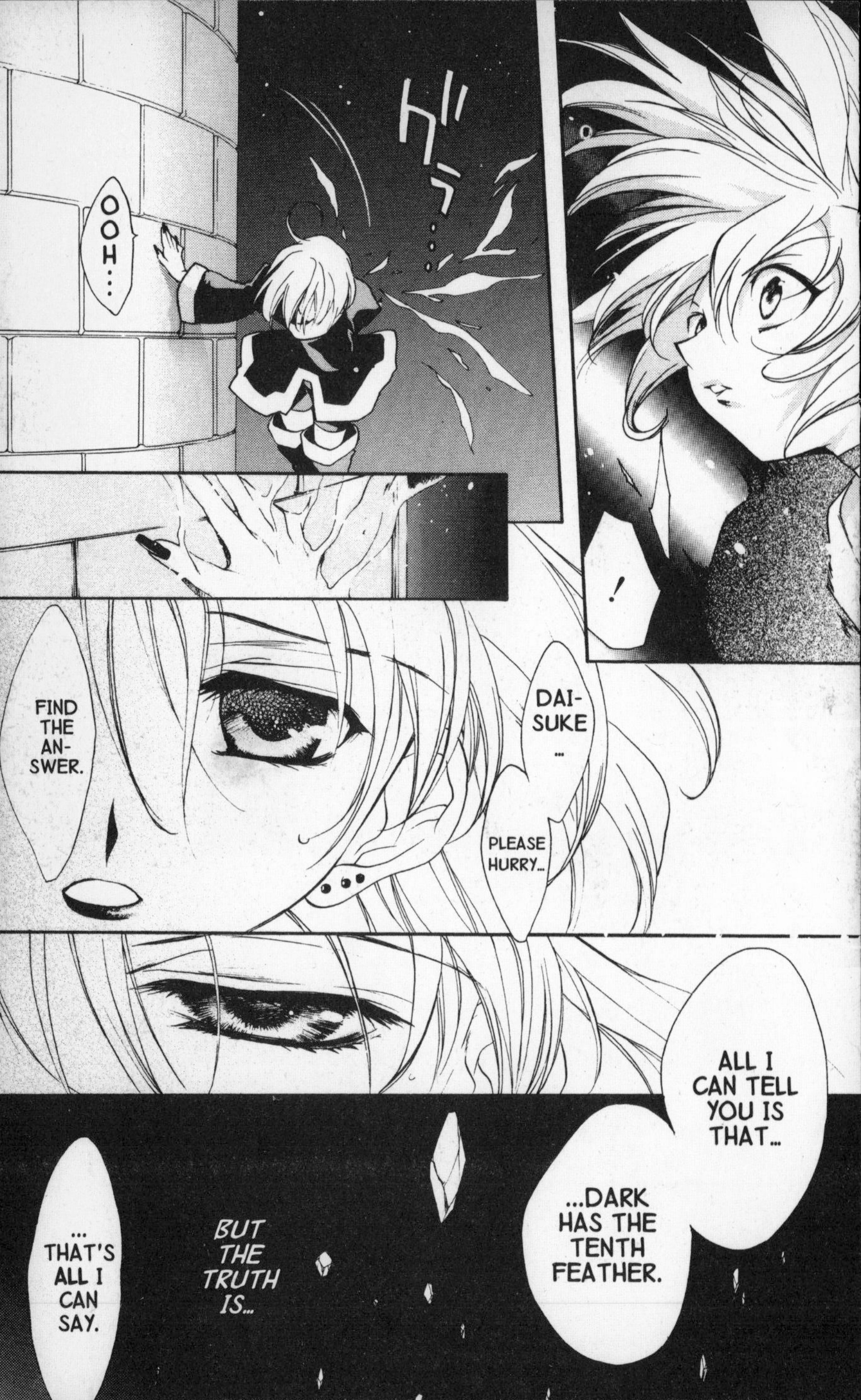
!
グラ…
OOH…
DAI-SUKE…
PLEASE HURRY…
FIND THE AN-SWER.
ALL I CAN TELL YOU IS THAT…
…DARK HAS THE TENTH FEATHER.
BUT THE TRUTH IS…
…THAT'S ALL I CAN SAY.

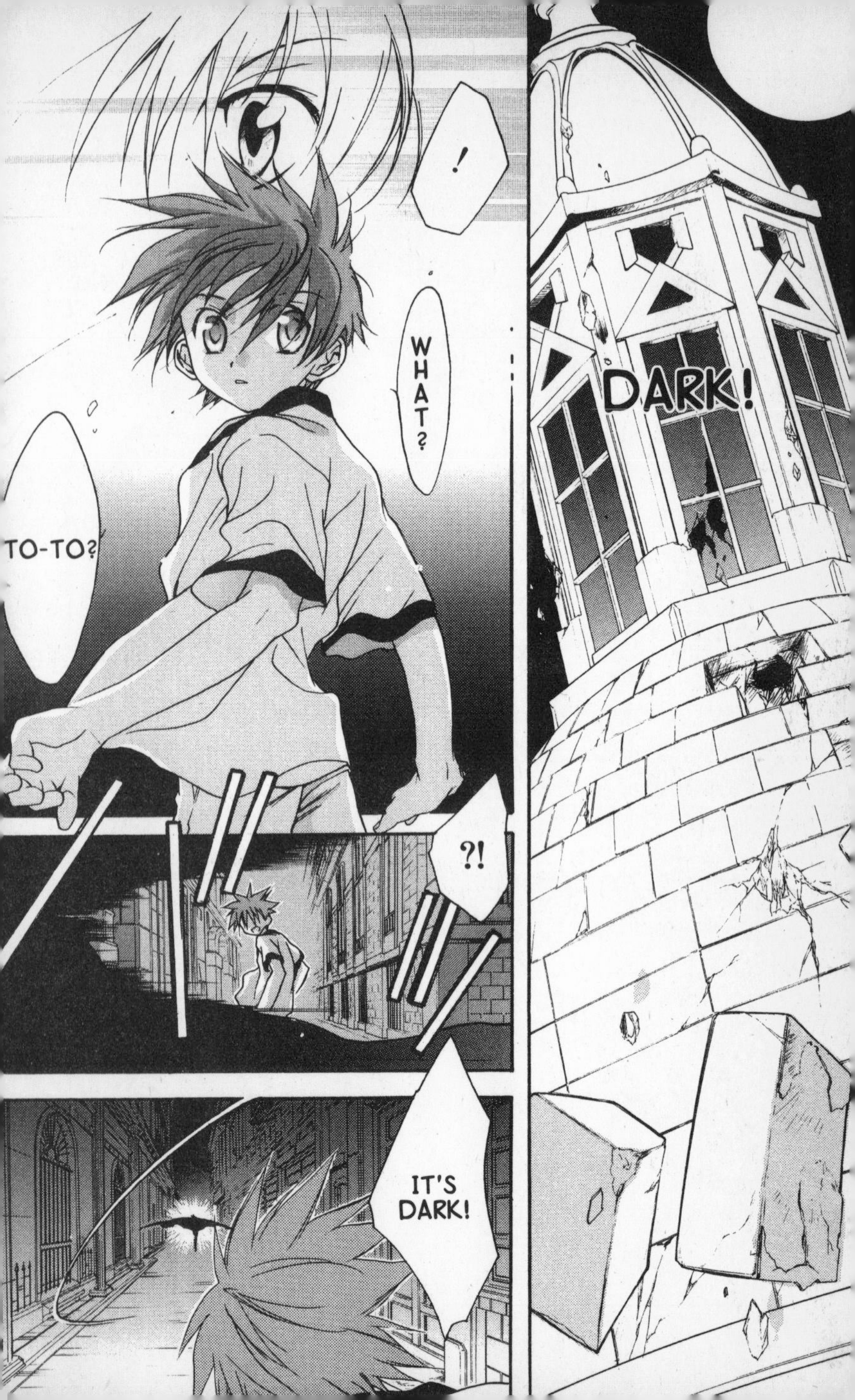
DARK!
!
WHAT?
TO-TO?
?!
IT'S DARK!

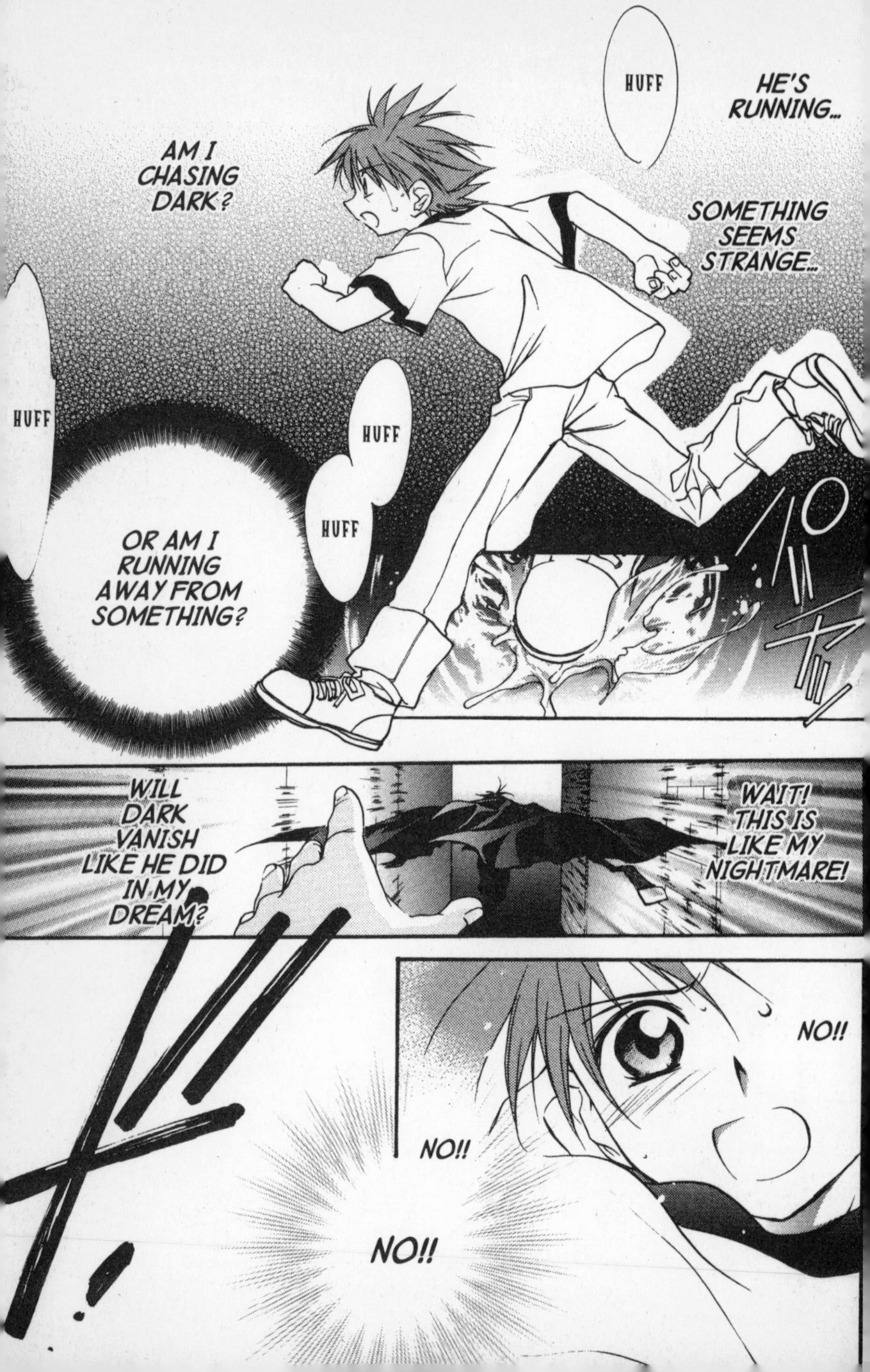
HUFF
HE'S RUNNING...
SOMETHING SEEMS STRANGE...
AM I CHASING DARK?
HUFF
HUFF
HUFF
OR AM I RUNNING AWAY FROM SOMETHING?
WAIT! THIS IS LIKE MY NIGHTMARE!
WILL DARK VANISH LIKE HE DID IN MY DREAM?
NO!!
NO!!
NO!!

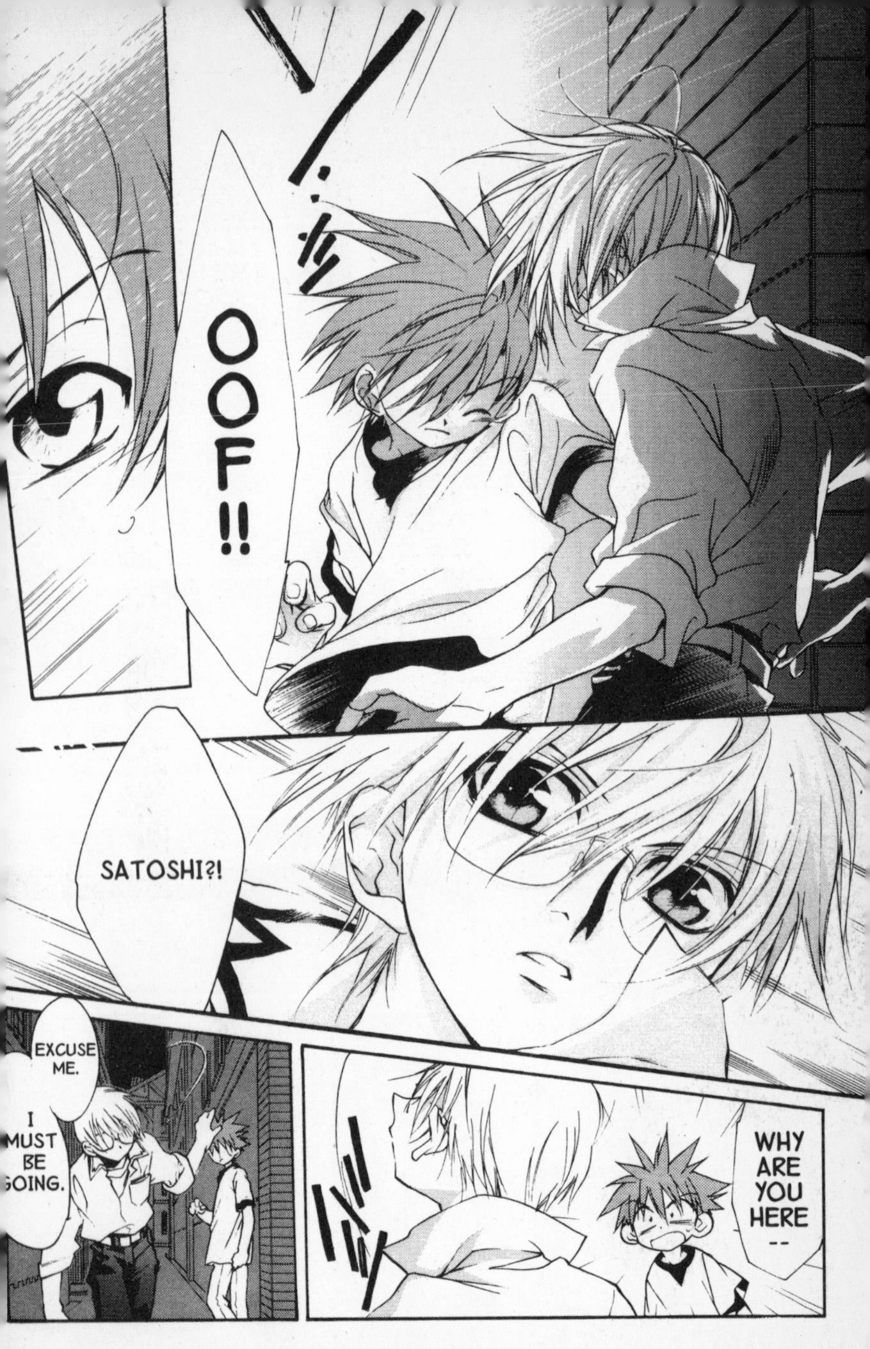
OOF!!
SATOSHI?!
WHY ARE YOU HERE --
EXCUSE ME.
I MUST BE GOING.

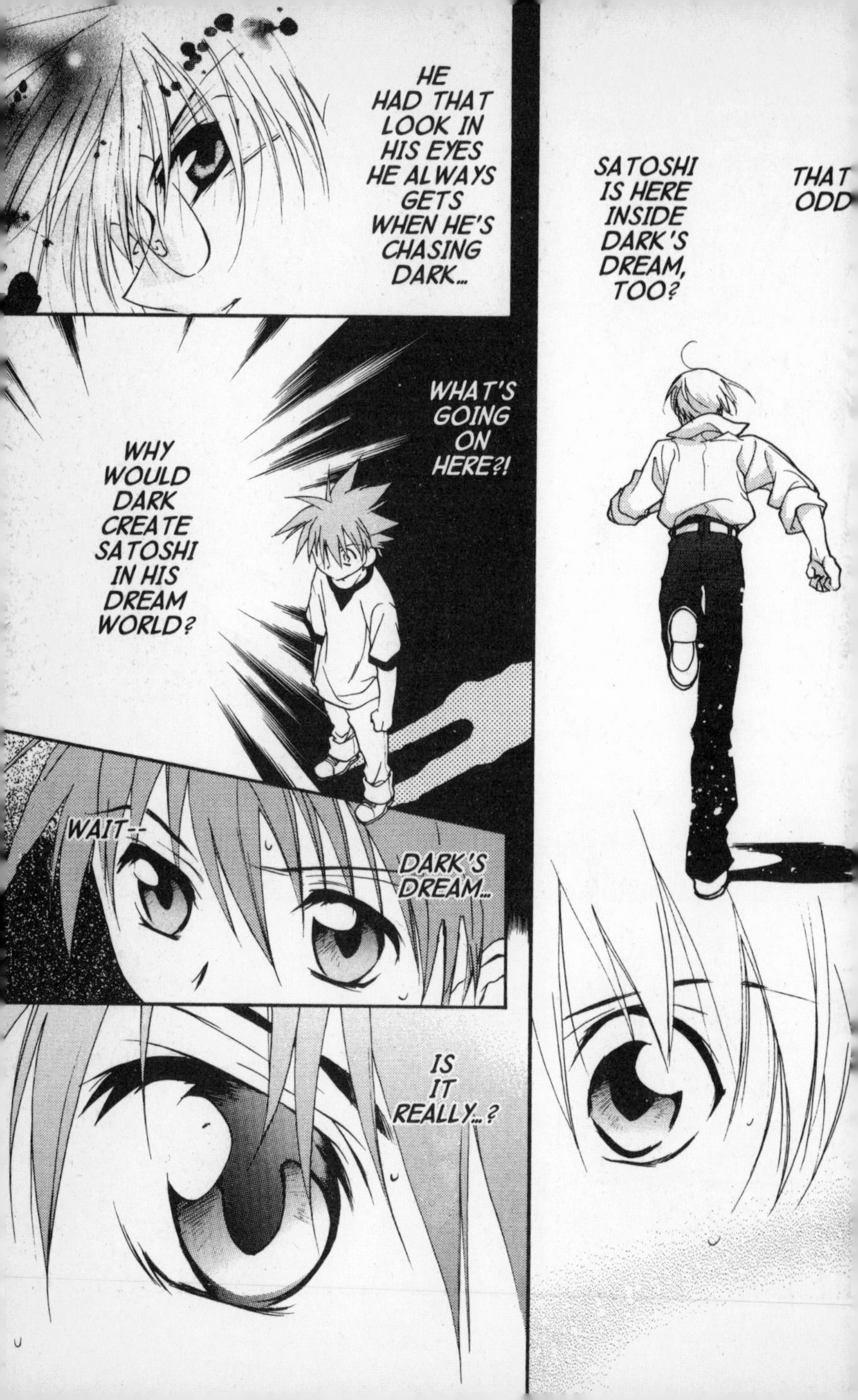
THAT ODD
SATOSHI IS HERE INSIDE DARK'S DREAM, TOO?
HE HAD THAT LOOK IN HIS EYES HE ALWAYS GETS WHEN HE'S CHASING DARK...
WHAT'S GOING ON HERE?!
WHY WOULD DARK CREATE SATOSHI IN HIS DREAM WORLD?
WAIT--
DARK'S DREAM...
IS IT REALLY...?

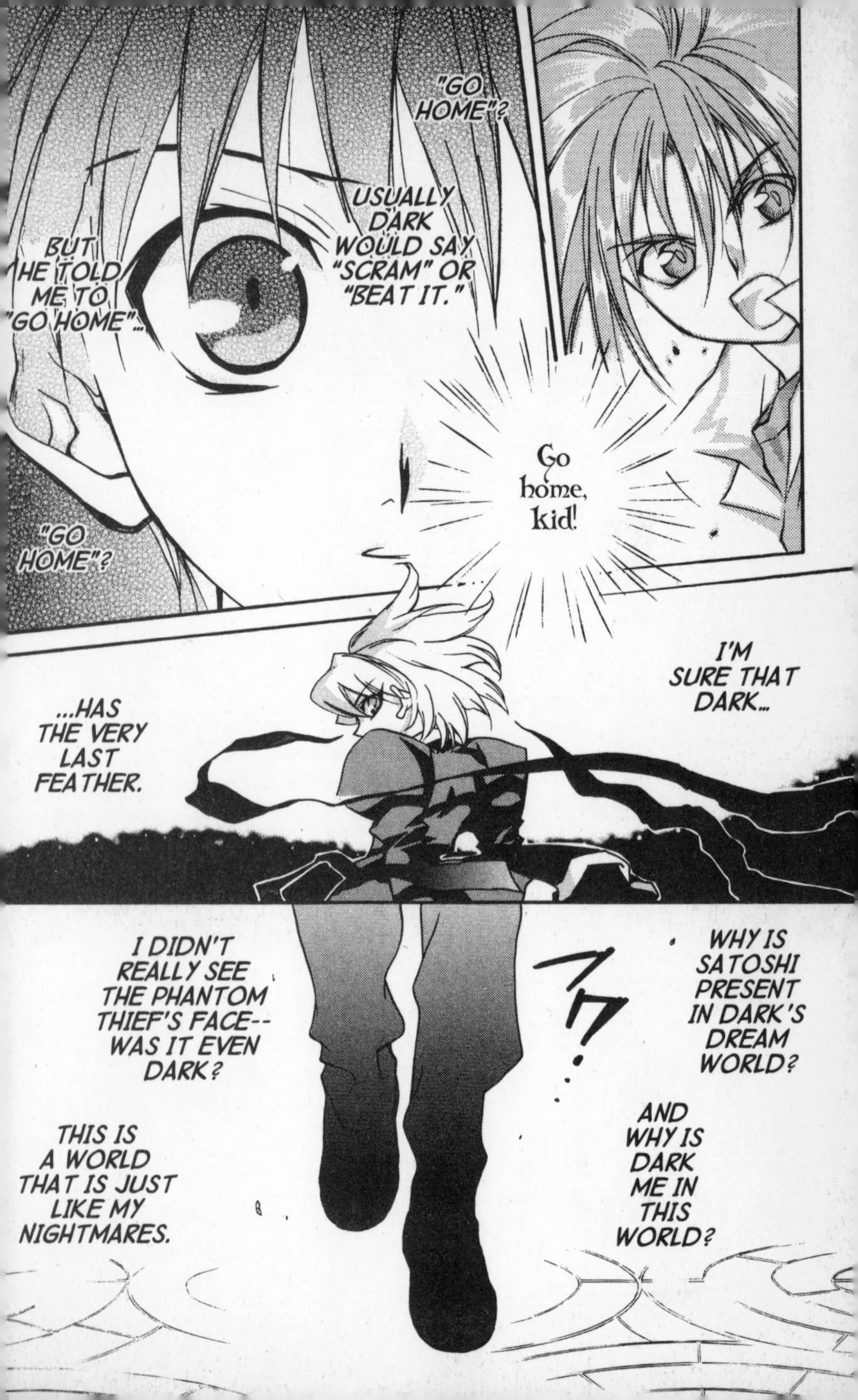
Go home, kid!
"GO HOME"?
USUALLY DARK WOULD SAY "SCRAM" OR "BEAT IT."
BUT HE TOLD ME TO "GO HOME"...
"GO HOME"?
I'M SURE THAT DARK...
...HAS THE VERY LAST FEATHER.
WHY IS SATOSHI PRESENT IN DARK'S DREAM WORLD?
AND WHY IS DARK ME IN THIS WORLD?
I DIDN'T REALLY SEE THE PHANTOM THIEF'S FACE-- WAS IT EVEN DARK?
THIS IS A WORLD THAT IS JUST LIKE MY NIGHTMARES.

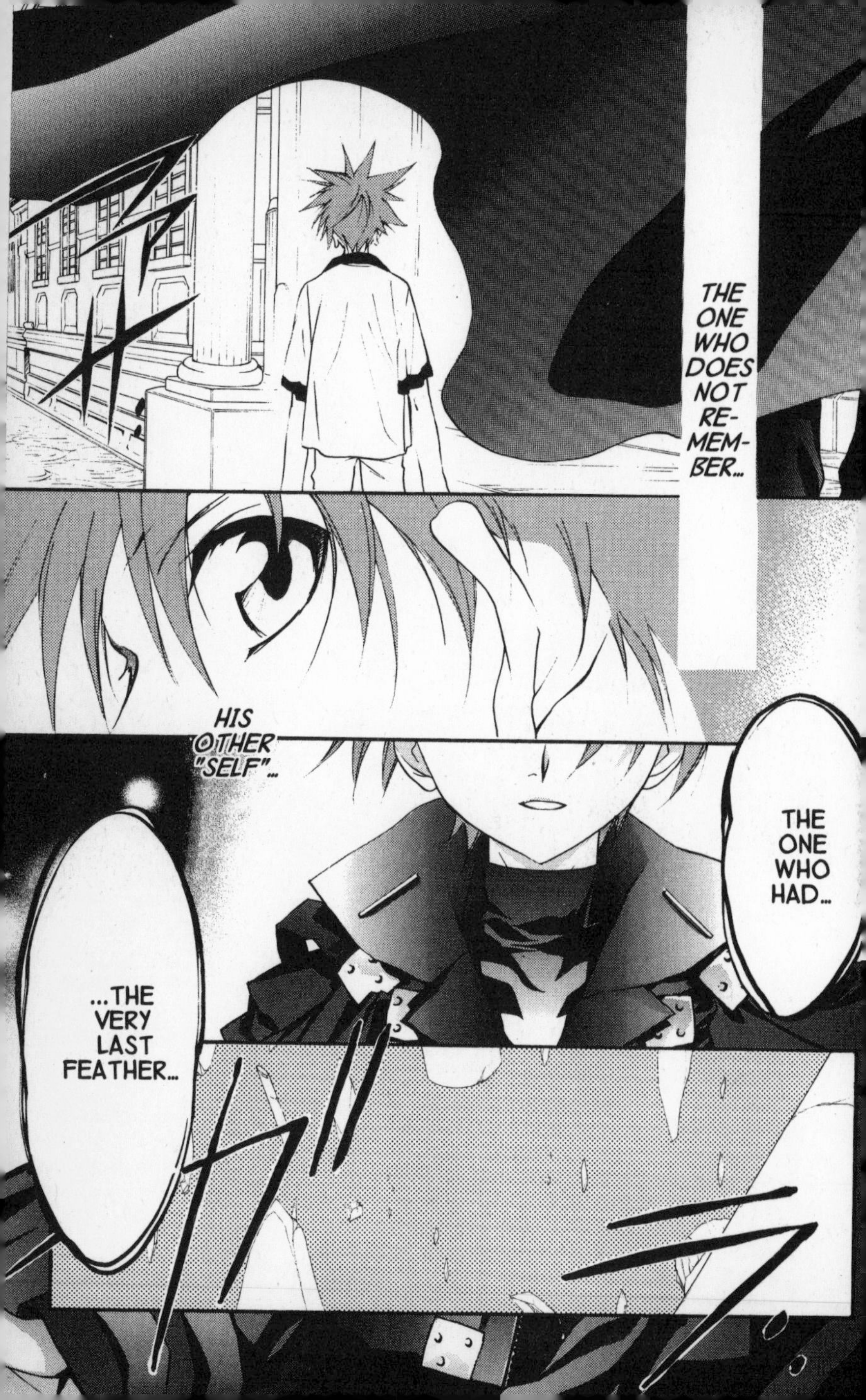
THE ONE WHO DOES NOT RE-MEM-BER...
HIS OTHER "SELF"...
THE ONE WHO HAD...
...THE VERY LAST FEATHER...

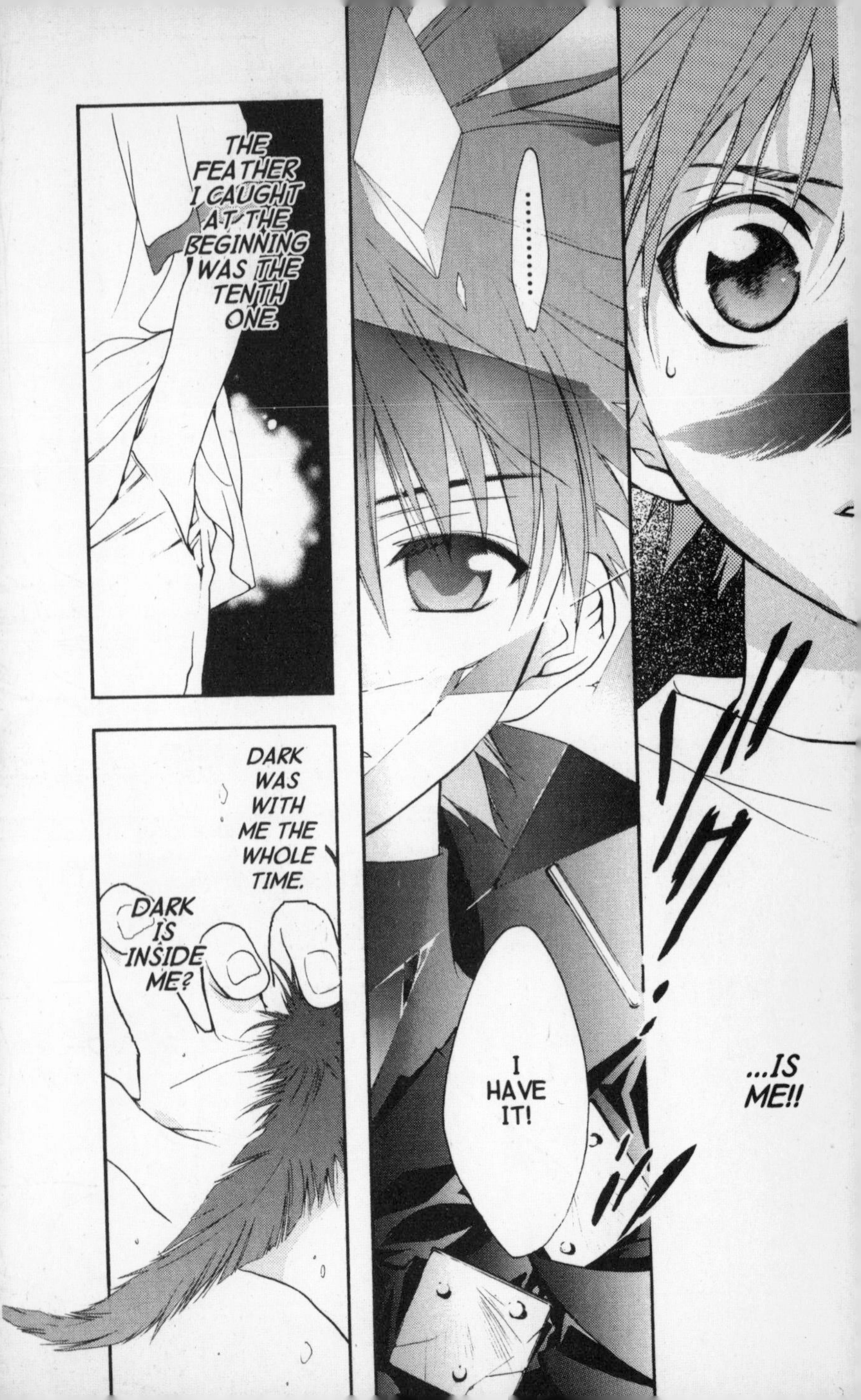
...IS ME!!
......
I HAVE IT!
THE FEATHER I CAUGHT AT THE BEGINNING WAS THE TENTH ONE.
DARK WAS WITH ME THE WHOLE TIME.
DARK IS INSIDE ME?

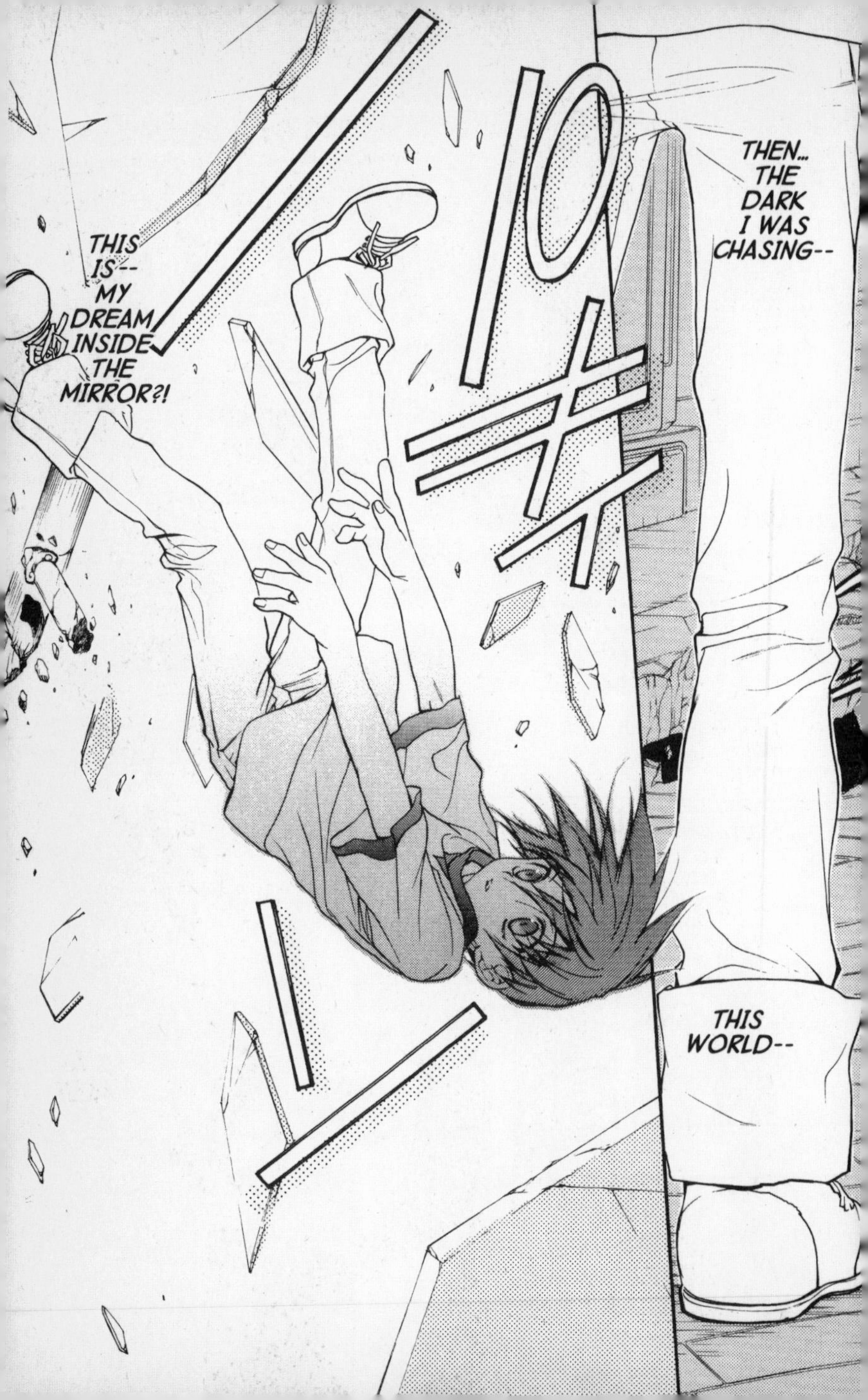
THEN... THE DARK I WAS CHASING--
THIS WORLD--
THIS IS-- MY DREAM INSIDE THE MIRROR?!

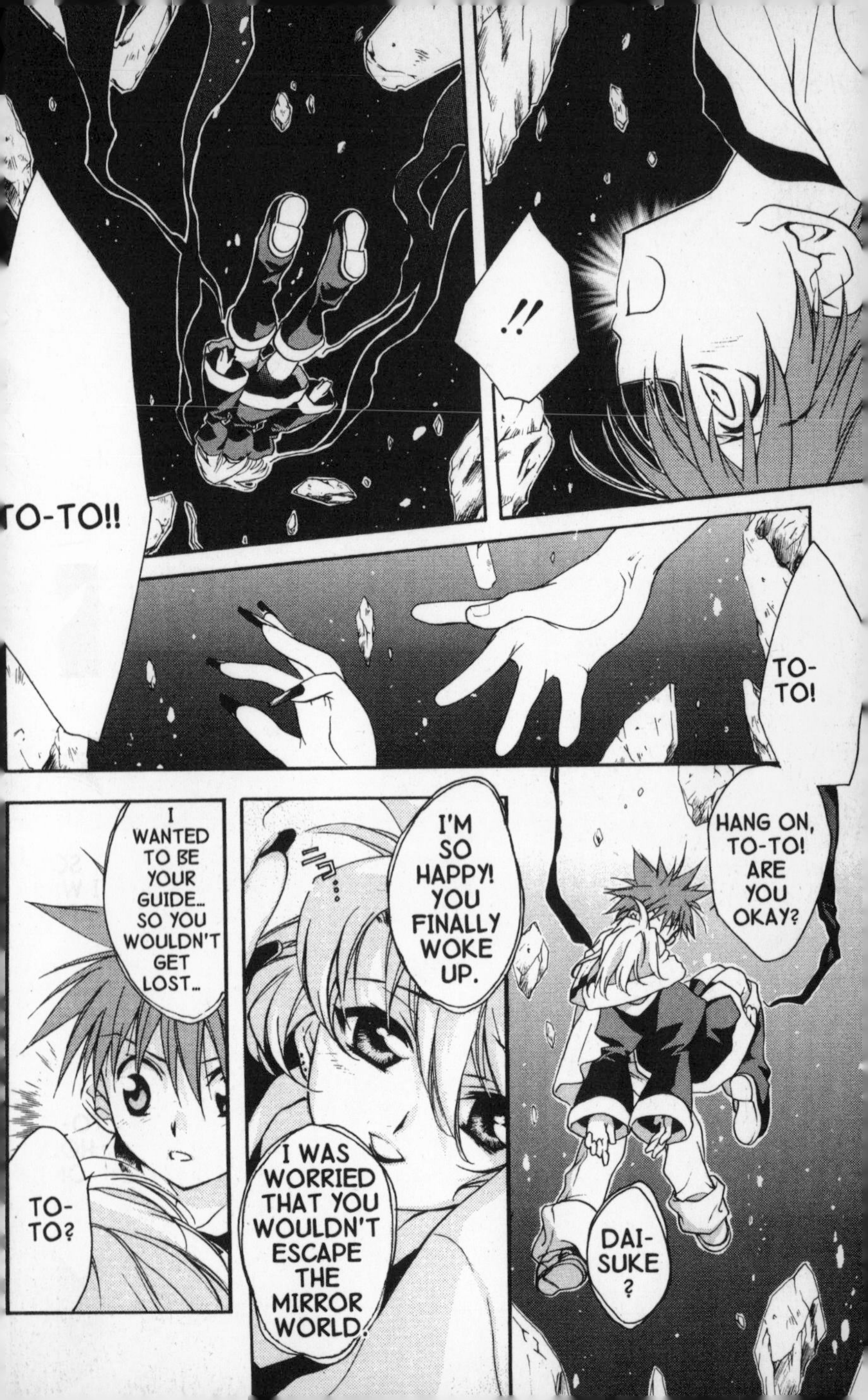
!!
TO-TO!!
TO-TO!
HANG ON, TO-TO! ARE YOU OKAY?
DAI-SUKE?
I'M SO HAPPY! YOU FINALLY WOKE UP.
I WAS WORRIED THAT YOU WOULDN'T ESCAPE THE MIRROR WORLD.
I WANTED TO BE YOUR GUIDE... SO YOU WOULDN'T GET LOST...
TO-TO?

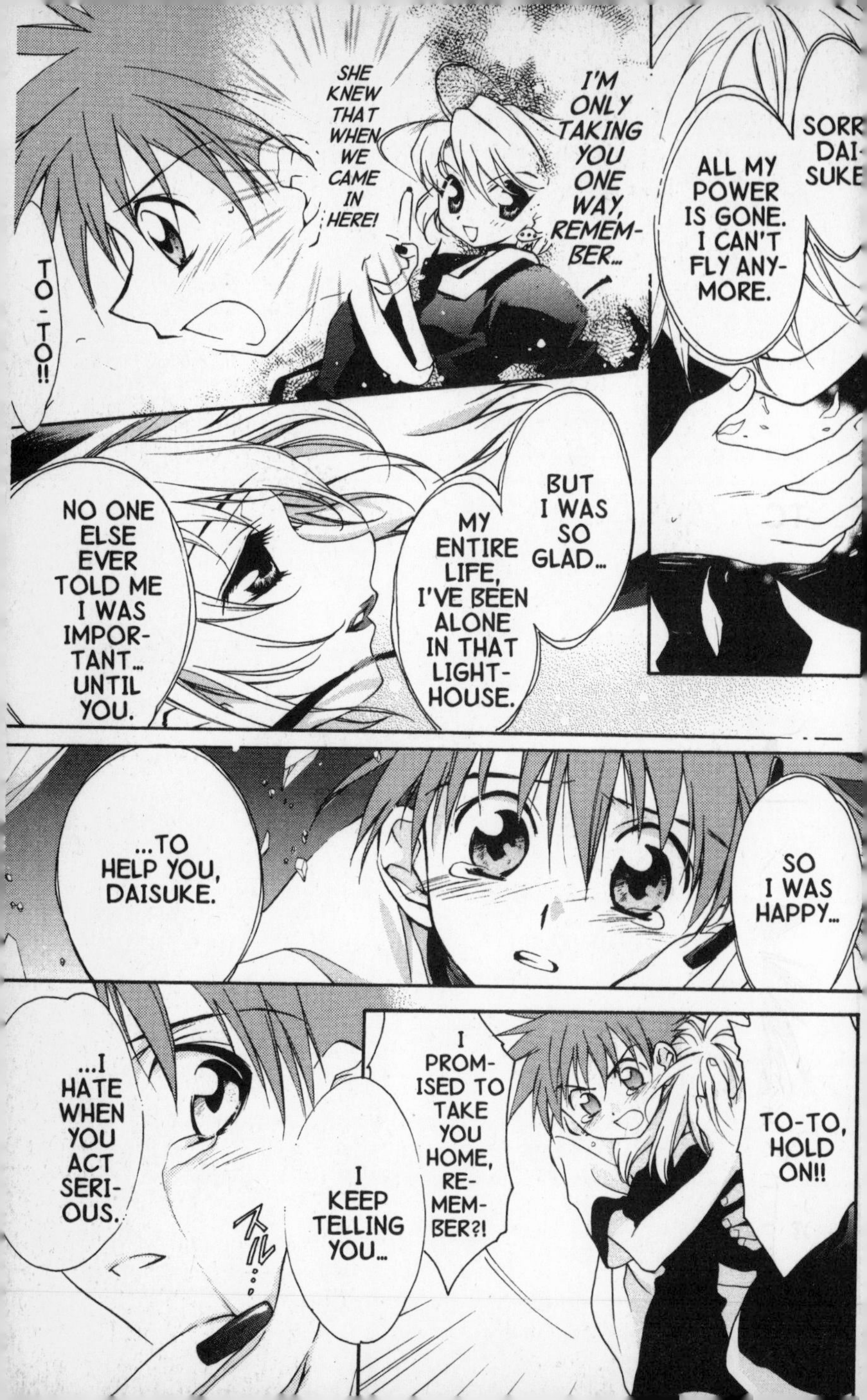
SORR DAI-SUKE
ALL MY POWER IS GONE. I CAN'T FLY ANYMORE.
I'M ONLY TAKING YOU ONE WAY, REMEMBER...
SHE KNEW THAT WHEN WE CAME IN HERE!
TO-TO!!
BUT I WAS SO GLAD...
MY ENTIRE LIFE, I'VE BEEN ALONE IN THAT LIGHTHOUSE.
NO ONE ELSE EVER TOLD ME I WAS IMPORTANT... UNTIL YOU.
SO I WAS HAPPY...
...TO HELP YOU, DAISUKE.
TO-TO, HOLD ON!!
I PROMISED TO TAKE YOU HOME, REMEMBER?!
I KEEP TELLING YOU...
...I HATE WHEN YOU ACT SERIOUS.

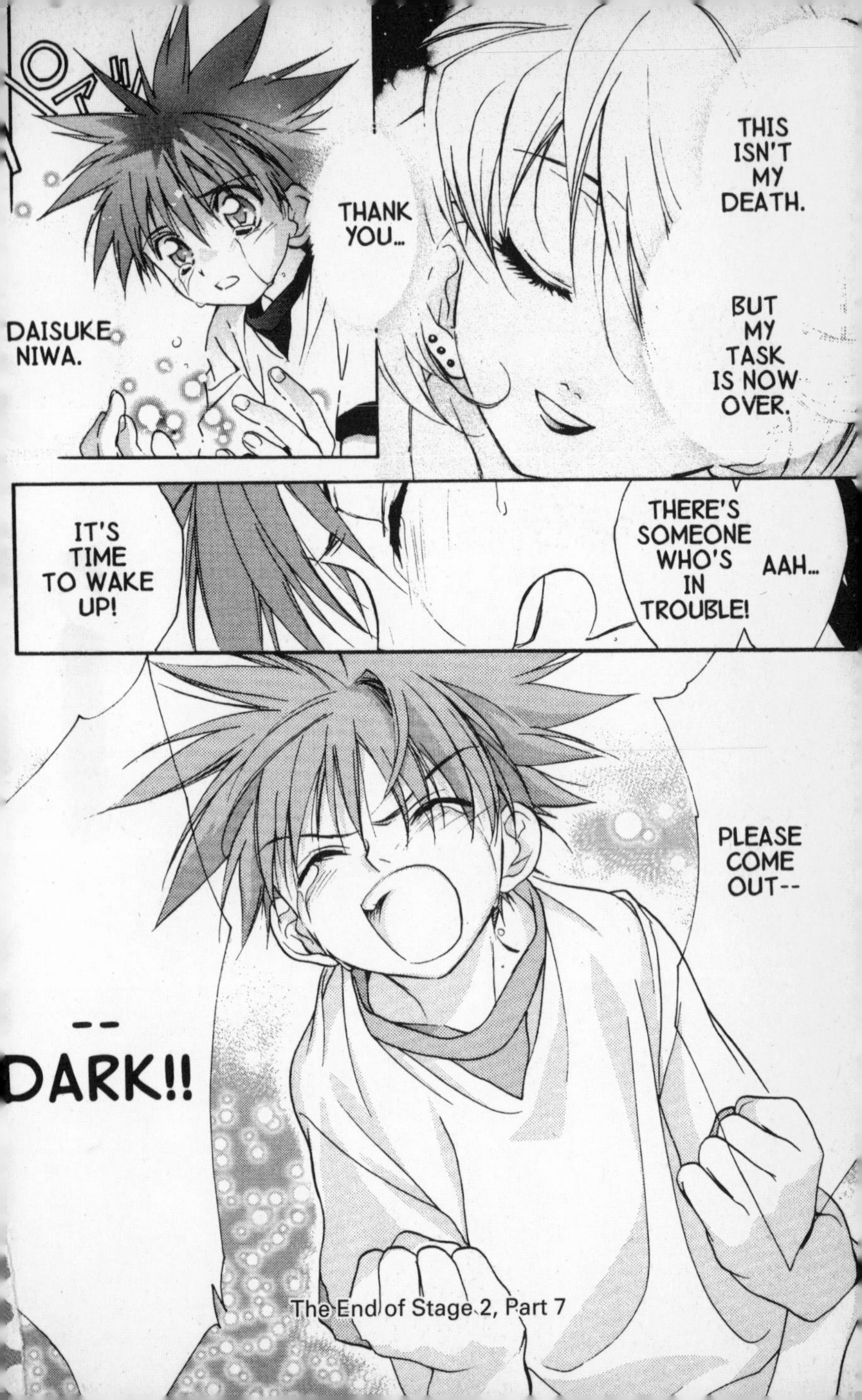
THIS ISN'T MY DEATH.
BUT MY TASK IS NOW OVER.
THANK YOU...
DAISUKE NIWA.
AAH...
THERE'S SOMEONE WHO'S IN TROUBLE!
IT'S TIME TO WAKE UP!
PLEASE COME OUT--
--DARK!!
The End of Stage 2, Part 7

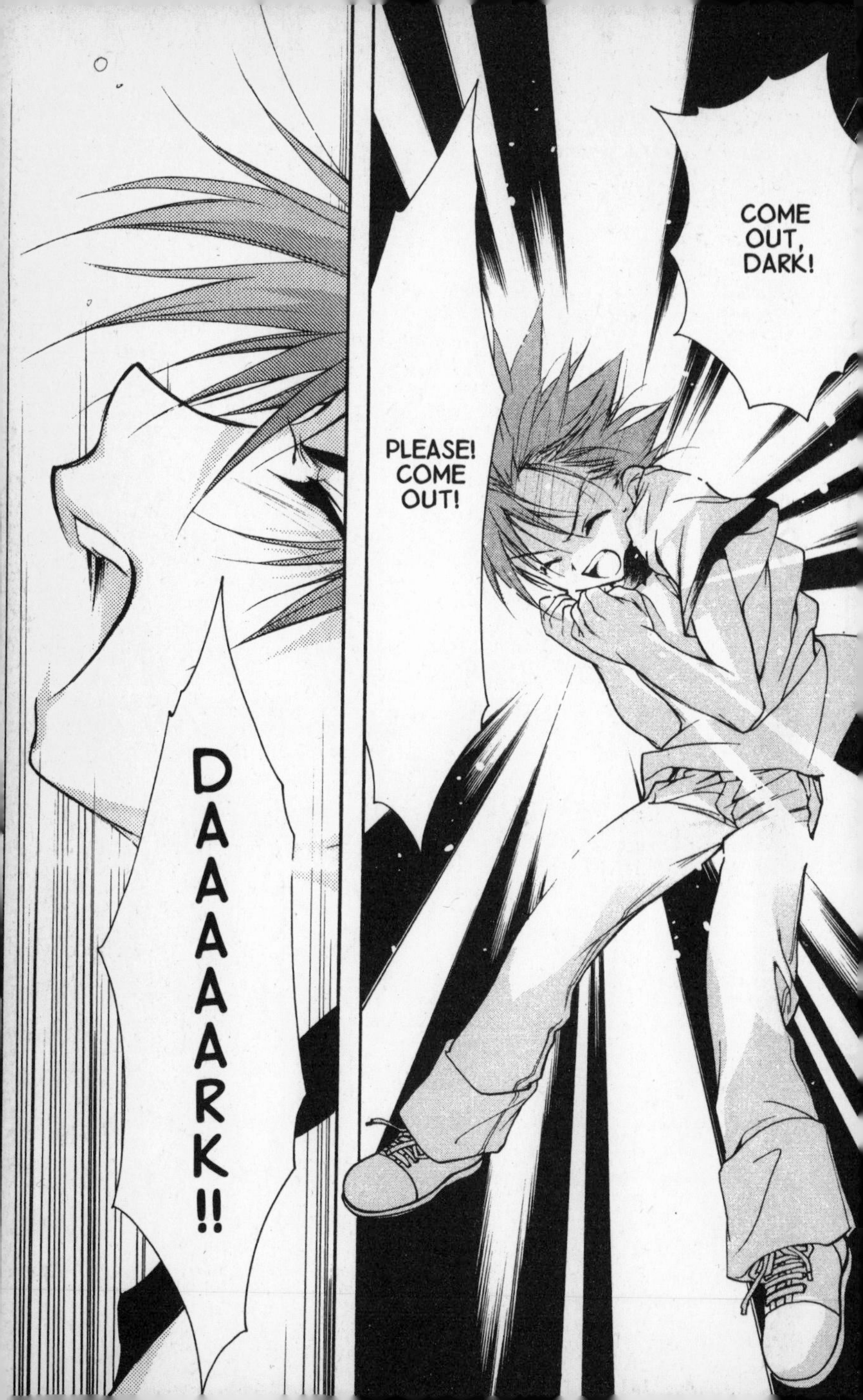
COME OUT, DARK!
PLEASE! COME OUT!
DAAAAARK!!

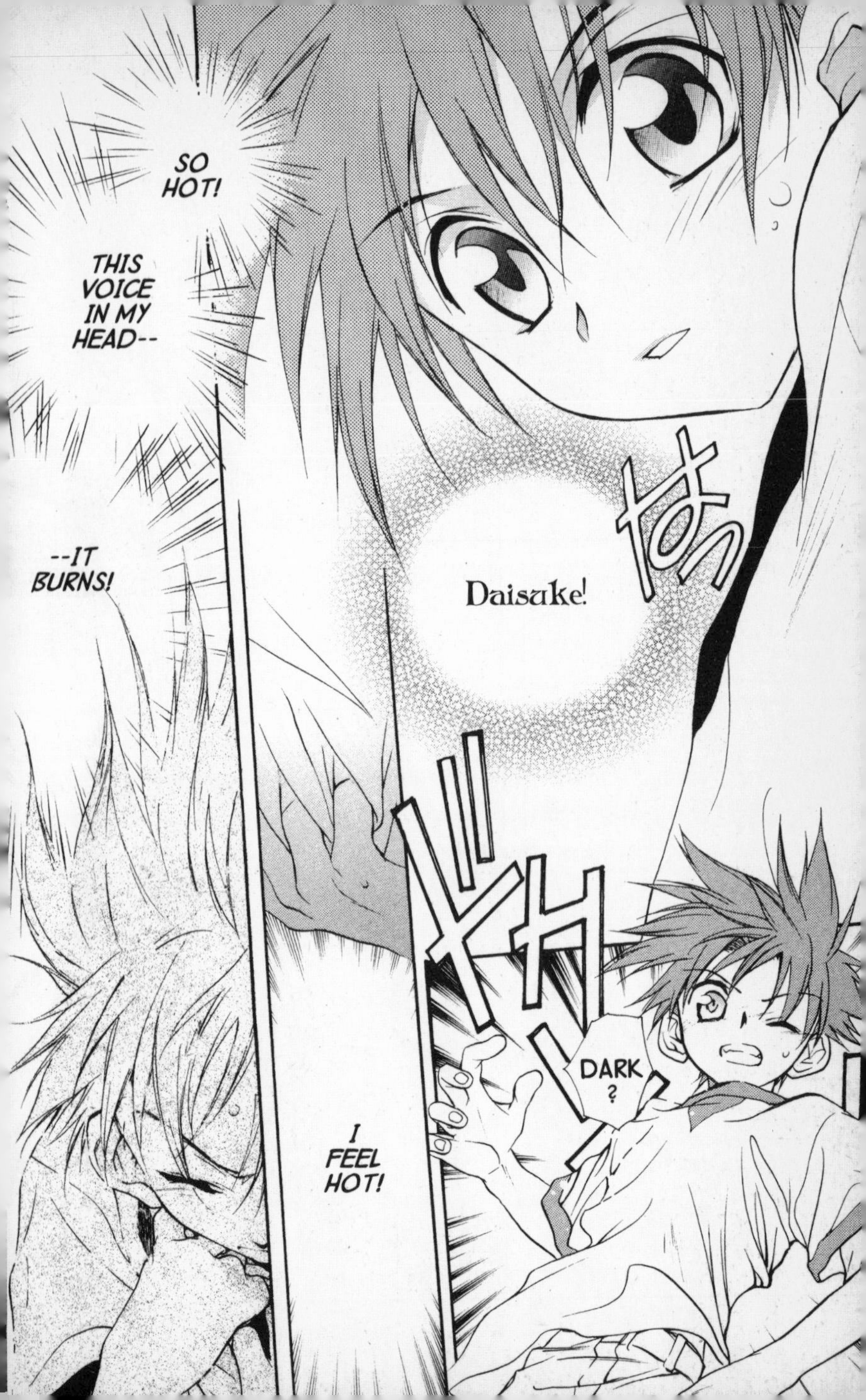
はっ
Daisuke!
DARK?
I FEEL HOT!
SO HOT!
THIS VOICE IN MY HEAD--
--IT BURNS!

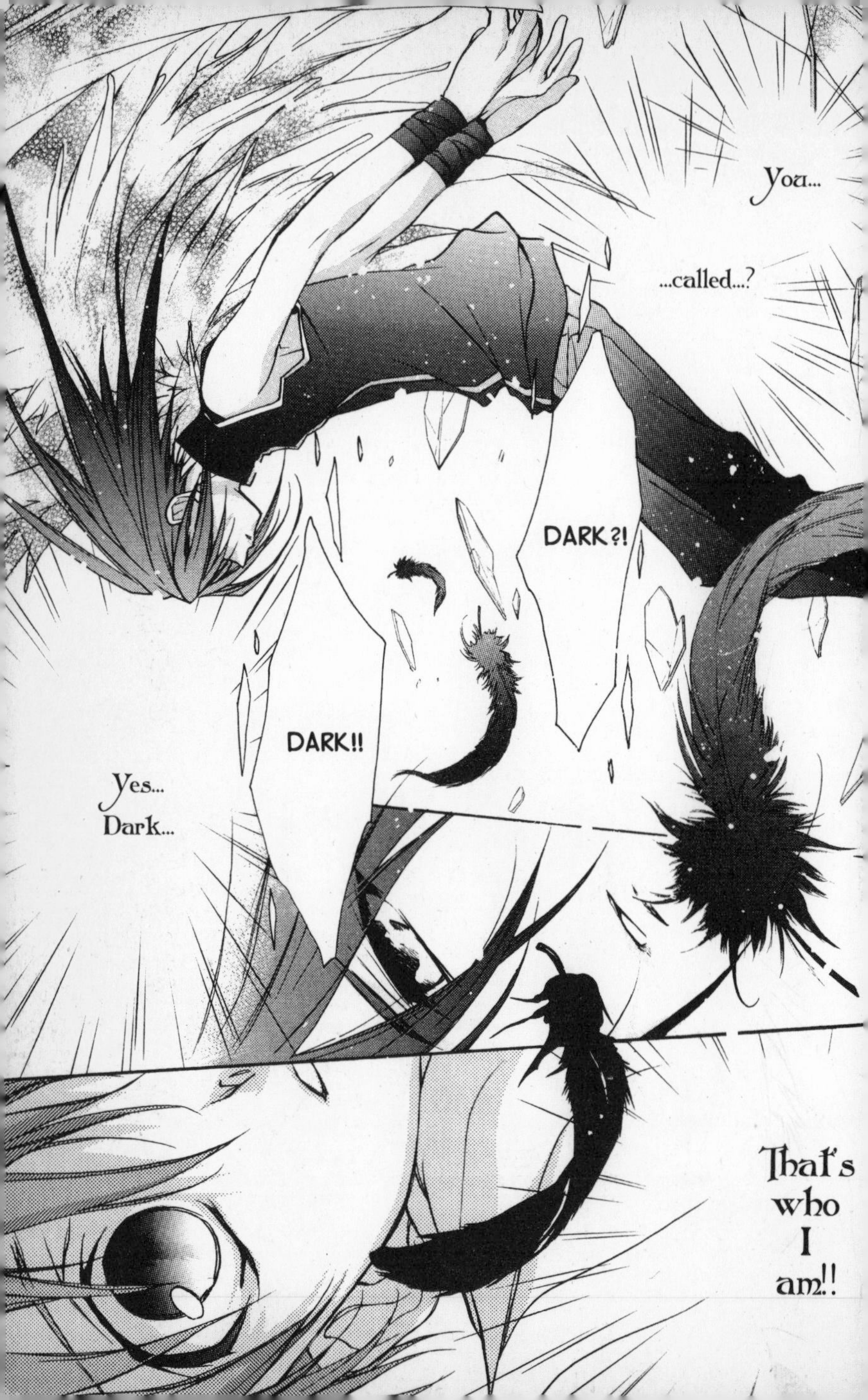
You...
...called...?
DARK?!
DARK!!
Yes... Dark...
That's who I am!!

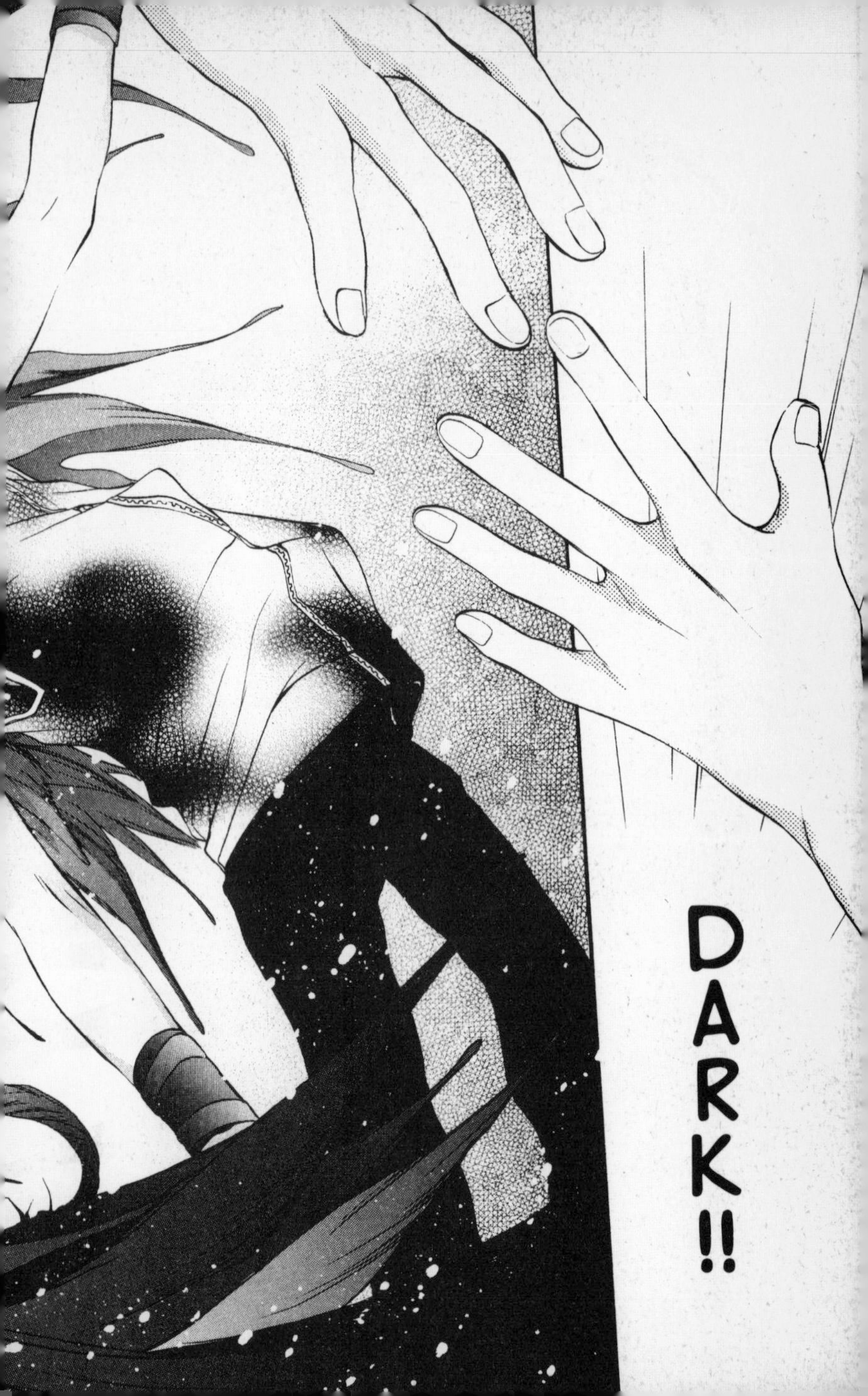
DARK!!

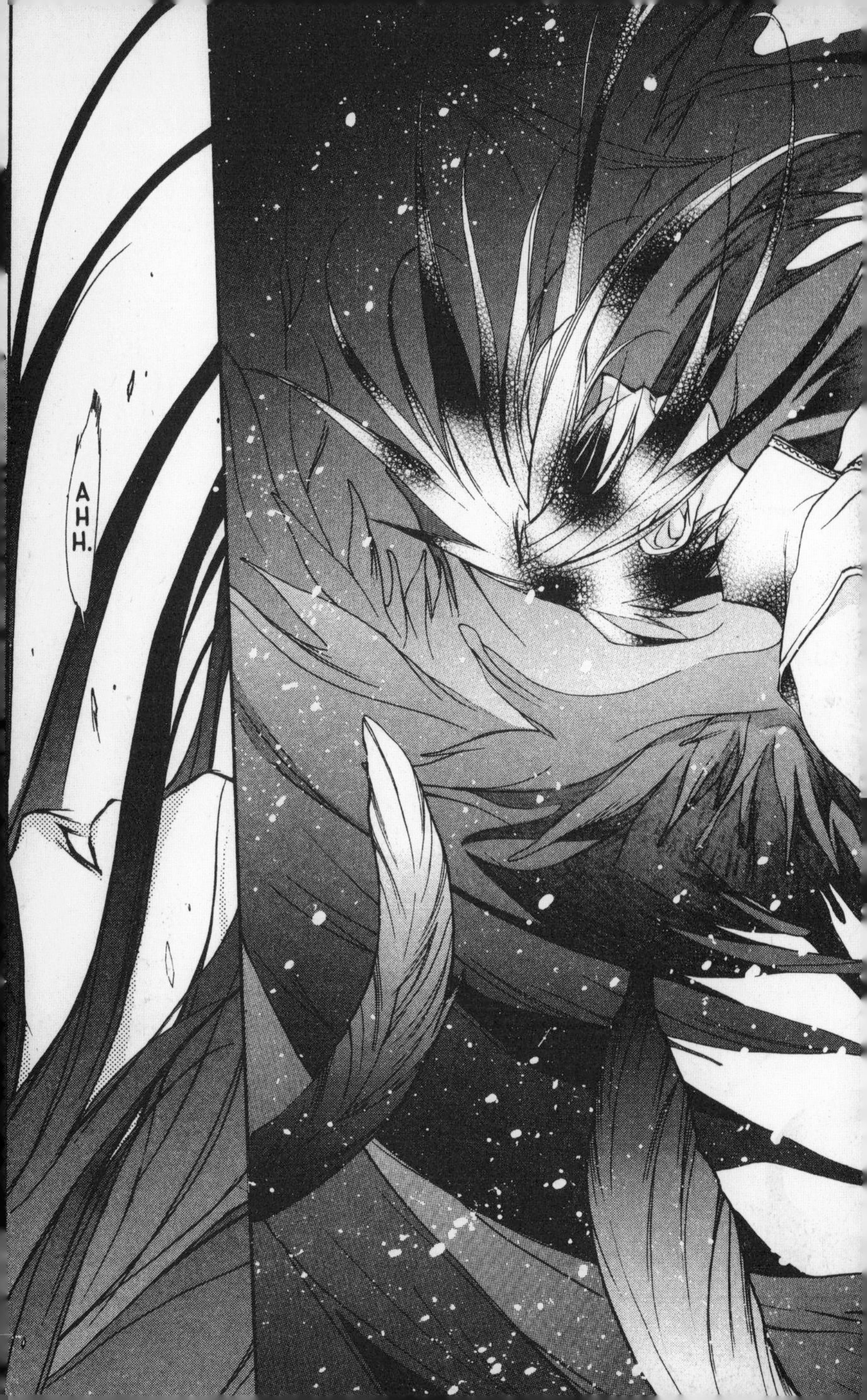
AHH.

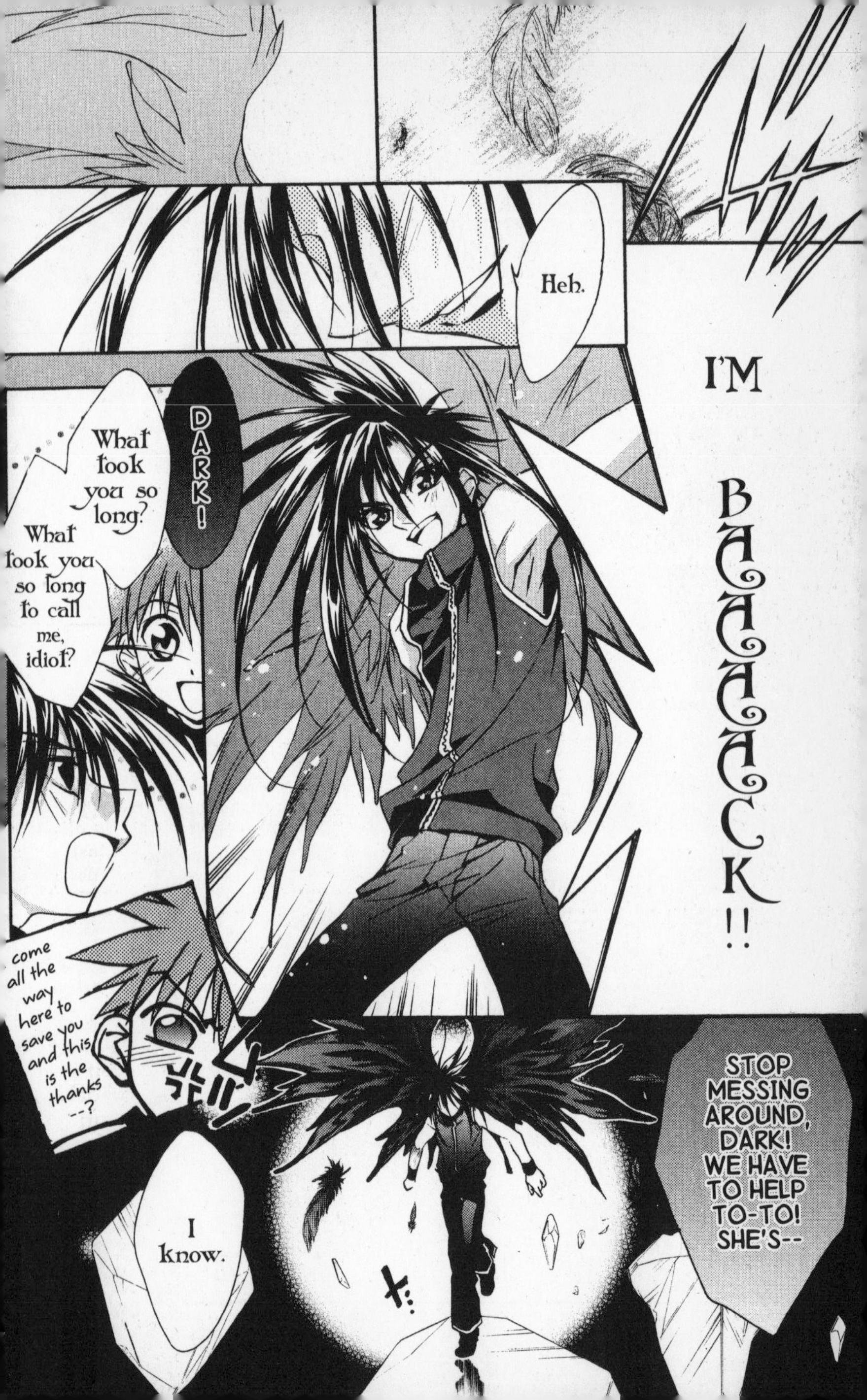
Heh.
I'M BAAAACK!!
DARK!
What took you so long?
What took you so long to call me, idiot?
STOP MESSING AROUND, DARK! WE HAVE TO HELP TO-TO! SHE'S--
come all the way here to save you and this is the thanks--?
I know.

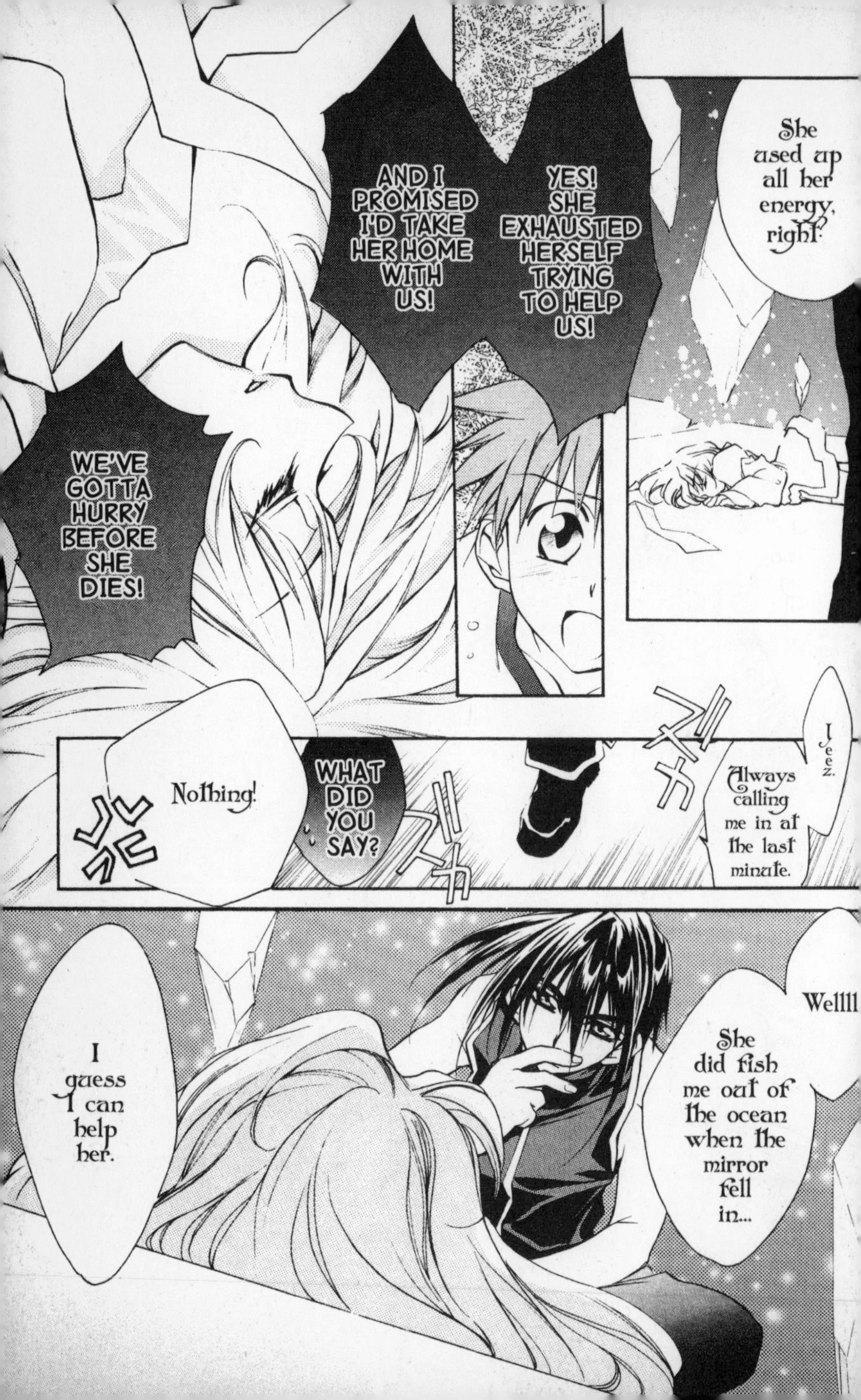
She used up all her energy, right?
YES! SHE EXHAUSTED HERSELF TRYING TO HELP US!
AND I PROMISED I'D TAKE HER HOME WITH US!
WE'VE GOTTA HURRY BEFORE SHE DIES!
Jeez.
Always calling me in at the last minute.
WHAT DID YOU SAY?
Nothing!
Wellll
She did fish me out of the ocean when the mirror fell in...
I guess I can help her.

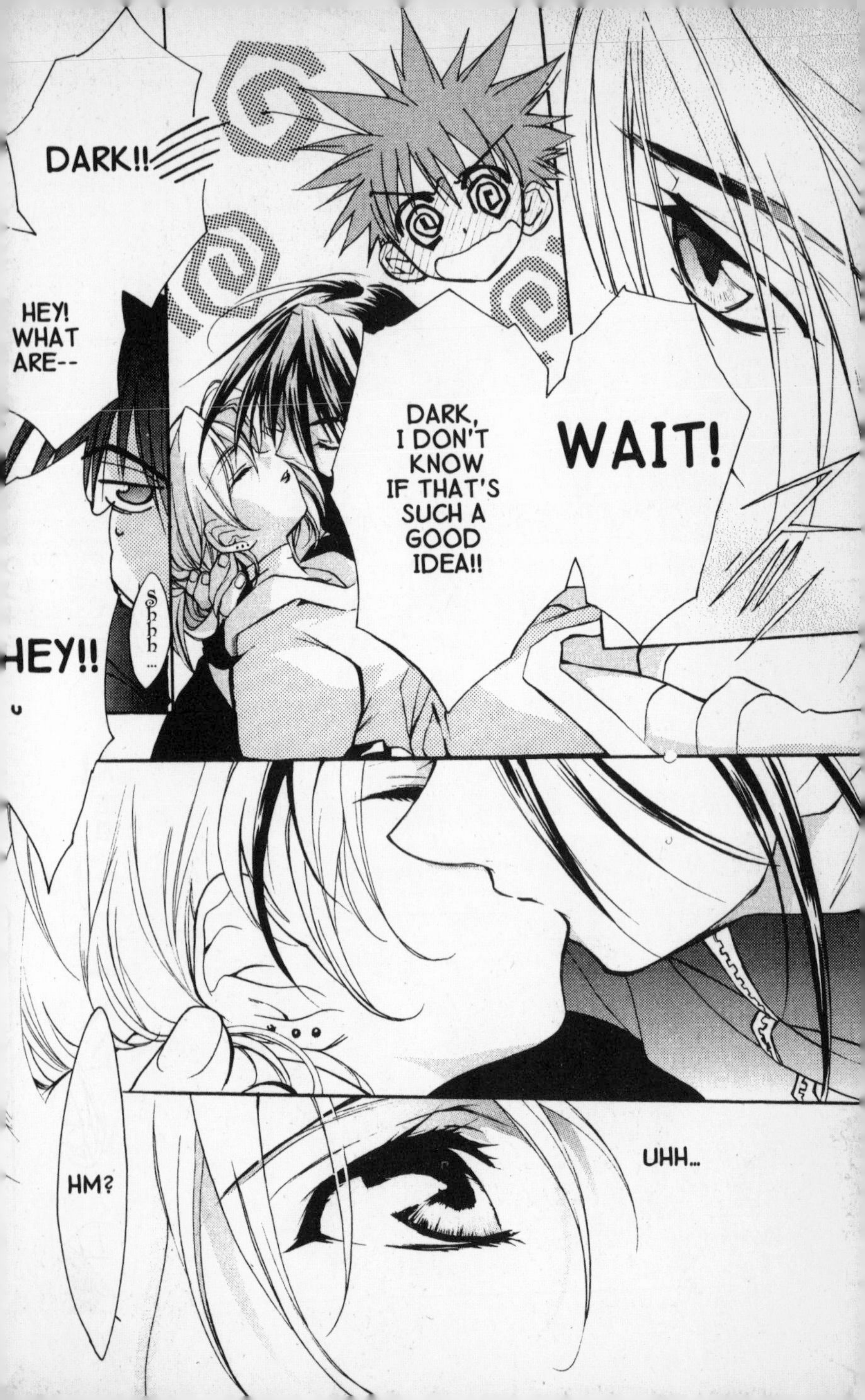
WAIT!
DARK, I DON'T KNOW IF THAT'S SUCH A GOOD IDEA!!
DARK!!
HEY! WHAT ARE--
Shhh...
HEY!!
UHH...
HM?

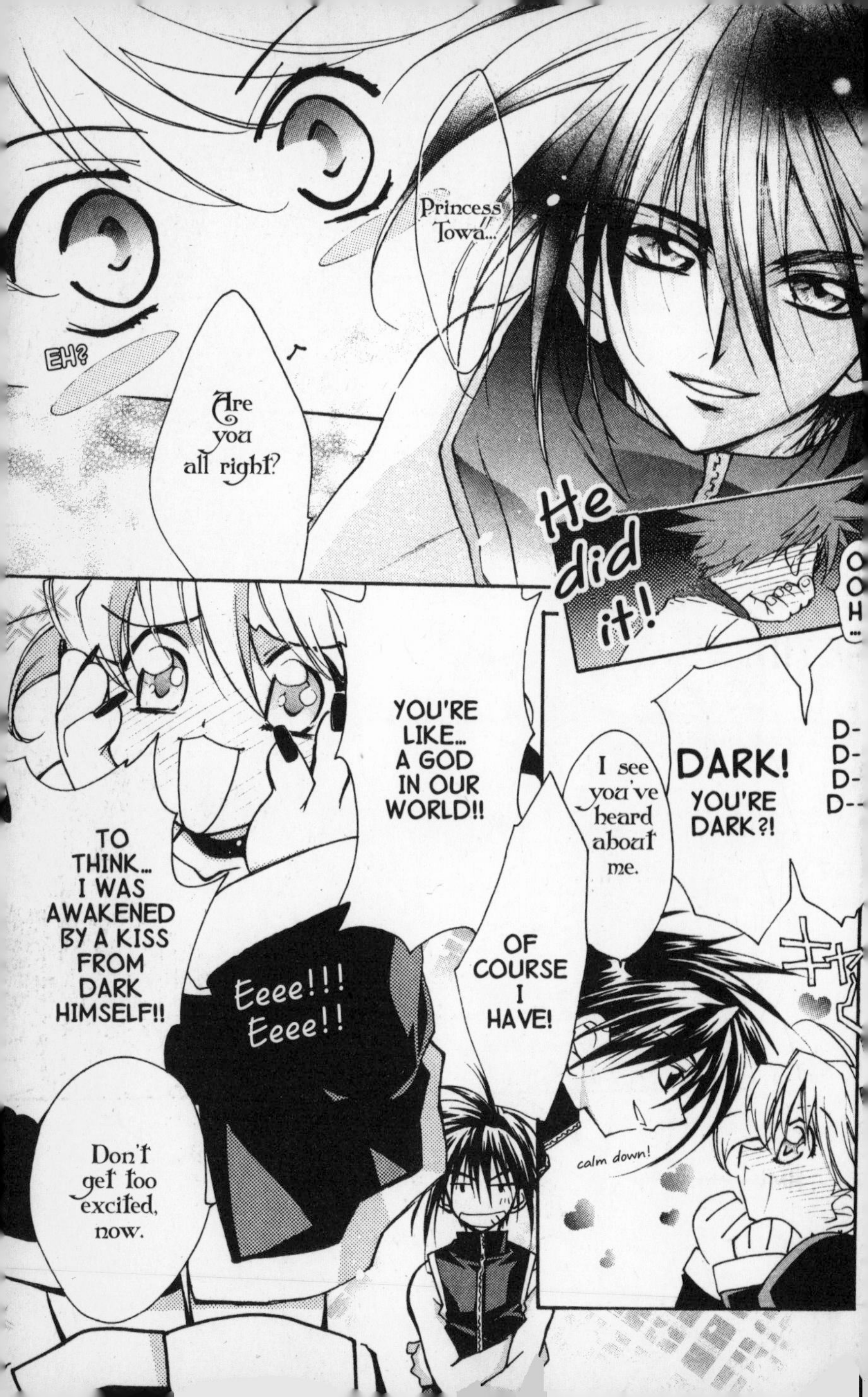

Princess Towa...
Are you all right?
EH?
OOH...
He did it!
D-D-D-D--
DARK! YOU'RE DARK?!
I see you've heard about me.
OF COURSE I HAVE!
calm down!
YOU'RE LIKE... A GOD IN OUR WORLD!!
TO THINK... I WAS AWAKENED BY A KISS FROM DARK HIMSELF!!
Eeee!!! Eeee!!
Don't get too excited, now.

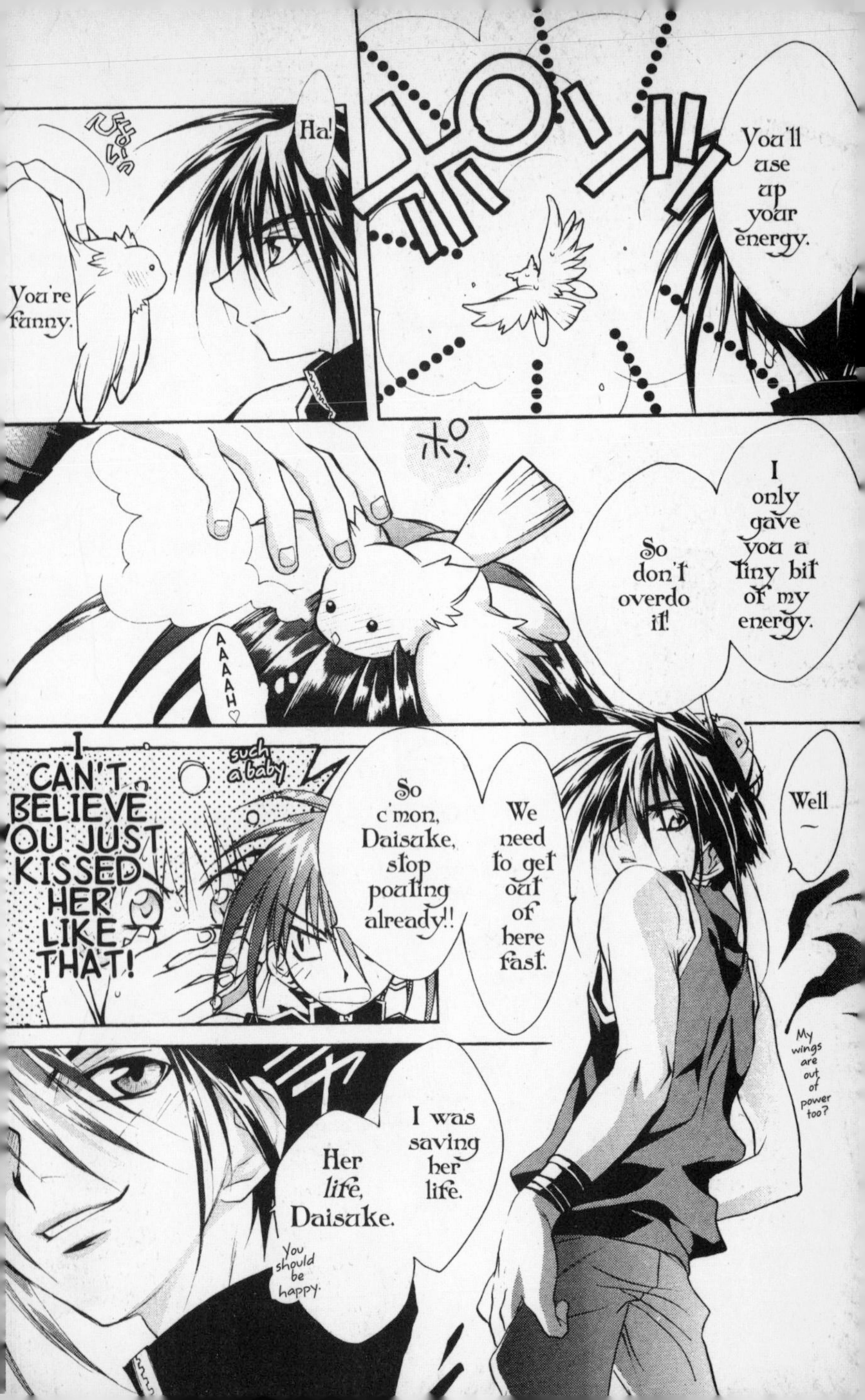
You'll use up your energy.
Ha!
You're funny.
I only gave you a tiny bit of my energy.
So don't overdo it!
AAAAH♡
Well ~
We need to get out of here fast.
So c'mon, Daisuke, stop pouting already!!
such a baby
I CAN'T BELIEVE OU JUST KISSED HER LIKE THAT!
My wings are out of power too?
I was saving her life.
Her life, Daisuke.
You should be happy.

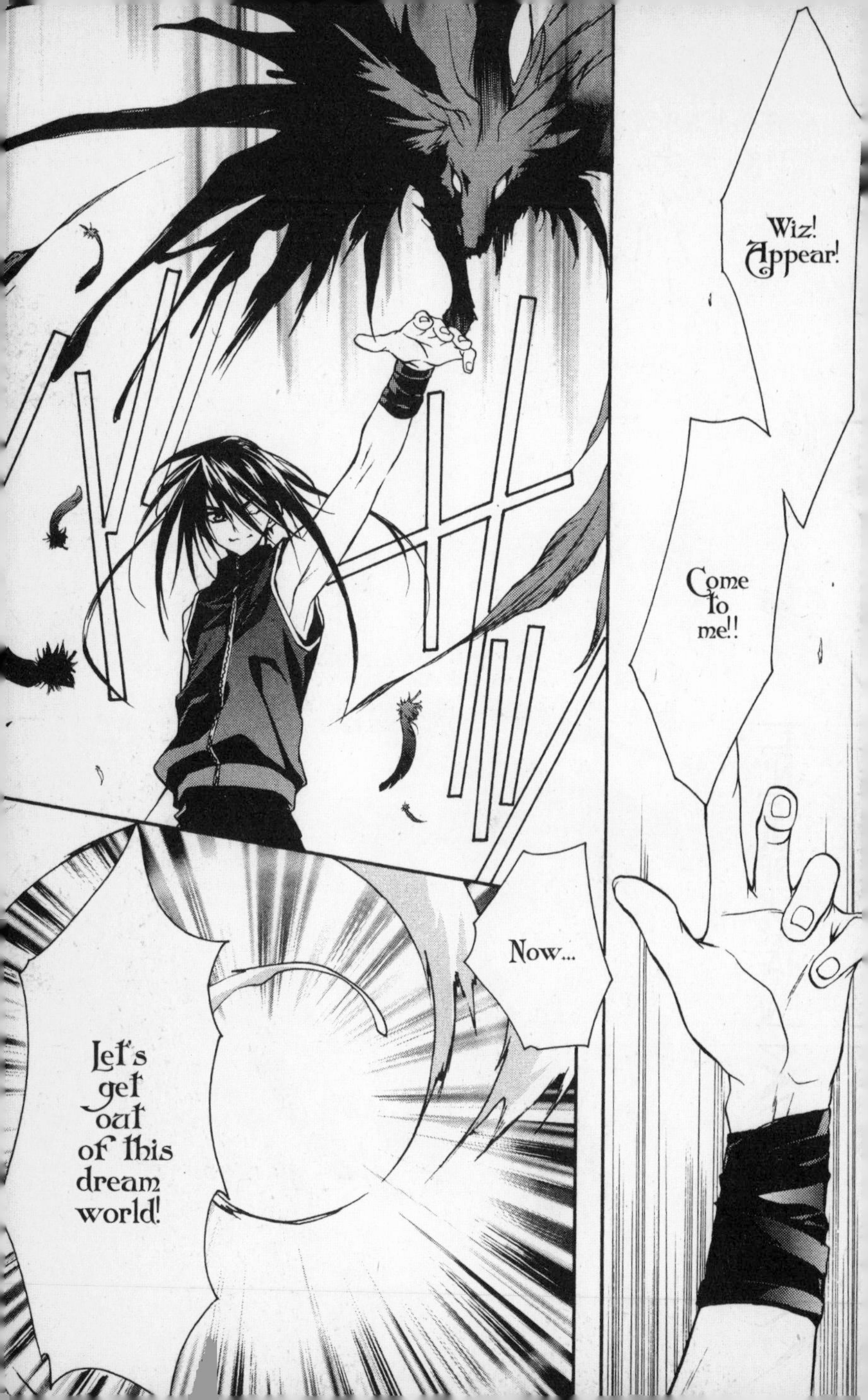
Wiz! Appear!
Come to me!!
Now...
Let's get out of this dream world!

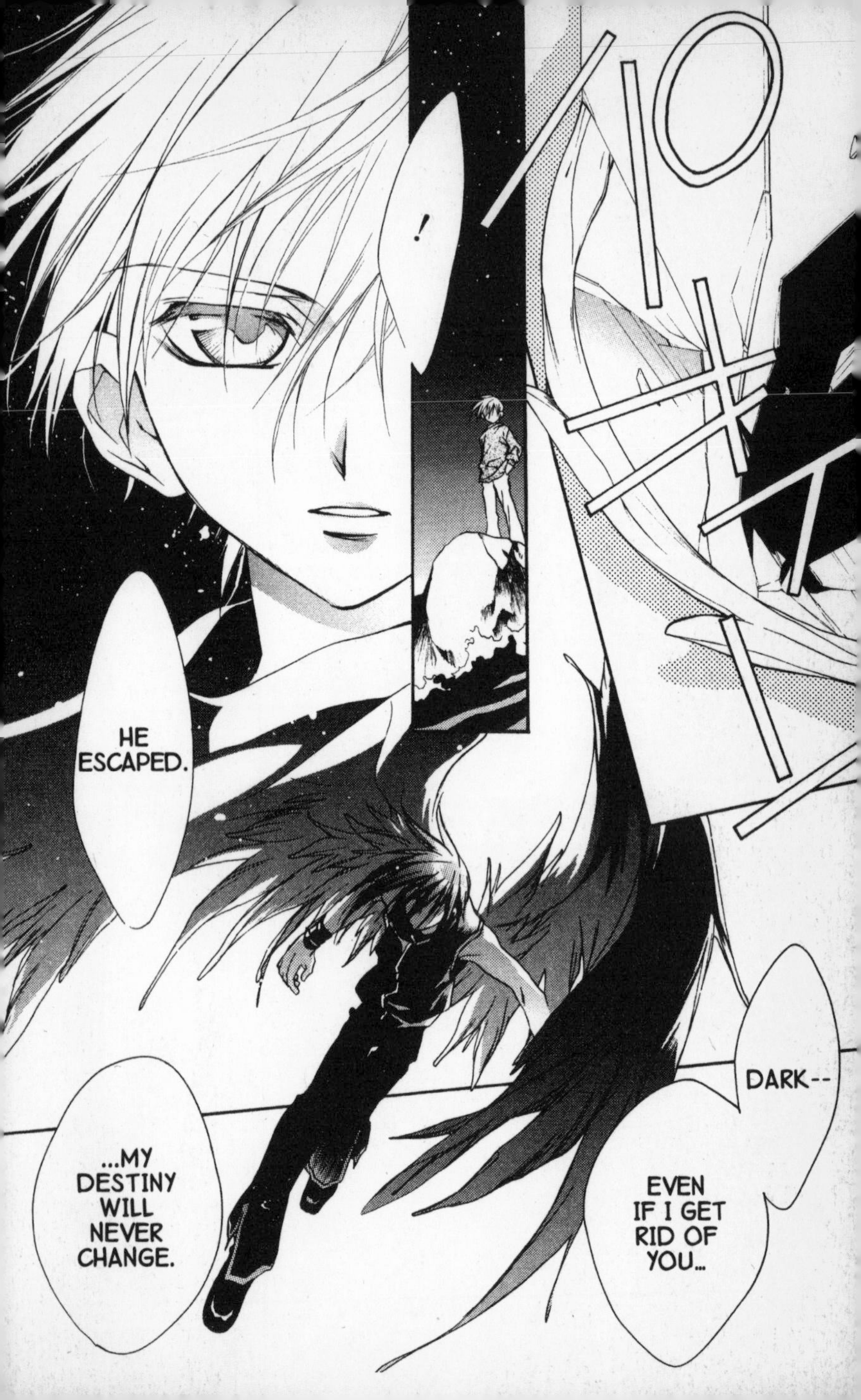
!
HE ESCAPED.
DARK--
EVEN IF I GET RID OF YOU...
...MY DESTINY WILL NEVER CHANGE.

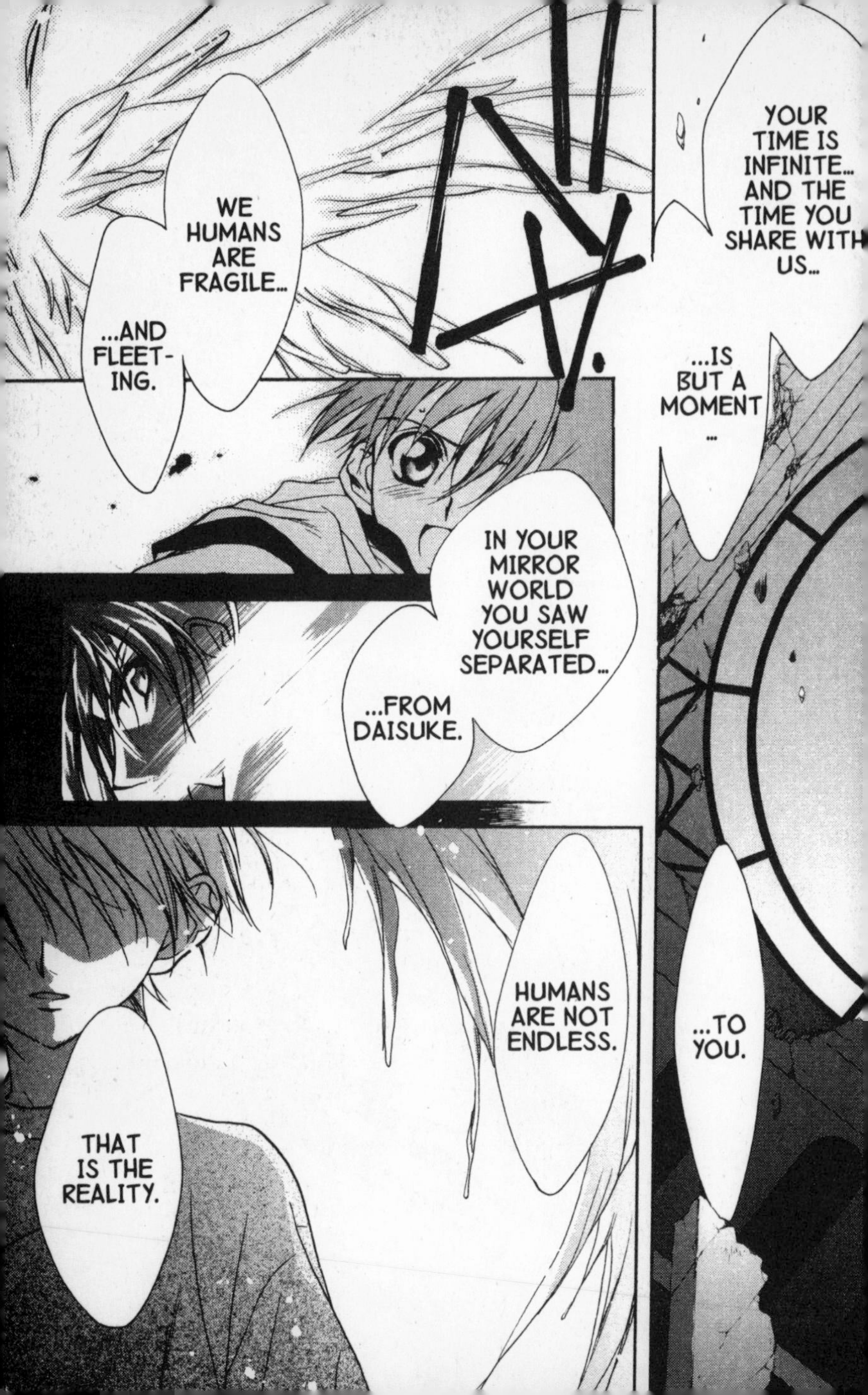
YOUR TIME IS INFINITE... AND THE TIME YOU SHARE WITH US...
...IS BUT A MOMENT...
...TO YOU.
WE HUMANS ARE FRAGILE...
...AND FLEET-ING.
IN YOUR MIRROR WORLD YOU SAW YOURSELF SEPARATED...
...FROM DAISUKE.
HUMANS ARE NOT ENDLESS.
THAT IS THE REALITY.

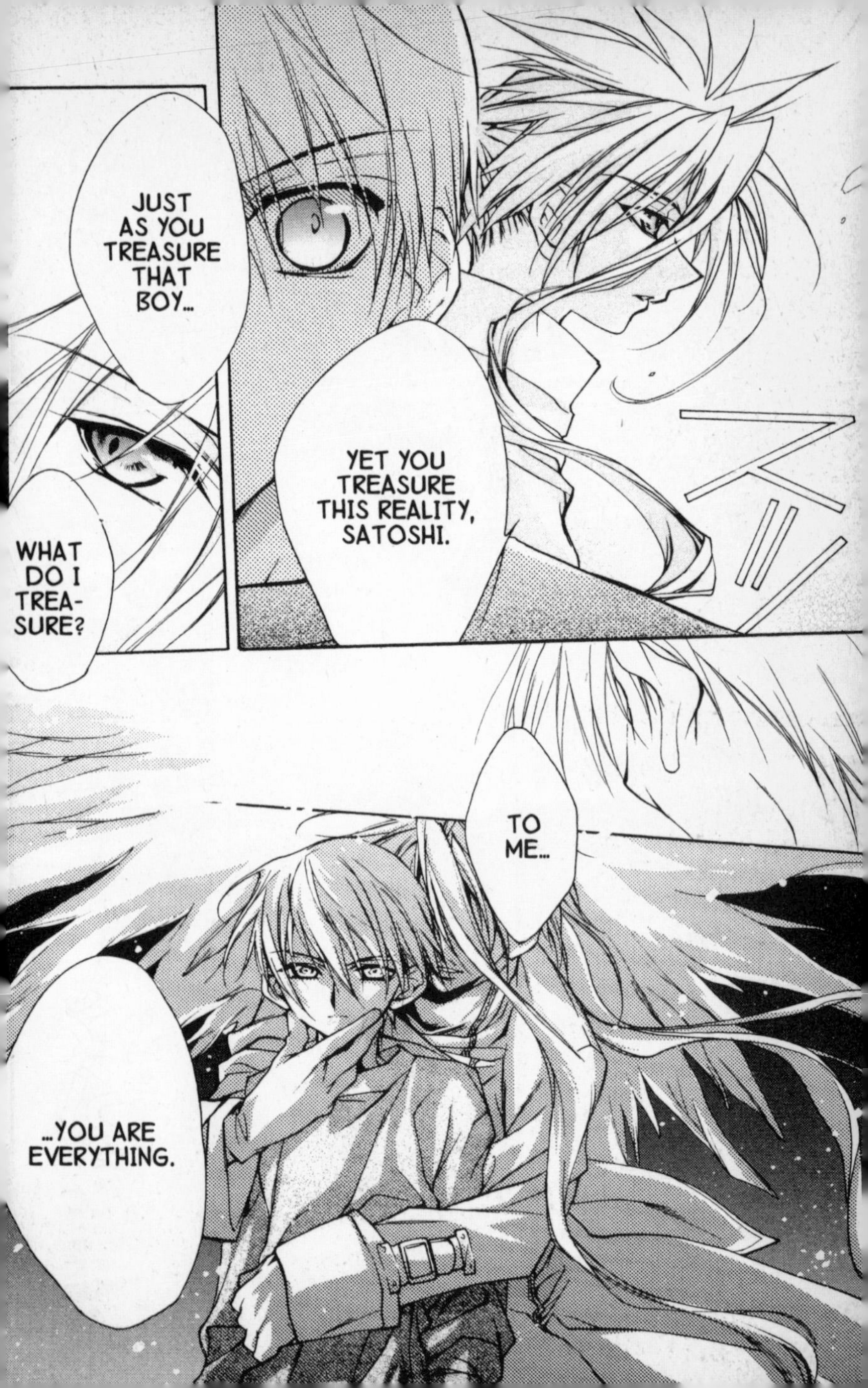
JUST AS YOU TREASURE THAT BOY...
YET YOU TREASURE THIS REALITY, SATOSHI.
WHAT DO I TREA-SURE?
TO ME...
...YOU ARE EVERYTHING.

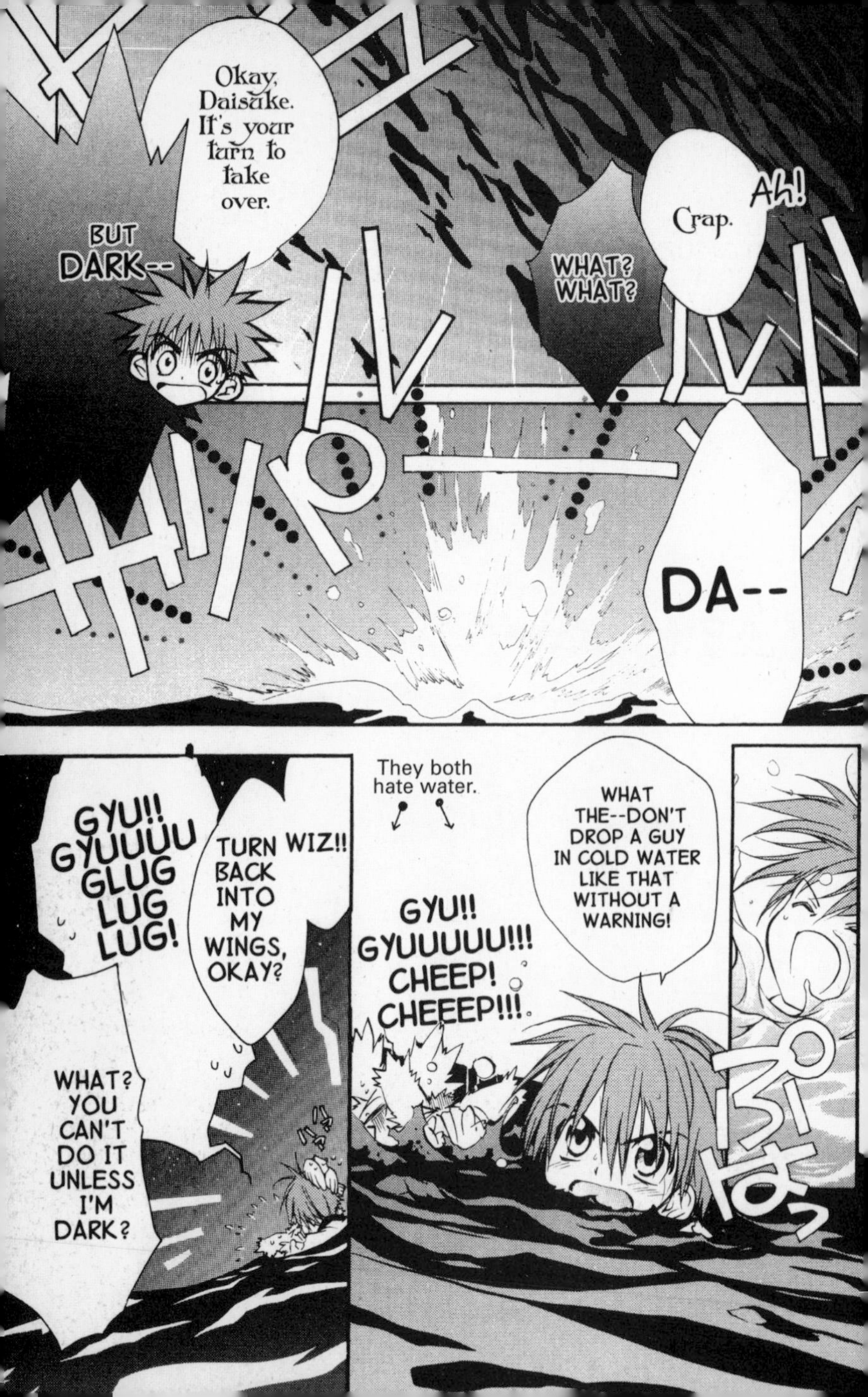
Ah! Crap.
WHAT? WHAT?
Okay, Daisuke. It's your turn to take over.
BUT DARK--
DA--
WHAT THE--DON'T DROP A GUY IN COLD WATER LIKE THAT WITHOUT A WARNING!
They both hate water.
GYU!! GYUUUUU!!! CHEEP! CHEEEP!!!
TURN WIZ!! BACK INTO MY WINGS, OKAY?
GYU!! GYUUUU GLUG LUG LUG!
WHAT? YOU CAN'T DO IT UNLESS I'M DARK?

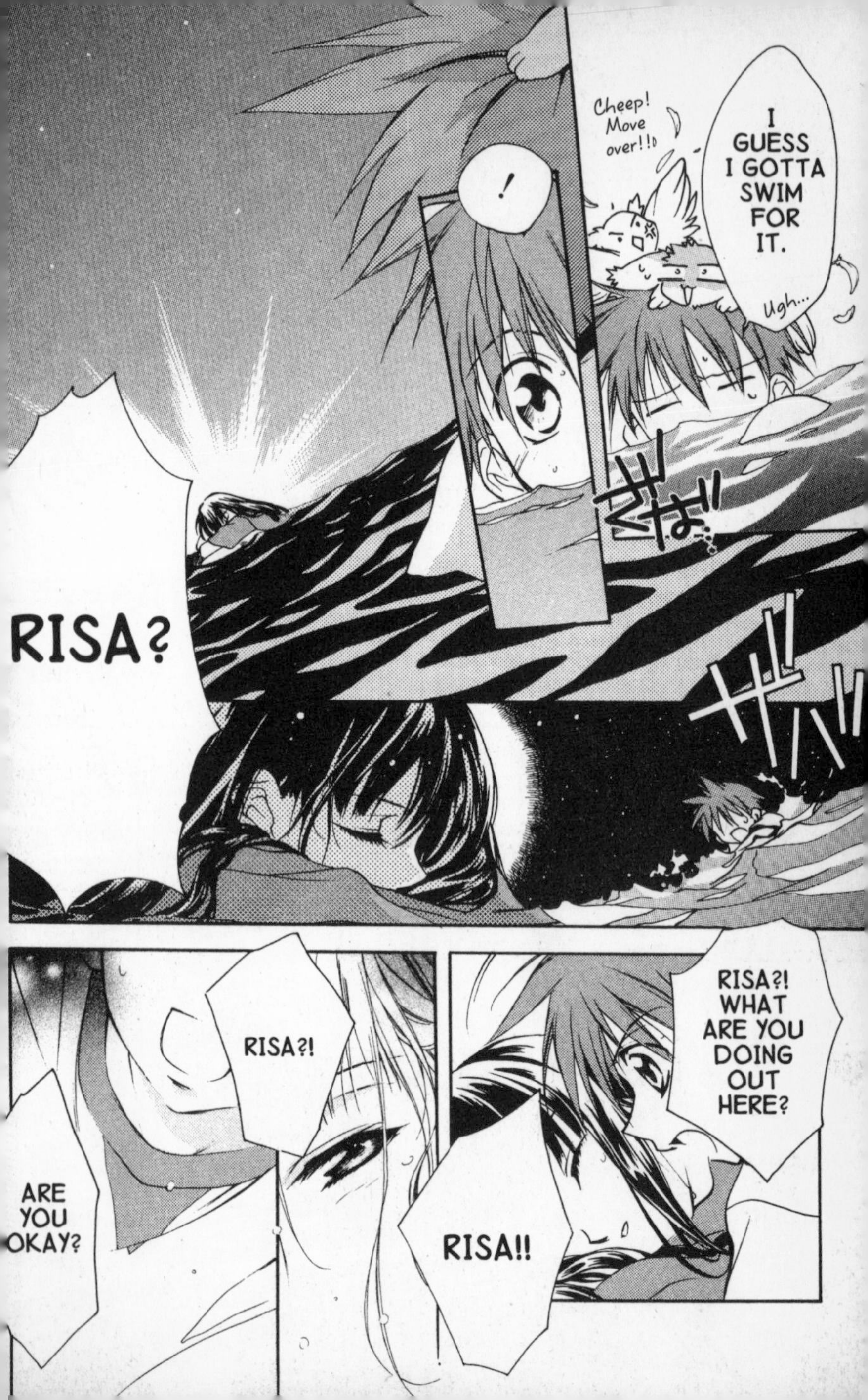
I GUESS I GOTTA SWIM FOR IT.
Ugh...
Cheep! Move over!!
!
RISA?
RISA?! WHAT ARE YOU DOING OUT HERE?
RISA!!
RISA?!
ARE YOU OKAY?

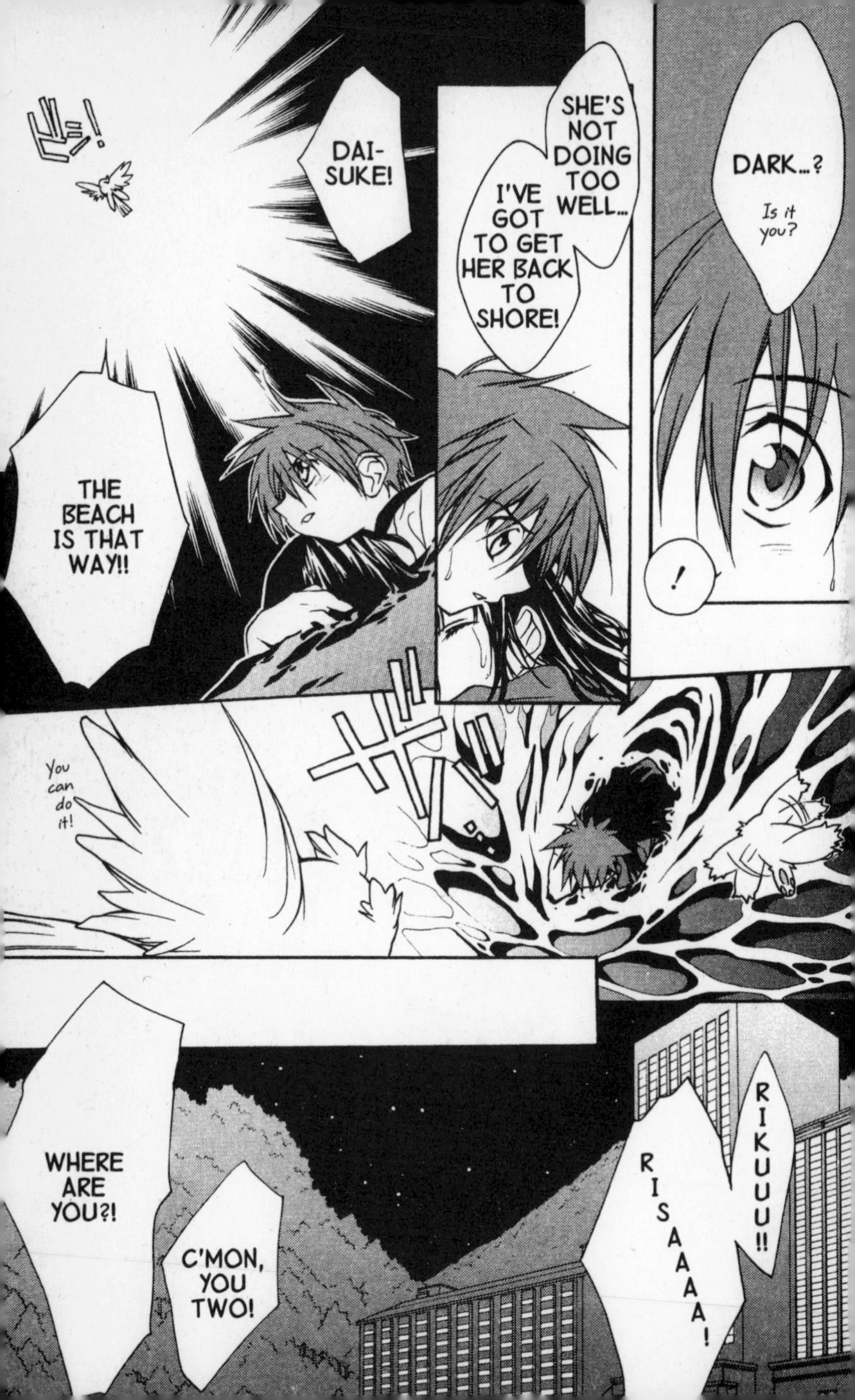
DARK...?
Is it you?
!
SHE'S NOT DOING TOO WELL...
I'VE GOT TO GET HER BACK TO SHORE!
DAI-SUKE!
THE BEACH IS THAT WAY!!
You can do it!
RIKUUU!!
RISAAAA!
WHERE ARE YOU?!
C'MON, YOU TWO!

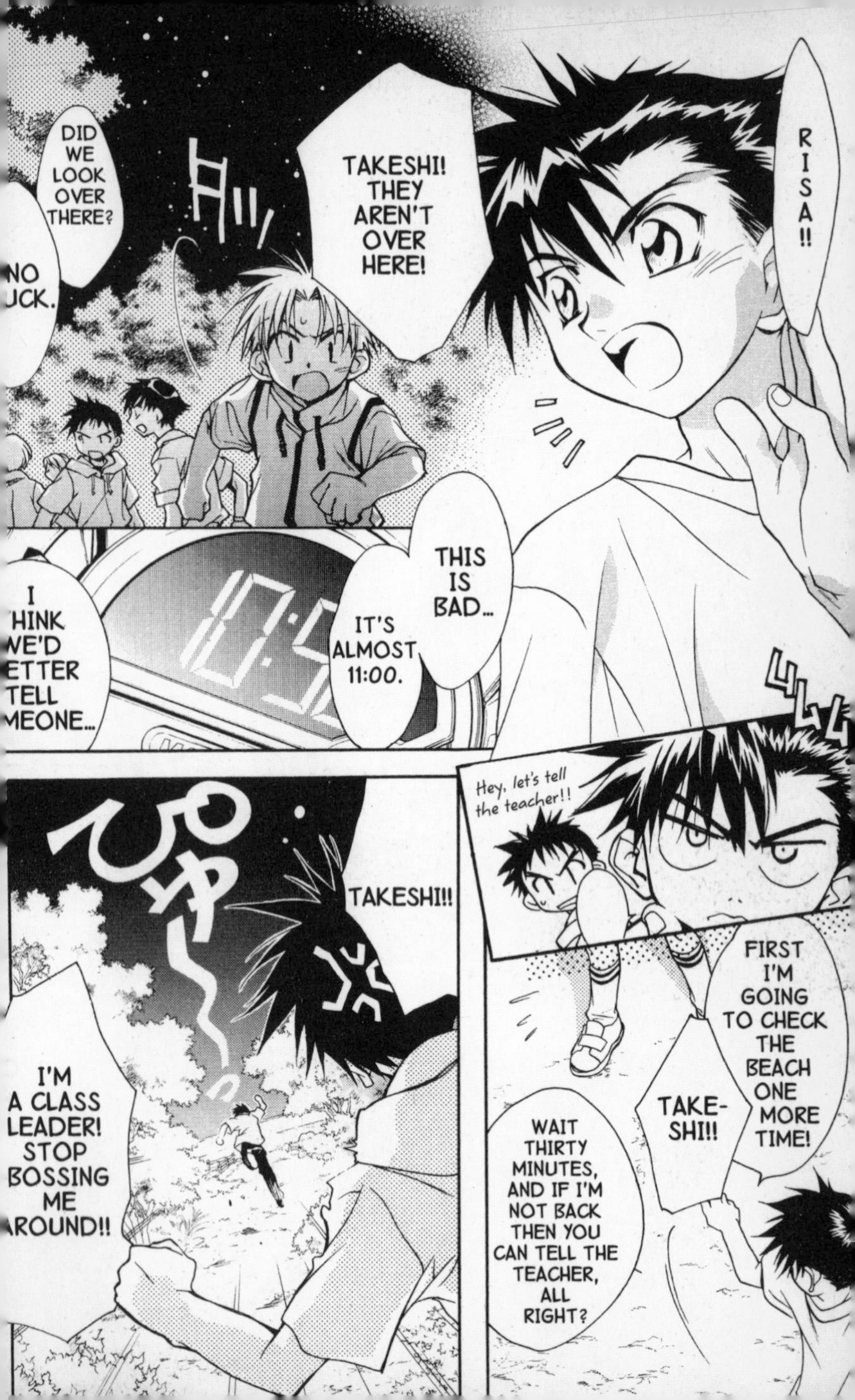
RISA!!
TAKESHI! THEY AREN'T OVER HERE!
DID WE LOOK OVER THERE?
NO UCK.
THIS IS BAD...
IT'S ALMOST 11:00.
I HINK WE'D ETTER TELL MEONE...
Hey, let's tell the teacher!!
FIRST I'M GOING TO CHECK THE BEACH ONE MORE TIME!
TAKE-SHI!!
WAIT THIRTY MINUTES, AND IF I'M NOT BACK THEN YOU CAN TELL THE TEACHER, ALL RIGHT?
TAKESHI!!
I'M A CLASS LEADER! STOP BOSSING ME ROUND!!

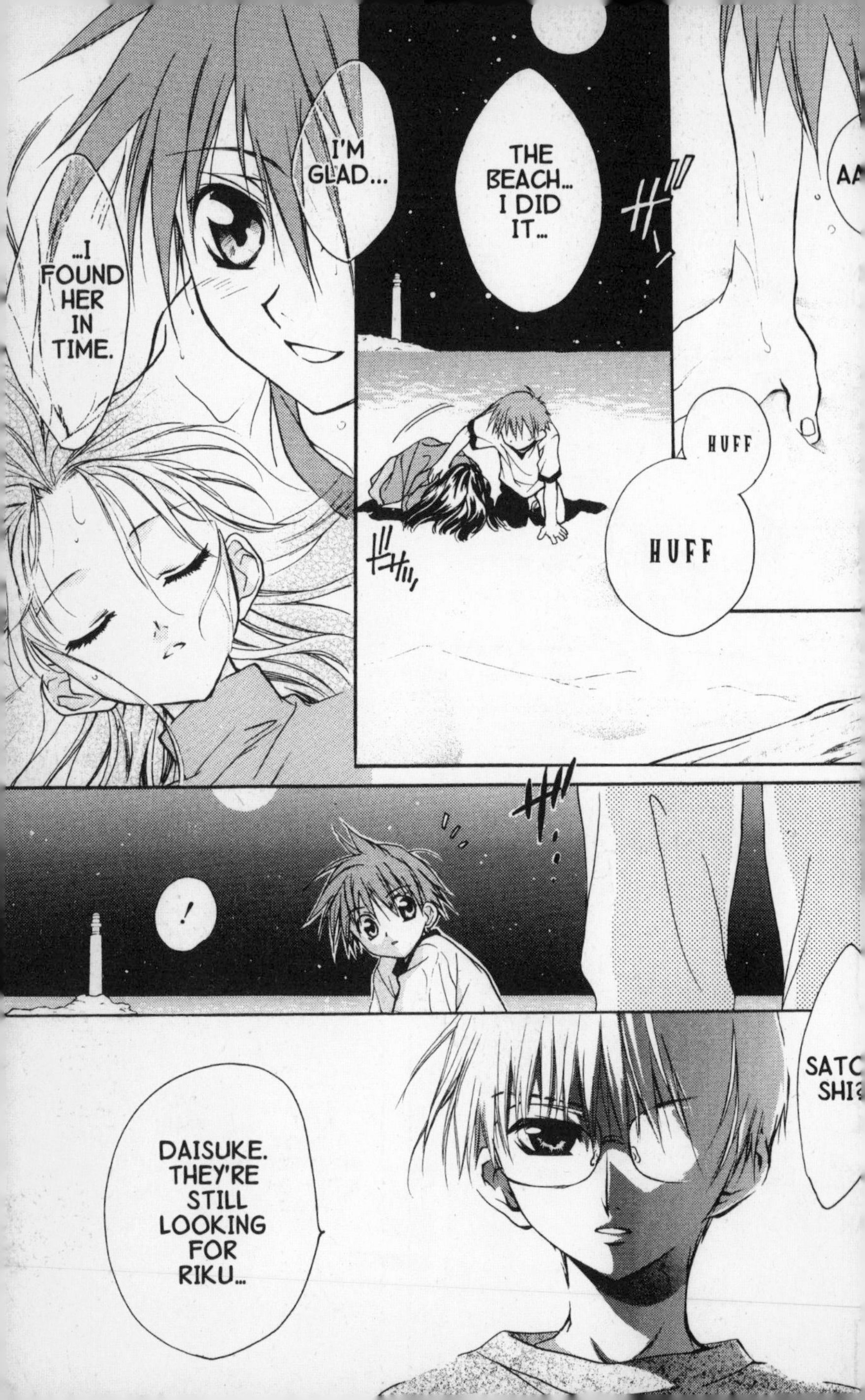
AA
HUFF
HUFF
THE BEACH... I DID IT...
I'M GLAD...
...I FOUND HER IN TIME.
!
SATOSHI?
DAISUKE. THEY'RE STILL LOOKING FOR RIKU...

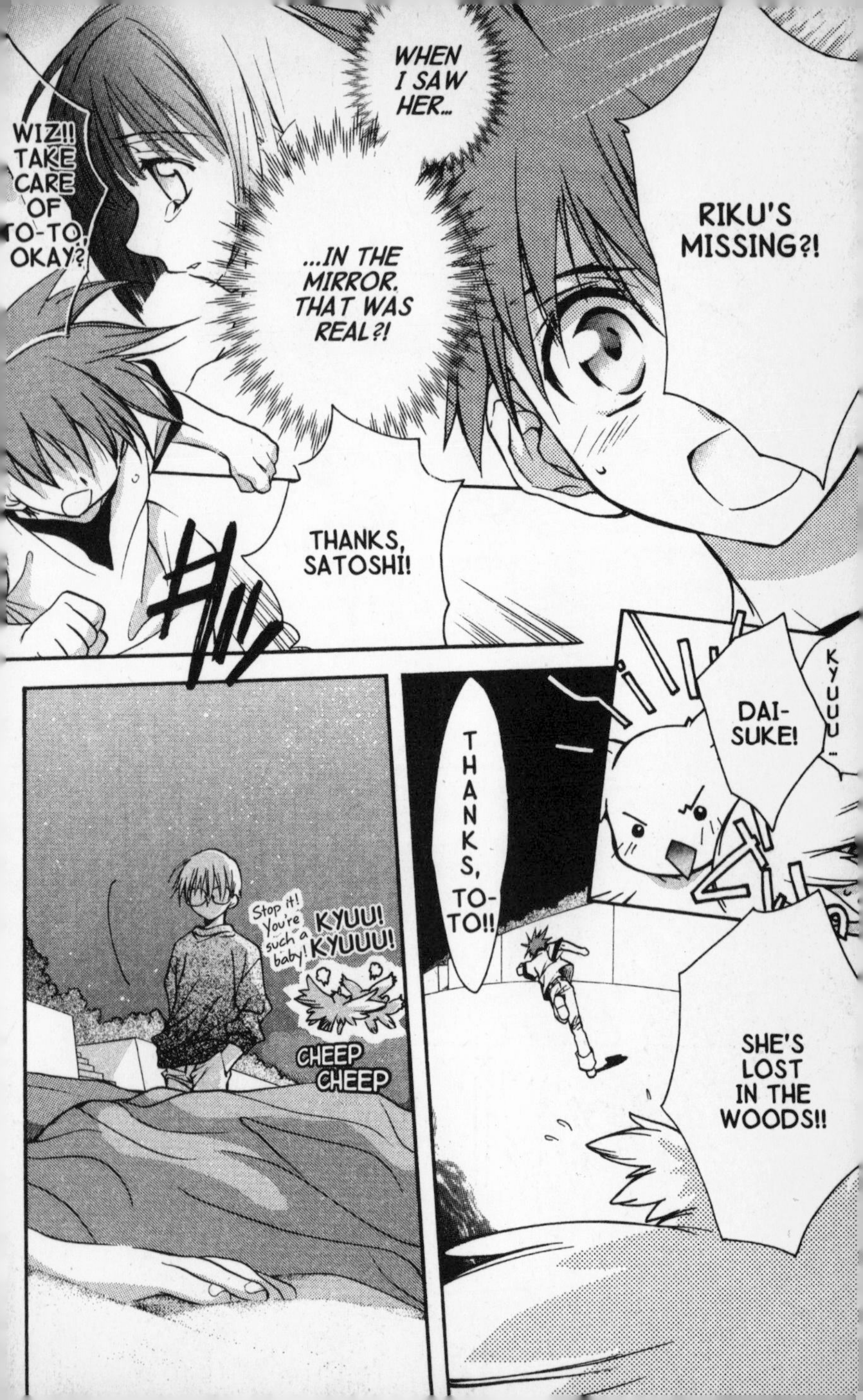
RIKU'S MISSING?!
WHEN I SAW HER...
...IN THE MIRROR. THAT WAS REAL?!
WIZ!! TAKE CARE OF TO-TO, OKAY?
THANKS, SATOSHI!
KYUUU...
DAI-SUKE!
SHE'S LOST IN THE WOODS!!
THANKS, TO-TO!!
KYUU! KYUUU!
Stop it! You're such a baby!
CHEEP CHEEP

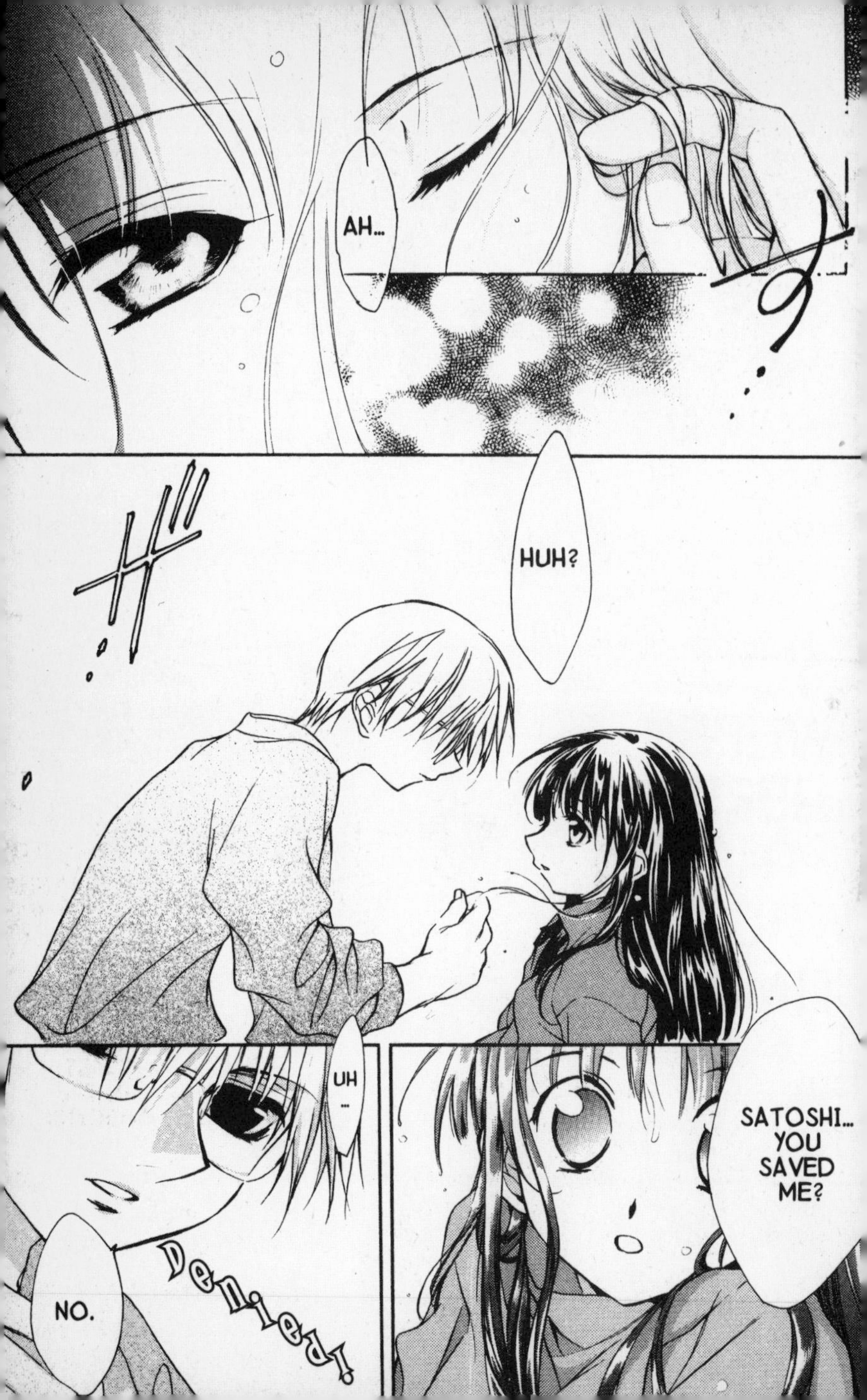
AH...
HUH?
SATOSHI... YOU SAVED ME?
UH...
NO.
Denied!

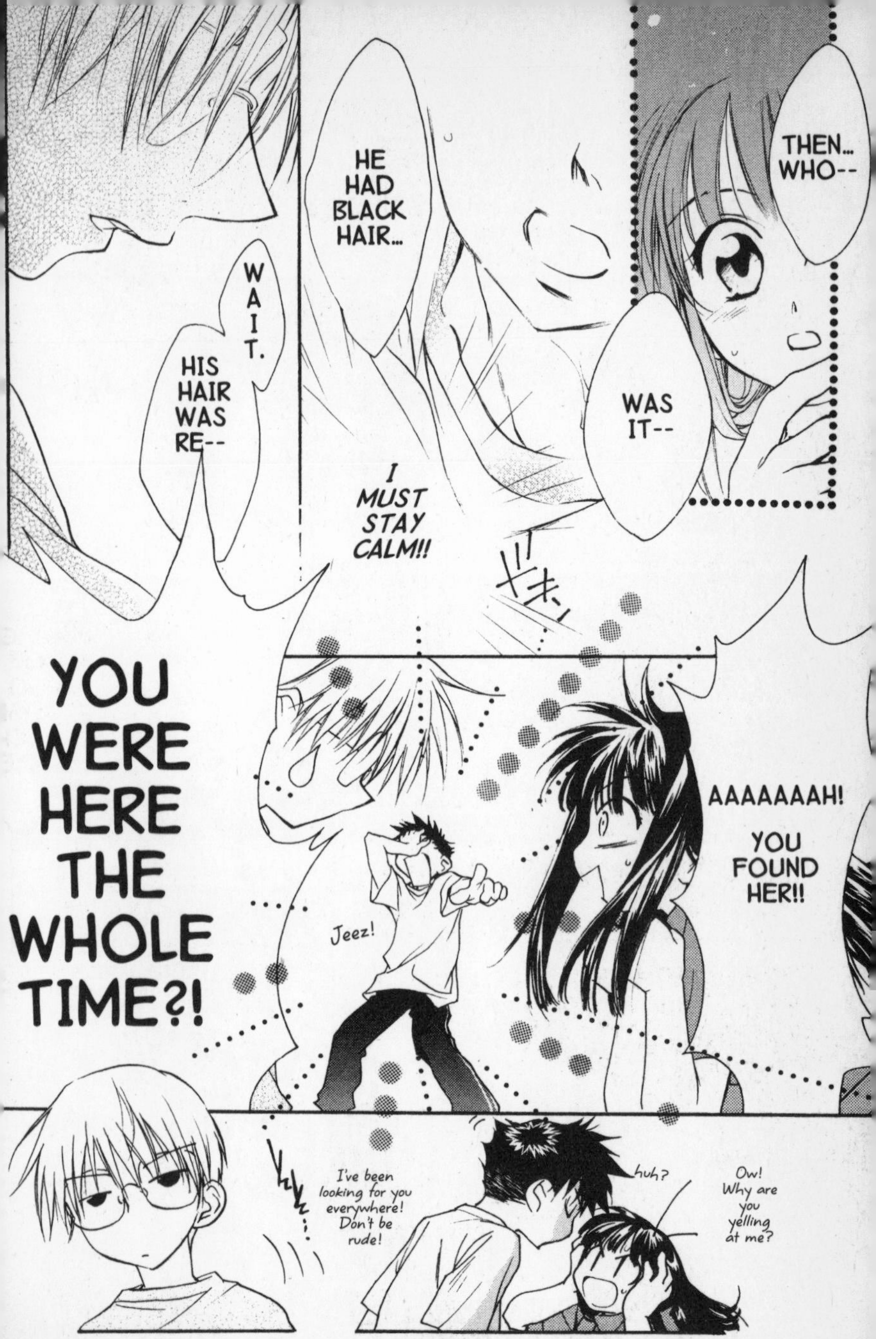
THEN... WHO--
WAS IT--
HE HAD BLACK HAIR...
I MUST STAY CALM!!
WAIT.
HIS HAIR WAS RE--
AAAAAAAH!
YOU FOUND HER!!
YOU WERE HERE THE WHOLE TIME?!
Jeez!
Ow! Why are you yelling at me?
huh?
I've been looking for you everywhere! Don't be rude!

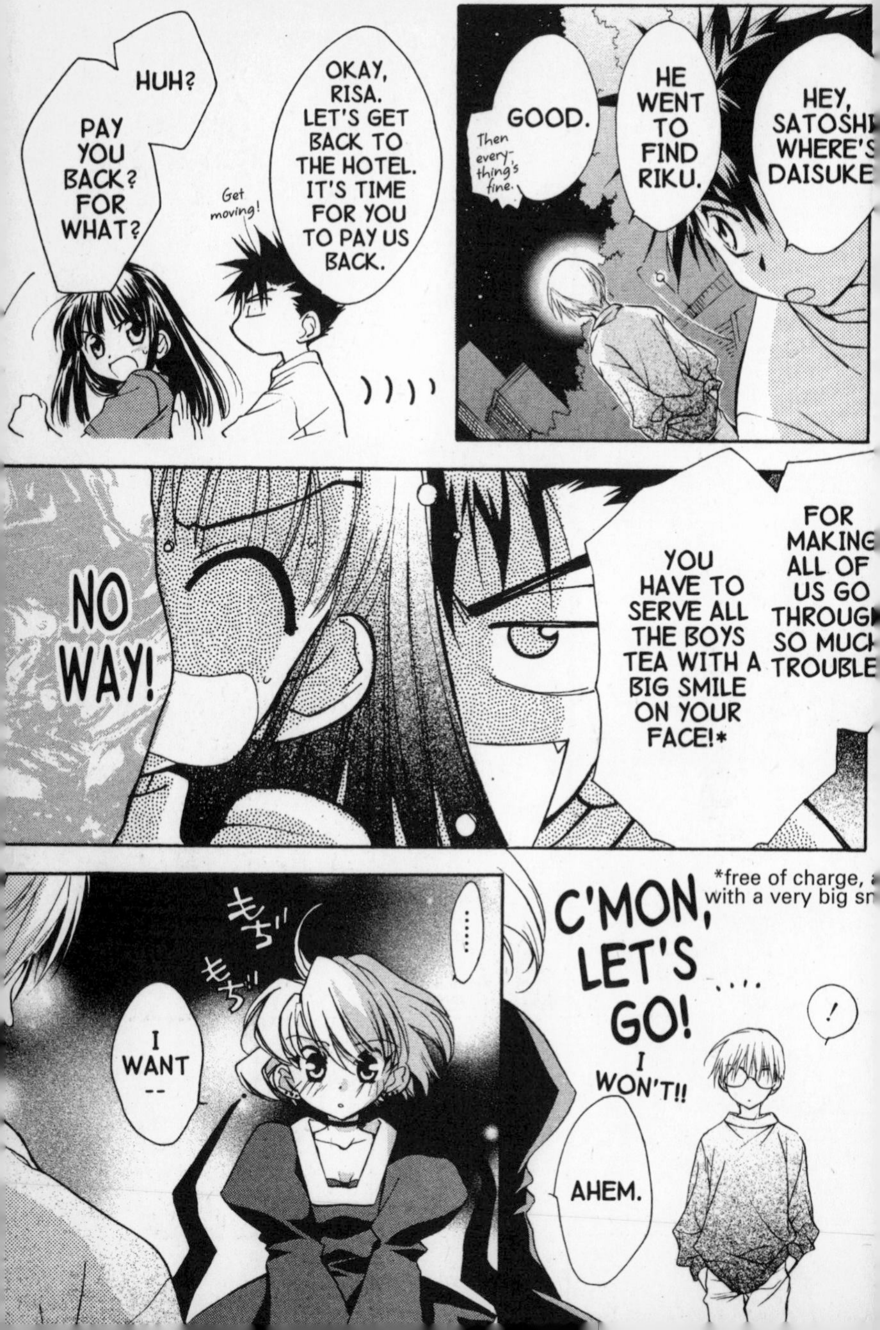

HEY, SATOSHI WHERE'S DAISUKE
HE WENT TO FIND RIKU.
GOOD.
Then every-thing's fine.
OKAY, RISA. LET'S GET BACK TO THE HOTEL. IT'S TIME FOR YOU TO PAY US BACK.
Get moving!
HUH?
PAY YOU BACK? FOR WHAT?
FOR MAKING ALL OF US GO THROUG SO MUCH TROUBLE
YOU HAVE TO SERVE ALL THE BOYS TEA WITH A BIG SMILE ON YOUR FACE!*
NO WAY!
*free of charge, a with a very big sm
C'MON, LET'S GO!
I WON'T!!
....
!
AHEM.
......
もぢ もぢ
I WANT --

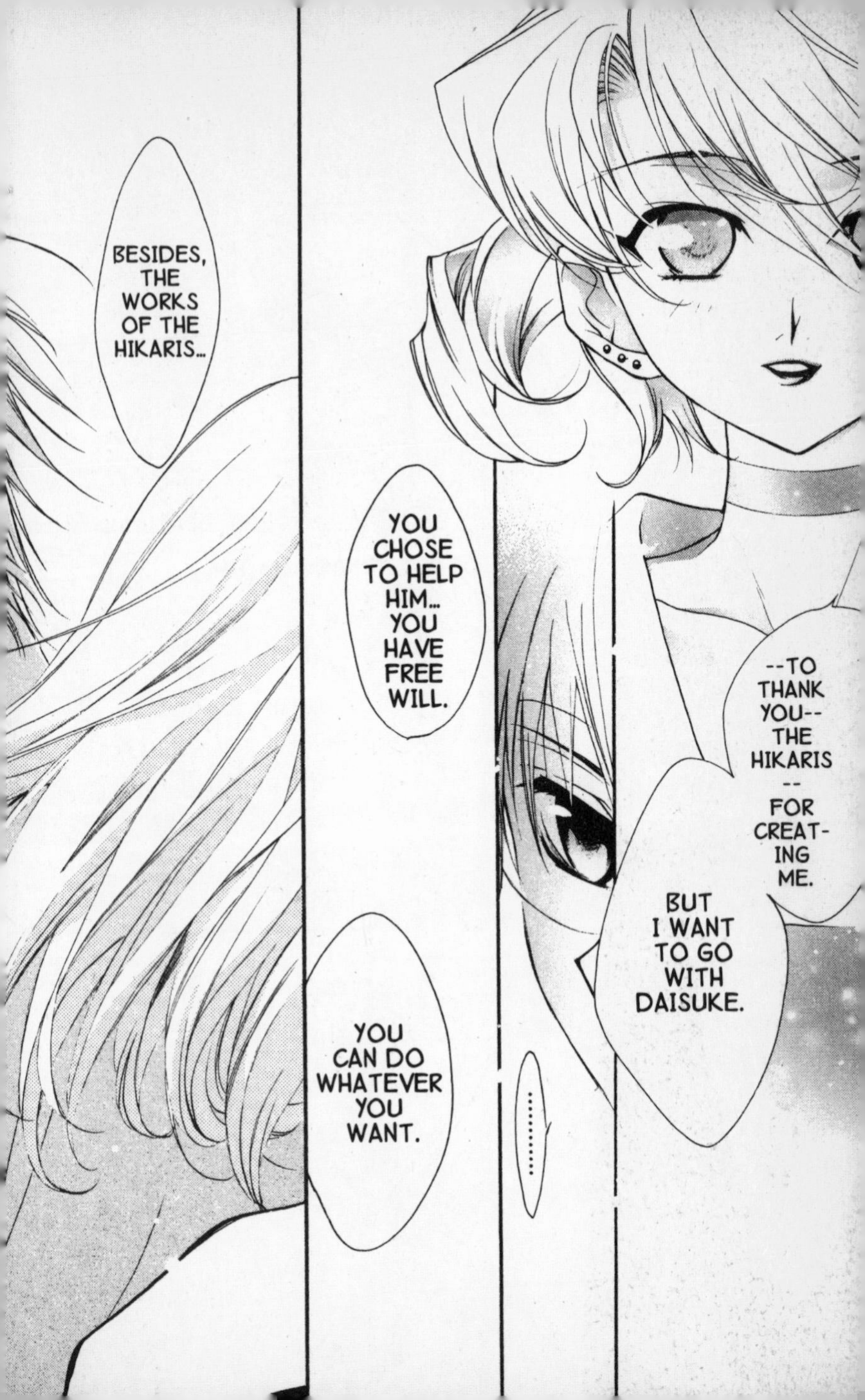
--TO THANK YOU-- THE HIKARIS -- FOR CREATING ME.
BUT I WANT TO GO WITH DAISUKE.
......
YOU CHOSE TO HELP HIM... YOU HAVE FREE WILL.
YOU CAN DO WHATEVER YOU WANT.
BESIDES, THE WORKS OF THE HIKARIS...

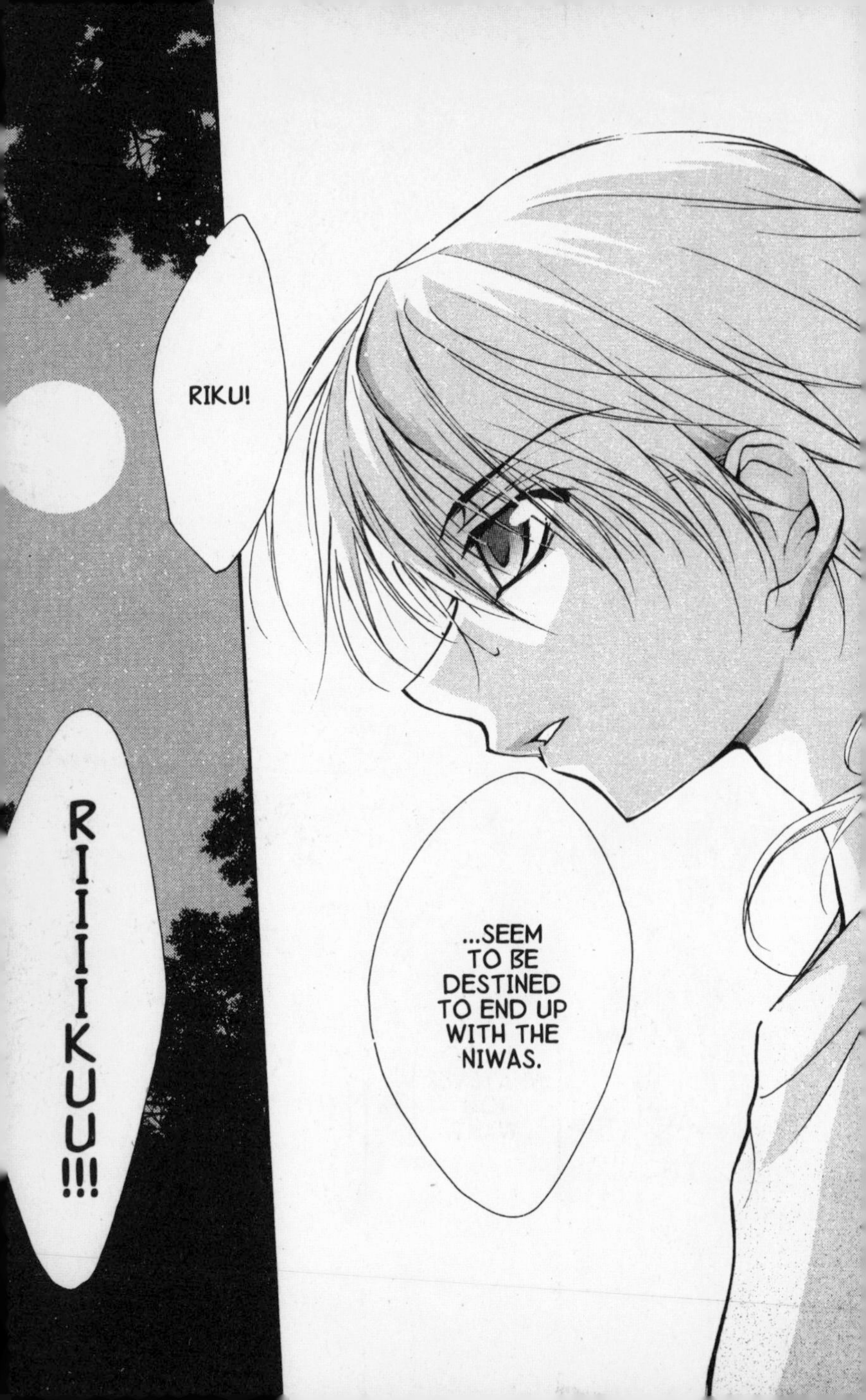
...SEEM TO BE DESTINED TO END UP WITH THE NIWAS.
RIKU!
RIIIIKUU!!!

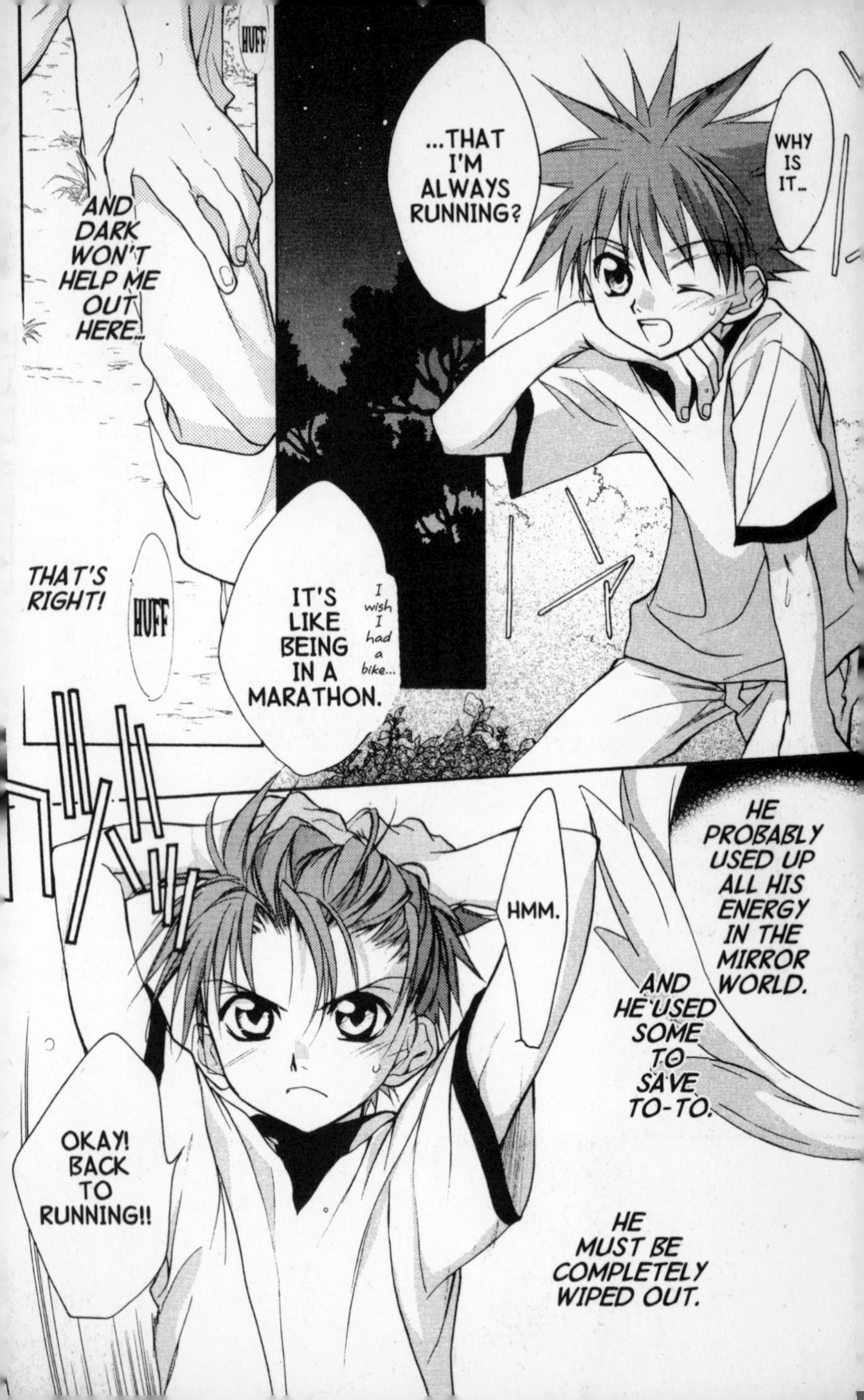
WHY IS IT...
...THAT I'M ALWAYS RUNNING?
IT'S LIKE BEING IN A MARATHON.
I wish I had a bike...
HUFF
AND DARK WON'T HELP ME OUT HERE...
HUFF
THAT'S RIGHT!
HE PROBABLY USED UP ALL HIS ENERGY IN THE MIRROR WORLD.
AND HE USED SOME TO SAVE TO-TO.
HMM.
HE MUST BE COMPLETELY WIPED OUT.
OKAY! BACK TO RUNNING!!

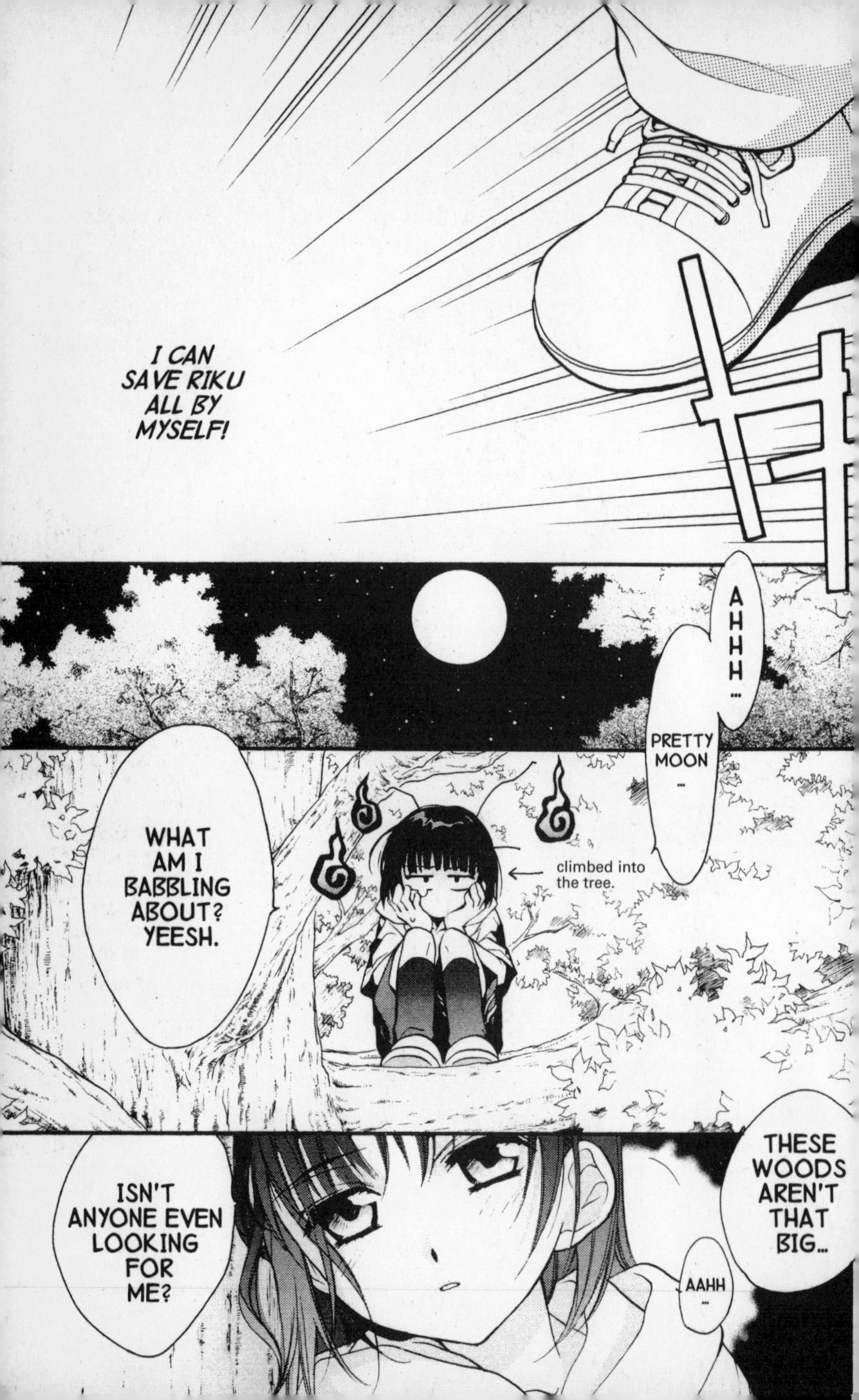
I CAN SAVE RIKU ALL BY MYSELF!
AHHH...
PRETTY MOON...
climbed into the tree.
WHAT AM I BABBLING ABOUT? YEESH.
THESE WOODS AREN'T THAT BIG...
AAHH...
ISN'T ANYONE EVEN LOOKING FOR ME?

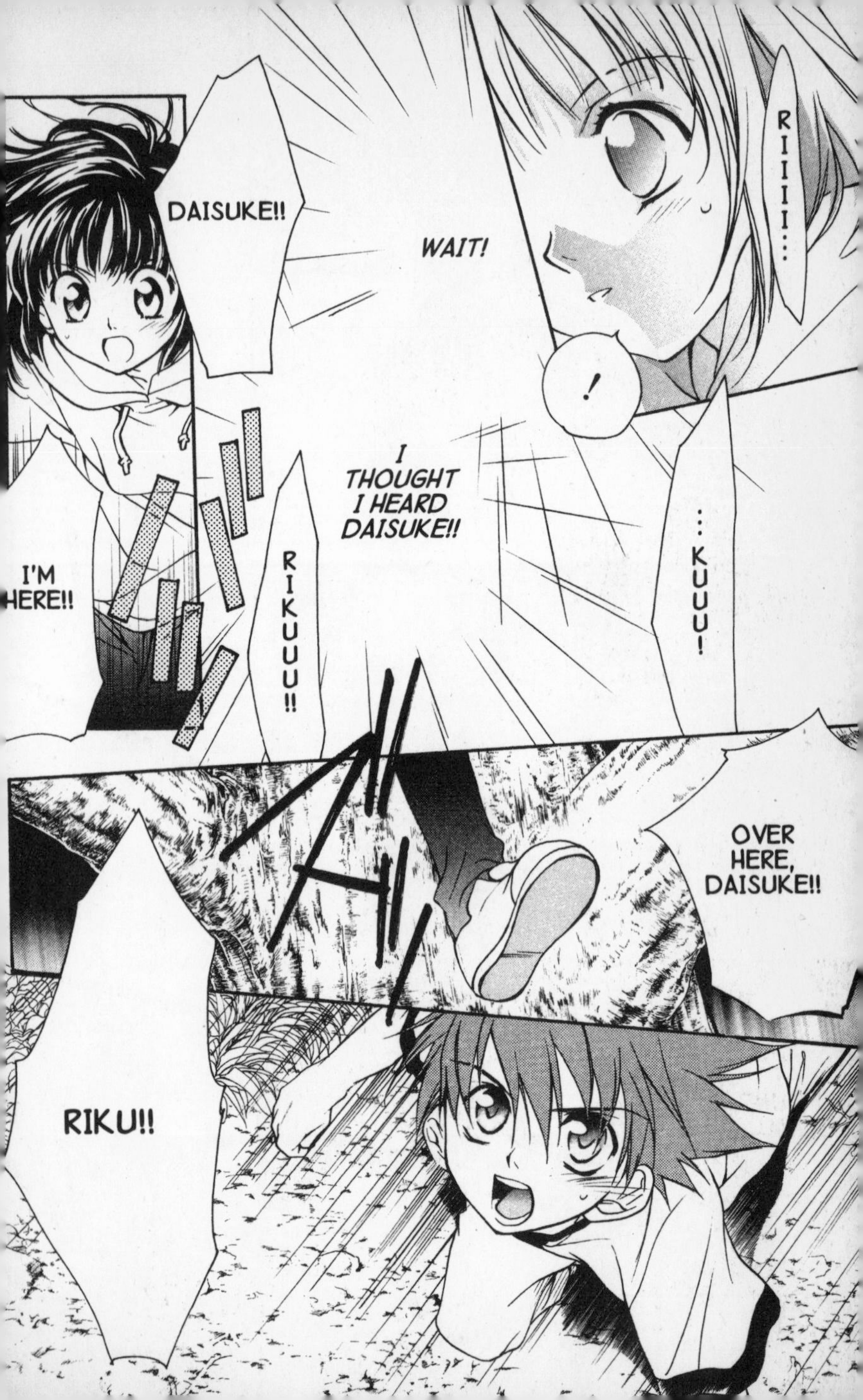
RIIII...
!
WAIT!
...KUUU!
I THOUGHT I HEARD DAISUKE!!
RIKUUU!!
DAISUKE!!
I'M HERE!!
OVER HERE, DAISUKE!!
RIKU!!

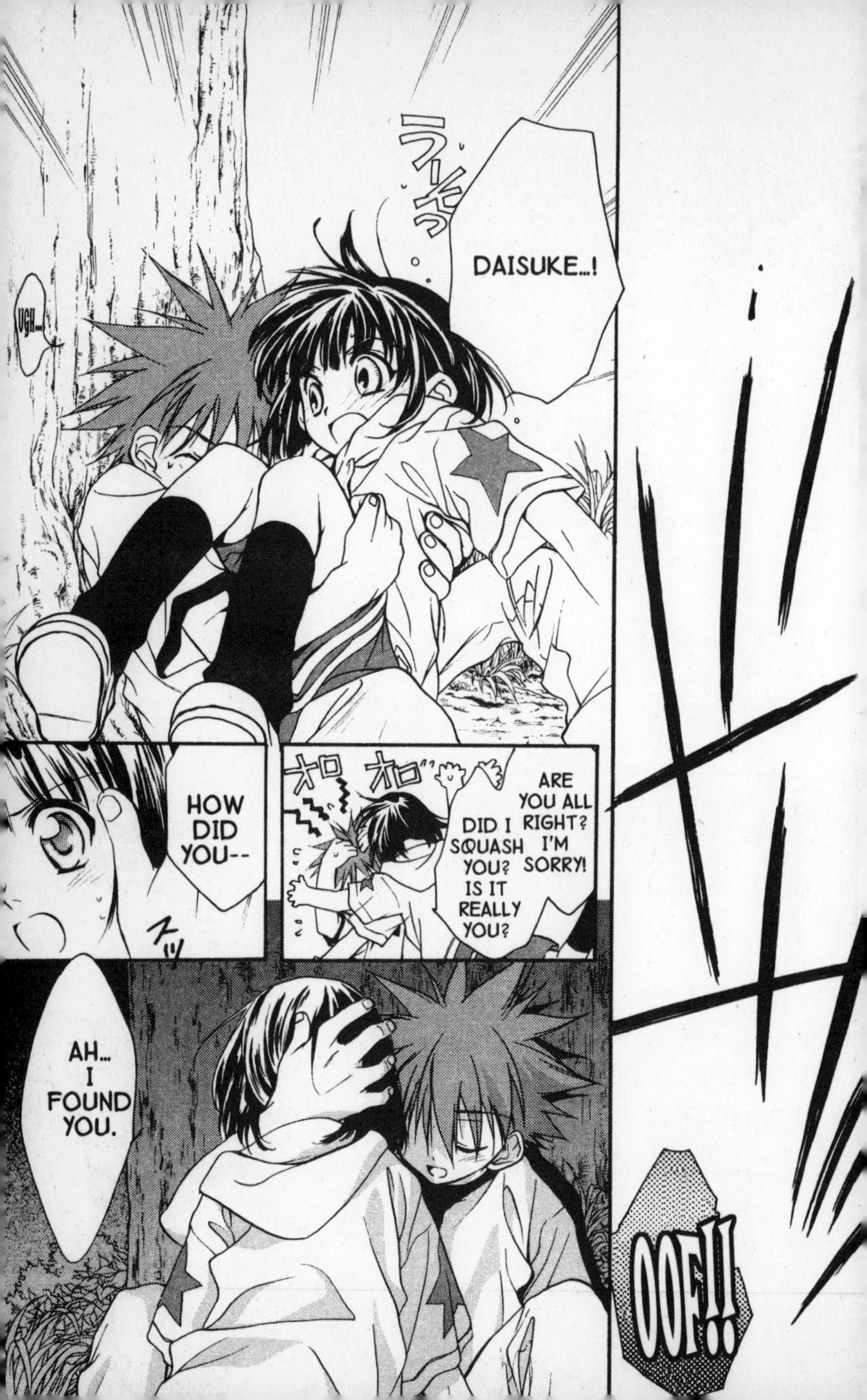
OOF!!
DAISUKE...!
UGH...
オロオロ
ARE YOU ALL RIGHT? I'M SORRY!
DID I SQUASH YOU? IS IT REALLY YOU?
HOW DID YOU--
スッ
AH... I FOUND YOU.

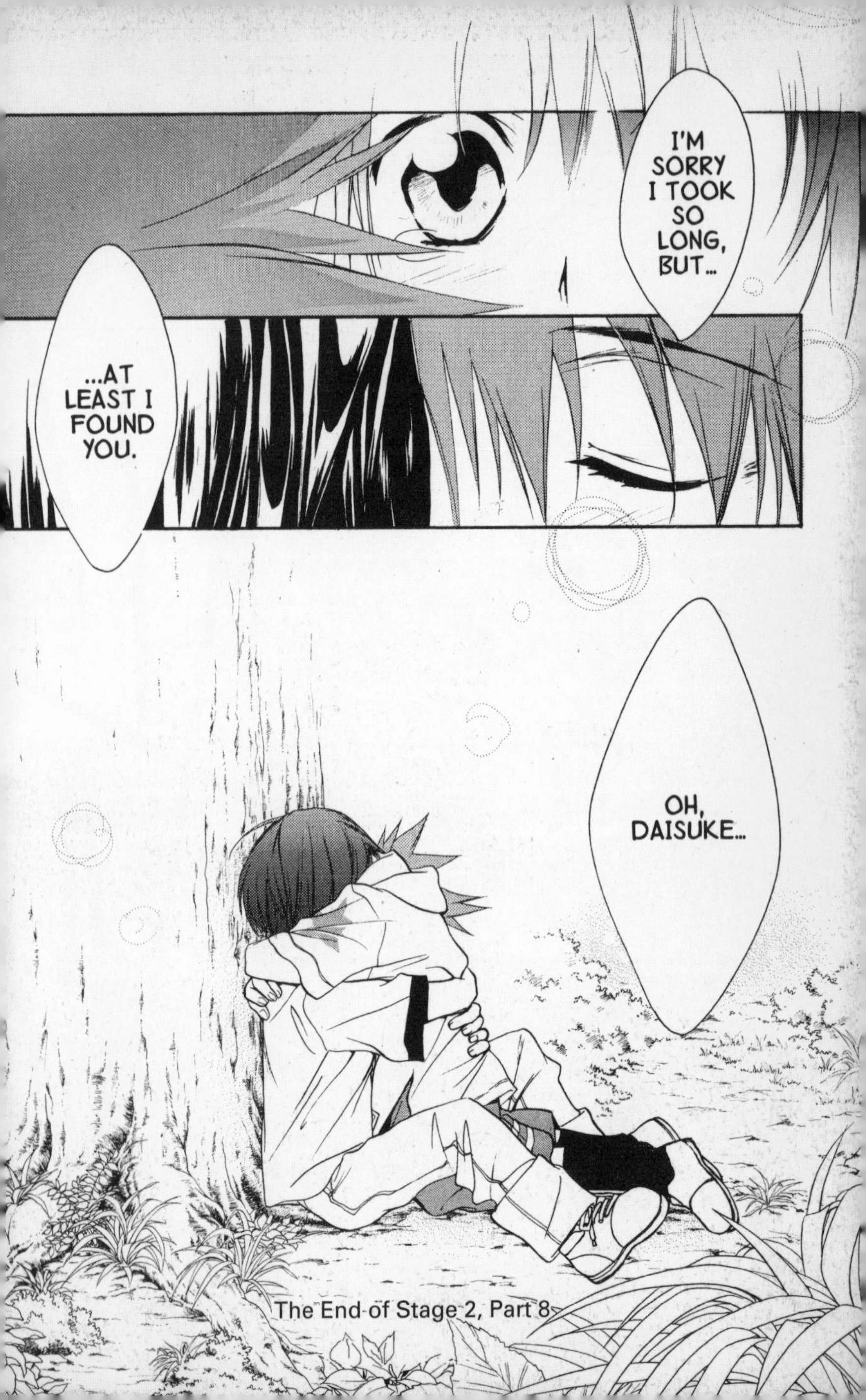
I'M SORRY I TOOK SO LONG, BUT...
...AT LEAST I FOUND YOU.
OH, DAISUKE...
The End of Stage 2, Part 8

D•N•ANGEL
THINGS TO COME...

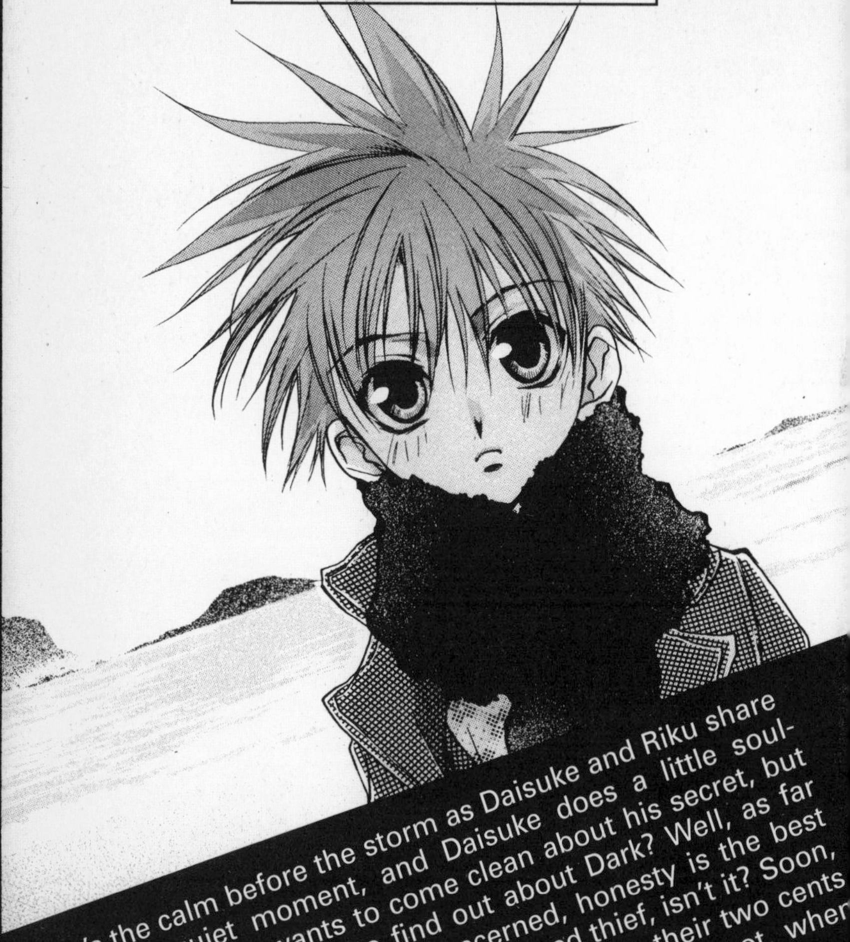

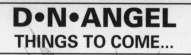

It's the calm before the storm as Daisuke and Riku share a rare quiet moment, and Daisuke does a little soul-searching. He wants to come clean about his secret, but is Riku really ready to find out about Dark? Well, as far as the Phantom Thief is concerned, honesty is the best policy—a bit odd for a self-professed thief, isn't it? Soon, the entire Niwa clan is on hand to put in their two cents on the subject—one that quickly becomes moot, when "Killer" Krad makes a frightening reappearance!

Be here for D•N•Angel Volume 6!
Hey! Come on, guys!!

ALSO AVAILABLE FROM TOKYOPOP®

MANGA

.HACK//LEGEND OF THE TWILIGHT
@LARGE
ABENOBASHI: MAGICAL SHOPPING ARCADE
A.I. LOVE YOU
AI YORI AOSHI
ALICHINO
ANGELIC LAYER
ARM OF KANNON
BABY BIRTH
BATTLE ROYALE
BATTLE VIXENS
BOYS BE...
BRAIN POWERED
BRIGADOON
B'TX
CANDIDATE FOR GODDESS, THE
CARDCAPTOR SAKURA
CARDCAPTOR SAKURA - MASTER OF THE CLOW
CHOBITS
CHRONICLES OF THE CURSED SWORD
CLAMP SCHOOL DETECTIVES
CLOVER
COMIC PARTY
CONFIDENTIAL CONFESSIONS
CORRECTOR YUI
COWBOY BEBOP
COWBOY BEBOP: SHOOTING STAR
CRAZY LOVE STORY
CRESCENT MOON
CROSS
CULDCEPT
CYBORG 009
D•N•ANGEL
DEARS
DEMON DIARY
DEMON ORORON, THE
DEUS VITAE
DIGIMON
DIGIMON TAMERS
DIGIMON ZERO TWO
DOLL
DRAGON HUNTER
DRAGON KNIGHTS
DRAGON VOICE
DREAM SAGA
DUKLYON: CLAMP SCHOOL DEFENDERS
EERIE QUEERIE!
ERICA SAKURAZAWA: COLLECTED WORKS
ET CETERA
ETERNITY
EVIL'S RETURN
FAERIES' LANDING
FAKE
FLCL
FLOWER OF THE DEEP SLEEP, THE
FORBIDDEN DANCE
FRUITS BASKET

G GUNDAM
GATEKEEPERS
GETBACKERS
GIRL GOT GAME
GRAVITATION
GTO
GUNDAM SEED ASTRAY
GUNDAM WING
GUNDAM WING: BATTLEFIELD OF PACIFISTS
GUNDAM WING: ENDLESS WALTZ
GUNDAM WING: THE LAST OUTPOST (G-UNIT)
HANDS OFF!
HAPPY MANIA
HARLEM BEAT
HYPER RUNE
I.N.V.U.
IMMORTAL RAIN
INITIAL D
INSTANT TEEN: JUST ADD NUTS
ISLAND
JING: KING OF BANDITS
JING: KING OF BANDITS - TWILIGHT TALES
JULINE
KARE KANO
KILL ME, KISS ME
KINDAICHI CASE FILES, THE
KING OF HELL
KODOCHA: SANA'S STAGE
LAMENT OF THE LAMB
LEGAL DRUG
LEGEND OF CHUN HYANG, THE
LES BIJOUX
LOVE HINA
LOVE OR MONEY
LUPIN III
LUPIN III: WORLD'S MOST WANTED
MAGIC KNIGHT RAYEARTH I
MAGIC KNIGHT RAYEARTH II
MAHOROMATIC: AUTOMATIC MAIDEN
MAN OF MANY FACES
MARMALADE BOY
MARS
MARS: HORSE WITH NO NAME
MINK
MIRACLE GIRLS
MIYUKI-CHAN IN WONDERLAND
MODEL
MOURYOU KIDEN: LEGEND OF THE NYMPHS
NECK AND NECK
ONE
ONE I LOVE, THE
PARADISE KISS
PARASYTE
PASSION FRUIT
PEACH GIRL
PEACH GIRL: CHANGE OF HEART
PET SHOP OF HORRORS
PITA-TEN
PLANET LADDER

08.20.04

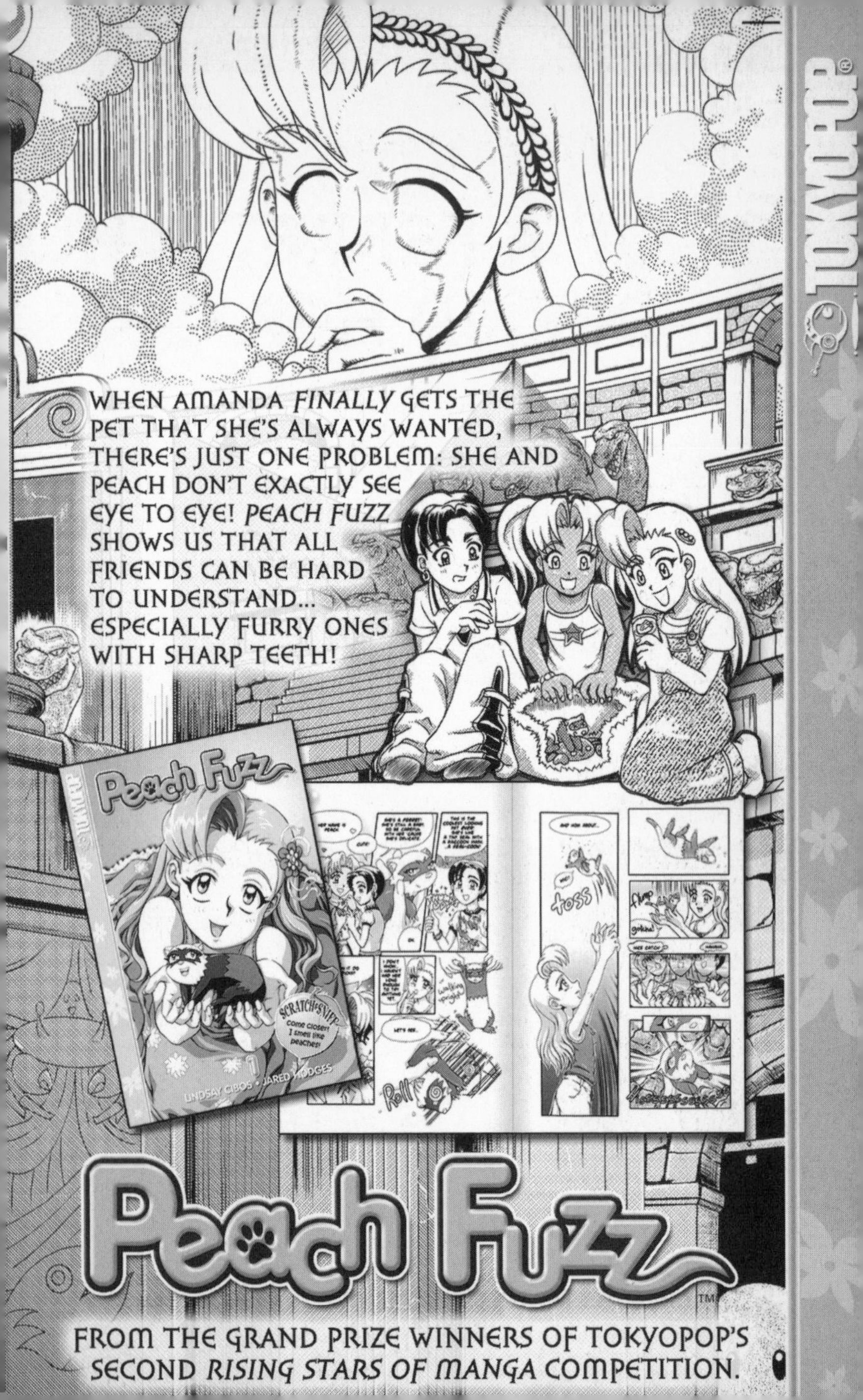

TOKYOPOP®
WHEN AMANDA *FINALLY* GETS THE PET THAT SHE'S ALWAYS WANTED, THERE'S JUST ONE PROBLEM: SHE AND PEACH DON'T EXACTLY SEE EYE TO EYE! *PEACH FUZZ* SHOWS US THAT ALL FRIENDS CAN BE HARD TO UNDERSTAND... ESPECIALLY FURRY ONES WITH SHARP TEETH!
Peach Fuzz
SCRATCH & SNIFF
Come closer! I smell like peaches!
1
LINDSAY CIBOS • JARED HODGES
toss
Roll
Peach Fuzz™
FROM THE GRAND PRIZE WINNERS OF TOKYOPOP'S SECOND *RISING STARS OF MANGA* COMPETITION.

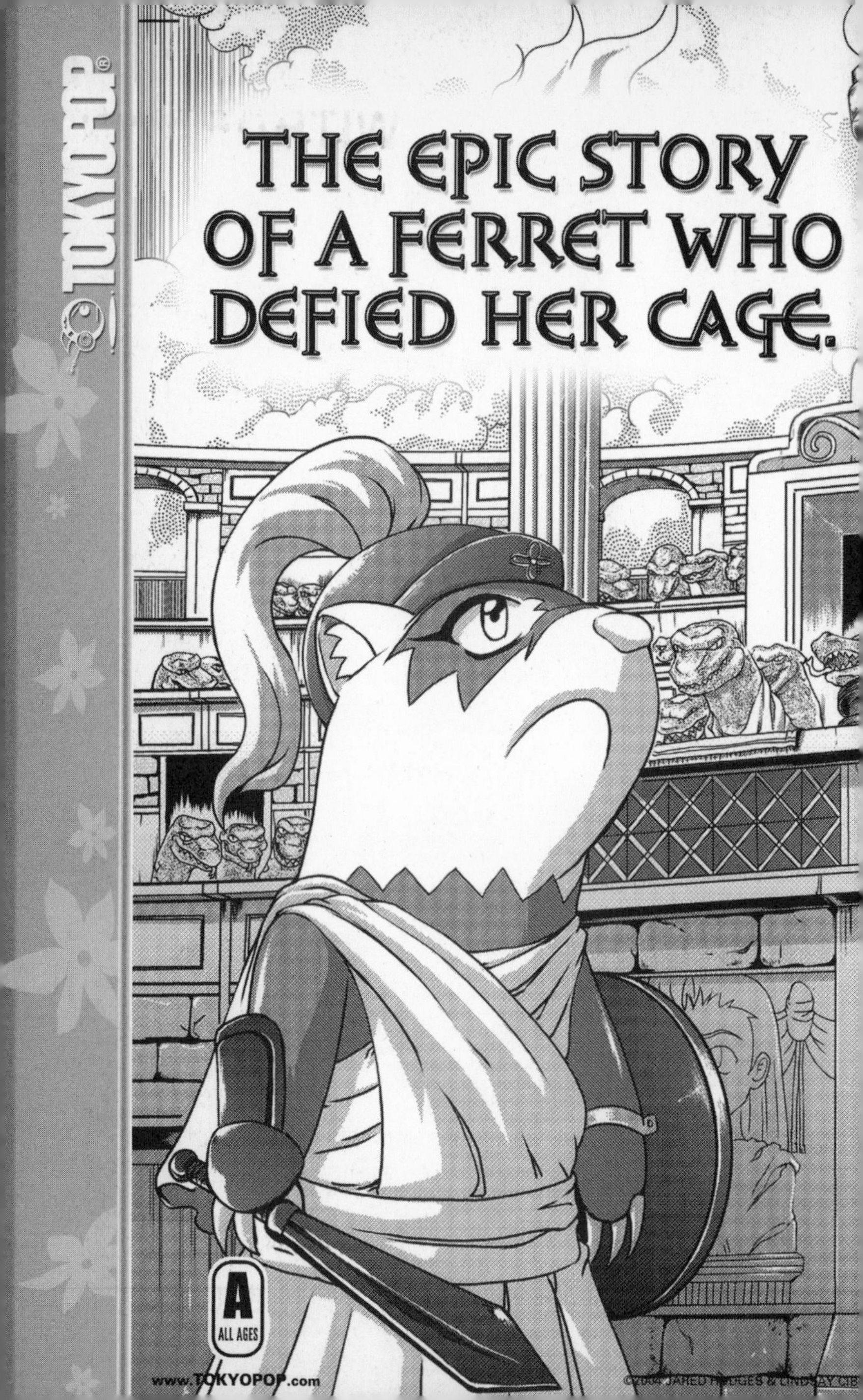
TOKYOPOP®
THE EPIC STORY OF A FERRET WHO DEFIED HER CAGE.
A
ALL AGES
www.TOKYOPOP.com
©2004 JARED HODGES & LINDSAY CIB

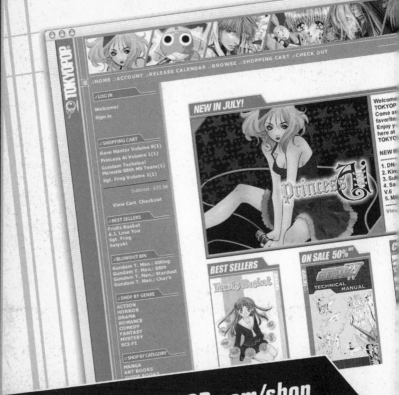

STOP!

This is the back of the book.
You wouldn't want to spoil a great ending!

This book is printed "manga-style," in the authentic Japanese right-to-left format. Since none of the artwork has been flipped or altered, readers get to experience the story just as the creator intended. You've been asking for it, so TOKYOPOP® delivered: authentic, hot-off-the-press, and far more fun!

DIRECTIONS

If this is your first time reading manga-style, here's a quick guide to help you understand how it works.

It's easy... just start in the top right panel and follow the numbers. Have fun, and look for more 100% authentic manga from TOKYOPOP®!